Esperanza, Or, the Home of the Wanderers
by Anne Bowman

Address:
HardPress
8345 NW 66TH ST #2561
MIAMI FL 33166-2626
USA
Email: info@hardpress.net

Esperanza; or, The home of the wanderers

Anne Bowman

He was comforted by seeing Jack bending over the prostrate figure of a man, and
apparently engaged in some friendly office to the stranger.

249. W. 404.

ESPERANZA;

OR,

THE HOME OF THE WANDERERS.

BY

ANNE BOWMAN,

AUTHOR OF "LAURA TEMPLE," "TRAVELS OF ROLANDO," ETC.

"Through tangled forests, and through dangerous ways,
  Where beasts with man divided empire claim,
  And the brown Indian marks with murderous aim."
                                        GOLDSMITH.

LONDON:
G. ROUTLEDGE & CO., FARRINGDON STREET;
NEW YORK: 18, BEEKMAN STREET.
1855.

PREFACE.

WHEN we propose to strengthen the character and inform the mind of the young, it is sometimes expedient to render the draught of instruction more palatable by the tempting addition of the *soave licor* of the poet. And thus, knowing the charm of fiction to youthful readers, I have endeavoured to blend lessons of useful knowledge and Christian truth with a narrative of adventure, and in the characters, the trials, and the fortunes of a numerous family, to point out that obedience and union, perseverance under difficulties, and trust in God, must produce enjoyment and peace. My earnest wish is, to impress on the minds of the young that all have a mission on earth; that none can begin too soon faithfully and earnestly to fulfil this duty; and thus, in whatever circumstances we are placed, we may

> "Make our lives sublime,
> And, departing, leave behind us
> Footsteps on the sands of Time."

A. B.

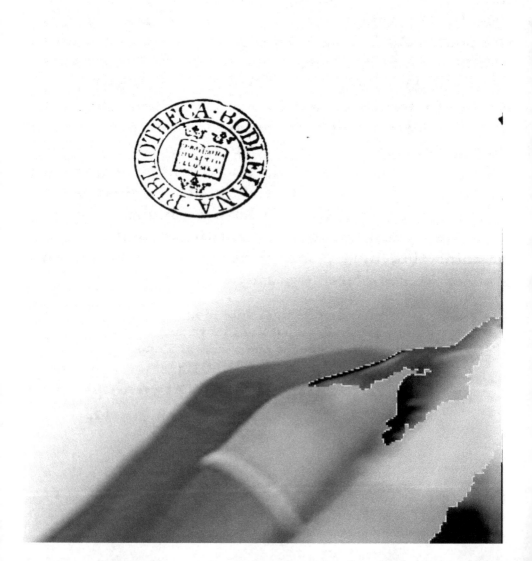

PREFACE.

When we propose to strengthen the _____
inform the mind of the young, it is _____
dient to render the draught of instr_____
able by the tempting addition of _____
the poet. And thus, knowing the _____
youthful readers, I have endeavour_____
of useful knowledge and Christian _____
rative of adventure, and in the _____
and the fortunes of a nume_____
that obedience and union _____
culties, and trust in God _____
and peace. My earnest _____

minds of the young that _____
that none can begin _____
to fulfil this duty _____
stances we are placed _____

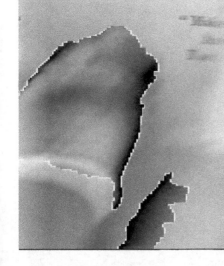

CONTENTS.

CHAPTER I.

CHAPTER II.

CHAPTER III.

CHAPTER IV.

CHAPTER X.

CHAPTER XI.

CHAPTER XII.

CHAPTER XIII.

CHAPTER XIV.

CHAPTER XV.

CHAPTER XVI.

CHAPTER XVII.

CHAPTER XVIII.

CHAPTER XIX.

CHAPTER XX.

CHAPTER XXI.

CHAPTER XXII.

CHAPTER XXIII.

CHAPTER XXIV.

CHAPTER XXV.

CHAPTER XXVI.

CHAPTER XXVII.

CHAPTER XXVIII.

CHAPTER XXIX.

CHAPTER XXX.

CHAPTER XXXI.

ESPERANZA;

OR,

THE HOME OF THE WANDERERS.

CHAPTER I.

The Merton Family. Vicissitudes of Fortune. Plan of Emigration. London. The Zoological Gardens.

"INDEED, dear papa," said Tom Merton, "I believe the best plan would be for us all to go out to South America."

"Most assuredly we must go," said his sister Matilda; "Tom and I have thought over the matter, papa; and we decidedly pronounce this to be the wisest measure for our advantage."

"I second the resolution," cried out Jack. "Charley says there is capital shooting on the mountains; besides, it would be rare fun to have a voyage. Fancy, girls, you see me looking down on you from the masthead; I know I shall turn out a regular sailor."

"I am quite sure, papa," added Mary, the youngest child, "that South America must be a pretty place, or cousin Charles would not like it; and the way to it will be easy, for Charley does not like any trouble."

Mr. Merton regarded his children with astonishment; he would never have dared to contemplate so bold a scheme himself; but now the possibility of accomplishing some such measure dawned on his mind, and, smiling at their earnestness, he promised to consider the plan.

Mr. Merton was an excellent scholar, an estimable

B

5-6

man, respected and beloved in his own small circle; he was no longer young, and yet he had never attained a higher rank than that of a country curate. In the small village of Winston, in a mountainous district in the north of England, he had been born; there he possessed a small estate, and there, since he left the university and married, he had continued to perform the duties of curate in a widely scattered parish; and, far from the world, had lived only for his books, his family, and his attached congregation.

Mr. Merton had married, as poor curates are wont to marry, a very pretty, very amiable, but undowered bride. Much older than his wife, he had yielded to her gentle nature, and indulged his Lucy as a father indulges a favourite child; till, though her sweet temper was unspoiled, her half-formed character was enfeebled, and her physical powers impaired; for the constant watchfulness of her tender husband had filled her mind with nervous fancies, and induced her to yield to indolent indulgence, till her health really suffered.

Mr. Merton had four children; Tom, who had proposed to his father the startling project of emigration, was fifteen years of age, and with his brother Jack, who was two years younger, had been for some years at one of the first grammar schools of the north of England, where they had attained a good knowledge of classics and modern languages,—where Tom had acquired a taste for natural history and science, and Jack had been the leader at cricket, foot-ball, and all gymnastic sports. The simple and inexpensive habits of Mr. Merton enabled him to lay aside the small income arising from his estate for the education of his sons, whom he ardently desired to send to the university, where he himself had acquired an honourable name.

The two daughters, aged fourteen and twelve, had been chiefly brought up by their maternal grandmother, an active widow, who lived on her own farm, and managed it skilfully and profitably. She sent her two grand-daughters to an excellent school, and spared no money in procuring for them the advantage of the best masters of the place; but in the vacations she undertook herself to teach them all the useful arts of domestic economy, as practised in a large farm-house. She was determined, she said, that the girls should be of more use in the world than their mother, her poor Lucy, who had first been spoiled by her own father, then married before she had learned to make a pudding, and, after all, been so indulged by her husband that she could now do nothing.

The girls were amused at the idea of mamma ever being thought able to make a pudding; now, she usually was in bed till after the puddings were made, and only rose from it to make a feeble exertion to attend to her flowers, or her pet canary. When she felt better than usual, she would sometimes make clothes for the poor, reclining on the sofa as she worked, and amused by Mr. Merton reading to her. But all the children were fondly attached to her, she was so mild and gentle; and even Jack the boisterous, looked penitent if, after indulging in some noisy diversion, he remembered poor mamma's headache. "I cannot bear to see her look so patient and pretty," said he, "and I know she never could scold me, much as I deserve it."

A cousin of Mr. Merton's, who was with him at the university, and was one of his earliest friends, had entered into commerce, traded in South America, and finally married an heiress in Valparaiso, and settled there as a merchant. He had lost his wife a few years after their marriage, and Mr. Merton frequently heard from him afterwards, but his letters were melancholy; he spoke of his own approaching death, and besought his cousin to receive and superintend the education of his only son, whom, though he must inherit a large estate near Valparaiso, he wished to be brought up an Englishman. Still it was a great shock

B 2

to Mr. Merton to receive a visit from a grave, severe-looking elderly man, who announced himself as Mr. Buchanan, the uncle of the late Mrs. Villars, and who added that he was instructed to consign to Mr. Merton, Charles Villars, the orphan son of the said Mrs. Villars, and her husband the late Mr. Villars, with the sum of £5,000, to be invested in the English funds, and applied to the education and board of Charles Villars, during his minority, he having now passed his tenth year, in such manner as Mr. Merton deemed just and expedient.

Then placing the handsome, pale, noble-looking boy in Mr. Merton's hands, giving him an inventory of his clothes, books, and toys, and putting a crown-piece in the child's hand, with an injunction not to spend it, he took leave, saying that pressing business called him to Liverpool; leaving Mr. Merton in a state of great agitation and distress, with a child of ten years of age in his quiet rooms at Cambridge.

"What in the world can I do with the boy here?" said Mr. Merton to his revered friend, the master of his college, Dr. Allan, who had made his usual evening call on him. "If he had been eighteen years of age, instead of ten, and had been grounded in the classics, I would gladly have carried him on; but this child, who is ripe in mischief, disturbs the course of my life, and fills me with unwonted terrors. His dog, the most unamiable of its kind, hunts cats into my rooms, growls at me if I attempt to caress him, eats my toast from the plate before me, and snaps at my legs, if I remonstrate. Unlike the canine race, the animal is cowardly, treacherous, and cruel. And the boy flings my cherished folios after the cats, and his boots at my bed-maker, calling this respectable female " Old Hag!""

Dr. Allan laughed at his friend's distresses, and pointed out to him the simple plan of sending the boy to school. "To-morrow, Merton," said he, "send him to school. He will there have his wants attended to, his mind stored, his manners polished, and his faults corrected."

And much against his wish, the spoiled boy was sent off next day to a school, where his nobler qualities were developed, his early failings subdued or corrected, and Mr. Merton was gratified with reports of his progress in learning. The following year Dr. Allan accepted the valuable living of Winston, and persuaded Mr. Merton, as this parish was his native place, to leave the university, and become his curate. But the parsonage of Winston was lonely, and the good curate soon introduced a young wife into it, and from that time Charles Villars spent his vacations at Winston ; and even after he went to the university, where, with good talents, he had taken a very fair degree for a young man of wealth, Winston continued to be his home when he chose to visit the country. After leaving the university he made a continental tour, and on his return had apartments in town, with no decided pursuit ; and though fond of society and a gay life, still seemed happiest in his long visits to his dear uncle, as he always called him, at Winston. But even if the mountain-home had its hours of dullness to the gay Charles Villars, it was very dear to all the Mertons, and it was only painful vicissitudes of fortune that could have induced them to desire to leave it.

The old friend of Mr. Merton, the rector of the parish, Dr. Allan, had recently died suddenly, and the living was bestowed on one who knew not Mr. Merton, and who dispensed with his services, for he should bring his own curate with him. At once Mr. Merton had to mourn the loss of his friend, and of his home. At once he found himself with a helpless wife, a large family, and a very small income, dependent on that small income for a subsistence. It might not have been difficult for Mr. Merton to obtain some other small curacy ; but he wanted energy to seek a new patron, and shrunk from the idea of taking up his

abode amidst new faces.   In the midst of his distress,
Mrs. Merton's mother died, and her son succeeded to
the property, a sordid and morose man, with a large
family. He instantly sent Matilda and Mary Merton to
their father, saying the girls had already had too much
of his mother's money spent on them, but they would
get no more.   With much murmuring, he reluctantly
paid to Mr. Merton the small legacy his mother was
enabled to leave to her helpless daughter, but Mr.
Merton saw, that in his distress, he must not expect
either advice or assistance from his brother-in-law.

It was at this time that Charles Villars came to
take leave of his dear friends at Winston.   He had
been summoned to Valparaiso by Mr. Buchanan, his
great uncle, who had brought him to England, and
who now entreated him to visit him, to settle the
long accounts of money matters, and to receive large
arrears due to him.   To Charles, so many years older
than his own children, Mr. Merton told all his sorrows and difficulties.   " Tell me, Charles, what shall
I do ? I feel like the unjust steward of the parable :
' I cannot dig, to beg I am ashamed.' "

" I have money enough for everybody, uncle," said
Charles, " and you should all have come up to town
and lived with me, but for this voyage.   Not that I
object to it ; for it will be something new, and the
wild sports of South America are splendid ; besides, I
am glad to leave town just now, for not a soul is to
be seen there at this dull season.   But I tell you
what we can do : you can go with me, my dear
uncle ; in fact, I believe you must go, or Uncle Buchanan will never believe I am the true Charles
Villars he delivered to you.   Besides, he writes to me
that he has built a new church on his own *haciendo*,
for his English labourers, and he orders a priest to be
sent out, as if he were ordering a bale of Manchester
cotton."

Mr. Merton shook his head, and pointed to his
family gathered round him ; it was then that Tom,

the philosopher of the family, suggested the plan of emigration in earnest.

"You need not consider the plan, my dear uncle," said Charles; "depend on my judgment; it is the right thing. Buchanan town will be glad to welcome you; and I rejoice particularly in the prospect of having the boys with me on the tedious voyage out. I have been quite out of spirits at the thought of my imprisonment for months in a dirty ship, redolent of tar and all manner of foul odours; subjected to the unspeakable horror of a cabin dinner with unknown, vulgar adventurers, and no one to sympathize with me. Now, if you go, I can tell all my distresses to my dear compassionate aunt, talk philosophy with you, learn practical navigation with the boys, and romp with the dear little girls. You must not send me out without you, uncle, for I can never fancy a home unless I have all this dear circle round me."

But it was many days, and after much reasoning and reflection, that Mr. Merton discovered, first, that the proposed scheme was possible; and, next, that it was desirable. At length he left all to Charles and Tom, and shut himself in his study, to mourn over the necessity of his banishment. With Mrs. Merton Charles had little difficulty: she wept bitterly, feeling oppressed by some great calamity, which she could neither comprehend nor bear to contemplate, but she had ever been accustomed to look on her beloved husband as infallible, and, as he agreed to the measure, she supposed it must be right. The only unusual exertion she made was to tell Nanny, her faithful old servant, that she must pack up her clothes, for they were going to leave their dear home.

"I reckoned as much, mistress," observed Nanny; "but how we are to get you shifted I can't see. Sure*lie*, master never thinks to carry us far away?"

"Charles says it will be thousands of miles, Nanny," replied her mistress, in a mournful voice, "and we must go in a ship, which I dread very much; but I told Mr. Merton that you must go with us, for what could I do without you?"

"That's the truest word you ever spoke, mistress," said Nanny, in a great state of irritation; "without me, indeed! I'd like to see anybody try it. But this, I'll be bound, is just Master Charles at his tricks. Set off in a ship—a pack of nonsense! How is I to be gotten into a ship, let alone a poor silly body like you!"

But Tom assured Nanny the thing was decided, and, after much grumbling, she began her fussy preparations. "And if we are to go, master," said she, angrily, to poor Mr. Merton, in his besieged retreat, "please to say when; for what with one fancy and another that Master Charles takes, everybody's time's taken up; and we hav'n't washed these three weeks; and let us have all clean wi' us, for I cannot see how folks can wash aboard ship."

But Matilda, who was great in household matters, and exceedingly fond of rule and management, undertook to direct the distracted Nanny, who loudly bemoaned her expatriation, but never for a moment considered she had the option of remaining. Finally, when all was ready, she bent to her fate like a wind-blown rush, and took leave of her intimates with the importance of a woman setting out on her travels. Tom's thoughtfulness and Matilda's management enabled them to select, arrange, and pack all things needful, without disturbing or annoying their abstracted father or feeble mother. A kind and honourable friend of Mr. Merton, who practised the law in the nearest town to Winston, undertook the sale of his furniture, and the management of his little estate, which, as the heritage of his family, he was reluctant to sell. The family then took a sorrowful leave of the weeping people, and, under the experienced protection of Charles Villars, set out for London, where they were to continue with him till all was provided for their voyage.

Charles was well acquainted with several South American merchants, who directed him in what manner to fit out the family for their new home; and they also introduced him to the captain of a vessel, comfortably fitted up, which was to sail in a few weeks for Valparaiso, round Cape Horn.

By the sale of Mr. Merton's furniture a sum was realized which enabled him to fit out the whole family well; and, by the advice of the friendly merchants, many useful articles of English manufacture were purchased, not being easily attainable at their proposed destination. Their wardrobes were filled with light summer garments suitable to the climate; but a warm winter dress was added for each, to be worn when they reached the colder regions during their voyage. Mr. Merton's books, with the addition of those of his children, filled one large chest, which Mr. Merton determined to have in his cabin, that he might guard with a jealous eye his most-treasured possession. Finally, Mrs. Merton's legacy of £500 was invested in the English funds; the dividends, and the rents of the Winston property, were to be transmitted to Mr. Merton at Valparaiso.

Whilst all these preparations were going on, Charles Villars, having first seen his young friends dressed with more attention to the reigning mode than they had cared for at Winston, pleased himself by gratifying their several tastes in seeing the wonders of London. Mr. Merton only desired to see Westminster Abbey and the church of the old Knight Templars; and there he would have spent the whole period of his stay in London; but his heart was touched when he found Nanny had seen nothing of the town, for the valet of Charles, a very fine gentleman, had declined the office of introducing the strikingly rustic figure of the Winston maiden to a London public. But Mr. Merton, regardless of Nanny's showy yellow gown and primitive black silk bonnet, led her through the streets, Jack undertaking to flank the party, for fear of mischief, and Charles and Tom following at a distance, lest, as Charles said, they should be mobbed by Nanny's followers. "I will buy her the smartest straw bonnet in Oxford Street," added he, "if she will give me that extraordinary coal-scoop she crowns her head with. I will send it to Mrs. Keeley ; and that bonnet would be the greatest hit of the season."

The girls did not at all comprehend why Mrs. Keeley should have Nanny's bonnet ; but of one thing they were quite sure, that she would never exchange her highly-valued best bonnet for a straw bonnet, whatever the fashion of London might require.

"We are now in St. Paul's Church-yard, Nanny," said Jack, in his character of *cicerone* ; "and that is the great St. Paul's Cathedral."

"Ye'll not tell me this can be a church-yard, master Jack," said the incredulous maiden, "with all these grand shops about it, and so many carts and carriages rattling over the graves. Nay ! nay ! London folks can sure*lie* never be so hardened as to keep their market-day with their poor dead under their feet !"

Her master quietly enlightened her on the subject of church-yards and cemeteries, and begged her to notice the cathedral.

"Is this your grand St. Paul's, that looks so bonny in picture-books ?" said Nanny. "Why, I see nothing but a great black wall ; it's not to be named on the same day as Carlisle Cathedral. I'd be very sorry to see you, master, minister of such a great, black, noisy place as St. Paul's, that's not a bit like a canny, quiet church. Come on, honeys, I cannot bide to see it. That's not a temple of God Almighty."

And so they went on through the mazy streets ; but Nanny, who had been struck with wonder at the first sight of London as a whole, was much dissatisfied with it in detail, and amused the children very much by her animadversions on the people, who, she declared, never could clean their windows or sweep their chimneys, and she classed all the London people together as dirty, ill-behaved, and altogether heathens.

Tom chose to visit the British Museum, and they spent several days pleasantly and profitably among the relics of past ages. At length, when the time for their departure was at hand, the girls petitioned for one day at the Zoological Gardens. Even Charles, sheltered by a cab, condescended to accompany the party, which included Nanny, to that attractive scene, though he felt rather alarmed lest he should encounter any of his fashionable friends while surrounded by such a rustic group.

The screams of delight which burst from the party can only be comprehended by those who have witnessed the first introduction of children to this fairy scene. Tom was perfectly absorbed; he followed the keepers, inquiring and observing, and made notes of the habits, the appearance, and the names of the animals. Jack, with less steadiness of character, and a somewhat exuberant vivacity, was wild with enjoyment. He planted himself in a menacing attitude before the cages of the ferocious animals, crying out, "Hollo, sir! if I had you in a wild forest, and had a good rifle in my hand, I promise you your chance would be small." The girls laughed at Jack's rhodomontade, and were delighted with the scene, but clung to papa with a little trepidation. Nanny, after a succession of shrieks, subsided into a stupid astonishment, gazing at everything in silence, with enlarged eyes; and Charles Villars, smoking a cigar, stood aloof, regarding his very much loved friends with an ineffable air of superiority, and wondering how in the world people could be so *green*.

At length Nanny's tongue was loosed. "Pray you, master, speak to me; I feel all of a maze! Save us! master, look at yon great black creature walking about among folk, just like one of our own black mountains setting off out of its place! And what will become of us all, master, if such like beasts

be roving about in that place we have to be sent
to ?"

"It is impossible, Nanny," replied Mr. Merton ; " it
is well ascertained that the elephant has never inhabited the new world in the postdiluvian ages.   I
doubt, even, if the elephant of the antediluvian world—
which the researches of geology have revealed to us,
walked, in those early ages, through the primeval
forests of our own island—was an inhabitant of America, or, indeed, if that vast continent had then been
called forth from the waters.   The doubtful remains
of an earlier world, the scanty and vague traditions
existing among the natives, the immense mass of
waters which still cover so large a portion of the continent, and the luxuriant vegetation which announces
the freshness of the soil, all proclaim that it is indeed
a new world, gradually emerged from the ocean."

Nanny curtsied with profound veneration of the
hidden meaning of her master's reply.   Mr. Merton
rarely measured the understanding of his auditors
when he gave words to his thoughts, but Nanny
was always content : " Master spoke grand," that was
enough, though his words might be really Greek.
But Charles was roused by his guardian's visionary
theory, and spoke to him.

"That is a refuted error, my dear sir.   I am certainly not prepared to prove that the elephant ever
inhabited America ; but the numerous gigantic organic
remains discovered, prove that the antediluvian America was the abode of wondrous land animals now
extinct—the huge megatherium, the scelidotherium,
a creature larger than the rhinoceros, the mylodon,
nearly as large, the toxodon, large as the elephant,
and several other extraordinary animals, whose teeth
indicate that their immense frames were supported
by vegetable food.   Thus, my dear uncle, the fact is
indisputable that before the vast continent was trodden by man, it must have been a gigantic Zoological
Garden."

" It may be so, Charles," said Mr. Merton, " but I should like to view these remains, that my doubts might be dispelled. But is it not extraordinary that the present *feræ* of America are certainly inferior in size to those of the Eastern continent ? "

" I cannot account for that fact," answered Charles, " for it certainly is a fact ; though you must not form your judgment of the lion and tiger of America, properly the puma and jaguar, by the wretched representatives of the species you see in confinement here. I hope I shall have the honour of introducing you to some noble specimens of the race in their native forests."

" I would rather not, I thank you, Charles," answered Mr. Merton, hastily ; " I should feel greatly alarmed at such an encounter. I prefer the contemplation of these ferocious beasts, when under the subjugation of man, the ruler on earth of the brute creation."

" I am going to take out a dozen choice rifles," said Charles, laughing. " You must let me put one into your hands, uncle, and you will have the better of the brute. The boys have already made their choice among them, and you shall have the best that remains."

" Did not my profession forbid me to shed blood," replied Mr. Merton, " I should still feel the same repugnance to the use of arms. I shrink from the sight of the weapon of destruction."

" Then we will be your body-guards, papa," said Jack ; " but come, leave your tedious discussions, and watch Nanny's delight at the sight of the parrots."

" Did ever eyes look on such another bonny bird as that ?" cried the astonished maiden. " Sure*lie*, Master Tom, this is like to be the king over all our poor bits of brown sparrows and black crows."

" Nanny, you understand nothing of the arrangements of ornithology," said Tom, somewhat pompously. " The sparrow and crow both belong to the *Passerine* order, the birds that feed on insects, fruits, or grains, and build their nests in trees or bushes, on the ground, or even in the habitations of men. The sparrow is of the family *Fringilla*, having short, stout, rounded bills, sharp at the point. The crow, of the genus *Corvus*, is distinguished by a strong convex bill and a rounded tail. Now, the parrot has no affinity to these birds ; it is of the order *Scansores*, the climbing birds, and of the family *Psittacidæ*, distinguished by hooked bills, fleshy tongues, and claws formed for climbing. These beautiful birds are found in the woods of South America of many varieties, and I shall have great pleasure in viewing them in a state of nature."

" Bonny creatures they are, for all their queer names," said Nanny, apparently satisfied with Tom's explanation ; " and a good schoolmaster you have had, Master Tom, to make you get off such long outlandish words."

" Never listen to Tom's crabbed descriptions, Nanny," said Jack, " but come with me, and I will show you some of the strange animals we may meet with in our new country."

And Jack showed Nanny the stately ostrich of America, the ponderous condor, the curious scaly armadillo, and the gentle llama. With the latter animal she was much pleased, declaring that she would not believe it was a wild beast, for it looked as quiet as the goats that skipped about on their own mountains.

" The llama we shall doubtless meet with," said Tom, " for vast herds of these animals are found on the mountain sides of South America. The llama is ——."

" Pray defer your discourse on the llama, Tom," interrupted Jack, " till we meet with one at large ; and just look after papa, for fear he should intrude into the den of the brown bear, who might not honour him with a pleasant reception. And, above all, keep him from the cage of the tiger, for I see the treacherous brute is on the watch to have a claw at some unwary observer."

" I believe," said Mary, " that Matilda and I could milk a llama as well as we used to milk the goats ; so remember, Nanny, if they cannot give us cow's milk at Valparaiso, we will keep a flock of llamas, have a dairy, and make our own butter and cheese."

Charles, who had not forgotten the enervating climate of Valparaiso, nor the languid disposition of the inhabitants, laughed at the little girl's schemes ; and assured her she must not condescend to do any household work at her new home, or she would never be regarded as a lady.

" Then, cousin Charles," said Matilda, " you, with papa and mamma, who like ease, must represent the aristocracy of the family. Mary and I like to be active, and I certainly intend to take the management of the house."

" That I am quite sure of," said Jack, laughing ; " but I protest, too, against being a lazy fine gentleman. I will hunt and shoot, and fish ; I am up to any kind of hard work, and would rather draw a carriage than ride in one."

" I should like very much to accompany you in your field sports," said Matilda ; " but I fear it will be necessary for me to remain at home to keep Mary at her useful employments. I have an ardent desire to pass days in the woods, watching the habits of the various birds, and the fairy-like insects, or collecting and arranging new plants."

" Well, well, Matilda," answered her brother, " you must sometimes take a holiday from the butter and cheese labours, and we will fly away to the woods and mountains, and spend the day among the birds and insects."

" And probably with the tigers and wild bulls, too," said Tom. " We must know a little more of the

woods round our residence, Jack, before we plan excursions into them. · But papa is weary, and I think
all our eyes must ache with gazing, so we had best
leave this charming fairy land."

CHAPTER II.

The Family leave England. Introduction to Dr. Lewis. Arrival
at Madeira. The Southern Cross. Rio Janeiro. Visit to
the country house of Don Alvarez. Departure from Rio
Janeiro.

" Oh, mistress! honey mistress !" said Nanny, on their
return from this, the most wonderful experience of
her life. " What a pity it is you are such a poor ail-
ing creature; you could not see yon bonny place,
that's more like a grand picture out of a great book
than aught real. And they're all alive, mistress,—
such creatures! Why, at Winston we want sending
to school; we ken no more than half of the things
God has made. There was a great, black, awful creature : one of his legs was bigger than Master Charles,
but he was as quiet as a lamb. And the bonniest
things, that I thought were great butterflies! But
Master Tom says they are birds, and we shall see lots
where we are going; and you shall have some, mistress, if we cannot get a *gold linnet*. But surelie, the
awfullest beasts that ever was seen was them monkeys. Would you think it, mistress, they sniggered
at me, and telled one another, and pointed their ugly
hands at me ; and Master Charles got me away from
them, for he said they had found it out as I was a
North-country body."

" No doubt they had, Nanny," said Charles ; " for
monkeys are knowing creatures. When we touch at
Rio Janeiro I intend to buy one, to amuse us for the

rest of the voyage, and you will find out what a con-
jurer the fellow will be. And now, dear aunty, all is
ready, and to-morrow we must embark; so take your
warm cloak, to be ready to wear till we get to a warmer
latitude, when you will have to relinquish it a while."

It was really a serious undertaking for Charles,
who was by no means fond of trouble, to get the
family and their extensive baggage safely embarked
in the *Maypo*, a commodious vessel, which was bound
to Valparaiso with a valuable cargo of British manu-
factures. Captain Russell, to whom they had previously been introduced, was a gentlemanly and
intelligent man, who was glad of pleasant society
during his long voyage. He introduced them to the
only passenger besides themselves that he had consented to take out,—Dr. Lewis, a young physician,
whose health had not been very good, and who, as he had
no ties to bind him to England, and was fond of travel
and of the study of Natural History, had decided to
go out to Valparaiso, where, if the climate suited him,
he purposed to remain and practise his profession.
Captain Russell appropriated two large cabins, surrounded by convenient berths, to the use of his passengers; and before the first twenty-four hours had
passed, Mrs. Merton, reclining on an easy sofa, and
surrounded by comforts, was almost reconciled to the
change. The cabin was much more luxuriously furnished, and kept cleaner and neater than their London
lodgings. A bookcase, filled with the light literature
of the day, supplied her with amusement; and she
listened with pleasure to the animated description
given by her children of the wonders of the ship.

But Dr. Lewis was certainly an unexpected addition
to the pleasure of the voyage. Every one acknowledged this. He had erudition enough to discuss
learned points with Mr. Merton; knowledge of society,
to render him agreeable to Charles; a taste for Natural
History, to delight Tom; medical science, to command
the respect and attention of Mrs. Merton; and a happy

C

good-nature, that won him the affection of the younger party.   He prescribed for Mrs. Merton, won her confidence, and by degrees succeeded in persuading her to make a little exertion, to walk about the cabin ; and before they had sailed ten days she was actually seated on deck ; supported by cushions, certainly, but enjoying the fresh breeze and the lively pleasure of her children at mamma's improvement.

"Do you know, Captain Russell," said Matilda, whose education had given her a little conceit, "I cannot see the use of that man remaining in such a dangerous position up at the top of that mast."

"But I see the use of it," replied the captain, good-humouredly ; "he is looking out for the appearance of land."

"Oh! I could see the land well enough from this spot, if there was land to see," said she, "without risking my neck by climbing up there.   I only wish we were in sight of land, for I should then beg of you, Captain Russell, to sail close to it.   It would be decidedly more agreeable to be passing fields and towns, as we do on a railway, than to sail for days with one unvarying prospect of water before us."

"'My dear young lady, pray mind your dolls and your crochet-work," answered Captain Russell, "and leave the management of the ship to wiser heads.   I am despotic here, and never allow any one to advise or censure."

"You silly goose," cried Jack, laughing, "don't you know that there is nothing a sailor dreads so much on sea as land—keep clear of land, and we keep clear of danger.   No likelihood of your seeing fields or houses for some time yet."

"Not before we reach Madeira, I hope," said the captain ; "there I intend to land and take in fresh water.   I have a sacred duty to fulfil there."

From Dr. Lewis they afterwards heard that Captain Russell had buried a wife and daughter in the lovely but melancholy island of Madeira—that forlorn hope of the consumptive patients of the bleak northern climates; and he wished to visit the graves of all he held dear on earth.

A few days after, they anchored opposite the port of Funchal, and were struck with equal delight and astonishment at the picturesque appearance of the shores, which are bounded by lofty cliffs, rising, in many parts, perpendicularly from 1,000 to 2,000 feet. Captain Russell proposed to his passengers to join him in his visit to Funchal, and they gladly accepted the opportunity of relieving the tedium of a long voyage by seeing a new country. The children leaped about in ecstasy, as they arrayed themselves neatly for their expedition. Mr. Merton was interested, Mrs. Merton passively willing, and Nanny, though she murmured greatly at all the trouble of preparation for a few days' absence from the vessel, was in her heart very glad to see grass and trees once more.

"Come, Villars," cried Dr. Lewis, "the boat is ready; what in the world can detain you now, when you were the most anxious of us to go on shore?"

In truth, Charles was under the hands of his valet; for to appear in his careless ship costume at Funchal, where they should assuredly meet elegant English society, was unworthy of Charles Villars. It was only the captain's positive assurance that he must be left behind, if not ready, that induced him to complete hastily his grand toilet; and he then sprung into the boat, arrayed in his fashionable English morning dress.

"Observe the ridges of the mountains," said Dr. Lewis to his young friends, "broken into mimic pyramids and towers, standing out so strongly against that clear blue sky, which you would fancy was never ruffled by a cloud. Can anything be more picturesque than those heights, and the deep and precipitous gorges which so abruptly sever them?"

There was some difficulty in landing on the stony beach at Funchal; but they were met by the noisy, bustling boatmen of the town, who accomplished the landing with much greater ease and expedition than the sailors from the ship, unacquainted with the coast, could have done. Sedan-chairs were waiting near the landing-place, in which Mrs. Merton and her daughters were placed; and Nanny, though very reluctantly, was induced to enter a similar conveyance. They were then borne by men to an hotel in the town, the gentlemen walking by their side.

The pretty town of Funchal stands in the midst of an amphitheatre of mountains, scattered over with groves of lofty and luxuriant heaths and brooms. White villas gleam through the rich verdure, and contrast pleasantly with the green cultivated terraces that surround the town.

After Captain Russell had left them, to make his melancholy visit to the graves of his family, the party spent the few days they remained in this beautiful place in rambling up the hills by roads hedged with geranium, hydrangea, and myrtle, passing through groves of orange and lemon, and vineyards purple with their rich produce. A little higher grew bananas, figs, and pomegranates; then they reached the region of the familiar fruits of England,—apples, pears, and peaches, though on the ground were still spread the melon, tomata, and egg-plant. Still higher, and only the potato can be cultivated.

Tom collected plants with untiring assiduity, and all enjoyed the delicious fruit. Dr. Lewis wished them to see something of the process of making the rich wine for which Madeira is famed; but time would not permit this; and, laden with as much fruit as they could conveniently stow, the gratified party left " fair Madeira's groves," and, returning to the vessel, pursued their voyage.

After leaving this island, Tom had several times the high gratification of pointing out to his brother and sisters the flying fish. These curious creatures were seen in numbers, skimming like swallows over the waves; sometimes they suspended their flight for a few seconds, then rose again, and were always pursued by the larger fish, which frequently leaped high out of the water, attempting unsuccessfully to seize their prey. These observations charmed the children till they forgot the monotony of the voyage. Then they passed within sight of the Canary Islands, and were amazed with a distant view of the lofty peak of Teneriffe, gilded by the sun, while the lower part was shrouded in clouds.

They were glad to adopt their light summer dresses now, and as they approached the burning regions of the equator, were rarely able to remain long on deck till the evening. After crossing the line, they began to look round for the peculiar novelties of the south; but it was not till they reached the 16° of south latitude that, on one delicious night, Dr. Lewis, the keenest observer, pointed out to the assembled family, in the clear heavens, the glory of the southern hemisphere, the Cross of the South.

" I am now content with my expatriation," said Mr. Merton, gazing with fervent admiration on the cruciform arrangement of the stars; " how often, in my quiet study have I longed to study the heavens of the south; especially I have desired to look on this constellation, the sight of which hushed the fears of the first voyagers on the unknown Southern Ocean, who hailed with astonishment and renewed hopes, the extraordinary appearance of the symbol of the faith of Jesus."

" Yes, papa," added Matilda, " and you taught me the beautiful passage in Dante, describing these *quattro stelle.* I have not forgotten it."

" But we do not understand Dante," said Jack, " and therefore, if you please, we will speak English, —the language of the sons of freedom."

But notwithstanding Jack's admiration of the English language, he had, with the rest of the young people, been studying Spanish and Portuguese for some weeks, under Mr. Merton, who was an accom

plished linguist; Charles Villars, who had not forgotten his early Spanish acquirements, undertook to
be under-teacher, for Mr. Merton was not skilful in
rudimentary instruction; and before they reached
Rio Janeiro, they were all able to understand and even
speak the Spanish, as well as a little of the language
common at that place,—the Portuguese.

With all the delight which youth ever experiences
at novelty, the young people stood on deck, looking
at the first land they had seen of a new world, as the
vessel entered the magnificent harbour of the city of
St. Salvador, usually called Rio Janeiro. As they approached the principal landing-place, the bright sunshine of that climate lighted up the splendid scene in
glorious beauty. The grand and spacious harbour,
with the amphitheatre of mountains, the rich tropical
woods and the fair white city, and scattered villas,
formed an unrivalled picture.

As soon as they landed, they entered an hotel near
the harbour, till Charles, accompanied by Captain
Russell, went to call on a rich Portuguese merchant,
who was a distant relation of his mother, and a friend
and correspondent of his uncle. He was welcomed
with ready hospitality by Don Alvarez, who insisted
on receiving the whole party during their stay at Rio,
and immediately dispatched his strange old picturesque carriage, drawn by mules, driven by a negro
coachman, to the hotel; and the Mertons, with Dr.
Lewis, were conveyed to the house of Don Alvarez, in
the city. The lower part of the house was occupied
as warehouses, the upper rooms forming the residence
of the family, when they were in town. At present,
his wife and daughters were at his *estancia*, or farm,
in the country, whither he proposed to conduct his
visitors, after introducing them to the novelties of a
city in a new hemisphere.

The Europeans were not long in discovering that
the greatest and most disagreeable novelty to them
was the prevalence of slavery. Slave domestics, slaves

carrying burdens, slave vessels in the harbour, and slave traffic in the markets, made them regard Rio with other feelings than those they had first experienced. Besides, a nearer view of the city robbed it of much of the first brilliant effect. The streets were narrow and ill-paved, the houses, public buildings, and even the royal palace, had a mean and gloomy appearance; though, in the better class of houses, the open balconies in front, filled with brilliant and fragrant flowers, imparted a degree of cheerfulness to their aspect. The churches, numerous and richly decorated, were built in a better style; but there was a want of grandeur in their appearance, and all felt disappointed. Nanny declared this foreign place was no better *nor* London.

" Well worth our own canny Winston," sighed she, " where else have we seen clean white cottages, and a bonny green wi' bits of bairns playing about on it? and folks there were no way shamed to do their own turn, and not sin *again* God by such sights as we look on here. God forgive them that use those poor black niggers no better than if they were cart-horses, and put decent women to shame by making these black creatures work openly int' streets, barely a rag to cover 'em. I like none of your grand cities."

But though the streets were dull and dirty, the party were charmed with a delightful promenade by the seaside, where numbers flocked every evening to inhale the refreshing breeze, and to rest or wander under shady avenues of lofty trees unknown in England, or only seen in the dwarfed specimens cultivated in green-houses.

" Do tell me, papa," said Tom, " is not this noble tree, which cannot be less than forty feet in height, the bread-fruit tree?"

" It is the *Artocarpus integrifolia*, is it not?" said Mr. Merton, appealing to Dr. Lewis.

" Certainly," answered Dr. Lewis; " it is commonly called *The Jack*, a native of the Indian Archipelago, but successfully cultivated here. The fruit is much larger than that of the *Artocarpus incisa*, which I see is also growing at a little distance from us ; but as an article of food, the large nuts are less agreeable to the palate. Both are, however, nutritious, and of priceless value in the Indian islands, where they are natives, supplying wholesome and pleasant food at all seasons. But see, Tom, here is a tree familiar to all who are learned in tales of travel ; the Mango,—*Mangifera Indica*, one of the most delicious of the tropical fruits, and handsomest of trees. I am truly glad we have had an opportunity of viewing these exotics in such a favourable situation."

"But do leave the trees now," said Mary, " and let everybody come with me to a charming market which is close by the avenue. There are hundreds of beautiful birds, far more extraordinary than those we saw at the Zoological Gardens. I never saw so many brilliant colours grouped together in my life. You might fancy you were entering a delightful flower-garden, and that all the flowers were alive. And do, Charles, listen to the extraordinary confusion of a hundred parrots all chattering at the same time."

"And doubtless," said Charles, " they are holding a very pleasant *conversazione*. Look at that old green fellow, he has noticed us, and now, with his head turned on one side, he is looking very significantly at his companion, and declaring his opinion of us. I will tell you what the impertinent knave says : 'I say, friend, what do you think of these new arrivals ? I see no style about them,—no brilliancy. Did you ever hear anything so discordant as their shrill, squeaking notes ? I conclude they must be some of the stupid wild geese, who have made a flight from their dark, cold homes, to bask in the sunshine of our bright world.' "

"Oh, Charles !" cried Mary, "I am too old to be that you can understand the language of birds, the gifted vizier in the wonderful Arabian tales.

Even papa, who knows all the languages of men, does not pretend to know those of animals."

" Well, calm your indignation, my fair cousin ; and to atone for my fault, I will purchase the critical fellow, and present him to you," said Charles. And Mary was in great delight to take home the handsome bird ; and she set about teaching it English on that very day ; for, of the known languages, the bird had, till then, only spoken Portuguese.

Captain Russell called next morning to announce to them that he should inevitably be detained a few days longer than he had proposed, for six of his best sailors had deserted, and he could hear nothing of them, though he strongly suspected that they had been tempted to enter an American vessel which had sailed the day before for California, as the captain of the ship had been offering high wages for the best sailors in Rio. Captain Russell had had several Portuguese sailors to offer their services, but, like a true son of John Bull, he had a great prejudice against the natives of any country but his own ; he was therefore waiting in hopes of meeting with English sailors.

The Mertons accepted the invitation of their host to pass a day or two at his country house, to which they were conveyed the same day ; and here they enjoyed in full perfection the beauties of tropical scenery. The climate in the country of Rio is delicious ; an equal temperature keeps up a perpetual spring, and neither winter nor summer withers or destroys the verdure. The house was large, airy, and richly furnished, and the ladies welcomed them with courtesy and kindness. They were well-bred and graceful, but seemed to possess few intellectual resources, spending the day in dressing, eating fruit, or playing on the guitar.

The young Europeans took great interest in looking over the farm, which consisted not only of grazing-lands, which fed multitudes of cattle, but also of a coffee-plantation of five thousand trees in full bearing, cultivated by slaves under the inspection of over-lookers.

"Do observe, Matilda," said Tom, "the elegance of the slender stem, the beauty of the white jasmine-looking flower, and the red berry, like a small cherry, all in perfection at the same time. How little I expected we should have had this gratification ; I am already delighted with America, where everything is so new and interesting."

"To enjoy to perfection the grandeur of new and foreign scenery," observed Dr. Lewis, " a man ought either to be a painter, to feel the pleasure of painting in his mind an ideal picture of the whole before him ; a geologist, to look with interest and admiration at the naked rock, and trace its gradual formation ; or a botanist, to whom every blade of grass is a page in the Book of Nature, and who perceives, amidst the wealth of vegetation, those minute distinctions which create the harmony of the whole."

There were certainly great attractions in a country residence in this delicious climate. The young men had riding, fishing, and sailing under skies ever clear and bright ; and the ladies reclined in bowers simul-taneously fragrant in blossoms and rich in fruits, play-ing, singing, conversing, but rarely reading. And when Captain Russell joined them to say they must be at Rio to embark next day, it was not without re-luctance they took leave of the glorious woods, where the trees, closing above, formed natural avenues, and the bright sunbeams shone through leaves of every shade, from the dark green of the stranger pine to the paler hue of the natives of the tropics. In these shades millions of gorgeous butterflies floated lazily on the air, and the long grass beneath their feet was noisy with the eternal chirping of the *cicada*.

But they were compelled to depart. Captain Rus-sell had manned his vessel, and, leaving behind him some English goods, had completed his lading with rice, cotton, and sugar. They took leave of their hospitable friends, and once more found themselves confined in the cabins of the *Maypo*, and sailing on the mighty Atlantic.

CHAPTER III.

Continuation of the voyage. Porpoises. Cape Horn. The mutiny. Dr. Lewis obtains the promise of liberty for his friends. They are put out to sea in an open boat. Perilous voyage on an unknown sea. Landing on a rocky coast.

FAIR winds and calm skies accompanied them on their voyage for some time. Captain Russell seemed to forget his sorrows in the society of the cheerful young people, and in listening to the words of pious consolation from good Mr. Merton. His vessel was well manned, for he had met with a party of eight English sailors, who professed a great desire to make the voyage round the Cape; and, only too grateful to find English hands suited to his purpose, the captain engaged them all, as they refused to be separated. He was perfectly content with their services; but the young Mertons regretted the loss of the good-natured fellows who had accompanied them from England, and they pronounced the new sailors to be cross, ill-tempered men.

There was little variety to amuse them for many days; but at length they had the pleasure of seeing an immense shoal of porpoises, extraordinary creatures, which, by a series of jumps, cut their way through the deeply-furrowed water. Mary, whose character was less reflecting than that of her sister, and whose geographical studies had not made a profound impression on her, was perfectly amazed at the great distance they had sailed, and that they were now only in the latitude of Buenos Ayres.

"Why cannot we land there at once?" said she; "it is but a little way across the continent to Valparaiso, which is nearly opposite; and we could soon cross to it by land, which I have no doubt would be much pleasanter than this dull voyaging."

"About a thousand miles, child," said Jack, laughing, " and no pleasant road either, if we may trust the travellers who have crossed the Pampas and the Andes. Mary; you had forgotten the terrific Andes, with their snow-crowned heights."

"Moreover," said Charles, "Buenos Ayres is not one of our stations; and good-natured as Captain Russell is, he would not, I believe, turn his vessel from its course to land us in the river La Plata. Therefore, my dear Mary, you must be content to voyage, like a good sailor, round the formidable stormy Cape."

And time went on, and at length they caught a distant view of high, bleak mountains, which, Captain Russell told them, were the inhospitable shores of Tierra-del-Fuego. All the young people were now anxious to behold the fearful Cape they must soon reach; the Cape of Storms, the terror of the early navigators, the rocky point which had frowned on many a scene of terror, woe, and death. They watched with interest for its appearance, and when, shrouded in mists, the lofty, black, barren rock was seen stretching into the sea, in gloomy sublimity, they felt awed by its neighbourhood, and Mary whispered to her more philosophic sister her dread lest the black mountain should draw the vessel towards it, and destroy them all, like the loadstone rock of the Eastern Tales.

Then Mr. Merton related to his children the perils of the adventurous Anson, and of succeeding voyagers, who followed his course, amid dangers and sufferings that tinged their adventures with a thrilling and romantic interest; nor did this great promontory, the worthy limit of a mighty continent, permit our voyagers to pass without some demonstration of its power. Many days of westerly winds and driving sleet, days of hard labour to the sailors, and alarm to the passengers, were passed before they left the Atlantic and entered the Pacific, in tempestuous weather, which retarded their northern progress, and made the most patient long for a termination of the tedious voyage.

The boys especially, who had enjoyed on the voyage to Rio the long stories of the good-natured sailors, and who spent many an hour in acquiring that knowledge of nautical matters, so fascinating to boys, were now rarely among the crew; for the surly manners of the new sailors prevented any intimacy with them. "Papa," said Tom, "I fear Will Hardy is a very wicked man; I heard him tell some of the sailors who left England with us, to 'never heed the bullying of the captain, but to stick to him: they would let the captain see who was master, and would have their pockets full of Californian gold before long.' I could not help speaking, papa; I said the *Maypo* was not going so far north as California; but before I could speak another word, he gave me a box on the ear, and bid me mind my own business, and speak when I was spoken to."

"I beseech you, my dear boy," said Mrs. Merton, in great alarm, "do not go near those dark, scowling men; I feel as if we were all completely in their power."

Dr. Lewis laughed at the lady's timidity. "Pray have no fears, my dear madam," said he; "rely on it, that in a well-regulated vessel the captain is a petty despot, and however numerous his crew or his passengers may be, all must obey his nod. But for your satisfaction, I will always accompany the boys when they visit the main-deck, and take care they have no disagreement with the men. I believe Will Hardy to be an audacious, violent fellow, but I do not think him dangerous."

"And yet, Dr. Lewis," observed Mr. Merton, "we have historical evidence that men, led astray by the love of gold, or the insane thirst for blood, have risen in mutiny, despising authority, and swept away from their path the innocent and the helpless."

"Take courage, papa," exclaimed Jack; "I will fight like a true-born Englishman, if we have a mutiny. Will Hardy is a saucy, revengeful rascal, and hates Captain Russell, because he was put into confinement for two days when he broached the rum-cask. I say, Charlie, where is the gunnery?"

"Really I cannot say, Jack," replied Charles, languidly. "My duelling-pistols I have, of course, in my dressing-case; but the fowling-pieces, rifles, and ammunition, I left to Wilson to pack. I believe I have a sword, or something of the sort, in the cabin."

"And I shall certainly not trouble your fine gentleman valet to seek for the rifles," said Jack; "but if you will give me leave, cousin Charles, I will turn over the baggage till I meet with them, and we will fit up an armoury here. What do you say to it, Dr. Lewis?"

"I have no objection to your plan, most valiant hero," said the doctor, "though I feel satisfied that it is quite unnecessary; we are under a secure government, Master Jack."

"I wish you may find it so," cried Nanny, who had been listening to their discourse. "I like none of that Will Hardy, he's just a born good-to-nought; and all them saucy chaps that came along wi' him, are no better than they should be. Didn't I hear him *incense* them about gold in lumps like a man's head that was to be had for picking up, if they were at the right place; and then he spat out his quid, and trampled it under his foot, and said, 'That, for the captain and his surly mate; this bonny ship is ours, my brave lads;' and then he swore such awful oaths, that he never would set his foot among them proud Spanish folks at Valparaiso, that I trembled again; and sure enough, I would have gone right to the captain, to tell him all; but poor body, he always seems so mopish and down-hearted, I pitied to make him worse."

"Truly, Nanny," said Dr. Lewis, "you are a keen observer; Captain Russell and I must some conversation about these reports of yours; but many mutinous words do not amount to an act of mutiny. Nevertheless, we will take care that Will Hardy shall go no further in his plans."

"Well it will be, if you can stop him now, sir," exclaimed Nanny. "He has some good *backers*, depend on it; and I wish in my heart we all had our feet set *cannily* on dry land!"

Though Dr. Lewis, to spare the feelings of the timid, had laughed at these tales, he did not feel altogether comfortable; and proceeding at once to the captain's cabin, he communicated to him the suspicious words uttered by Will Hardy and his associates. The captain, absorbed in the remembrance of his domestic afflictions, spent much time in his cabin, and had never, himself, noticed any signs of insubordination among his crew; but, startled by the report of Dr. Lewis, he immediately summoned his mate, repeated the facts, and demanded his opinion on the matter. The mate, a trustworthy and excellent seaman, was, nevertheless, a stern and severe man, disliked by the sailors. He frowned at the recital, declared that he believed Will Hardy to be a desperate villain, ripe for any crime; and proposed that the captain should immediately order him into irons.

"That I would certainly not advise," said the cool-headed Dr. Lewis. "The expressions used by him, might only be idle words to terrify the children and Nanny; in which case the punishment would be severe, if not unjust; and if the men should really mean mischief, such a proceeding might be dangerous, and likely to hurry matters to a conclusion. But we must all be watchful and prepared, till the suspected men can be got rid of."

"The knaves know well enough what they are about," said the mate; "nothing of this was heard till we had passed the Cape, where we might have landed them; and they defy us to do it now, three hundred miles off any port."

Captain Russell, now thoroughly roused, went on deck immediately with the mate, and Dr. Lewis returned to his friends. He found Jack already arranging his armoury, and after admiring his promptitude, he ventured, without alarming them unnecessarily, to suggest the prudence of arranging all their most valuable possessions in such a manner as to make their removal convenient, in case they should be driven to the necessity of lanching the long boat, to escape from the disorderly crew.

A loud noise of voices, and trampling of feet on the deck, announced a crisis at hand, and the young men armed themselves, to defend their parents and sisters. Nanny, quite in her element, when active measures were needed, scolded the whole party for leaving England, abused the captain and his crew, kicked about the boxes, declared she ought to have been told about the *shifting* days before; but worked actively, and made every one else work, all the time. Once more she corded the boxes that had been opened, collected the knives, forks, and spoons from the table, and put them into her capacious pockets, tied a tea-kettle to the top of one box, and a large iron kettle to another. Finally, she drew the blankets from the beds, and made each person wrap one round him, and was just attempting to roll up a mattress, when the door flew open, and two men entered, bearing the ghastly figure of Will Hardy, covered with blood, with one arm hanging useless, broken by a ball.

"Here's a job for you, Mr. Doctor," said one of the men; "look after Will, and set him right. We can't spare him."

"Rash and wicked men!" cried Mr. Merton; "what are you about? Know you not that you are violating the laws of God and man?"

One of the ruffians replied by pointing a pistol at the speaker. Dr. Lewis dashed it from his hand, and said in a commanding tone, "We are all armed, and if you injure a person in this cabin, you shall die, and your leader must perish for want of assistance. Spare my friends, and, by God's help, I will save his life."

"Give me some of your drugs," groaned the sufferer, "to stop this pain, and let me have the use of my limbs again; and I swear to you, you shall all go free."

The doctor made a sign to his friends to leave all to him; then, with the assistance of the young men, and of Nanny, who could not, however, forbear groaning out her disapprobation of the deed, he extracted the ball, set the arm, placed the exhausted sufferer on a sofa, and dressed his wounds. He then prepared an opiate to administer to him.

"What's that stuff you are going to give me?" asked Will.

The doctor explained to him the nature and the effects of the draught. The man was silent for a few minutes, and then said,—

"Do you mean to stay, and be one of us, Doctor?"

"I do not understand you, Will," answered the doctor; "I know there has been some altercation; but where are the captain and the mate?"

"Never you mind," said the wretched man; "they'll never put irons on another poor fellow: they've got their due."

Dr. Lewis was inexpressibly shocked; he saw murder had been committed. On further inquiries, the man did not deny the fact; and when the good doctor reminded him of his perilous state of soul and body, he found him hardened in guilt and scoffing at repentance.

"You may as well speak out, and say whether you will join or not," said the reckless villain. "Think of yourself, man; for if you send me to sleep, ten to one but my *chaps* cut all your throats, that you mayn't have a chance of turning informers."

"Then, certainly, Will," said Dr. Lewis, calmly,

D

" I not only refuse to become an accessary to mutiny
and murder, but, if I should be spared to reach any
shore where the laws of civilized nations are recognised, I should consider it my first duty to report
your lawless proceedings to the proper authorities."

Will swore dreadfully when he heard the resolution
of his doctor, who only noticed it by reminding him
that the excitement of anger would endanger his life.
He was silent for a few minutes, and then said:—

" You have done your best for me ; and I swore
you should escape with your lives ; so I will give you
and these white-faced loons a chance. Call Jack
Allen."

Jack Allen was summoned, and received orders
from his commander to put out a boat, to let the passengers have such of their property as they chose to
take, as well as a cask of water and one of biscuits, with
a bag of rice ; to see that they embarked immediately,
and then to send them off to their fate. These orders
were mingled with execrations and fiendish laughs.

It was with fainting hearts that the half-distracted
party collected their moveables and went on deck, the
ladies trembling and not daring to look round, lest
they should see some bloody record of crime. Their
boxes were lowered into the boat. Jack and Tom,
taking care to bring the rifles and ammunition, descended to arrange all in some order. Dr. Lewis
once more visited his patient, gave proper directions
for his treatment, administered the anodyne, and then
went with all speed on deck, anxious that no delay
should prevent their escape from that blood-stained
vessel, though the alternative was to plunge into
unknown dangers.

Mr. Merton, with his wife and daughters weeping
and terrified, first embarked, and were followed by
Nanny. Dr. Lewis looked round for Charles, who
was calling out loudly for his valet. He was answered
by a laugh of derision from a group of the sailors,
who were watching the departure of the passengers.

At length the elegant Mr. Wilson turned round, and, with a supercilious air, inquired who was calling on him.

" Come, Wilson, be quick," cried his master, impatiently ; " look after my portmanteau and dressing-case, and follow me immediately."

" Thank you, Mr. Villars," said the man, sarcastically, " but I have had quite enough of servitude. I am your master now ; and I would recommend you, for old acquaintance' sake, to jump into the boat and make off before the wind changes. If Will goes this bout, you will all have to follow your friend the captain, depend on it, and he was sent to sea without a boat. A good voyage to you all. I'm off with the jolly rovers, to lead an easier life than I did with you and all your tantrums."

Dr. Lewis seized the arm of Charles, and forced him away, for he saw the men were regarding him with an evil eye. In another minute they were all in the boat, and before the rope was loosed, Wilson threw the portmanteau down, exclaiming, " There, that's more than you deserve ; but I know you like a bit of dress ; and after all, you're not a bad fellow, if you wouldn't give yourself such grand airs."

The crew gave three cheers as the little boat parted from the vessel, and Mrs. Merton, covering her face, cried out, " Heaven preserve us ! What will become of us ! We shall all be lost on this dark ocean which spreads before us, without a landmark of hope !"

"Papa, do you and Nanny just look to mamma," cried Jack ; " she is very pale ; but she need not fear. Depend on it, Tom and I will row away as hard as we can from those desperate fellows. See, here are oars and sails. We want nothing, papa, but stout hearts and a fair wind."

" Brave boy !" said Dr. Lewis ; "I have little nautical skill, but I will try to help you. And here is Mr. Villars."

" Oh ! Charley is a first-rate hand," said Jack.

. D 2

" Why, at Cambridge he was always A 1 in boating-matches.　We may rely on him as a sure help."

"Really, boys," said Charles, in a languid voice, "I fear you rely on a broken reed.　Consider how many years have passed since I addicted myself to such violent plebeian exercises.　I will try an oar; but I apprehend that, as my gloves are of peculiarly delicate kid, they will soon be worn out by the friction, and I shall thus be wholly incapacitated."

"How exceedingly absurd you can be when you choose, cousin Charles," said Matilda.　"But no one cares for your affectations here.　Go on rowing, and when Charles's gloves are worn out, Mary and I will work at the oars without gloves."

Charles laughed at this spirited rebuke, and, somewhat ashamed, took up an oar, and began to work vigorously, without any thought of his gloves.　The four young men continued for an hour to row, without further aim than to lose sight of the fatal vessel. When this was really done, Mr. Merton, speaking for the first time, laid his hand on Tom's arm, and said,

" My dear children, pause a moment, and let us consider, first, where we really are, and next, what port or shore we ought to endeavour to reach.　You are all exhausting your strength without any definite aim.　It may be that we are rushing into greater dangers than those from which we have escaped."

Dr. Lewis fortunately possessed a small pocket compass, and, on duly discussing the business, he recommended that they should immediately make to the east; for, as they could not be far south of Chili, if they did not land in some hospitable port, they might, at all events, find shelter and aid to reach a civilized country.

But night came on, and, exhausted with their labours, they hoisted a sail : the wind blowing strong from the south, drove their little bark for many hours northward.　They watched alternately during the night, and morning light revealed to them, high above a heavy mist, that shut out all below them, the snow-crowned heights of the lofty Andes, gleaming at a great distance to the east.

But, remote as this was, it was still a landmark; and their delight was great at the prospect of leaving that deep, dark ocean, which, though it had yet been tranquil, might in a moment rise and overwhelm them. They made a breakfast on biscuit and water, a very necessary refreshment, though it did not accord with Charles Villars's notions of "a good breakfast," and then once more resumed the oars, using every effort to approach the coast. But the wind did not favour them, and their exertions seemed all in vain; they passed rapidly over the water towards the north, but did not appear to get nearer to the shore.

Charles forgot his affectation, and worked so hard, that he not only wore out his gloves, but the skin came off his hands, and still they saw no land, but the dark and mist-enveloped mountains looming through the clouds. Nanny relieved Charles at the oar, and her hard hand bore the labour well. Even Mr. Merton and the girls tried a few strokes while the boys rested, and by their unskilfulness created a laugh, which was beneficial to all.

"Do you think, papa," asked Mary, "that we are near Robinson Crusoe's island? I should very much like to land on it, if we could be quite certain that the savages were not there."

"Alas, my child!" replied Mr. Merton; "though we have no means of ascertaining our position with certainty, I fear we may reckon on being at least eight degrees south of that charming region; and, should we succeed in landing on any island in this inhospitable climate, it can only be a chill and barren swamp."

"We will try, if possible, to reach the mainland," said Dr. Lewis; "for if we are even compelled to land on a desolate shore, we may go on to the north till we arrive at civilized spots. Take courage, Mrs. Merton,—you are surrounded by brave protectors ; we have freedom, a good boat, provision, and a calm sea. Rely on our arms to bring you to port."

Mrs. Merton did not certainly complain, but her look of suffering and misery gave great pain to her husband and children. Nanny at length, out of patience, added her sharp remonstrances to Dr. Lewis's soothing assurances.

" I cannot bide this, mistress," said she. " See how they are all toiling like so many slaves, and not a bit of skin left on their poor hands ; and I wonder what you, poor helpless body, could do without them. Sit up a bit, I say, and look *cheery* at the lads : it's enough to break their hearts to see your down-heartedness."

Nanny's words were not without effect on the dependent Mrs. Merton ; she roused herself to take some interest in their arduous work, and their unwearied look-out to the east. At length they were encouraged by the discovery of a dim hazy line of coast, towards which the continued south wind prevented their direct approach. Many rocky islands were scattered round, but they seemed barren and desolate, and, surrounded by breakers, were inaccessible to the little boat.

After many hours' struggling and labouring at the oars, they got near enough to observe, that gloomy dark rocks, perpendicular and lofty, guarded the coast, and were half-shrouded with a heavy mist. Here it seemed impossible to land, and the most courageous felt a sinking of the heart. Their spirits and strength alike failed, but still they rowed on, to survey the coast as near as they durst venture to approach it. The lofty heights were covered half-way down with dense clouds, which defied the fierce wind which now began to blow, and remained immoveable.

" Here we cannot land," observed Lewis ; " let us push on, as long as we can hold the oars, along the coast. Surely we must reach a more promising spot than this."

They were now evidently in a large gulf, and passed more islands, all barren and desolate. Darkness was coming on, the wind suddenly changed, and blew furiously from the east, forcing them towards the rocky and dangerous coast. They abandoned themselves to despair; they believed their destruction inevitable, and expected every moment to be swallowed up in some eddying whirlpool, or dashed on the sharp rocks that guarded that inhospitable coast.

"My children," said Mr. Merton, "our death is certain; let us lift up our souls to God."

They abandoned their oars and knelt down to pray; even the thoughtless Charles joined them devoutly. They prayed earnestly and fervently; and God heard them. They rose from their prayers with calmness and resignation; they had been driven nearer to the coast, and the keen eye of Dr. Lewis detected a narrow inlet. He called on them to resume their oars, and they rowed with hope and cheerfulness, and at length brought their frail boat safely into the inlet, which seemed to be the mouth of a river. They laboured with pain and difficulty to ascend the stream, which rushed between high cliffs overhung with trees. At length they reached a patch of sandy beach, on the north side of the river, which permitted them to land; and a large beech-tree which grew on the spot enabled them to secure the boat, by mooring it to the trunk.

CHAPTER IV.

The gloomy Shores below the Andes.   The Cave of Refuge.
   Domestic Arrangement.   The Morning Survey.   The Failure
   of Provisions.   The Fishing Expedition.   Shooting in the
   Woods.   The Water-fowl.   The Return of the Fishing-party.

THEY looked round, and perceived by the dim light,
that they had landed on a spot scattered thickly with
dwarfish trees and bushes, backed by steep wooded
rocks, rising one above another, and spreading on towards the lofty Cordillera, piercing the clouds.

The first care of the children, after removing Mrs.
Merton from the boat, almost insensible from cold
and terror, was to form for her a dry resting-place, by
spreading their blankets and cloaks on the beach, till
they could find some sort of shelter from the chill and
moist night air.   The boys then, with Dr. Lewis, ascended the banks, and looked round for some place of
refuge, but in vain ; they could see nothing but the
dark jungle ; and they decided, therefore, to return and
unlade the boat, as well for the security of their property from accidents, as to obtain the means of raising
a temporary tent with the sails.

While the young men were occupied in removing
the casks and boxes beyond the reach of a rising tide,
Matilda and Mary had made their way through, or
rather over, the thick jungle, till they reached a cliff
grown over with luxuriant creeping plants.   Passing
along the face of the cliff, Mary, in stooping down
to disentangle her dress, discovered a very low opening.   Through this she crept fearlessly, and finding it
into a spacious cave, she did not wait a moment,
returned to her sister ; and they flew lightly back
air friends to announce their happy discovery,

Mary assuring her mamma that her cave was quite as good as that of Robinson Crusoe.

"But I cannot live in a cave," ejaculated Mrs. Merton in a tone of depair ; " go on, my children, and leave me here to die."

"A likely thing, indeed, for us to do!" answered Nanny. " Come, mistress, brisk up a bit, and some-how or another, we'll get you on to see what sort of a place these sharp bairns have picked us out."

"Besides, my dear Mrs. Merton," said Lewis, " we have the use of our hands, and we should none of us choose to sit down idly to dwell in a cave. But we shall be glad to make this cave our hotel for the night, if it be habitable, and if we can find no better shelter ; for you must allow, my dear Mrs. Merton, our need of shelter is urgent."

" But I shudder to think on the danger which my child has run," said Mr. Merton. "Why did you venture alone into a place which probably may be the den of a bear, or some other ferocious beast, from whose claws you have been providentially preserved?"

"But I believe, papa," observed Tom, "that none of the *ursi* are found in South America. We are informed that the black bear, an animal that feeds on fruit, roots, and honey, is common in North America down to the Isthmus of Panama ; the dangerous grisly bear, the terror of man and beast, ranges the Rocky Mountains, spreading destruction as he goes ; but this monstrous and ferocious animal has never yet, I believe, been found in the woods of the Andes."

" Tom is quite correct," said Dr. Lewis, " and we need not have any fear of intruding on a bear."

" Of course not," said Mary : " I should certainly have seen the owner, if there had been one, for I looked keenly round. And I am quite sure you will be all delighted with the very comfortable lodging I have selected for you."

Dr. Lewis and Tom had carried Mrs. Merton be-tween them, and they soon reached the rock ; but when

they were shown the low narrow entrance, they all
shrunk back, a little startled.   At length Lewis and
Jack crawled through, carrying with them some dry
branches, and having struck a light, they kindled a
fire and surveyed the cavern.   They decided that it
would, at any rate, be desirable as a shelter for the
night, as it was spacious, dry, and airy, from numerous loopholes in the rock.   In walking round, they
discovered a wide opening not far from the first,
which would afford a more convenient entrance,
though it was quite concealed by creeping plants on
the face of the rock.   Through this opening they
emerged and joined their anxious friends, who had
become alarmed for their safety.

On the representation of the two surveyors, the
whole party ventured to enter.   Mrs. Merton shuddered as she gazed round on this vast dungeon, and
Nanny screamed loudly at the sight of some bats
flitting about, disturbed by the light; but the conviction that this dry and secure shelter was their only
refuge from the dangers of the night, reconciled the
most fastidious to minor inconveniences.

All now was bustle and activity.   While Nanny
settled Mrs. Merton on a couch of cloaks, Mary and
Matilda collected dry twigs, and soon raised an enormous fire ; and as the cave was floored with dry fine
sand, it really looked comfortable.   Dr. Lewis suggested the prudence of removing all their effects to
this place of safety, and, with the assistance of Tom,
Jack, and Charles, accomplished this work of great
labour ; then, after Nanny had filled her kettles with
fresh water from the river, they rolled pieces of rock,
to secure the two places of entrance.   Then Jack
declared their castle was impregnable.

The largest chest was selected for a table, smaller
boxes formed seats, and they sat round the fire, enjoying the warmth till the tea-kettle boiled.

"I took care of the tea and sugar," said Nanny,
" for I knew, mistress, you would get on badly without

them, if we got among the savages, like what the little lasses read to me, wild *creaters* that eat raw flesh like brute beasts. But, laws me! Matilda, honey, haven't I gone and never thought of teacups!"

"I am quite astonished at you, Nanny," answered Matilda. "Now, observe how thoughtful I have been. Reflecting on our probable wants, I took care to bring away six of the small tin cups of the cabin, which we disliked so much to use there; but I considered they could be carried with less danger than glass or china, to serve out the water in the boat. Now we shall be compelled to use them for teacups; and everybody ought to thank me for my prudence."

But everybody did not thank Matilda; on the contrary, her brothers laughed at her vanity; Mr. Merton began seriously to consider some theory for the correction of conceit and vanity; and, above all, Dr. Lewis, the friend and instructor of the clever little girl, shook his head reprovingly; and this made her feel a little ashamed of her boasting. Nor was she much gratified to see her mamma's disgust at the sight of tea served in a tin cup, made in a kettle, and without milk. But fatigue and cold compelled her to swallow the tea; and it was astonishing to see the exhilarating effect produced on the wearied voyagers by their simple supper of tea and biscuit.

After supper, all hands were again at work; the boxes were piled up to form a separate bedchamber for the gentlemen, and for his couch each had his blanket. The single mattress they had been able to bring away was spread for Mrs. Merton; the cloaks and blankets made beds for the little girls. Mr. Merton read prayers, with more than usual devotion, with a special thanksgiving for their deliverance from the dangers of the sea. Then Nanny made up a good fire, and they lay down and slept as soundly as if the cares of to-morrow were nothing.

But the dawn of morning brought serious thoughts to every heart, of the first step to be taken in their

strange position.   Dr. Lewis rose with the light,
called Charles and the boys, and with them left the
cave to look round at the prospect the light of day
should reveal to them.   They climbed the most acces-
sible part of the cliff, till they reached a sort of platform covered with jungle, over which they walked for
some distance.   Tom found that this thicket consisted
of barberries, covered with fruit not yet ripe, arbutus,
and dwarf beech-trees ; and he was satisfied, for he
should here obtain new botanical specimens.   Their
progress was soon arrested by still higher cliffs rising
towards the mountains.   They walked forward towards
the north for a few hundred yards, and at length an
open vista showed them the mighty Pacific breaking
against perpendicular cliffs on the one hand, whilst on
the other side rose the frowning barrier of the Andes.
There was a stern and gloomy air of solitude in the
grand scene ; and it was with much awe that even the
young and thoughtless boys looked upon hill rising
above hill, all thickly clothed with dark woods, and
all, apparently, untrodden by man.

"It seems impossible to penetrate farther inland,"
said Tom, "especially for females ; and dear mamma
would certainly die of fatigue or fright if she attempted
it.   Would it be possible, Dr. Lewis, for us to ascend
the river in the boat ? "

"Certainly not, for any distance," answered Lewis.
"It is plain that the river flows from the Cordillera,
and must be a torrent higher up, where a boat would
be useless.   I see no means of our leaving the retreat
which has sheltered us, but returning to the boat,
descending the river, and making another struggle
against the perils of the ocean."

Charles shrugged his shoulders, and protested
against such madness ; and even Tom and Jack, whose
love for the sea it required much to quell, looked sorrowfully at their lacerated hands, and had evidently
no desire to take up the oars again.

"I don't see why we should not cross the Andes,"

said Jack, stoutly; "other travellers have done it, and why should not we try? Let us make a litter, and turn the oars into poles for it; it will be ten times easier to carry mamma than to tug at the heavy work of rowing."

"Your proposal is exceedingly absurd," returned Tom. "Do you not perceive that, to cross these fearful mountains, we must pass over the region of perpetual snow; and without guides, mules, or horses, we should inevitably be lost."

"At all events, my dear boys," said Dr. Lewis, smiling at their discussion, "I believe we must try the ocean before the mountain. But let us return now, and petition for some breakfast, for I, at least, am very hungry."

They returned laden with dry brushwood for fuel, as a propitiation to the household goddess, Nanny, whom they found active and busy, and rather more amiable than she had been the preceding evening. Mrs. Merton had reminded her that one of the chests contained a silver tea-service, a present from Charles Villars, when he came of age, to his kind and gentle aunt, who had valued it too much to leave it behind her. Nanny grumbled a little about the *fash* of opening boxes; but, being assisted by the cheerful girls, the cords and nails were soon removed, and the silver teapot and sugar-basin, and a damask tablecloth, taken from the box. The breakfast-table was spread, and though the tin cups did not harmonize with the glittering silver equipage, the strange medley only increased the merriment of the party. Mary declared she had never enjoyed a breakfast so much; the tea was so good made with fresh water, and the old dry biscuits seemed fresher since they were removed from the close ship; and, to complete the table-service, Dr. Lewis produced three small silver cups, which had formed part of the fittings of his medicine-chest, and which were now presented to the three ladies. The tea might have been better with milk, but the voyage had accustomed them to this privation.

Nanny was pleased with her stack of fuel, and, in very good humour, said, "Now, as soon as you've done your breakfast, one of you must go to the butcher's shop, and get me a joint for dinner, for I tell you there's none here for you."

This was a melancholy fact that no one had thought of, and Charles drew such a long face at Nanny's words, that Mary burst into an incontrollable laugh, for which her sister reproved her, and assured Charles that he need not feel unhappy, as she had no doubt she should be able to contrive something for dinner. These words increased the merriment of the young party.

"Bring out your wand at once," said Jack, "and begin your incantation, most potent fairy. Summon the slaves of the wand, and order them to provide a sumptuous dinner, well cooked,—be very particular about the cooking, for Charley is difficult to please."

But when the laughter subsided, the stern reality of the case appeared somewhat gloomy, and they set about discussing their situation seriously. After Mr. Merton had received a full account of the expedition of the morning, Dr. Lewis added:

"Now, my dear sir, I should like to have your opinion on the steps necessary to take; for as it appears we have unfortunately landed on an uninhabited and apparently uninhabitable shore, we shall be compelled to make further exertions. My own persuasion is, that it would be desirable to extend our voyage northward, if possible, till we may be enabled to reach one of the ports of Chili."

"Oh, Mr. Merton!" exclaimed his alarmed wife. "I trust you will never consent to such a plan. I would sooner die here than enter that dreadful boat again. I cannot endure the sea. Why should we not go inland? Surely, if we persevered in going forward, we should at length meet with some human beings to pity and help us. Or I will even be content to remain here: wretched as this cave is, I can endure it better than the terrors of the sea."

"Why is it impossible," asked Mr. Merton, much distressed at his wife's agitation, "to travel north by land along the coast? I am of opinion that such an experiment should first be tried. I have, in fact, myself no love for maritime adventure, and would gladly remain on the shore, and in the quiet retreat to which the mercy of God has conducted us."

"Papa was not cut out for a sailor," said Jack. "But, Dr. Lewis, wouldn't it be a good plan to have a look at the shore by daylight?"

"I was about to propose this plan," replied Lewis. "I hope Mr. Merton will not object to our taking the boat down to the mouth of the river, and making a survey of the coast. We might be able to discover some more favourable landing-place, and, at all events, catch a dish of fish for dinner."

"There's some sense in that!" exclaimed Nanny. "Take your rods and nets, my good lads, and be off, and see to get some trout, or maybe a salmon, and we'll not starve. But you'll not get me into either boat or ship again—I'll bide with mistress. This is but a sad jail of a place; but if I had just a bonny cow, and a bit of a poultry-yard, I could bide here ten times sooner than in your crazy boats, or among such murdering sailor chaps. Lord save us!"

Dr. Lewis was disappointed at the reluctance shown to the plan, which he still considered the wisest; but, hoping that time would reconcile every one to it, he profited by a reluctant permission extorted from Mr. Merton, and arranged the fishing-party. Charles had one of his common fits of indolence, and declined to accompany them; but Tom and Jack soon produced all their fishing-tackle from the great chest, and, with Dr. Lewis, entered the boat, and with very little labour rowed down the stream.

They were no sooner out of sight, than Charles felt a little ashamed of his idleness; he took his rifle from the case, looked out his powder and shot, and asked Mr. Merton if he thought there would be any good sport in the woods.

"I am unfortunately unable to ascertain the latitude we have reached," answered Mr. Merton: "had we landed as far north as the fertile country of Chili, you might have obtained birds, curious and valuable. On the coast the penguin (*Diomedea chilensis*), a link between the tribes of the air and the ocean; or by the rivers the beautiful flamingo (*Phœnicopterus chilensis*); besides the condor and ostrich, and the innumerable variety of humming-birds."

"Get us a fat goose, or a couple of ducks, if you can, Master Charles," interrupted Nanny. "I shouldn't know how to set about cooking *them* birds, with such crabbed names."

"I will try for something eatable, depend on it, Nanny," said Charles, laughing.

"And I will go with you, Cousin Charles, to pick up the game, and to search for eggs," said Mary.

"If there are any eggs to be found," said Matilda, "your giddy head will never discover them. I must go myself, of course, and then I can take care of you. But in case we should lose our way, we ought to have a post with a signal erected here; and that I certainly shall not attempt to rear."

"That I will undertake," cried Mary. "If Nanny will lend me her scarlet cloak, you will see what an admirable signal I will hang out."

"I request you to leave the matter in my hands," said Matilda, gravely; "I will consider it over ——"

"No time for consideration. Dinner must be provided, and Charles has the game to shoot, so up I go," cried the active little girl, as, catching the lower branches, she swung herself up a beech-tree; and, climbing like a squirrel, she tied the cloak to the highest bough.

Charles was now thoroughly ashamed, and as he held out his arms to assist her to descend, he said:

"Dear Mary, what an idle fellow I am! But you shall never climb a tree again; you have given me a good lesson."

Attired in the close, warm cloth dresses which had been provided for the colder part of their voyage, and which the moist climate, even in the summer season, rendered very necessary, the sisters set out with Charles to make their way up the wooded cliffs,—no easy task : the tangled underwood obstructed their steps, and on the summit of the first hill they entered a wood of tall beeches, mingled with a noble tree, which Charles recognised as the winter's bark ; and they were glad to see also the graceful birch, and a sort of fragrant laurel. In the midst of this wood they heard the strange notes of a variety of birds, and Mary, in great astonishment, cried,—

"How very strange, Charles, that the birds of America should have a different language from those of Europe. I am certain that little fellow is a redbreast ; he hops up to us as familiarly as our own dear English redbreast ; but they would never understand each other, for the note of this pretty creature is more like the bark of a dog than the song of a bird."

" This must be the *Pteroptochos rubecula*, I rather think," observed Charles ; " but you must ask your scientific brother Tom to describe it to you, Mary, for I am too idle to become a lecturer. But, see, there is a flock of birds of the same family running along the ground. These are more like game than your redbreast, and I shall certainly have a shot at them."

Charles soon killed half a dozen of these little creatures, which resembled fieldfares, but had longer legs. Mary then besought him to desist, for she declared it was a positive sin to destroy so many lives for one meal.

" Let us return to the banks of the river," proposed Matilda. " I am positive I saw wild fowl up the stream ; and wild ducks would make a more substantial dinner than these small birds."

To this proposal Charles willingly assented, for in truth he was more fatigued by walking along the entangled brushwood than the light and active girls,

E

and he hoped to find a clearer path on the banks of
the river. They found the shores overgrown with
reeds, and the water covered with wild ducks, geese,
and petrels ; the beautiful kingfisher also dipped now
and then into the stream, and then withdrew to its
nest among the reeds.

Charles was quite satisfied with his prospect of
sport, and thanked Matilda, as he loaded his fowling-
piece, for being such a capital pointer.

" I did not think of your sport when I directed
you here, Charles," returned she, honestly ; " all my
consideration was for the larder."

And Charles soon provided plentifully for the
larder, while Mary crept about among the rushes, and
filled her pockets with eggs. They were now heavily
laden, and the road was very rough ; but Charles
roused himself to unusual exertions ; cut some stout
branches, to supply the sisters with good walking-
sticks, and then suspending his heavier game on the
end of a third pole, he placed it over his shoulder, and
with slow steps they made their way homewards,
guided through the mazy woods by Mary's scarlet
signal.

They reached the cave very weary, long after midday,
and found that the voyagers had not yet returned, and
that Mr. and Mrs. Merton were in great anxiety about
them. But the wearied party were too hungry to be
able to wait dinner for their friends. It was quite a
sufficient trial of their patience to wait the process of
cooking the game ; but there was no help for it ; so
the girls assisted Nanny to pluck the small birds,
which were then broiled on sticks laid over the fire,
dished up on some smooth beech-leaves, and eaten
with biscuit and salt, a bag of the latter forming part
of Nanny's spoil when they left the vessel. The
knives and forks she had pocketed at the same time
were now invaluable ; but even her prudence had forgotten to secure plates, a most offensive omission in
the eyes of the fastidious Charles, and a great discom-

fort to Mrs. Merton; but to the light-hearted girls, only an excellent joke, at which they laughed so heartily, that the dinner was, in the end, enjoyed by all.

But as more guests were expected, and the little birds were all eaten, it was necessary to turn to the large wild ducks they had brought in. Nanny looked at these ducks with dismay, and a strong expression of disgust on her countenance, which moved Mary to laughter, a liberty Nanny resented by becoming very angry.

" Did ever anybody living set about cooking such a heap of outlandish things ? " exclaimed she, wrathfully, as she seized and began to tear the feathers from one of the birds. " Them that likes may eat 'em, but they'll not catch me poisoning mysel' with such oily, fishy creatures. And please to say, Master Charles, how they are to be roasted ? "

Matilda suggested that the birds should be made into a stew, and the iron kettle was suspended over the fire, the ducks cut up, and with salt and a little rice, made into a savoury dish.

But Nanny's ill-humour was not subdued. She began by sharply reproaching Mr. Merton for letting people *wheedle* him to leave home; then she accused Charles for taking their passage among a den of thieves. As to Dr. Lewis, she declared he must have lost his senses, to bring them to such a landing-place, a place so bad that nobody had ever built a house there. The sisters were scolded for tearing their frocks, " going scrambling about like lads ; " and finally, she said, that if the youths did not return soon, they should fast; she had no notion of slaving for them, when they could stay out whole days on their pleasure.

But Nanny's wrath, though loud, was never lasting or serious ; she had recovered her composure, and was announcing that the stew was completed, when the voices of the fishermen were heard singing the " Canadian Boat Song" as they rowed up the river. The harmony of the three voices had a pleasing effect in the solitude of these dark woods, and filled the eyes of Mrs. Merton with tears. She was even roused to go outside the cavern to wait the arrival of the voyagers; the rest of the family hurrying to the strand to receive the light-hearted party. They had filled the only basket they had brought from the ship with large trout and a fine salmon, and at the bottom of the boat lay a quantity of very large oysters which they had found on the rocks at the sea-coast.

This addition to the store of provisions was hailed with great satisfaction by Matilda and Nanny, the careful housekeepers; and even Charles, though he had dined before, assisted in swallowing a few oysters, in order that the large convenient shells might be used as plates for the stew, which the hungry guests applauded as the most savoury of dishes, never once objecting to the fishy flavour.

CHAPTER V.

The Sea or the Mountains? A Second Exploring Voyage. Cannibals of South America. A Walk up the Banks of the River. The Wild Goose.. The Potato. The Voyage determined on. Visit of the Indians. Loss of the Boat. Proposed Flight.

AFTER they had dined, Mrs. Merton anxiously asked if they had discovered any mode by which they could be released from their present dreary, damp solitude, without incurring the misery of a sea voyage.

"Ah, Mrs. Merton!" said Dr. Lewis, "if all were constituted like you, there would be an end of maritime discovery. I know you will not be sorry to learn that, on reaching the coast, we found most formidable obstacles to our further progress by sea, unless we could contrive to improve our little boat. This is an undertaking, however, beyond our power, even if we had possessed more mechanical tools than Tom's small carpenter's chest contains. The coast is guarded by a reef of rocks, which we have only avoided by a miracle, and which threaten destruction to any who should attempt to cross them. The opening through which we must have passed last night we could not discover, for the breakers foamed to a great distance from the coast. By the aid of my glass, I made out several small islands at a distance; but the danger would be very great of any attempt to reach them; and as far as I could judge, they are probably barren and uninhabited. We had intended to put out our boat as far from the shore as we could do it with safety, to obtain a wider survey, but the tide was ebbing, and we found the undertaking hopeless to-day; to-morrow we will choose a more favourable time. But everything now convinces me that the mainland is our best, I may say, our only hope."

"The mountains, you might as well say, Lewis," observed Tom; "for we are certainly even now on the Cordillera, which extends down to the ocean. What is your opinion, papa?"

"I believe, my son, that your observation is correct," said Mr. Merton. "It is a source of great regret to me that we are deprived of the means of ascertaining our position; but from the observations I have made on the form, and the productions of the coast, I would venture to pronounce that we must have landed on the rock-bound shores which extend far south of the country of Chili—the very base of the Andes. We are probably in the latitude of forty-two or forty-three degrees, a locality full of dangers and difficulties, and offering little to interest the inquiring mind."

"Then, the sooner we leave it the better, papa," said Jack. "We must either rig up our little craft to

fit her for a breeze, or we must pack up our property,
and set out across the Andes."

"How very absurdly you talk, Jack," said Matilda;
"you propose to scale the lofty Andes, as if they
were our Westmoreland hills. I am of opinion that
you would find this no easy undertaking yourself;
and for us, it would be impossible. How could dear
mamma ever be got up those precipitous mountains?"

"The best conveyance for mamma," said Tom,
"would certainly be a litter, carried by mules."

This observation was received with a burst of mirth,
which somewhat disconcerted the speculative youth;
and Matilda added, "You might as well have suggested that we should make the journey on an
elephant, Tom, which we are just as likely to meet
with here as a mule."

Mrs. Merton sighed over her helplessness, which
occasioned so much care to her children: she almost
determined to exert herself a little more; but the habit
of inaction, in which she had so long indulged, is one of
the most difficult of despotic habits to subdue. After
considering and discussing many measures, nothing was
decided on, except that the boat-party should revisit
the coast next morning, to make a further survey.
Charles again excused himself from the toil, saying,
he would go out and shoot some more ducks; and
the young ladies sat down to mend their tattered
garments.

A store of provisions was made up for the voyagers,
consisting of ducks, cooked as well as ducks could be
cooked with such inadequate means, and a small
supply of biscuit. They set out in high spirits,
laughing at Charles, who, at the same time, sauntered
lazily out with his rifle, half ashamed of his idleness,
but not energetic enough to overcome it.

After the little girls had tired of their needlework,
Mary said, "I wish, dear mamma, that you would try
to walk up the banks of the river. There are beautiful trees and flowers, and you would be amused to

see the quantity of ducks and geese on the water, a little higher up. Certainly, the ugly dark-grey ducks are very unlike our dear pretty ducks at home; and the geese are as dingy as the ducks; but we saw one beautiful, proud-looking, old white gander, that would have delighted Nanny,—he was so like Old Clark, that we left at Winston."

"Oh, Miss Mary," cried Nanny, quite softened by the remembrance of her favourite, "Old Clark was no common gander, he was a knowing fellow: folks said he was cross and spiteful; but, if it please God I should ever see Winston again, so sure will Old Clark come up and put his *neb* into my hand for a bit of bread. Now Clark knew folks as well as if he had been a Christian; but what can these creatures know in this outlandish place, where I'll be bound they've never set eyes on man or woman before we were so unlucky as to come among them."

"And no great luck for them either, Nanny," said Mary, "for cousin Charles makes cruel havock among them with his rifle."

"Ay, there again!" replied the irritable maiden; "he's just like the rest of you: not a bit of thought for what's to happen to-morrow. There he goes on; firing away all his powder, and that over a heap of poor skinny things, that smell so strong there's no touching them. What will he do if a lot of them black savages come to eat us all up? God help us! There's no more shot to be come at here!"

"Nanny, you are quite right," observed Matilda. "Indeed, I have been considering myself the imprudence of this wanton waste of ammunition, and I shall certainly remonstrate severely with Charles when he returns. Not that I would encourage you, Nanny, in the absurd idea that any of the natives of the continent of America are cannibals. This has been distinctly proved; has it not, papa?"

"It is more than suspected," answered Mr. Merton, "that the Fuegians, a people only separated by the

Straits of Magellan from the great continent, and
even some of the continental tribes of South Patagonia,
make no scruple in feasting on the flesh of their
slaughtered prisoners of war.   Moreover, recent
voyagers have narrated more frightful deeds of bar-
barity among these tribes, especially in Tierra del
Fuego.   The natives themselves allow that, in seasons
of famine, they murder and devour the aged women
of the tribes.   The poor victims, knowing the fate
that awaits them on such occasions, always flee, to
hide themselves in the woods ; but they cannot escape
their famishing hunters, who seize and strangle them,
or hold them over the smoke of a fire of green wood,
until they are suffocated ; and then cut up the body
and feed on their infernal repast.   But I am persuaded this barbarous custom does not exist so far
north as our present position.   Neither should we be
endangered, who are enemies to none of our kind ;
and the profusion of provision around us, prevents
any possibility of our falling victims to the famished."

"Nevertheless, it would not be desirable to come
into contact with any of these uncivilized people,"
observed Matilda ; "and we cannot have a better place
of concealment than this snug cave."

"But surely, Mr. Merton," said Mrs. Merton, in
great alarm, "you do not apprehend that there is any
probability of encountering those wild Indians, of
whose deeds of blood you have so often read to me ?
I should die at the sight of one of those savages."

"Have no fears, mamma," replied Mary ; "I shall
insist on Charles making wooden lances for Matilda
and me.   Then look at the number of armed men we
could raise.   Depend on it we should be a formidable
troop to oppose.   But come out now, mamma, and
look round you, and you will be satisfied no Indians
have ever visited this quiet solitary spot, nor is there
any temptation for them to come."

Mrs. Merton was persuaded to venture, and she
agreed that the solitude appeared never to have been

broken ; and, supported by her husband and children, she walked along the banks of the river as far as the sandy beach extended, but took fright at the difficulty, when her feet became entangled in the brakes of fuschias, covered with crimson blossoms, that frequently hung quite over the river. She wished to return, but the sound of Charles's rifle at no great distance encouraged her to remain. She sat down on a piece of rock, while Mary raised her clear voice to summon the sportsman, who soon came up to them, with his bag full of game, and a dark-looking goose swung over his shoulder.

"I have shot the goose, rather than its mate," said he ; "for I thought it looked younger, and might be more tender ; though certainly the appearance of the snowy-white gander was more tempting."

"I perceive," said Mr. Merton, "that this bird is the *Anas hybrida*, remarkable for the contrast in colour between the male and female birds. The latter is black, except that the tips of some of the feathers are white, and the bill and legs red. The male bird is of a pure white, with gold-coloured bill and legs,—a beautiful creature. These birds are remarkable for their attachment and constancy, and are always found in pairs, not in flocks."

"Then I am really very sorry, uncle," said Charles, "that I have severed the bonds of union ; but the necessity of the case must plead my excuse. Matilda declared to me this morning, that her affections were set on a roast goose. Speak, peerless manager of the household,—Is not this the truth ?"

"I am very glad, indeed, Charles," replied Matilda, who had been examining the vegetation around ; "for this low shrub has the smell and taste of sage, and is doubtless the herb called by the Indians *palghi*, of which we read in South American travels. This will be a sort of seasoning for the goose. But, papa, come here, and tell me, is not this the flower of the potato ?"

"It is, undoubtedly, that most valuable plant, my child," answered Mr. Merton. "The potato is certainly a native of South America. This is not, however, the locality in which I should have expected to discover the *Solanum tuberosum*, which usually selects a dry and sandy *habitat*. I doubt much that the tubers will prove fit for food."

"Nevertheless, papa, I should advise that we make the experiment," said Matilda.

Mary immediately seized the rough plant, and endeavoured to pluck it from the ground with her hands, but was not successful. Charles laughed at the vain attempts of his determined little friend, and went to her assistance. He produced a large knife, and soon dug up about a dozen good-sized potatoes of an oval form.

"We must have more, dear cousin Charles," cried Mary. "Nanny will be so delighted to see real potatoes, that she will be half-reconciled to our dismal cave."

Charles was not very eager to undertake the labour of digging, but his good-nature prevailed, and they soon filled up the game-bag with a good supply of potatoes.

"And now," cried Mary, delighted, "I will carry home a couple of these huge rhubarb-leaves, to dish the game and fish upon."

"This plant is not the rhubarb," observed Mr. Merton; "but, if I do not err, it is the *Gunnera scabra*. If it be so, the stalks, like those of the rhubarb, are eatable. You must cut some for the examination of Dr. Lewis, whose profound botanical knowledge far exceeds mine. And by all means take some of the leaves, which are rather more suitable for table-covers than dishes, for some of them must be eight feet in diameter, and, as you see, nearly circular."

They selected some of the smaller leaves, but left the stalks for another expedition, for they were now all laden with new treasures; and Mrs. Merton being quite weary, they set out homewards.

" And very good-looking potatoes they are, for a poor place like this," said Nanny, when she had looked over their several acquisitions. " And a bonny goose too, Master Charles, if it hadn't been so black ; and if I knew how to get it roasted, we could make out a decent dinner to-day."

Matilda showed Nanny how to spit the goose on a long stick, of which one end was sharpened, and stuck in the ground before the fire. By turning this simple spit occasionally, the goose was roasted perfectly. The salmon and the potatoes were boiled, and all served on the large leaves. The repast was duly praised ; the salmon was really excellent ; but Nanny murmured much at their bringing home sage and no onions. Surely they might have found some : sage and onions were not likely to be far parted. Still the goose, though somewhat meagre, was enjoyed ; and though the potatoes were rather watery, no one complained. The sole regret was for the absent, who did not return till evening, and were then so weary, that it was only after taking some refreshment that they were able to speak of their voyage.

After a good supper, Jack said, " Now, Nanny, take care that you and these girls rise early, and set to work briskly. Pack up everything ; cook all the provisions you have. Tom and I will go to the wood and scratch up a bag of these wonderful potatoes. We will fill the water-cask higher up the river, where the tide does not reach ; and then we will ship our cargo, and set out on our voyage of discovery."

Mrs. Merton turned very pale, and looked imploringly at her husband, who turned to Dr. Lewis, and said, " My boys are young and rash, my dear friend ; it is on your cooler judgment I rely for our safety. Do you think it prudent to leave the security of land, to risk a voyage in a small and crowded boat, and without a definite plan or object ?"

" I do indeed think this the most advisable plan, situated as we are," answered Dr. Lewis. " Even now, in summer, the climate on this coast is damp and probably unhealthy. The chance of our seeing any vessel is very improbable ; and should we remain in this moist and murky atmosphere until winter, our situation would be intolerable. We must make some efforts to escape from it. Taking advantage of the current from the river, we sailed out to-day, with little difficulty, a mile from the shore. I could thence, with my glass, distinguish a small island, the shores of which appeared woody and verdant. It is this island we propose to reach ; it will not be a long or danger-ous voyage ; and even should the island, as I suspect, prove uninhabited, it will probably afford us a more agreeable and healthy abode than our cave, and we shall be in a situation to hail any passing vessel. At all events, if we find it unsuitable to our wants, we can extend our voyage to some other spot, for I have no doubt it is one of the Archipelago islands, which lie off this coast."

The arguments of Dr. Lewis were convincing ; and, however formidable the undertaking, the sisters were content, and the youths sanguine. Mrs. Merton, as usual, yielded to the wishes of her husband ; and Nanny's murmurs were overpowered by the voices of the majority. After Mr. Merton had performed his sacred duties, and added an especial prayer for the blessing of God on their perilous undertaking, they lay down to rest, after the fatigues of the day, full of hope for the morrow.

About midnight, Dr. Lewis was roused by unusual sounds, and, starting up, he approached one of the crannies in the face of the rock, and, listening atten-tively, he heard voices and the neighing of horses. He went forward from his sleeping-place towards that part of the cave used for the kitchen, and was glad to see the fire was extinguished, for he was fearful some escape of smoke might have betrayed their place of concealment. He reflected a moment, and then de-cided on cautiously awaking the family, one after another, to prevent the danger of any sudden alarm.

P. 61.

Dismounting from their horses, they fastened the bridles to trees, and all entering
the boat, they pushed forward down the river.

His information caused them all much anxiety; but Lewis enjoined silence, and mounting on a chest, he contrived to reach an aperture, that, by the hazy light of the moon, gave him a view down to the river. He distinguished a party of Indians mounted on horses. They were tall men with flowing hair, clothed in long mantles, of a peculiar form. He could not ascertain their number, for they were crowded together on the spot where the boat was moored, and had evidently been arrested by the sight of it.

They were speaking rapidly in their own language, which Dr. Lewis did not understand; but one man, who seemed a leader, used several Spanish words in his discourse, and often alluded to *los Christianos*.

Dr. Lewis thought he could comprehend from this man's words that the sight of the boat had alarmed them; that they suspected many Spaniards had landed on the coast, and that they must bring their warriors to conquer and destroy them. The words of the leader seemed to occasion much pleasure to the rest, who uttered wild cries; then, dismounting from their horses, they fastened the bridles to trees, and all entering the boat, they pushed forward down the river.

When Dr. Lewis announced this movement to his anxious friends, the boys were in such indignation against the robbers, that he had some difficulty in preventing them from crying out and rushing from the cave after their boat. But he pointed out to them the madness of endeavouring to arrest an armed party, of unknown number, and the certainty that such an attempt must bring danger, if not destruction, on all.

They waited in great anxiety for about twenty minutes, when, concluding the strangers had really departed, Dr. Lewis left the cave, accompanied by Charles, who, in this emergency, was really roused to action. The moon was still up, and they were able to see that the boat was really gone, and that six horses

remained, tied to the trees, in all probability till the
Indians returned in formidable numbers. The rest of
the family were immediately summoned to hold a consultation on this important and vexatious event.
Jack, who had actually shed tears for the loss of the
boat, on the very eve of the projected voyage, bright-
ened up when he saw the horses, and he exclaimed,—

"I know mamma will prefer travelling on horseback to making a voyage, and we have a right to
these horses, in exchange for our boat ; have we not,
papa ? "

"I am glad, my son," replied Mr. Merton, "that
you feel a doubt on the subject, for the horses are
not legally or justly our property. They have been
left here by their masters, in good faith, to be reclaimed on their return, when they may possibly
restore the boat."

"But, papa," said Tom, "it is more probable that
they will return with a formidable body of warriors,
to massacre us, or to carry us off as slaves. It seems
to me a perfect folly to wait here for their arrival,
when we have a chance of escape by means of the
horses."

"I doubt the equity of such an act," observed Mr.
Merton.

"I believe we may consider it doubtful," said Dr.
Lewis ; "nevertheless, my good friend, our case is
urgent ; we have a fearful responsibility in the care of
your young and helpless family, and I am decidedly
of opinion, that on certain conditions, we are justified
in using the horses of the robbers. This we will promise to do. Should we be so fortunate as to reach a
place of safety, we will turn the animals loose ; and if
they have been well treated by the Indians, depend
on it their sagacity will point out to them the road
to their former friends. We will therefore, sir, with
your permission, return to the cave, and make our
preparations, for no time must be lost."

Mr. Merton yielded to the majority, but remained

unconvinced that they were acting right. They returned to the cave discussing various plans, all ending in the same conclusion, that they must leave the spot before the return of the Indians. As to Mrs. Merton, she really felt overjoyed at the capture of the boat, notwithstanding the alarm of the Indian visitors; such was her dread of the sea; nor did an equestrian journey seem so terrible to her, timid as she was; for, among her native hills, her usual mode of travelling had been on horseback, seated behind her husband.

The first consideration on their return to the cave was, whether it was possible to remove the contents of the boat on the horses. They were reluctant to abandon any part of their property in their uncertain situation; and it was determined to make the attempt.

" The carpenter's chest, which was one of Charles's generous gifts to Jack and me," said Tom, " I cannot consent to leave, though it certainly feels rather heavy."

" We will lighten it a little by taking out the two axes," said Jack, " for I have a notion we shall need them to cut our way through the woods. I hope we shall distance the rascals. What a lucky thing it was that we tore the sail so clumsily under that overhanging beech-tree last night, and that I was so prudent as to bring it up to the cave for the girls to mend, for the thieves will be some time in performing their voyage without it; though, poor wretches, I doubt very much whether they would understand how to hoist a sail if they had one."

" And a very lucky blunder it was too, Jack," replied Dr. Lewis, " that you brought it up rolled round the mast, for we must certainly place it on one of our horses, to form a tent which may shelter us from the dews of night during our wanderings, till we meet with more comfortable accommodation; but you had better not mention this plan to Nanny just now, for she looks rather irritated by the sudden demands on her exertions, and doubtless expects to rest at some convenient inn to-morrow. I would propose that the black horse, that looks elderly, and I suspect, has a blind eye, should be given up entirely to papa and mamma. It will certainly require the three strongest animals to carry our baggage, and we must arrange as well as we can with the two remaining."

"Positively, Lewis," said Charles, "you must let me have an animal of some sort. I am no pedestrian."

"Very well, Charles," replied Lewis, "but you must take a lady *en croupe*,—Nanny, *par exemple ?*"

"I will take Mary," answered Charles, hastily. "Mary and I have often had a scamper together at Winston; I will leave Nanny to you, Lewis."

"I have no objection in the world to walk," said Lewis, "and Jack has offered to be my companion; we must add Nanny to our party, and Tom must take Matilda on the remaining horse. If Nanny gets tired, we must perch her on the baggage-horses."

"See which *on* us will tire first," said the valiant maiden. "But here, *honeys*, come and take a bite before you set out, while I fill a bag with what we have left."

Cold ducks, cold goose, and salmon, with some potatoes, were placed in Nanny's bag. The large water-cask was to be filled at the river before they diverged from it. Breakfast was concluded, and then Mr. Merton performed the morning devotions with unusual fervour, and all rose from their knees with gratitude for the mercies God had bestowed on them, and a firm reliance on Him for the future.

CHAPTER VI.

The Departure. The Lasso and Bolas. The Ascent through the Mountain Forests. The Parrots. Strawberries. The Guanaco and Condor. Failure of Provisions.

"FAREWELL," cried Mary, "our good cave of refuge! And if we cannot find nests, as the birds do, among the trees and rocks, we can still come back, after the Indians are gone, to this quiet retreat. You boys have axes, you might cut down some of the trees, and we would plant gardens and make a comfortable home. What do you think of my plan, Cousin Charles?"

" I cannot say that I approve of it, Mary," replied Charles. " I have no taste for caves generally; I abhor this dungeon in particular; and if our evil fate drives us once more to seek such a shelter, I trust the mountains may afford us a more cheerful abode than this."

" Nevertheless, Charles," said Lewis, " I think it would be a measure of prudence to conceal the entrance, lest we should unfortunately again be glad of such a place of refuge."

This was soon accomplished; the baggage was brought out, and pieces of rock piled before the openings secured them from observation: the horses were brought up and laden. They were strong animals, apparently well trained; each had a bridle of hide, and a sort of saddle made of skins, with the hair uppermost; to each saddle was attached the lasso, and the indispensable set of bolas, so useful in the Indian chase. The lasso was a thong forty feet long, formed of many strips of hide of a regular thickness, plaited

F

together; it was quite pliable, from having been rubbed with oil. At one end was an iron ring, about an inch and a half in diameter, through which the other end of the thong was passed; thus forming a running noose.

The bolas were three balls of stone, probably iron pyrites, covered with hide, and attached to the ends of three thongs of plaited hide, about four or six feet in length. The balls were about the size of a hen's egg. Charles and Dr. Lewis were both skilled in the art of throwing the lasso and the bolas, and undertook to teach Tom and Jack, when circumstances permitted it. Beneath the beech-tree, where the boat had been moored, Jack was delighted to find three long Indian lances, which the Indians had probably found inconvenient appendages in their voyage, and had abandoned until their return. These lances were made of bamboo, about fifteen feet in length; they were headed with iron, skilfully sharpened, and were really formidable weapons. Charles and Tom, the equestrians, took possession of these arms, and, when mounted on their noble horses, with their ladies seated behind them, and poising their long lances gracefully, they rode off from the cave, Matilda declared they resembled the knights-errant of old, sallying forth in search of adventures.

The cushions and cloaks, which had formed their couches, had been strapped upon the horses to make commodious seats for the ladies, and with some contrivance they managed to carry away all their possessions. The cavalcade then, in the dim light of breaking day, moved slowly up the banks of the river for about half a mile, till they reached a convenient spot, when they filled the water-cask. From thence they diverged to the left, and passed with great toil over the entangled underwood. Jack and Dr. Lewis led the way, as pioneers, armed with axes, with which they cut away any extraordinary impediment; then followed the mounted party; the baggage-horses, which were fastened to each other in single file by ropes, brought up the rear, led by Nanny: there was no danger of their running away, heavily laden as they were.

They continued gradually to ascend through the wood as much as they were able, but their progress was necessarily very slow; and, though they continued moving onwards till noon without rest, Dr. Lewis calculated that they had not journeyed more than twelve miles. The sun was now so scorching that they were unable to go on, and, worn out with fatigue and anxiety, they gladly hailed the appearance of a small clear spot which offered pasturage to their horses; and beneath the grateful shade of a spreading beech they made their first halt.

The poor horses were unloaded and secured to the trees by the long lassoes, the cloaks and cushions were spread on the ground, the dinner was heartily enjoyed, and then the wearied party lay down to sleep, and had two hours of profound repose.

They rose refreshed and ready to proceed, and, relieved from immediate danger, began to look around and admire their new and romantic situation. Buried in the lonely woods that clothe the sides of the majestic Andes, far from all human-kind, homeless wanderers as they were, they enjoyed their adventure. The woods resounded with the notes of thousands of strange birds; bright-coloured and luxuriant plants wound round the dark pines, the beeches, and the still unknown forest-trees around them, and the weather was calm and pleasant. Once more they set out, but now in cheerfulness and hope.

"But why do you, our trusty guides and pioneers," asked Mr. Merton, "conduct us thus gradually from the coast, for I observe our course is continually N.E. ? My own opinion would have induced me to continue to travel along the coast till we reached some town, or, at all events, some fishermen's huts."

"I fear, my good sir," answered Dr. Lewis, "that the people on this savage coast are not industrious enough to become fishermen, or to build huts. Charles and I know something of these shores, which are in this part indented by long arms of the sea. If we did not leave the coast, we should be compelled to pass round these arms,—a labour of time, even if it were possible, which I doubt, for much of the coast is so rocky, that I do not believe it would be passable. We have therefore concluded it most advisable to ascend as high as we are able, in order to escape these impediments. I dare scarcely speculate on our success, for the forest is so intricate that I dread lest our animals should be exhausted with the labour of struggling through it. But I have remarked a sort of track from our resting-place, which I am now taking : I have no doubt it is made by the wild cattle which frequent the mountains, and which, like ourselves, have discovered the convenience of this plot of pasturage. You perceive the track is sufficiently beaten to render it passable, and if we should meet a wild cow on our way, I will show the boys the use of the bolas."

They went on toiling through the mazy woods with more confidence than before, following the track of the animals for five hours, when they reached a rapid, but now shallow river. After the first melting of the snow in spring, this brawling stream must certainly have been an impassable torrent ; and they congratulated themselves that the season was so favourable for their expedition. Here they found a convenient spot beneath the trees for their night's rest. The horses were unloaded and secured ; then the young men formed a sort of tent by suspending the sail over the lower branches of a tree, and the mast of the boat fixed in the ground. The boxes formed a barricade in front, and blankets were hung at the sides. A fire was then lighted, and the unanimous opinion of the party was, that the tent was ten times more comfortable than the cave. Nanny and her young assistants boiled the kettle, and a refreshing supper was made on tea and biscuit. The hungry youths petitioned for a cold duck, but the prudent Nanny was inflexible. "Where's the dinner to come from to-morrow, if you eat the ducks to-night?" was her question; and, though they promised to procure game next day, she put no trust in them. So they gave God thanks for his mercies, and went to rest; two of the young men watching alternately during the night, for two hours at a time, to keep up the fire, and to guard against the approach of any wild animals.

The night, however, passed without disturbance, and at early dawn they assembled at prayers, after which they took a scanty breakfast, loaded the horses, refilled the water-cask, and moved onwards. They began already to feel the air clearer and drier than on the low moist shores they had left; and even the languid spirits of Mrs. Merton revived in the brisk morning air. Nature was waking from the sleep of night, the leaves were rustling in the light breezes, the bright blossoms were opening, the small birds were twittering on the low bushes, deeper in the woods was heard the richer music of unknown tribes; the huge condor was sailing over their heads, and, strangest sound of all, the chatter of the parrot reached their ears on all sides. The plumage of this bird, which varies so remarkably according to its *habitat*, was in these woods of a dusky green, assimilating so well with the foliage amidst which it was perched, that it was very difficult to distinguish it. Jack and Tom were now initiated in the art of throwing the bolas. Their instructors showed them how to hold one ball in the hand, whirling the others round with great rapidity above the head, then sending them with a certain aim, revolving through the air, to wind round the victim, crossing each other, and binding so closely that the game was prostrated or crippled till it was easily secured. After many ineffectual attempts and laughable failures, the boys attained some skill, and Jack had the glory of bringing down two fine parrots, which he dispatched remorselessly, and presented them to Nanny to cook for dinner.

Her repugnance to cook the birds was very great, and loud were her murmurs. " Well, Master Jack, it's not for me to speak, I know.   One certainly doesn't know what one has to come to in this world ; and little do our folks at Winston think that we are driven to eat a poll-parrot !"

But the " poll-parrots" were, nevertheless, most excellent food roasted, on a stick, and everybody thought Nanny very niggardly because she had reserved a second couple, killed by Dr. Lewis, for supper ; for she declared she had little else to give them.

Mr. Merton examined the birds with interest, and said, " My reading has not acquainted me with the peculiar species of *Psittacus* to which these creatures, on which we have dined so luxuriously, belong.   Can you assist me with your knowledge, Dr. Lewis ?"

" The bird," answered Lewis, " is the *Psittacus jaquilma,* a migratory species, which inhabit the Andes during the summer, while in the winter, flocks of them descend into Chili, destroying the produce of every field they rest on.   Fortunately, their visit is not till after the harvest, or the whole country would be laid waste.   You will observe this is one of the most elegant of the parrots, with its long pointed tail ; and I think we must all agree that it must be one of the most delicious when cooked."

" And after such a delicious dinner," said Matilda, " I can offer you a most delicate dessert."   And she led them to a bank perfectly scarlet with large ripe strawberries.

" Truly," cried Mr. Merton, " this is the *Fragaria Chilensis,* which derives its name from that delicious perfume which doubtless led you, my child, to discover it.   And this provision is spread here, in this lonely mountain-forest, to feed the birds, who abide here, in the midst of abundance, and unmolested."

" I very much doubt their lives being secure, papa," said Jack.   " Observe yon carnivorous condor hovering over our heads : he would soon pick our bones if we were in his power ; and, wanting richer prey, he will make no scruple of devouring his lesser brethren by scores."

The enjoyment of the dessert made up for the scanty dinner; even Nanny smiled as she ate strawberries as large as a hen's egg, and of rich flavour; and she declared the fruit looked as if it had been grown in a Christian country.

But next morning, when they resumed their journey, the thoughtful and prudent of the party could not but feel much anxiety for the future. They had certainly not yet met with any distressing impediments or annoyances, but their slender stores daily decreased ; the birds were an uncertain dependence, and famine threatened them. Another day passed ; no game offered itself for the skill of the sportsman to be exerted on, and their spirits began to droop. To complete their trouble, a cold rain came on, and compelled them at an early hour to seek such imperfect shelter as their rude tent afforded. Then a keen wind rose, scattering their fire, which they found it impossible to keep up ; and they ate their dry biscuit, moistened in water, with heavy hearts, and, covered with cloaks, tried to rest.

After a watchful and shivering night, they rose early, and, as the rain had ceased, they set out before breakfast, to escape from the chill atmosphere of the damp tent. As they rode along, Charles asked, in a mournful tone, " Do you think, Matilda, you could screw nothing more from Nanny than that hateful prison fare, bread and water, for breakfast ?"

" No, indeed,. cousin Charles," answered Matilda, half-sobbing, " it is quite impossible ; we have nothing more, except a little rice. I do think, Charles, you might have provided us with some game before this. But we are very unfortunate. In all the histories of shipwrecked and deserted families that I have read, they always had deer or goats, or wild birds; or they met with everything they wanted in some wrecked stores on the coast. It would have been better not to have left the coast ! Here we can find nothing. To be sure, *I* did find the strawberries.''

Mary laughed merrily at the complaints of her disconsolate companions, and said, " Look well about among the rocks to-day, Matilda ; perhaps you may find the entrance into Aladdin's cavern, and if we could get that ' Genie of the Lamp ' under our control, wouldn't we make him bring us a good supper ? "

Matilda did not like her sorrows to be laughed at, and she was about to reply, when Dr. Lewis made a signal for the cavalcade to halt, and beckoning Charles and Tom to come forward, he silently pointed out to them a herd of curious-looking animals, browsing on a patch of rushy grass, which grew on the mountain-side.

The uplifted finger of their cautious guide stopped the exclamations that were ready to burst out ; he silently directed his young allies to arm themselves with their bolas, and the anxious party then crept slowly towards the herd. Dr. Lewis stopped them when they had approached as near as he considered safe, as it would have been vexatious to have alarmed and dispersed the animals ; they then whirled the balls rapidly above their heads, and flung them at their unconscious victims with some skill, considering the little experience they had had. One animal, whose hind legs were wound round by the bolas sent by Lewis, fell down, struggling hopelessly ; a second received the bolas of Jack round its neck, and after tossing its head wildly, and uttering an odd neighing cry, made off after the rest of the herd, which had fled in confusion at the first alarm. Jack was greatly mortified at the loss of his bolas ; but as they had two spare sets, this was not of so much consequence.

The whole party now proceeded towards their valuable spoil ; but, before they reached the spot, an enormous condor descended rapidly from above upon the fallen animal, and had already commenced his feast by devouring the eyes, when they came up. Regardless of their cries, the voracious creature continued its foul repast; but, not willing to lose the precious spoil, and doubting the probability of securing the marauder with the bolas, Jack fled back to the horses, and returning armed with his Indian lance, he drove the powerful animal from its prey, and slowly and reluctantly it winged its heavy flight.

"I regret," observed Tom, "that we were unable to secure the condor, a bird no less remarkable for its habits than for its magnitude. The immense extent of its wings when spread, and its peculiar and ravenous mode of tearing out the eyes of its victim, are all that we have been able to observe of its characteristics."

"And that must suffice for the present, Tom," said Dr. Lewis; "for, however we may desire to collect specimens of natural history, we must remember and compassionate our already heavily-laden beasts. A condor would have been no slight addition to their burthens. But I do not object to load them for a day or two with the produce of our bolas to-day, for I suspect we shall find this animal worth the labour of carriage.

The animal was dispatched, the legs tied together, a branch cut from a tree and passed under them, and then Tom and Jack bore the spoil with great pride towards the anxious party who were waiting for them. Nanny gave a sharp look of suspicion at the unknown creature, as they placed it on one of the baggage-horses, shaking her head doubtfully; and Tom the *savant*, and even Mr. Merton himself, looked a little puzzled.

"This animal," said Mr. Merton, addressing Dr. Lewis, who was walking by his side, "must be of the llama family—of the genus *Auchenia?*"

"You are correct, sir," replied Dr. Lewis; "it is the guanaco, an animal remarkable for the length and slenderness of its neck, its thin rat-like tail, and its foot, so admirably adapted for climbing the mountains.

You observe that the foot consists of two springy toes completely divided, a strong short hoof, pointed at the tip and hooked downwards, like a claw. The hoofs are compressed at the sides, and are concave beneath, to enable the animal to climb securely. I trust we shall meet with more guanacoes, and then we shall be in no danger of famine."

"Why, you won't tell me that the flesh of that queer-looking beast is fit for a Christian to eat?" said Nanny.

"It is greatly superior to mutton," replied Dr. Lewis; "and I know your excellent cookery will enable us to make some capital dinners on it."

There was much rejoicing at the sight of such an abundant supply of food sent to them; and they rested at an earlier hour than usual, that they might have time to skin and cut up the guanaco. The skin, which was covered with fine long soft hair, they plunged into a little stream near their encampment, to cleanse it thoroughly. Beneath the skin lay a large quantity of fat, part of which they used to rub the skin, in order to keep it pliable; after which it was spread over one of the horses to be dried. Dr. Lewis, as the best anatomist, was appointed butcher to the community; and he cut up the guanaco, Nanny declared, as well as if he had been bred to the trade; and from that time she looked with added respect at the doctor.

The steaks which were broiled for dinner were pronounced delicious; even the fastidious Charles, converted to reason by privation and the mountain air, declared he had eaten worse venison; and, after they resumed their journey, the travelling larder was carefully watched, lest another condor should descend and rob them of their treasure.

The guanaco was a large animal, and lasted them for many days, for in the high region they had reached, the cool air preserved it from corruption. But it was finished at last, and then several days succeeded when dry biscuit, scantily doled out, a few eggs found in some hollow tree, and an occasional parrot, constituted their insufficient diet. They concluded that they must now have travelled above one hundred miles, with very little repose, indifferent food, and through unbroken solitudes ; but they were totally ignorant of their locality, for the thick forests, though the trees were more stunted than those of the lower regions, were yet high enough to shut out entirely their prospect in every direction ; and Mary was certain they must have entered one of the enchanted woods of the fairy tales, from whence the intruders could never escape, but were doomed to wander there through the remainder of their lives. Alternately they climbed the steep and rough sides of the mountain, and then descended into some wooded valley, sometimes of great extent, again to ascend, and again to find another valley, yet ever gaining some higher part of that wonderful mass of mountains. The valleys were the *oases* of their journey. There they ever found shelter, fuel, and fresh water, the latter occasionally more abundant than they wished, for their overladen beasts were little able to ford a river. Sometimes they fell upon the dry bed of a river, which the melted snow from the Upper Andes would probably, in the spring, fill with a rushing torrent. They were then glad to exchange the struggle through the entangled brushwood for the comparatively easy path the rough and stony bed of the river afforded them, till some yawning chasm or insurmountable precipice compelled them once more to return to their forest road.

The poor horses had become wretchedly emaciated from hard labour and scanty food. The patches of rushy grass found here and there on the mountain-side afforded them an insufficient pasturage ; and the party contemplated with dismay the melancholy prospect of being left without any mode of conveyance in that dreary wilderness.

The air had now become cold in the evening, for an early autumn had set in ; and as they crowded round the fire, for which they had still the means of always procuring fuel, watching the boiling of the kettle which was to furnish them with their slender supper of one cup of tea, in addition to one biscuit each, all they could venture to consume from their remaining store, Matilda, unable to restrain her complaints, turned to her father, weeping bitterly, and said, " Oh ! papa, what will become of us when the biscuit-bag is exhausted ?''

" God can spread us a table in the wilderness, my child," said the good man. " He has saved us from the danger of assassination, from the perils of the ocean. He sheltered us from the bloodthirsty Indian, and has guarded us from the ferocious beasts of the forest. He has given us health and strength to endure our fatigues ; and, if we continue to pray to him, he will not forsake us.''

" I have especial reasons for gratitude to the Divine Mercy," said Mrs. Merton, " for I feel my health and strength daily improve with the mountain air and the wholesome exercise ; and I have had time to reflect, in our long journey, on my wasted life. I hope, my dear children, I have not been an unkind mother ; but I have been unfaithful to the trust God has placed in me. If he spare us all from the perils that surround us, I hope to begin a new life, and endeavour to atone for my past errors.''

The children had all remarked with pleasure the improvement in their beloved mother's health, and they now rejoiced with grateful hearts to hear her acknowledgment of restored strength and energy. They forgot their scanty supper in the joy of their hearts, and their evening devotions were doubly fervent in their gratitude.

CHAPTER VII.

Loss of one of the Horses. Jack's Expedition through the
Woods, followed by Dr. Lewis. Extraordinary meeting with
a Stranger. The Hut in the Wilderness. The Family
assembled. Commencement of Almagro's Story.

AFTER a cold and bleak night, the active family
arose to resume their toils, and to their great vexation
found one of the baggage-horses so weak and emaciated as to be quite unable to carry his burthen, and
they reluctantly left him on the spot of pasture. Tom
and Matilda were therefore compelled to relinquish
the horse they had always ridden, to which the baggage was now transferred, and the dismounted pair
joined the pedestrians. The procession moved on
very slowly, for they had now descended into one of
the many valleys of the Cordillera, and the thicket
became more intricate every yard they proceeded.
Jack, always more active and ardent than the rest,
was many yards in advance, when Dr. Lewis, the
second pioneer, saw him spring forward, and plunge
into a thick wood of loftier trees than they had lately
met with, which clothed an abrupt steep on the left
hand. Alarmed, lest the adventurous boy should encounter any danger, Lewis hastened forward to follow
him. On reaching the wood, he found the face of the
rock apparently inaccessible; he called out loudly,
but receiving no answer, he endeavoured to follow the
steps of his daring companion. By the broken and
separated branches, and the trampled underwood, he
was enabled to trace the rash youth; but the labour of
the ascent was excessive.

After pursuing the track for some distance in great
anxiety, he was struck with amazement at hearing the
report of a gun. He knew Jack carried no firearms, and

he paused for a moment in astonishment and dismay, which was increased when he heard heavy groans at no great distance from him. He did not venture to call out again : he had a vague fear that Jack was murdered, and rushed onward to avenge his death. He reached a descent as precipitous as that up which he had scrambled, and an opening in the trees enabling him to look below, he was comforted by seeing Jack bending over the prostrate figure of a man, and apparently engaged in some friendly office to the stranger.

They seemed the sole inhabitants of the valley, for all around was still and silent, and Dr. Lewis once more ventured to call out, and was answered in a cheerful tone by Jack. He descended the cliff with considerable difficulty, and found himself on a little open plain, covered with rushy grass, and scattered over with large fragments of granite. On the grass reclined the form of a dark-complexioned man, who appeared to be suffering greatly.

" Poor man ! " cried Jack, in great excitement ; " I do believe his arm is broken by the fall. Only think of a tumble over that precipice upon these terribly hard stones ! How lucky it was you followed me, doctor, for you must set him all right. And what a capital thing it was that the poor fellow did not shoot me instead of the guanaco."

This was all a mystery to the doctor ; Jack was never very lucid in his explanations, and was now labouring under unusual excitement. Lewis therefore requested him, while he examined the state of the sufferer, to give him some intelligible account of the accident.

" This is the story, then," said Jack : " I was a good way before you, and close to the wood, I heard a rustling among the trees ; I could not stand that, famished as we were, so, with my bolas in my hand, I pushed up through the bushes, and I soon saw before me a guanaco, doubtless the sentinel of the herd, browsing on a little bare spot in the wood. I stole near him as cautiously as I could, spun my bolas round, and whirled them fairly round his neck. He alarmed his friends without loss of time, setting up the loud neigh that offends Nanny's ears so much, reminding her, as she says, that she has been forced to cook and eat horse-flesh. Well; I stooped down to crawl under a high bush that was between me and the guanaco, and at that moment a shot was fired behind me, which would certainly have done for me if I had been standing upright. As it was, the shot entered the shoulder of the beast, which was then struggling to release itself from the bolas. Half-maddened with the pain, it leaped over the bush, and over me too, and, rushing forward towards the precipice, dashed against its destroyer, and hurled him with itself over the steep. I heard his dismal groans, and descended to help him; but when I found him in this bruised and bleeding condition, I was quite in despair, and was considering what I ought to do, when you dropped in so luckily. And after all, the guanaco has escaped, and carried off my bolas. There go two sets among the brutes, and how shall I replace them?"

"We will make his hide furnish us with bolas, if we can secure him," replied Lewis. "But now, Jack, make your way back as speedily as you can to the rest. Request them to wait for us at the foot of the steep, and do you return without delay with my box of instruments and medicine-chest. We must not abandon this poor man to die alone in this dreary wilderness. Doubtless, he has some habitation near at hand; if we could discover it, we would remove him, for he may have anxious friends expecting him."

Jack set out with his usual alacrity, and Lewis, having ascertained that the arm of the stranger was much fractured, sought for a tree, from which he was able to peel the bark in one piece sufficiently large to form a cradle for the disabled limb, which he bound in it for the present, deferring any important operation until he was removed.

It was not long before Jack returned with the boxes, accompanied by Tom and by Nanny, who, on hearing of a case of distress, volunteered her services, and took care to bring a large blanket with her. Dr. Lewis commended her prudent forethought, as the blanket would form the best litter they could contrive. He then made the man inhale some strong volatile, which roused him from his stupor; he opened his eyes, gazed round with mingled astonishment and terror, and muttered a few words of entreaty in the Spanish language.

Lewis immediately addressed him in that language, and demanded where his home was?

The stranger seemed to comprehend him, and faintly articulated some disjointed sentences, which seemed to indicate his unwillingness to disclose his place of abode. " Let me die here ! " he added after a pause.

Dr. Lewis, who not only understood, but spoke the language of the stranger fluently, asked him why he objected to be removed to his friends.

" Friends ! " cried the unhappy man. " Alas ! I have none ! "

" Then we will be your friends," cried Jack, impetuously, in very indifferent Spanish. " Tell us where you live, and we will carry you home."

The man gazed around him with a scrutinizing glance, which softened as it fell on Jack, whose almost unintelligible words he seemed to comprehend, for he pointed out to him a small opening in an opposite wood as the road to his dwelling. They lifted him carefully, placed him on the blanket, and thus bore him, as he directed, through thickets which covered a gradual descent of about a mile, when they entered on a wide, open plain, watered by a clear stream from the mountains. Facing the east, and supported against a rocky cliff, was a low hut, rudely constructed of boughs of trees, and roofed with skins. But their sole care now was the poor stranger; they took little notice of the spot, but gladly entered the humble abode. They found a tolerably comfortable room, lined with furs, and furnished with some seats of wicker-work, and a rough block of wood for a table. In one corner was a heap of dried grass covered with guanaco skins : this was the bed of the stranger, and here they placed him, now in a state of insensibility, from the pain occasioned by his removal.

The humane Dr. Lewis, with the assistance of the young men, soon reduced the fracture of the arm, dressed the wounds and bruises, which were numerous and of a serious nature ; and when his patient recovered from his fainting fit, Lewis administered some composing medicine, and had the satisfaction of seeing him sink into a profound sleep.

Leaving the sick man to the care of Nanny, they sat down to consider over their own plans, and to speculate on the strange situation of the solitary stranger. The little valley in which the hut was placed was covered with the mossy grass peculiar to the mountain hollows, and on this pasturage a handsome mule and two tame llamas were browsing. Portions of the plain, fenced with interlaced willow wands, were cultivated with maize, or Indian corn, now ripe, potatoes, and beans. The hut was large enough to accommodate the whole party, and, as the increasing gloom of the atmosphere portended a storm, Dr. Lewis decided that they were entitled, at least, to a temporary shelter ; the boys were therefore despatched to conduct the whole caravan, if possible, to this secluded spot, an office delightful to the young messengers, who agreed to be silent about all the wonders, especially about the llamas, the sight of which would be such a pleasure to their sisters.

Nanny had, in the meantime, been examining the contents of the hut with some curiosity. A quantity of *charqui*, or dried meat, was suspended from the beams, and on a shelf were placed some unskilfully wrought wooden bowls. One of these was filled with

G

fresh water; the other contained milk, which **Nanny** regarded wistfully. She inquired how long the man would sleep, as, of course, they had no right to touch his property without his leave.

Dr. Lewis laughed at her impatience, and told her he hoped it would be some time before his patient waked to offer them hospitality; but in the mean-time she might, at all events, make a fire from a large pile of dried sticks, which stood outside the hut, for these sticks could be easily replaced from the woods. This employment occupied her longer than she ex-pected, and with groans and lamentations she denounced the savage mode of building a house with-out a chimney or a window, except a hole in the roof, through which the smoke might escape if it chose, and through which the rain did choose to enter.

The rain now began to fall heavily, and two hours elapsed before the wet and weary party, after a most difficult journey, reached the hut, astonished with all they heard and saw, and most thankful for the shelter. Jack was in high spirits,—he had recovered his bolas. Tom had remarked a condor pouncing down on a par-ticular spot in the wood, and deviating from their direct course to reach that place, they found the condor just attacking the dead body of the guanaco, which had been the cause of the poor stranger's accident. After a fierce contention with the condor, the boys succeeded in rescuing the prize, and dragged it off in triumph. It was a large animal, and they were much fatigued with their exertion; but all were thankful for the abundant supply thus obtained.

All hands were ready to skin and cut up the gua-naco, but Mr. Merton would not permit any part of the flesh to be used till the stranger, to whom the spoil rightfully belonged, should wake, and give them permission to appropriate it. They were therefore compelled to content themselves with tea, which, after their exposure to the cold rain, was a great refresh-ment; and when the stranger opened his eyes, he gazed with astonishment on the large party collected round his table; he turned an inquiring glance on Dr. Lewis, who explained briefly to his patient the situation and the destitution of the party. He pointed to the guanaco, and inquired why they had not satisfied the cravings of nature by cooking some of the flesh. Charles, who was well acquainted with the people of South America, and spoke the Spanish language fluently, recognised the stranger as a Guacho, or Spanish American, though he now appeared in a half-savage state. Charles spoke to the Guacho, and told him Mr. Merton's scruples about touching the game which was not strictly their own.

The stranger smiled, and said, " The food which God has scattered over the mountains and amid the forests is common to all mankind. Enjoy the provision he has given you. For myself, I only desire water. Bring me a draught from the stream which flows at the north of the valley."

Jack readily rushed out through the pelting storm, and soon returned with a bowl of fresh water for the feverish patient. Some steaks were then cut from the guanaco and broiled, and the famishing family made the first hearty meal they had eaten for many, many days. They gave the Guacho some tea, with milk and sugar, which, however novel to him, he enjoyed much in his present weak and fevered state. He entreated them to milk the female llama, which had come bleating to the entrance of the hut. She was admitted, and Nanny, assisted by the two girls, milked a llama for the first time.

The Guacho seemed to contemplate his unexpected guests with a mixture of quiet wonder and pleasure; and before he sunk to sleep again, under the composing influence of the narcotic, he used the accustomed Spanish compliment with simple and forcible earnestness, entreating them to consider his house and all his possessions as their own.

Humble as the hut was, it seemed a palace to the

wanderers on that stormy night. The baggage was
brought in, the horses tied to the trees with long
lassoes, which permitted them to feed, and then the
blankets and cloaks were spread to form the usual
couches under the unusual shelter of a roof. It was
a night of peace and enjoyment, and their prayers rose
to God full of the gratitude they felt for his mercy.

Tom and Jack watched alternately by the bed of the
stranger, who slept quietly all night, and did not wake
till Nanny had fulfilled her household duties with all
the enjoyment she ever felt in household duties, and
breakfast was in preparation. Dr. Lewis found the
sick man already in a fair way of recovery, though stiff
and sore with the bruises he had received. The fever
had left him, the arm was going on well, without any
appearance of inflammation ; and after the kind surgeon had bandaged the limb in bark, and made a sling
of a shawl belonging to Mrs. Merton, the patient was
permitted to sit up and take some milk at the happy
breakfast-table.

The sun shone out, and the question of departure
was faintly alluded to ; but Dr. Lewis peremptorily
refused to leave his patient so soon, and it was agreed
that they must remain at least another day, a salutary
rest for the poor horses, as well as for themselves.
Charles then requested the Guacho to explain the
reason of his seclusion in this wild and solitary
valley.

"I seek," said the stranger, sternly, "to hide myself
from the foes who have rendered my life dark and
dreary as the long night of winter. Yet would I not
flee from them, did I not dread, that, instead of the
death I desire, they should doom me to the slavery I
abhor."

"But why do you speak of foes ?" asked Mr. Merton. "The Christian calls no man his foe."

"I was born the son of Christians," said the
stranger, "and by holy baptism I was also admitted
into the Church of Christ, by the name of Almagro.

I have forgotten the forms of my faith; but I have not forgotten that I was taught to forgive my enemies, as I hoped my own sins might be pardoned. Therefore I would not slay the savage and cruel Indians, who have robbed me of all I loved; but I cannot love them—I must call them enemies."

Mrs. Merton caught the word *Indios*, though she did not understand Spanish, and, turning to Dr. Lewis, she asked him, shuddering, if the man was speaking of any Indians near this place. After Lewis had assured her of the perfect security of their retreat, he requested the stranger to relate to them his sorrowful story. Almagro sighed, and commenced his tale in Spanish, mingled with some Indian words, but it was sufficiently intelligible to most of the family, who had long been studying Spanish, and was at intervals interpreted for the benefit of Mrs. Merton and Nanny.

" In the wide plains of the Pampas was the home of my birth. My father prided himself on bearing the name of Valdivia, and my brother Pedro and I learned at an early age to reverence the name of our heroic ancestors, by whose valour and prudence Chili had been conquered and civilized. Many a long evening we listened to my father, with breathless attention, as he related to us the traditional history of the wonderful expedition of the intrepid Valdivia, from Peru to the southern boundary of Chili. He told us how, with a handful of brave soldiers, the warrior subjugated nations, and founded cities, one of which still bears his honoured name; how he made his way, at first with little molestation, through stubborn and independent Araucania, reached the southern tribes, who thenceforward abhorred the Spanish name, and founded the city of the frontiers. He concluded by describing the desperate valour which led the hero, with slender forces, to enter the field against the mighty army of the brave Araucanians; and we shed many tears over the defeat and the tragic fate of the illustrious and unfortunate warrior.

" From my father we learned that Valdivia, during his prosperity, had liberally bestowed large tracts of the conquered country on his officers. To his noble relative, our ancestor, he had assigned a rich allotment, on the east of the Andes, where a colony was formed, which flourished long and prosperously. But the Indians of the south, maddened by the tyranny and oppression of their Spanish rulers, who had scattered, enslaved, or destroyed whole nations, vowed to be revenged, and implanted in the hearts of their children an implacable hatred against Europeans. From time to time they stole on the devoted colony with devastation and destruction. Finally, the few families that remained, fled from certain massacre to the Pampas, and built scattered huts ; trusting that their poverty might save them, if they were discovered by their inveterate enemies.

" Generations had been born, and had died in peace, in the simple dwelling of my father. It was a lowly hut of wicker-work, thatched, and shaded by peach-trees, which surrounded it and overhung the porch. We seemed to be cut off from all communication with man ; yet my father, ever haunted with fear of the Indians, had constructed a sort of fortification ; a fence of the tall and impenetrable cactus, which inclosed the hut and the corral which contained our cattle. We lived in security, peace, and affluence, for we had cattle and horses, more than we needed, always in the corral. At three years of age, Pedro and I could climb by the tail and mount the young colts ; at seven we were horsemen ; and then learned to whirl the bolas, and cast the lasso. We brought the llama from the mountains, and my mother wove us garments from its long hair ; and when we succeeded in securing the fleet ostrich, we adorned our heads with the plumes.

" My father taught us, as he had been taught, to read and to write ; and from my mother we learned to play the guitar. Every evening the lonely hut on the Pampas resounded with our hymns to God; we were a family of love, and peace dwelt among us.

" But a cloud fell on our happiness; when my brother was about twelve, and I ten years of age, we remarked to each other that our father had become moody and reserved. We had no music, nor would he allow us, as usual, to follow him to the chase. He employed us at home, either in drying the beef for *charqui*, or preparing the wool for my mother to spin. Of her we felt afraid to make inquiries, but we saw she looked anxious and unhappy.

" One day my father entered the hut in great agitation, ' My wife and children,' cried he, ' we must leave this beloved spot; we must abandon the home of our fathers !' We were struck with consternation, and my poor mother sunk back, pale as ashes, and powerless to speak. ' For a long time,' continued my father, ' I have observed, in my hunting excursions, the track of the abhorred Indians. I ought to have fled at once from the presence of the destroyers; but I was reluctant to leave this beloved spot, and I weakly hoped their appearance in this part was accidental; but this day has confirmed my worst fears. I had imprudently ventured on the open plain, when, to my dismay, I beheld at a great distance a nume- rous party of our dreaded foes, galloping forward with all the regularity of disciplined troops. I made a hasty retreat, and was, I trust, unobserved; but no time must be lost; our retreat is no longer secure, we must prepare at once for flight, and for defence.'

" With breaking hearts we set about collecting a few necessaries, and some valuable family memorials; my poor mother was quite incapable of directing or aiding us, and we performed our mournful task in agitated silence. We placed our packages on our best horses, armed ourselves with the few weapons we possessed, our knives and spears; and were pre- paring to take a reluctant farewell of our dear home, when a shrill and yelling cry pierced our ears. It

was the first time we had ever heard that sound, but
we recognized it at once as the unmistakeable signal
of woe and massacre.   My mother fainted, sinking
down on the earth from whence she was never more
to rise.   The Indians attempted no parley; in a
moment the inclosure was blazing in every direction.
The terrified animals broke furiously from the corral,
and rushed through the flames, to be secured by the
enemy.   My father, in distracted hesitation, bent over
the prostrate form of my beloved mother, absorbed in
the thought of her fate.   At that moment the Indians
penetrated the inclosure, and the leader, springing
forward, with one blow of his club, laid my father
dead at his feet.

"I shrieked with horror, and was immediately
seized by an Indian and bound on the back of a horse ;
but my bolder brother rushed forward and wounded
the chief with his spear.   I saw him overpowered ; I
saw him share the fate of my father and mother : all
were cruelly butchered.

"Overcome with horror, I lost all consciousness ;
and when I revived I found myself still bound on
horseback, but far distant from the scene of slaughter.
The robbers had brought away all our cattle and moveable possessions, and were journeying towards the
Cordilleras.

"I was for some time speechless with astonishment
to find myself still living.   Then, as the terrible remembrance of the past moved me, I demanded, with
loud cries and entreaties, that they would release me
from my bonds, that I might return to my desolate
home.   They either did not understand, or did not
regard my words ; except that by blows they enforced
silence.   And thus harshly treated, ill-fed, and heart-
broken, I travelled on with these men of blood and
robbery for many bitter days, among the dangers of
the wild and rugged mountains.   But I have little
recollection of this : I had become almost as insensible
as the rocks around me.   I heeded not my present

sufferings ; I had no care for the future ; the affections, the hopes of my life were buried in the past.

"But I was young, and life was strong within me; the privations and perils of the mountain journey were passed, and my captors brought me to their dwellings. They were a marauding tribe, under the dominion of a ruler who governed several of the mountain tribes of the Araucanians, who inhabit the foot of the Andes. To this chieftain I was sold, or presented as a slave ; and though no longer free, I was not cruelly treated. I was now placed among warriors, and my master, the *Toqui*, as he was designated, of the province, had me taught the use of the bow, the sling, and the pike ——"

"But," interrupted Jack, "I never understood that any of these wild Indian tribes had regular governments and disciplined warriors."

"The Indians of the Pampas," replied Charles, "are wild and uncivilized, but the Araucanians have ever been a brave independent people, and, in the maritime provinces, have a shadow of civilization. And Araucania can boast a splendid history, scarcely less glorious than that of Carthage. Pray, Almagro, tell this incredulous boy what sort of fellow your Toqui was."

"Cadeguala, the Toqui," answered Almagro, "was a man of noble and martial appearance, with a complexion little darker than yours, young gentleman, which is perhaps now deepened by exposure to the sun of summer. I had seen no man but my father, till I beheld the ruthless Indians, whom I shrunk from with abhorrence ; but I looked with wonder on Cadeguala, clothed in his flowing poncho, curiously wrought with coloured flowers, and bordered with rich fringes. I fancied that he must resemble one of the princes of Europe, of whom my father delighted to read."

CHAPTER VIII.

Continuation of Almagro's Story. The Dwellings and Habits
of the Araucanians. The Death of the Toqui, and the Flight
of Almagro and Carielpa. The Burning Mountain. Escape
to the Mountains, and the Birth of Zara. The Fatal Visit of
the Indians, and Death of Carielpa. The Wanderings of
Almagro. Conclusion of his Story. Plan of Crossing the
Andes. The Earthquake, and its Consequences. Jack's
Expedition to survey the Ruins.

"Will you tell me, Almagro," asked Matilda, in
tolerably good Spanish, "what kind of houses the
Araucanians inhabit, and what is their food?"

"Our dwelling," answered Almagro, "which was
the best of the scattered village, was built of mud, and
thatched. It was of great extent, and had two en-
trances in the front, which admitted light and air; two
openings at the back led to the kitchen, a detached
building. One side of the apartment consisted of
sleeping-places, separated by divisions made of cane,
and having bed-places raised some height from the
floor. On the opposite side the floor was raised to
form seats. Carpets, rugs, and low tables completed
the furniture of the dwelling.

"In the kitchen were the fire-hearths, earthen pans
and pots, and baskets. For the table they have gourds
separated for bowls and dishes, and large muscle-
shells, brought from the coast, for spoons."

"How I wish we could find some gourds," cried
Mary. "How delightful it would be to make bowls
and bottles, as they did in the Swiss Robinson Crusoe."

"We have certainly not yet reached the latitude
where the gourd is found," observed Tom. "The order
Cucurbitaceæ is rarely met with beyond the tropics."

"Pray don't be so pedantic, Tom," said Jack; "and do, dear Almagro, continue your story."

"I must tell the young lady," continued Almagro, "that we had excellent food, for the Toqui was a rich man. We had milk and bruised corn, potatoes and pompions, food quite new to me. We had *charqui*, and even poultry, which were domesticated, fed on grain, and when fattened, were killed and eaten! Many a tear did Carielpa, the little daughter of the Toqui, and I shed when some favourite fowl was slaughtered by the women, and she would have famished rather than fed on that food, for she had a tender and loving heart.

"The mother of Carielpa was dead; she had been a Creole, and the pure blood of Spain predominated in the mingled current which filled the veins of the child. The Creole mother had lived long enough to teach her daughter to compassionate the Christians, whom the people hated; and to believe in the Christians' God.

"The beauty of Carielpa realized to me my dreams of angels; I could not believe that mortal women were so lovely. Moreover, she was kind to me, and in return I assisted her in the labours which the custom of the Araucanians inflicts on the females. When my own duties of attending to the horses were completed, I assisted her to bring the loads of maize and wheat from the fields, which were entirely cultivated and reaped by the women. We conveyed the sheaves to the threshing-floor, a piece of ground swept clean and enclosed with rails. We spread the corn over the earth, and a number of horses were then turned into the enclosure, and driven round till the straw was broken into pieces and the grain fell from the ears. The broken straw was collected and carried away; the grain was then exposed to the wind, which bore away the chaff, and the valuable corn left on the floor was gathered and stowed in bags of hide.

"The lenity of Cadeguala permitted me several hours' recreation every day, and in these happy hours the gentle Carielpa was my companion. She wept with me over my tale of woe, her bright eyes sparkled with sympathy when I repeated to her my father's histories of the past ; and she rejoiced that she was, like me, of Spanish blood. Then we tried to remember the prayers taught to us by the mothers we had lost, but the words had faded from our memory. We feared this was sinful, but we talked of the Heaven where we hoped to meet the lost, and we worshipped God with our hearts.

"As I grew older, I became strong and active; I loved the chase, and learned the art of war, but my spirit rebelled against the practice of arms, lest I should be called on to use them against my own countrymen, for I could never forget I was a Spaniard ; and though I could not see Carielpa frequently now, I never forgot to remind her, when we met, that we were of kindred blood, and were bound to love each other. This bond of amity reconciled me to my life of servitude, for though I was a slave, I was no longer alone in the world,—Carielpa supplied to me the kindred I had lost. Every year increased our attachment ; but it was not till the Toqui had announced to his daughter, that she was to be the wife of a neighbouring chief, that we felt the extent of our love, and the impossibility of our separation.

"It was Carielpa herself, who announced to me this terrible arrangement. Never shall I forget that agitated meeting under the calm moonlight. The whole scene rises now before me. I see the beautiful girl standing trembling under the algarob-tree, the thorny branches of which were then weighed down with the large yellow pods of fruit. I see her in the loveliness of that eventful night ; her turquoise-coloured *chiamal* flowing to her feet, fastened to the shoulder by a silver brooch, and round her slender waist by a sash and silver buckle. She was grace itself, and needed no ornament ; but custom induced her to wear the large silver ear-rings, the necklace and bracelets of brilliant stonés, and the jewels in her flowing tresses.

"I have heard enough, Carielpa," cried I, in frantic despair. "Leave me now for ever! To-morrow I follow the Toqui in his expedition across the Cordilleras against the Tehicelhets; I will cast myself upon the lances of these barbarians, and perish on the plains. Why should I return here to see you the wife of another?"

"'Be calm, Almagro,' answered she. 'It is the wish, the command, of Carielpa, that you should return to her. The Toqui loves his daughter, and will not sacrifice her happiness. Let Almagro bow to the laws and government of Araucania. Let him become a great warrior, and the Toqui may then adopt him as his son.'

"I had no hope of such a happiness; nor could even my love for Carielpa have bribed me to abjure my faith and my loyalty to my country. I departed in moodiness and despair on the ill-fated expedition. Many days after I returned,—the harbinger of sorrow. We had been overpowered by the numbers of the Pampas Indians, defeated and scattered. A small number escaped by a pass of the mountains unknown to the enemy; I was one of this unwelcome party, and by my endeavours, we rescued, and brought with us, the body of our leader, pierced with many wounds.

"The grief of my Carielpa for the loss of her noble parent, was aggravated by the knowledge that the Toqui who was to succeed him, was the man to whom she had been promised, and who already insisted on his right to claim her as his wife. This claim she determined to escape; and during the days of her mourning we met in secret, and arranged our flight. We had frequently heard of a missionary priest, who had been permitted to reside at a remote station at the foot of the Cordilleras, and we determined to seek his abode, and ask his counsel.

"I prepared two of the fleetest horses, and in the

dead of night we mounted and fled unnoticed. Silently
and swiftly we passed onwards for many miles, with
throbbing hearts, and many an anxious glance behind
us. As the morning light rose dimly, we looked upon
the green hills and fertile plains we were leaving for
the dark and dismal forests of the Cordilleras. But it
was a flight from slavery to freedom, and we chose it
without hesitation. As I was gazing fearfully at the
distant scenes we had passed, my eye rested on that
lofty snow-covered mountain, from which is seen to
rise thick smoke and gleams of light, night and day ;
a mystery which the Araucanian cannot explain, but
looks on, and trembles. We must have been twenty
miles at least from this much-dreaded spot, when suddenly a tremendous explosion, such as no mortal ear
surely ever before heard, shook even the ground
where we stood, riveted with horror. Then we saw
volumes of red flames burst from the distant mountain, pour down its snowy sides, and shine through
the dark woods below ; from whence they spread
rapidly over the plains below.

" ' We have offended God by our flight,' hoarsely
murmured Carielpa. ' His judgment is pursuing us !
We are lost for ever ! '

" I sought to calm the agitation of my beloved, but
I, too, believed the day of doom was at hand. Still,
with the instinct of human weakness, we urged on
our horses for many miles up the steep side of the
hills to escape that fiery torrent. Before the day
closed we reached in safety the dwelling of the good
priest. He welcomed us as his children, calmed our
fears, explained to us the wonders of that volcanic
eruption which he had also contemplated, with interest ; finally, he united us in the sacred bonds of
marriage. He advised us to seek the concealment of
some lone valley in the mountains till pursuit should
be over ; then we might descend to the Pampas and
commence the Guacho life, which I had so often
described to my Carielpa.

" Through the means of the good father, we obtained such necessaries as we might require; we exchanged our horses for mules, as better fitted for mountain travelling; I obtained arms and ammunition; and with light hearts we set out on our perilous journey.

" For many days we travelled, resting beneath the trees, or in the caves of the mountain. At length, tempted by the charms of a little verdant valley, which seemed to have been a solitude since the creation of the world, we chose it for our home. There I built a hut; I chased the puma and the alpaga, and with the skins of these animals lined the walls of my dwelling. I caught the vicuna, and the ingenious hands of Carielpa formed useful garments of its fur.

" I cultivated the ground, planting the seeds obtained from the good priest; and even among the mountains we had potatoes, beans, apples, peaches, and abundance of maize for our daily food. I captured the young llamas; domesticated them, and they gave us milk to add to our wealth. We lived in plenty and in happiness; our labour was light and pleasant, for we worked for ourselves; and, blessed with each other, we desired no society.

" To complete our happiness God bestowed on us a lovely girl. It was not till then that we felt how precious our own lives were, and learned to tremble at an unusual sound that might portend danger to us, and make our dwelling desolate. But years passed, and we were spared, and our Zara sprung up in grace and beauty. She learned to climb the mountain, in order to capture the docile parrot, or the delicate humming-bird; or to bring to us her little basket filled with gigantic strawberries. Sweet Zara! she was our humming-bird! the bright creature that floated among the flowers! the joy of our calm existence!

" She was nine years of age, and we no longer thought of the sorrows of the past, or the dangers of

the present; our thoughts were all absorbed in plans
for the happy future of our darling. One day, never
to be forgotten, she had climbed the mountain to
watch a nest of young parrots that had been her care
for weeks. I was engaged in reaping my harvest, and
my Carielpa was assisting me to bind and bring home
the sheaves. For some time we did not notice the
protracted absence of our Zara. It was the mother's
heart that first caught the alarm; she left me, and
with nervous agitation proceeded to call loudly on her
child. None answered! she fled back to me, to beseech me to follow the dear wanderer. I smiled at
her fears, but her word was my law, and I set out up
the mountain side in the child's track. I pursued it
beyond the spot to which she usually rambled; suddenly a cold terror assailed me, for I saw the track I
was on was that of horsemen. For a moment my
breath failed me; then I shrieked out the name of my
child, but in vain; all was still. I rushed desperately
on, in the too-plainly marked track; I climbed the
steep heights, and at length, in a deep gorge, I caught
a distant view of a large body of mounted Indians,
galloping at full speed. Alas! alas! even at that
great distance, I marked amid the band of naked,
dark robbers, the flowing scarlet poncho of my child!

"I sprung wildly after them, but every moment
rendered the distance wider between us. In a few
minutes I lost sight of them, and I knew that I
should see my child no more. I flung myself on the
ground, and, in the bitterness of my despair, called
on death. Then, starting up, I mechanically retraced
my homeward steps, and, bursting into the hut, in
wild and broken words declared to my Carielpa our
fatal bereavement.

"May God forgive me for the deed, for I was mad;
but he has visited me for the sin. My tender wife
looked wildly on me, and fell at my feet, bathed
in the blood which flowed from her mouth. Then I
saw that my rashness had murdered her; and, in

remorse and agony, I raised her, and applied those herbal styptics that Nature has provided for our weakness; she partially revived; and I prayed her to live for my sake, to save me from the bitter reflection that I had been her murderer. I even tried, with a sinking heart, to offer her hopes; but she shook her head, though she was unable to speak.

For days and weeks I watched over her, and in my painful anxiety I sometimes even forgot my first great sorrow. But God had ordained me heavier trials still. She, who was all that was left me in life, faded and died in my arms. I could not weep; I hung over her for hours, scarcely more alive than herself. At length I roused myself. I shrouded her fair form in the bright garments of her maidenhood; I dug her grave amid the flowers she loved, and marked the spot with a rocky slab, on which I carved her name.

" Then I fled from that desolated Eden: I loaded the mules and llamas with my few effects, and wandered from spot to spot amid the mountains, ever searching in vain for my lost child. I have crossed the lofty heights and descended to the Pampas. I have been chased by the savage tribes of the mountain and the plain, and have escaped by miracle.

" Years elapsed, when, wearied and hopeless, at length I reared a hut in this lone valley, far distant from my first sweet home: the grave of my peace. Here I have moodily fulfilled the necessary duty of providing for my subsistence; but with my hopes my affections were chilled. I could not love even the gentle llama that gave me food, or the familiar birds that built their nests beneath my roof. Existence was a cheerless and melancholy duty; and when your humanity prompted you to save my miserable life, my first feeling was regret that you had not left me to perish."

" Do you still continue to regret it, unfortunate and presumptuous man ?" asked Mr. Merton.

" I do not, reverend man," replied Almagro. " Your

H

mild counsels and holy persuasions have led me to
believe that God has spared me for some special purpose. I am content to live, that I may fulfil the
duties required of me. Tell me, then, what I ought
to do?"

Mr. Merton was an able theorist; but he looked
towards Dr. Lewis, on whose practical wisdom he
greatly relied, to answer the demand of the stranger.

"I think, Almagro," said Lewis, "that Mr. Merton will agree with me in recommending you to
attempt a more useful course of life. You certainly
cannot return into Araucania in safety; but you are
active, you have the means of removing yourself from
this solitary spot, and it is your duty to do so. God
has created man to help his fellow-creatures. You can
surely make your way to some region of usefulness,
as we are endeavouring to do."

"I have accidentally discovered a pass across the
Andes," replied Almagro. "It is probably yet unknown to any one else. It is full of difficulties, and
at a considerable distance from this spot; but I can
guide you to it. Yet even should we reach in safety
the foot of the mountains, vast solitudes and manifold
dangers would still lie between us and the abodes of
civilized man. Before us would stretch the dreary pathless Pampas, haunted by the destroying Indian, and by
the demon of famine. Can God lead us through that
wilderness?"

"Man of little faith!" said Mr. Merton. "That
God whose protecting hand miraculously conducts and
preserves us day by day, can make for us a pleasant
path through the wilderness, and bring us to a haven
of peace and rest, if we trust in him."

"And now I know, papa," said Jack, "that it was
God's providence that sent me into the thicket after
the guanaco, that I might help poor Almagro when he
got that terrible fall. What a fortunate thing it was, for
if he goes with us, we shall be such a happy party."

"I fear my gloomy presence will not add to the hap-

piness of the party," said Almagro ; " but I am summoned from my solitude, and am content to obey."

After this arrangement was agreed on, the family
consented to remain some days at the hut, till Almagro should be sufficiently recovered to travel. But
none were idle : the little girls, under the direction of
Nanny, attended to the llamas, milked them, and even
tried, by the rude process of shaking the cream in an
empty cask, to produce butter. It was but an imperfect success ; but they were greatly delighted to set
the half-coagulated result of their labour before Mrs.
Merton and Almagro, the two invalids of the party.

The young men hunted the vicuna, instructed by
Almagro, with some success, and caught parrots in
plenty. They reaped the ripe maize, thrashed it, and
stored it in bags of hide. They dug up the potatoes,
gathered the beans, and packed all the provisions that
were not perishable, in readiness for their long journey.
Two of the five horses, which they had with great difficulty brought to this spot, were still too feeble for use ;
the remaining three had recovered wonderfully, from
rest and plentiful food ; but Almagro had great doubt
of their being useful in the difficult journey before
them. He proposed that the two strongest animals
should be laden with part of the baggage, the remainder to be placed on the llamas, who were accustomed
to carry burthens. On his own excellent mule he had
great reliance, and this was to be given up to Mrs.
Merton ; the rest of the party were to walk. This
project could not be accomplished without great toil
and fatigue, and their progress must necessarily be
very slow ; but a little consideration induced them all
to agree to it.

Almagro was now quite well ; and the preparations
were all completed. The packages were neatly tied in
guanaco skins ; a quantity of guanaco flesh was dried
and added to their store ; and on this, the last day they
proposed to spend in the hut, Nanny declared they
should have a feast. She made some cakes of pounded

maize mixed with cream, to be baked on the hearth; while Matilda and Mary set out to the wood on the mountain side, behind the hut, for a basket of ripe strawberries.

The cakes were ready and the kettle boiled, and Nanny was beginning to be cross, when the little girls entered hastily and in great trepidation. "We have brought you no strawberries, mamma," exclaimed Mary; "we were so much frightened by the sound of roaring from the rocks. I believe we must have been near the den of some wild beast."

Mrs. Merton, in great alarm, begged that nobody would leave the hut, and that some barrier might be placed before the open entrance.

"Indeed, mamma," said Matilda, "my opinion is that Mary is wholly mistaken. The noise certainly was not the cry of any animal; it was more like the moaning of wind confined within the mountains."

Charles uttered an exclamation. Dr. Lewis silenced him with a significant glance, and then turning to Mrs. Merton, he assured her that there were no dangerous animals in the valley; but to satisfy her, Charles and he would examine the spot pointed out by the young ladies. At her desire they took their guns, and stepping into the open air, both at the same moment looked at the sky: it was calm and serene, and they breathed more freely.

But on reaching the rocky side of the mountain, they distinctly heard a low rumbling.

"It is the certain indication of an approaching earthquake!" cried Charles.

As he spoke they felt the ground beneath them vibrate.

"Let us return," said the doctor; "we can do nothing to help ourselves; we must pray for God to preserve us amid the dangers of these fearful mountains."

Before they reached the hut the sky was black with thick clouds and the rain began to fall violently; the llamas were trembling at the entrance of the hut, and followed the gentlemen into that shelter.

The family were all in great consternation, for they had felt the shock, and the truth could no longer be concealed. Now the earth was still, but the rain poured in torrents, penetrating the roof, extinguishing the fire, and ruining part of Nanny's festive cookery before she could rescue it. But it was of no consequence; no one had any appetite, and they enjoyed Nanny's rich cakes "no more than if they were eating the corn out of the husk," as she grumbled out.

A few minutes after, another loud rumbling, succeeded by a more violent shock than the first, announced that the danger was increasing. The weakest were now the bravest, and Mr. and Mrs. Merton, deeply imbued with the faith which alone can strengthen in adversity, and relying with simple and earnest love on their Saviour, called on the rest to unite with them in prayers of submission to the Divine will.

"Why should we not yield up our lives to Him who gave them," said Mr. Merton, "as happily in this remote wilderness as if we died on a bed of down, under a silken canopy? He ordains all wisely; let us submit in faith and hope."

While they were kneeling, listening to the prayers and pious exhortations of Mr. Merton, a terrific crash was heard. They shrieked involuntarily, for they believed the end of all things was at hand. It was truly the rending of mountains, of which huge masses came thundering down the steeps. The earth heaved violently, and they all fell prostrate. The frail hut tottered, but remained uncrushed, though the light at the entrance, which was at once door and window, was shut out. They were enclosed in a mass of rocky fragments.

For some minutes they remained motionless, expecting instant destruction; but all was still and silent. Then Mary, in a tone of awe, whispered, "Mamma, dear mamma, is this the Day of Judgment?"

Mrs. Merton burst into tears, and Mr. Merton then ventured to look fearfully round to ascertain the

extent of his loss.   All were safe; the fragile hut
stood firm amidst that "wreck of matter;" and one
after another the awe-struck and humbled Christians
rose from the earth to thank God for their preservation.

Comforted and resigned, they looked round, and,
through an opening in the roof, saw the light, which
convinced them they were not entirely buried. Through
this opening the rain poured in, and it was salutary
employment for them to remove their packages to a
dry corner of the hut, and to place the water-cask
beneath the opening, at once to prevent an inundation,
and to secure the precious fluid their imprisonment
prevented them from otherwise obtaining.

There was certainly something frightful in the rocky
barrier which obstructed their escape from the hut; but
their chief terror now arose from the repeated shocks,
which continued during the day at intervals of half an
hour.   Night brought no respite or rest; and at midnight a most extraordinary rocking of the earth was
accompanied by such a deafening sound of subterranean thunder as the artillery of man's invention could
never have produced.

For some hours after this violent shock no sound
was heard but that of the pouring rain, and the roar
of torrents rushing from the heights.   Fear, long
watching, and abstinence had stupefied them all so
much, that it was only when the daylight glimmered
faintly through the opening above that they rallied,
and began to hope that the terrors of the awful visitation were passed.

At the desire of Dr. Lewis they took some food,
and, revived by the refreshment, proceeded to action.
The timid, crouching llamas were fed with some maize
straw, which had been fortunately brought into the
hut, and were then milked.   The overflowing water-
cask was removed, and, to exclude the rain, they were
compelled to close the opening with hides, thus shutting
out the light, which rendered their captivity still more
dismal.   They made small openings in the side walls

of the hut, but in vain, for immoveable rocks seemed to enclose the hut on all sides. This was a melancholy prospect; but, at all events, no attempt at escape could be made during the heavy and incessant rain.

They continued as tranquil as their distressing situation permitted them to be for three days, occasionally feeling tremblings of the earth, but no more great shocks. At the end of that time the rain ceased, and they ventured to remove the covering from the roof. The air was most grateful to them, and Nanny once more lighted a fire, that they might have the refreshment of a warm breakfast.

"And now, papa," said Jack, "you must send me out through the roof; and I hope I shall return with the olive-branch in my mouth."

It was not without much persuasion that the timid parents consented to an expedition which was absolutely necessary, and which Jack, light and active, was best fitted to undertake. He was enjoined to be cautious and observing, and to return speedily, and was then assisted by his friends through the opening of roof, which was widened to allow him to pass.

They waited with considerable anxiety to hear his report of the state of things, and very soon were thrown into a state of great alarm by hearing a doleful cry from the boy, who seemed to be at some distance from the hut. The distracted parents looked at their friendly counsellor, Lewis, in dismay, their minds filled with images of danger and death.

"Charles," said Lewis, "I leave the honour of this enterprise to you. You are lighter than I am, and can scale the roof with less risk. You must take your lance with you, for it may aid your descent. But I do not apprehend any danger to the impetuous boy, my dear friends; his cry was rather that of sorrowful astonishment than of alarm."

CHAPTER IX.

Charles follows Jack.   Melancholy Effects of the Earthquake.
Release from the Hut.   Commencement of the Ascent.
Bridge-building.   The Bearded Bird.   Return of Niger.
The Lake among the Mountains.   The Snowy Region and
its privations.   The Pass.

CHARLES was not unwilling to redeem his character
from the reproach of indolence ; he was, moreover, sin-
cerely attached to his favourite companion Jack, and
anxious to assist him.   He passed through the opening, and over the roof without mischief, and descended
over the fragments of rock which half buried the hut.
He looked round, and was struck with wonder at the
strange scene the late smiling valley presented.   Immense stones, which had been hurled from the
heights, lay scattered, or piled around : no vestige of
cultivation remained ; the whole plain was a mass of
chaotic confusion.

On making his way forward, over rent rocks and
uprooted forests, with considerable difficulty, he at
length reached Jack, who was sitting weeping on the
summit of a pile of stones.

" Well, Jack, my good fellow," cried his friend,
" Is this your olive-branch ?   What has happened to
you ? "

" Oh !   Charley, I cannot help crying when I
see all this," replied the boy.   " Those huge rocks
lying against the hut, we cannot move, and dear
papa and mamma can never cross them.   And I
actually believe, Charley, that the poor horses are
laid dead beneath these great rocks, for they are no-
where to be seen ; and without them, we may remain
for ever shut up in our dark prison."

Jack was not of a desponding character, but terror

and confinement had quite subdued him. Charles was compelled to use greater energy than was usual to his indolent nature, before he could rally the usually buoyant spirits of his young friend. He suggested brighter hopes, and engaged Jack to accompany him to examine the state of the hut. The immense mass of rock which had fallen before the entrance, being higher than the roof, had shielded it from further dangers. The back of the hut originally rested against the rock, and the ends were half buried in piles of stones. The pile at the south end had fallen about two feet from the hut, and the narrow pass left, induced them to hope an escape might be made from this end.

They raised one of the uprooted trees against the hut to form a ladder, and their return was thus easily effected; and hailed with joy by the family, notwithstanding their melancholy report. Jack declared that he could not help crying out when he saw the poor dear horses were missing; he had forgotten that he should alarm them.

"But I was glad," added he, " when I saw Charley, for he knew what ought to be done at once. But, papa, how can we get on without our good horses?"

"They were not our horses, Jack," answered his father, " and I have felt no peace of mind since we brought them away. God has punished us for the act by depriving us of our ill-gotten treasures. The poor animals may have fled into the woods; and I wish that I could be assured that they had returned to their true owners."

This wish was not heartily responded to, for Jack and Tom had not forgiven the Indians for carrying off the boat. Dr. Lewis observed, that all animals have an instinctive knowledge of an approaching earthquake, and that doubtless they had fled to a less dangerous situation.

"My faithful mule," said Almagro, " the companion of my days of misery, will certainly return to me, if he be living. Besides, the two llamas have been trained to carry burthens, and will be very useful in our journey. Fear not, kind fellow-Christians, God has saved us in the earthquake, and will not leave us here to perish."

"Well, then, Almagro," said Jack, " we must begin by pulling down this wall at the south end of the hut."

"Allow me to suggest," said Tom, " that such a proceeding must inevitably let down the roof upon our heads. We must first prop the rafters, and then, the opening should be carefully arched to make it secure."

"Or what would you say, Tom," said Dr. Lewis, smiling, " if, since the hut can be no longer habitable, we should commence by taking down the roof, and thus avoid the danger of it falling upon us, or the necessity of an arched outlet?"

The plan was approved, and Almagro consented to the destruction of his hut. "I had hoped," continued he, " that after we had abandoned it, it might, at some time, have afforded shelter to other distressed wanderers; but this is a necessity."

The removal of the thatch and rafters that formed the roof was soon effected; after which the end wall was demolished. They had now light and air sufficient, but the accumulation of stones, trees, and soil, before the opening, formed an obstacle difficult to surmount. But a little contrivance and industry smoothed the difficulty. At the part, where the pile of rubbish was lowest, they shovelled the soil and formed an inclined plane, which it was easy even for Mrs. Merton to cross. Wearied with labour they sheltered themselves as well as they could, and lay down to take their last night's rest within the walls of the hut.

As if it had had an instinctive knowledge of their intention, the lost mule waked them early in the morning with its welcome braying. Almagro started up to meet and caress his faithful friend, which was in good condition, and quite uninjured. They all now commenced with alacrity the labour of the morning. They moved to the least encumbered spot of the plain all their packages, loaded the two strong llamas, reserving the lightest burthen for the female, which was least able to carry. A load of skins was placed on the mule, on which Mrs. Merton was seated, while her husband led the animal.

All being ready, Almagro took a last look at the hut he had inhabited for so many miserable years, and they moved in a tedious and perilous manner over the impediments in their way. As they proceeded they still found the way obstructed by scattered rocks and broken trees, and they were continually obliged to deviate in order to avoid them. At length they reached the stream which bounded the valley, but found, to their consternation, it had become a torrent, which, confined by steep rocky banks, was now deep and impassable—a roaring and foaming river. They looked at Almagro for counsel.

"It is absolutely necessary," said he, "that we should cross this stream in order to reach the pass. It may be many days before this torrent subsides; more rain may even fall and keep up the impetuous waters. Laden as we are, it is impossible to ford the stream; we must therefore make a bridge."

"I know something of the principle of bridge-building," said Tom, with a sage look, "and I pronounce that such an undertaking would take too much time; though we have abundance of materials close at hand."

"How very simple you are, Tom," said Jack. "Of course Almagro did not mean that we should build a grand stone bridge, like London Bridge; so you need not tire the girls with a lecture on piles and arches."

"I should not be tired of a scientific lecture," said Matilda, "if it was applicable to our case; but give us your plan of a bridge, Jack."

" Just a lot of smooth planks laid across the river,
and then shorter ones placed crosswise, to make it
firm.   There you have my bridge," said Jack.

" Which would require more time and labour than
we can give, and better tools than we possess," said
Lewis.   " I suspect that Almagro's bridge will be
more simple."

Almagro explained his plan ; then the animals were
released from their burthens for rest and refreshment ;
the tent cover was suspended over two opposite pieces
of rock, and under its shelter dinner was prepared,
while the young men set vigorously to work on their
bridge.

They easily found a prostrated tree long enough to
span the narrow torrent ; they lopped off the branches,
and drew it to the bank.   Then, steadying one end of the
trunk against a piece of rock lying at the brink, they
raised the tree by long ropes of twisted thong, and let
it fall across the stream.   Their first attempt succeeded happily, and they prepared and lowered a
second tree in the same manner.   A little distance
intervened between the trunks, but Almagro, accustomed to cross streams on these slight bridges, passed
over quickly, and assisted them with his sound arm to
place the trees side by side.   This bridge, about three
feet across, was sufficient for the agile boys ; but the
timidity of Mrs. Merton obliged them to fill up the
hollow in the middle with broken branches and brushwood.   It was then perfectly safe : Jack ran across
several times to show its stability ; then the mule and
llamas were led over, and finally Mrs. Merton submitted to be carried across by Dr. Lewis, who was
tall and strong.   The rest of the party had no fears ;
and they very soon had their tent again raised on the
opposite shore, which they preferred, lest any new
storm should carry away their bridge ; and without any
disturbance they spent the first night of their journey.

They were waked by the chattering of the parrots,
and the charming song of an unknown beautiful little

bird, which Jack captured and brought to the tent, that the naturalists might give it a name.

" I should say it was a canary-bird," said Tom, " if it be possible to meet with a canary-bird in the Andes."

" Or if a canary-bird ever wore a black velvet cap on its head, as this pretty creature does ?" said Matilda. " I pronounce that it resembles more our English goldfinch in its note and plumage than the canary. Am I not correct, papa ?"

" Who ever saw a goldfinch or a canary with a long beard, like this curious warbler ?" said Jack. " I think it must have been some venerable old hermit of these woods, transformed by some wicked sorceress into a bird."

" It is certainly not the goldfinch, Matilda," said Mr. Merton, " though it must be one of the same family, the *Fringillidæ;* but I am not so well versed in the ornithology of South America as our friend Dr. Lewis, who doubtless can tell you the species."

" It is the *Fringilla barbata,*" said Lewis, " remarkable for the beauty of its plumage, the melody of its song, and the singularity of its venerable black beard. You may observe that the throat is covered with black hair, which increases in length every year the bird lives, and I believe its existence generally extends to ten years.   From the length of its beard, we may conclude our captive has reached extreme old age, yet you hear its voice is undecayed.   It builds in the rocks a nest of small stones and feathers, and feeds, like the rest of the *Fringilla* family, on the seeds of plants.   I would advise you now to release it, Jack ; we shall have more pleasure in hearing its notes when it is in freedom, and I presume you have no design to roast and eat it."

There was a general cry of horror at such a suggestion : the creature was too charming to be eaten ; and finally, Jack was persuaded to set it at liberty, as they could not preserve it, unless they took the trouble to make a cage for it, and even then it must be an incumbrance in their toilsome journey.

The road by which Almagro conducted them led along the side of the mountains, ascending gradually; and though it was rugged and entangled with thicket, was less bewildering than their former aimless course. As they reached a higher region, the trees became stunted and thinly scattered, and the pasturage still more scanty. They rarely found any birds for food, but had no fear of famine, for they had still a large stock of dried meat and maize, and the mountain springs were unfailing. They also carried some straw for the animals, when they should have ascended beyond vegetation.

But they did certainly wish for some fresh meat, after many days' slow travelling; and they looked anxiously out for the appearance of the guanacoes, but in vain; till one night, when they were preparing to rest under the shade of a projecting rock, Jack declared he heard the step of a guanaco. They all remained silent; the trampling was distinctly heard; the bolas and lassoes were made ready. Then a loud neigh was heard—the guanaco was at hand—and they ranged themselves about to intercept the welcome visitor. A minute elapsed, then a rustling was heard in a thicket behind them, and out sprung a horse!

"It is our faithful Niger!" cried Jack; and they all recognised with pleasure the stoutest of their lost horses, a great favourite with the boys. He was much improved in condition, having evidently led a life of ease and plenty during his travels.

"He must have followed us for some days," observed Charles, "for I have more than once fancied I heard a distant neighing. Poor fellow! how glad he seems to be to see his friends again, little thinking of the reception he so narrowly escaped."

"And now, papa," said Mary, "as Niger has given himself up voluntarily to us, I suppose we may conscientiously keep him?"

Mr. Merton paused, and then agreed that they should use Niger as their own; for as he understood the horses which roamed over the Pampas were common property, they should not infringe on justice by appropriating this wanderer. Niger was therefore provided with a saddle of skins, and Mr. Merton mounted him, carrying his daughters alternately behind him. The rest of the family were supposed never to be tired of walking, though this was a mistake; for night after night they encamped weary and footsore, and sat down to patch their dilapidated shoes, in the best way they could, with pieces of hide.

But they all continued in excellent health and spirits; Mrs. Merton was so much stronger, that she now took her turn to walk for an hour, while Nanny took her place on the mule; and Almagro's arm was perfectly well. They were now little interrupted by the thicket, for vegetation had decreased to a few half-dried shrubs and some scattered blades of grass, —insufficient pasturage for the hungry animals. The shrubs were collected to light the evening fire, under some sheltering crag; or, better still, in some cave, when they had the good fortune to meet with one, for the nights were intensely cold: this cold was not, however, detrimental to health, as they all experienced.

From time to time they passed over the ridges of the mountains into some of the numerous valleys of the Andes, where they found better shelter and herbage. But still before them rose the gigantic form of the principal Cordillera, which, like a monster wall, seemed to shut out the world beyond, and to reach to heaven. The trembling girls inquired of Almagro, if they should have to ascend to that snow-crowned summit; but he assured them that would not be the case, but begged them to collect in the valley all the dry roots and grass they could obtain, as they would probably meet with no more vegetation or fuel. They now ascended the banks of a stream, on a sort of pathway, left by the passing-off of the waters of the last winter's snows, which must in the spring have swollen that slender stream into a torrent. Slowly and patiently man and beast toiled up this rugged ascent for hours, till they reached a ridge of rocks, where a shelving spot allowed them to light their fire, and take rest and refreshment, and to give their poor animals the last straw they possessed.

Morning showed them, beneath their resting-place, another valley or basin, green with a slight vegetation, towards which they gladly proceeded, and allowed the animals to crop the few blades of grass. Crossing the valley, which was about two miles in width, they encountered a broad and rapid river. It looked dark and deep ; but there was no choice ; they must attempt to ford it, for there were no materials here for making bridges, even if the river had been narrow enough for such an attempt. Dr. Lewis undertook to try the stream by riding over on the mule ; he was an excellent swimmer, and therefore did not mind the risk. He found the water not more than four feet deep, but somewhat dangerous from its rapidity ; but he succeeded in carrying the party over, one at a time, behind him. The llamas and horse were reluctant to enter the water ; but they were attached in a line by ropes ; and Dr. Lewis, leading the way on the untiring mule, drew the line across the river. There was much struggling and noise, but no damage ; and, after a little rest to recruit them after their fright, they pursued their weary way.

The road they now took wound along the sides of the mountain above a precipice. The narrow path was scattered with stones, which rolled beneath their feet, and rendered it dangerous and painful to pass over them. They looked down into hollows filled with snow, for now verdure was no more seen, while still above them the snowy summits towered to the clouds, dazzling their eyes and depressing their hopes.

They seemed to have passed the limits of animal or vegetable life, and were shocked to meet with the skeleton of a horse, left in all probability by the Indians in crossing the destroying mountains. The only living creatures they saw were the giant condors, hovering over their heads, flapping their huge wings, and watching for their expected prey. Mrs. Merton was in constant dread of these birds; and, in truth, it would not have been difficult for these monstrous creatures to have attacked and overpowered any of the enfeebled party.

"Oh, Almagro!" cried Tom, "I can go no farther; my shoes are worn out, and can be mended no more: I am sick and weary; and unless we had wings, like yon hideous condor, we could never mount to those snow-covered heights."

"My feet are bleeding too," said Jack; "but I should not mind very much for that, if it was not so cold; and we cannot make a fire for want of fuel. We might, to be sure, burn the tent-pole."

"That we must certainly not do," said Lewis. "Under the shelter of this projecting rock, by the aid of the pole and sail, we can raise our tent, and then, wrapped in our blankets and cloaks, we must try to forget our toils and troubles. Besides, Almagro will satisfy you, Tom, that we shall not be compelled to ascend to yon snowy pinnacles before we reach the eastern descent of the Cordilleras."

Almagro smiled, and assured Tom that he hoped in another day to bring them to the pass; an assurance that revived their drooping spirits. They then made a good supper on a mixture of *charqui* and pounded maize, boiled to a sort of jelly, which Nanny, warned by Almagro, had prudently prepared before the fuel failed. The famished animals were supplied with a handful of maize each, a little milk was obtained from the llama, and then, thanking God that they had still food, shelter, and safety, they heaped all the covering they could obtain over them, and slept peacefully.

Jack, in spite of his sorrows and his sore feet,

I

waked them up early next morning with a hunting-song. His spirits never flagged ; he was the best worker, and the most good-natured assistant of the party. It was Jack who pounded the *charqui* when Nanny was tired ; he fed the animals, rolled up the blankets for his mother and sisters, and sometimes for Charles too. It was he who delighted Almagro with wonderful stories of English customs and English happy homes ; and it was he who, when every one was desponding, cheered them with his gay laugh and merry song.

"Come here, Master Jack," said Nanny ; " I have long thought of it, and just take my clogs to walk in. I have a pair of good shoes yet, and that's more than some can say. You laughed at me for bringing my clogs, and now see what a good job it was."

The fact was that Nanny, never to be persuaded that her future home was to be entirely unlike her native home, had, in order to provide against all emergencies, brought amongst her stores a pair of the wooden-soled shoes worn by the mountain peasantry of Westmoreland ; and these *clogs*, as they are pro-vincially called, she had worn in her toilsome pil-grimage. This had been a most fortunate experiment, for Nanny's feet had suffered less from the journey than those of any one else ; and Almagro's admiration of the *clogs* had been so great, that he had declared, as soon as they had reached the region of wood again, he would certainly make a pair of clogs. Even Charles, who had destroyed a great part of his collec-tion of light, elegant, London boots, looked with envy on Nanny's *sabots*, and admitted that he might him-self have been tempted to endeavour to fabricate a pair of clogs, if the summit of the Andes had not been a locality so extremely unfavourable to the operations of shoe-making.

"On ! on ! chattering boys," called Lewis, "and let us take advantage of the bright sunshine to follow Almagro to the highest point of our pilgrimage."

The highest point, the long-sought-for pass, was the flat summit of a peak, where the snow lay for ever. In the midst of the plain was a wide frozen lake, evidently the crater of an extinguished volcano. They gazed on it with astonishment and awe, wondering how many centuries had passed since it had poured its devastating fires down to the plains. They found several shells in a calcined state scattered around, amongst which they recognized the oyster, conch, and perriwinkle shells.

" It *surelie* must have been some of the fairy folks," said Nanny, "that have fetched these bonny sea-shells all the way up these weary hills, and have laid them up here for their own *bairns*."

" And now that we have found them, Nanny," said Jack, " who knows but one of the good fairies may hop out of a conch-shell, and turn it into a coach drawn by fiery dragons, to carry us over the mountains ?"

" Don't you talk nonsense, Master Jack," said Nanny, "before folks that know things. Here's Master Tom, now, will know out of his books how these sea-shells came to be lying so far from the sea."

" These shells, Nanny, are probably antediluvian, the relics of an earlier world," began Tom, gravely.

" Which, in plain language, means, Nanny," interrupted Dr. Lewis, laughing, " that these shells were brought here by the great Deluge, of which you read in your bible."

" Doubtless," said Mr. Merton, " this is the fact, for we know that the animals which inhabit the plains, and the fishes from the depths of the sea, were alike deposited on the summits of the highest mountains, when, at the word of God, the waters covered the whole earth. The ignorant savage, wherever he is found, acknowledges the fact of the Deluge ; but the Christian knows that the sin of man brought this fearful visitation on the world. Let us contemplate its traces with awe and trembling, beseeching our heavenly Father to have compassion on the frailty of humanity, and to spare us and our children from the punishment our sins ever deserve."

CHAPTER X.

The Eastern View from the Pass. Commencement of the Descent. Expeditious Despatch of the Baggage down the steep. The Caves. The Snow-storm and its results. Privations. The Chase of the Guanacoes. Jack's Perilous Adventure in the Snow.

On each side of the pass rose the lofty walls of still higher mountains, which the family believed they never could have surmounted, but must have perished in their wanderings, but for the guidance of Almagro. The plain extended for two miles beyond the crater; it was scattered with broken and pulverized fragments, which rendered walking difficult and painful, even on the level ground. At length they reached the termination of the pass, and looked down on the wondrous scene of the eastern descent. Mountains below mountains were spread before them, separated by deep hollows filled with snow, into which it appeared to them a single false step might precipitate the unfortunate traveller. The eye ached with gazing on the vast and widely-spread declivity, which terminated in a blue haze— the undistinguishable Pampas.

The eastern descent is more abrupt than that of the west, and every step is attended with danger; yet still it was with extreme satisfaction that they took the winding downward path, which was more distinctly marked than any they had yet trodden. They rested for the night on a level spot, with aching limbs, and the inspection of their diminished stores did not tend to cheer them. The dried meat was quite exhausted, and the maize, which they were obliged to share with their famishing animals, was nearly at an end.

But the morning light, after a night of repose, renovated their spirits, and they set out with bolas and lassoes in readiness, hoping to fall in with the guanacoes, and, in the ardour of search, they almost forgot their fatigue and hunger. For some time they pursued a monotonous zig-zag path, unbroken by any appearance of life, till at length they met with a few withered plants of grass scattered among the broken fragments and patches of snow. These afforded a feast for their exhausted beasts, who picked up every leaf in their reach.

Though the air was keen and transparent, Dr. Lewis expressed his satisfaction that none of the party, not even Mrs. Merton, had suffered from that difficulty of breathing which is so frequently produced by the rarity of the atmosphere in these lofty regions. There was still another danger to which they were liable, and this, Almagro explained to them, was the reason he wished so especially to expedite their descent. This danger was the chance of a fall of snow, which not unfrequently occurrs among these mountains, even in the early autumn. He pointed out, several hundred feet below them, a basin of table-land, surrounded by mountains, which he was anxious to reach, for he knew that several caverns existed on that spot, which would afford them safe and convenient shelter for the night.

This valley could only be attained by a long and circuitous path : and Almagro proposed that they should relieve the feeble animals from their burthens by sending the baggage down the steep. This was an experiment Mr. Merton was unwilling to consent to, as he considered it extremely hazardous, but his children were very anxious to see the adventure ; and Dr. Lewis, the grand counsellor, assuring Mr. Merton that he might implicitly trust the prudence and experience of Almagro, he was at last induced to consent.

The tent and pole being first confined by a rope, were allowed to glide a little way down the steep ; then the rope was withdrawn, and they quickly descended to the level below. The boxes and bags followed, watched with great anxiety, and all reached the bottom in safety ; though Nanny railed furiously at Almagro, who fortunately did not comprehend her words, for his madness in sending the bag with the pans and kettles " to *topple* down the mountains in that *unnatural* manner." The relieved animals uttered joyful cries, and went on their way cheerfully, the old llama being now followed by a little tottering young one, which was born on the summit of the Andes, and had entered very early into a life of toil.

The deviations of the road now hid the baggage from their sight ; then nothing could divert Nanny from the idea that they should find all their property carried off by Indian robbers ; and when, after a long journey, they reached the valley, and she looked over the packages, she seemed surprised that nothing was missing.

Almagro pointed out to them some openings in the face of the opposite mountain, which he assured them led to spacious caves, where he had often rested in his wanderings. They followed him across a plain thinly scattered with the long, rushy grass of the Andes, till they reached the entrance of one of the caves.

"In this place," said Almagro, " I have frequently lodged in my expeditions to the Pampas; and two years ago I left here some stores against my return, but, travelling far to the north, I crossed the mountains by another pass. It is possible we may still find them."

They passed through the narrow entrance into a lofty and spacious cavern, by no means gloomy, for many apertures above the entrance admitted light. In the midst were the traces of a fire, and in one corner was a heap of brushwood, which Almagro recognised to be his own, the remains of a prudent provision he had made for crossing the mountains, and left there till he should return. Beneath the fuel remained, untouched and uninjured, a bag of guanaco skin, containing a good supply of maize.

It would not be possible to describe Nanny's delight at the sight of the maize ; she had been greatly prejudiced against this grain when she first saw it, but she now hailed it as good provision. Her good-humour was only of short duration however, for, on removing a shawl from her head, she suddenly recollected that her friend Jack had induced her to take off her stiff, black silk bonnet, which was no protection from the cold, and to supply its place with the shawl, while he had placed her bonnet, she now believed, in one of the bags. And it was so; the bonnet was found, under the pans, kettles, and heavy baggage, crushed flat.

It was impossible to resist the provocation to mirth which Nanny's flattened bonnet presented, and the shrieks of laughter from the young party were loud, and extremely irritating to the aggrieved damsel; but Mrs. Merton quietly reproved them, and promised Nanny, if it pleased God to grant them a permanent resting-place, her first care should be to make her a new bonnet.

"If we should come to any fields of grain," said Matilda, "I am well skilled in plaiting straw, and I have no doubt, mamma, I could succeed in making Nanny a better bonnet than you could."

"When did Miss Matilda Merton ever doubt that she did not do everything better than everybody else?" said Jack. "Here, then, successful young lady, here are my bolas. Go forth, and entrap a guanaco for us."

Matilda was annoyed by the sarcasms of her lively brother, and was about to make an angry reply; but she saw that her father looked serious, and that her friend Dr. Lewis shook his head at her, and she reflected that perhaps she had boasted a little in her assertion, and had better say no more.

Mrs. Merton's gentle words had somewhat allayed the vexation of Nanny, and she commenced the pleasing duty of kindling a fire once more. In the meantime the youths went out to unharness the animals; then, directed by Almagro, they proceeded to an adjoining cave, where he pointed out to them a bundle of dried grass and maize-stalks, which he had left there on his last journey.

"Hurrah!" cried Jack, "Let us give the poor beasts a good feed."

"Stay, my young friend," said Almagro. "Consider; the animals will find sufficient grass in the valley for their subsistence to-night; and some unfortunate travellers may chance to pass this way in the winter, when the snow has hidden all vegetation. Then this scanty supply may enable them to save the lives of their beasts, and thus they may themselves have the means left of escaping from the death of famine which hovers over these mountains in the winter season." As he spoke he pointed to the skeleton of a mule, which lay a few paces from the cave, a victim in all probability to the perils of the Andes.

"You are right, worthy man," said Mr. Merton, who had joined them, "Charity requires that we should bestow a portion of the blessings we possess with prudence and discrimination, in order that we may benefit those who most need our aid. We must use with economy the store made for the unfortunate. Would that our means allowed us to add to it."

At the suggestion of Almagro, they removed the provender to the cave in which they designed to lodge themselves, leaving the adjoining cave open, in case the inclemency of the night-air should induce the animals to seek a shelter. Tom and Jack undertook to carry the burthens; as they left the cave an animal fled swiftly past them; but not so swiftly as to escape the ever-ready bolas of Almagro, who secured the fugitive, and entered the cave with his welcome prize.

It was the large hare of the Pampas, sometimes, but rarely found in the valleys of the Andes. It must have weighed twenty pounds, and was a most seasonable relief under the present circumstances. After

THE HOME OF THE WANDERERS.

Almagro had skinned the animal, he commenced the cleaning of the soft downy skin, of which he planned to make a pair of warm boots for Mrs. Merton, with the fur inside.

The girls milked the llama for their present refreshment, and Nanny in the mean time made a stew of the hare and a little maize. She had still a good supply of salt, and the supper, impatiently waited for, was pronounced by the hungry party to be the perfection of cookery. After supper they rolled large stones to defend the entrance, and, arranging their packages and couches conveniently, offered up their prayers, and slept in peace.

But soon after midnight Dr. Lewis was waked by the loud howling of the wind, and the rattling of stony fragments whirled down the steep, mingled with the neighing and bleating of the alarmed animals. He listened awhile, and then turned to rest, thankful that they had such a secure shelter; but the storm, increasing in violence, once more awoke him, and he found Almagro standing at the entrance of the cave, where, between the rocky fragments with which they had formed an imperfect barrier, the snow had forced its way and lay scattered on the ground.

"This is what I have ever dreaded," said Almagro. "These fearful *temporales*, the sudden storms of autumn, are death to the unfortunate travellers who are exposed to them. God has graciously granted us a protection from the tempest, and He alone knows how long we may need it, and how we shall subsist in this desert."

Charles Villars now joined the alarmed friends. He had heard fearful tales of these hurricanes, which bring down the snow suddenly from the summits of the mountains, entombing man and beast in an untimely sepulchre; and greatly agitated, he watched with them the falling snow till daybreak. When the dismayed family were assembled, and had removed the stones from the entrance, they found the snow lying two feet deep already, and falling as furiously as ever, while the raging wind threatened destruction to all who were exposed to it.

"This is, indeed, terrible!" said Mr. Merton. "My children, let us pray for the tempest-stricken wanderers, perishing unaided and unprepared, while we thank the gracious God who has spread his rocks to shelter us in the storm and the whirlwind."

After prayers they had a consultation on their position.

They were certainly in perfect security from the danger of the storm, but it might be of long continuance; their provision was scanty, and there was no probability of their having the means to augment it. However Mr. Merton forbade all despondency, and entreated them to rely firmly on the providence of God, who had ever helped them.

They breakfasted on the remainder of the stew to save their fuel; but soon after the cold became so intolerable, from the wind blowing over the accumulated snow, that they were compelled to light a fire, and to crowd round it for warmth.

The hardy boys, less susceptible of cold than their sisters or their parents, rambled about among the many caves which branched from their lodging. They discovered that the whole series of these caverns communicated with each other, and in their wanderings they entered a division which they found to be tenanted by their animals. It was the cave they had left open for the poor creatures, which had gladly resorted to it in the storm. In a remote part of the cave Niger and the mule were standing together, trembling violently, but the llamas, more accustomed to mountain hurricanes, were lying peacefully near the entrance.

As the snow was whirling into the cave with great violence, the youths rolled some stones before the opening to form a partial screen, for the caves were in the lower mountain, and faced the wind and storm.

They procured a small quantity of food for the beasts from the larger cave, and then the llama was milked, which made a pleasant addition to their slender provision. The water-cask was empty, but so long as they could make a fire, they were sure of a supply of melted snow; and after all, as Jack said, this was a nice holiday for both bipeds and quadrupeds.

But for three more days and nights the snow continued to fall without intermission, and their spirits began to droop, for privations of every kind threatened them. They might, certainly, have killed the poor llamas; but besides the impolicy of destroying their faithful servants, and the cruelty of the deed, they would have reaped little benefit by it, the creatures having become mere skeletons from their insufficient food.

"I don't think there would be so very much harm," said Matilda, "in our having a good stew made of the young llama. It is of no use, and it certainly consumes a great deal of the mother's milk."

"And who has so much right to the milk, Matilda?" demanded Jack. "Not you or I; though we may like it very well. Then, as for eating the pretty, gentle, playful young llama, I shudder to think of it. I shall expect next, that you will wish to make a stew of me; a proceeding I shall by no means consent to, though you are the manager of the housekeeping."

"But, my good friend, Jack," observed Lewis, "remember the heavy responsibility of a housekeeper, who is expected to provide and has not the means. Do not be severe on Matilda, who is only thoughtful and careful for the future, and looks round her with a prudent calculation."

"But Matilda should remember," said Mr. Merton, "the beautiful lesson we read this morning, 'Behold the fowls of the air; they sow not; neither do they reap or gather into barns; yet your Heavenly Father feedeth them.' This was not written to encourage neglect and idleness, but to repress covetousness, and too much care for the events of the morrow, which God holds in his Almighty hand."

Matilda had always a defender in Dr. Lewis, who appreciated her energy and usefulness, and who sought, with a friendly hand, to correct her foibles of presumption and self-conceit.

On the fourth morning, the sky was clear, the wind had subsided, and the snow ceased to fall.   They removed the stones from the opening, and looked out with astonishment and dismay on the wonderful scene of the mighty mountains, covered, as far as the eye could extend, with one shroud of frozen and untrodden snow.   They remained some time contemplating this dreary waste in silence.   Then Mary said, " Cousin Charles, we shall be quite famished, if some hero does not venture out to hunt for us.   We saw the guanacoes in a higher region than this, and I think such bold hunters as you all are ought to find them here. Who will volunteer for a foray ?"

Charles was usually very obliging to his favourite friend, Mary, but he now looked dismally on the bleak prospect, shrugged his shoulders, and drew his cloak round him, without reply; but Jack, in a moment, slung a pair of bolas round his neck, and, with a long lance in one hand, and a lasso in the other, was ready to lead the way.   Mrs. Merton was in great alarm at the project, but Dr. Lewis said—

" Have no fears, Mrs. Merton, it will warm us all to have a run over the snow, which appears to be quite hard; I will lead the expedition, and will take care no one is imprudent.   Arm yourselves, then, and follow me, gallant gentlemen !"

Jack shouted for joy, and, with Almagro, followed Lewis.   Tom was less prompt; he began an argument to prove that the guanacoes would certainly descend to the uncovered plains, rather than remain on the snow, where they would be famished; but the bold hunters set out without him, and Charles, now thoroughly roused to the chase, said, " Well, Tom, we cannot escape the thing—we are in for a run, so we must try and intercept a herd on its downward journey."

After they had proceeded a few hundred yards, Dr. Lewis observed that the snow had become softer, as the valley was more open in this part, and the sun was now shining forth. He recommended them therefore to try the ground before them with a lance, and to proceed slowly. They had reached a jutting cliff, which projected considerably forward, when Jack, always eager, bounded before his prudent leader, and passed round the angle of the rock. They heard him give a low whistle, from which they concluded he had found game, and following him round the cliff, they saw, with great satisfaction, a herd of guanacoes, about thirty yards before them, pushing their noses into the snow, and struggling to obtain the scanty vegetation buried beneath.

Tom was beginning to explain the cause of this remarkable refutation of his theory, but Dr. Lewis, in a whisper, commanded silence and caution. Caution was a word never understood by Jack the rash, who was already whirling the bolas over his head, and springing forward, he disappeared from their sight in a moment beneath the snow.

The shock to the assembled friends, who fully expected he had gone over some tremendous precipice and was lost, cannot be described. For a moment they were mute and paralyzed: then the prudent leader, drawing Charles back, who was preparing to follow his friend, probed the ground, and found they were all within a yard of the edge of the descent. He called out loudly—a moment of silent anguish succeeded—then they saw the point of Jack's lance appear above the snow, about five yards from the spot where they were standing. This was a pleasant sight—they were sure he was living—but they were not sure he might not perish before they could find

the means to extricate him.   Dr. Lewis called out to
Jack to widen the hole through which he had passed,
by carefully moving his lance round, while they made
ready to assist him.   They lashed the two remaining
lances firmly together, to form a strong pole, and
then fixed to the end a long and strong lasso, brought
out by Almagro, for the pupose of drawing home the
the game they might kill.   They passed the lances
over the snow till the lasso fell through the opening,
then Dr. Lewis called out to Jack to secure the noose
firmly round his waist, and to endeavour to ascend
the snow, while they would assist him by drawing the
lasso.

They could not hear his reply, but they perceived
by the agitation of the pole he was complying with
their advice.   Then they drew the lances gently forward till they felt a resistance, when it was necessary
to manage with caution, for it required great strength
and a firm grasp to prevent the lances from slipping
from their hands.   By slow degrees they secured a
hold of the lasso, which they grasped firmly, leaving the
boy to make exertion for himself.   At length his dark
head and pale face were just seen above the surface
of the snow, and a shout of joy burst from their lips ;
at that moment a violent jerk caused the lasso to
slide through the hands of Charles and Tom, who
were foremost in the line, and the dear head disappeared again.   A cry of grief followed, but Lewis and
Almagro, who were behind, and still had a firm hold,
encouraged them to resume their attempts, and to
draw the lasso gently and firmly.   In a short time
the head once more appeared, and Lewis directed the
boy to lie down on his back, and suffer himself to be
drawn through the yielding snow.   This was a slow
and difficult process, and poor Jack was nearly suffocated in his perilous transit ; but he was at length
landed safely out of danger, pale and exhausted, with
aching arms, and a sprained ankle.

For some time he was unable to speak, and they

stood round him, watching him in great anxiety, and grieved that they had no restorative to give him. At length, with a kind of sob, he spoke—

"All right! Now be off after the guanacoes, and leave me here."

It certainly was a great temptation, for the guanacoes, apparently unconscious that their enemies were at hand, were continuing their unprofitable employment, burrowing under the snow for the poor herbage. The hunters could not see them so near without making some effort to secure them, destitute as they were of provision. Almagro, accustomed to hunting, even over the snow, had been sounding the ground from the cliff, and came to report that the chasm into which Jack had fallen did not extend more than ten yards below the spot, where there was a safe pass forward.

Encouraged by this good news, they set out, leaving Jack seated on the snow. Bolas and lassoes were made ready, and they succeeded in approaching to within ten yards of the animals, unnoticed. Then a sort of suspicious movement was observed among the herd, when the hunters immediately sprung forward, and bolas and lassoes were flung with all the skill they could command. Great was the confusion, and loud the neighing cries. The animals dashed off in different directions at first, and Tom was overthrown by a large animal, and dragged for several yards by his own lasso, which he had cast round the neck of the animal, and continued to grasp firmly. Almagro, who had captured a noble animal with his bolas and despatched him, saw Tom's situation, and ran to his assistance, piercing the guanaco with his lance. Lewis was unsuccessful, and the bolas of Charles, to his great mortification, were carried off by a guanaco in its triumphant retreat.

However, they had much reason to be satisfied with the success of the hunting, for it was no easy task to drag the two heavy animals over the softened snow to the place where Jack was waiting them. They found him in high spirits, notwithstanding the pain of his ankle, for he had also a prize to display. As he was sitting still and silent on the snow, a hare had ventured so near to him that, by the aid of a spare set of bolas which lay near, he had entrapped and secured it.

They were now furnished with an abundant provision ; but, as the labour of drawing the guanacoes to the cave would have been exhausting in their weakened condition, Almagro set out, and soon returned with the mule and some strong hide ropes, by means of which they harnessed the animal, which drew their spoil, and at the same time carried on its back the disabled Jack.

When the triumphant procession reached the mouth of the cave, past hardships and present perils were alike forgotten in the joy of success. The girls cried out with delight, and Nanny held up her hands in astonishment at the sight of such unusual abundance. Mr. and Mrs. Merton alone were calm, but they were not the less truly thankful.

"I think, Master Jack," said Nanny, with some indignation, "that this poor dumb creature had work enough to pull such a load, without having you perched a-top of his back."

"That's quite true, Nanny," answered Jack, "and I could not have had the heart to do it, but I have had a roll in the snow ; and shall have to trouble you to bathe my swelled ankle, and then you shall hear the adventure of Jack the guanaco-killer."

Nanny was always kind and willing in a case of distress. She soon had Jack placed on a mattress. His ankle was examined, and, under the direction of Dr. Lewis, bathed and bandaged ; then he began his story.

"Truly, it's very little indeed that you girls know of the dangers of a hunter's life. When I sprung after the guanacoes, and plumped down over the precipice, feeling myself sink through the snow, I certainly did think I should see you no more, and I began to say my prayers. I stopped, at last, on some hard snow, which, I dare say, has lain there for many a winter; but, except that I had a peep of the blue sky through the tunnel I had made, I was pretty nearly buried alive; and had no hopes of ever getting out, it was such a long way to the top. Still, as soon as I felt my feet on firm ground, I could not help trying to climb, but I slipped down directly, and the snow came tumbling after me, filling my eyes and ears till I was blind and deaf; nor did I like to try any more, for fear I should bury myself completely. I attempted to call out, but I dare say nobody could hear me, for my voice sounded, to my own ears, as if I was speaking through a quill.

"At last I thought of raising up over my head my long lance, which I luckily held in my hand when I went down. Then I heard dear Dr. Lewis calling to me, and I began to think things were not so bad. I knew now what they were about, so I began to make ready for another attempt. I planted my lance firmly in the ground, took out my knife, and dug some holes in the side for my feet as high up as I could reach, for near the bottom the snow was tolerably hard. But I laughed for joy when I saw the good stout lasso come dangling down, and very soon I had my head and arms through the noose.

"I now grasped the lance to support me, and got up capitally for some feet; but when the snow got softer I had great difficulty in climbing, and felt glad of the support of the lasso. Besides, when I had nearly reached the top of my lance, I had to tug it out, for I was determined not to leave it behind me in that doleful pit. I got it out, and pushing it upwards, I used the lower end to plunge in the snow at the side, and that steadied me a little.

"How my heart beat when I got my head above the snow; but in my joy I forgot my prudence, and made a

K

jump; the soft snow gave way, and I should have gone to the bottom again but for the lasso, by which I hung suspended, like the sign of the Golden Fleece, at Winston. A desperate tug the good folks at the side must have had. Luckily I got my feet rested again before the lances could break, or before I was quite pinched in two, and, with a little more scrambling, reached the opening, from whence I was drawn like a log of wood by my good friends to *terra firma.*"

"You were always a *miraculous* boy, Master Jack," said Nanny; "and see now what trouble you've brought on us all with your unthinking ways. Another time you'll maybe look before you jump."

Jack laughed, as he promised obedience to Nanny's wise counsel; and she spared him further reproaches as she looked at the hare he had brought, of which she was now making a stew. Jack claimed the skin of the animal, that he might, under the direction of Almagro, solace his confinement by attempting to make boots for his sisters, similar to the comfortable pair Almagro had made for Mrs. Merton.

CHAPTER XI.

Preparation of *Charqui.* Almagro's Plan of Descent rejected. An Unpleasant Nocturnal Visit. The Sledge Expedition. The Lower Valleys of the Andes. The *Pino de la Tierra.* The discontent of Charles Villars.

ALL were now busily engaged. The wool was shorn from the guanacoes and placed in a bag. Then the animals were skinned, and the hides spread out on the snow to be cleansed, after which they began a large preparation of *carne secco,* the useful *charqui.* Pieces of flesh were cut in long slips, about four inches broad, and one-third of an inch thick. Some of these slips were suspended outside the cave, to be dried by the sun and air; others were hung in the smoke of the fire. The meat thus dried will keep good for a long time ; it is generally prepared for cooking by beating it between two stones to make it tender, and then stewed.

The fat of the animals was melted, and stored in bags of hide ; and Mr. Merton proposed that if they should be providentially released from their confinement before they had needed to encroach on this useful provision, they should leave at least some portion of this store in the cave, for the benefit of other unfortunate travellers.

But days passed, and there still seemed no hope of their proceeding on their journey. The snow, partially softened by the noonday sun, was again hardened by the night frosts, and rendered more slippery and dangerous.

After drying part of the guanaco flesh, they had lived on the remainder, and still had a good portion buried in the snow before the cave to keep it fresh ; but they had been unable to procure more, for the early snow had driven all the animals to the lower valleys. The monotony of their cavern life was depressing. At first Jack had amused himself by making two very neat pairs of boots for his sisters, instructed by Almagro. They were made of the skin of the hare, the fur inwards, soled with the hide of the guanaco, and sewed with threads made of the same material. Then all the shoes and boots were mended with patches of hide, and no more work remained to be done.

Almagro frequently went out. He had climbed to the summit of the mountain in which the caves were hollowed, and he assured them that from thence there was a gradual sloping descent, smoothly covered with snow, which led to a level valley two or three hundred yards below ; and this descent, he pronounced, might be safely and rapidly accomplished on a sledge, which he would make of the skin of a guanaco. This plan was at once rejected by the timid Mr. Merton, and Mrs. Merton shuddered at the very idea of such a startling scheme.

But Almagro was pertinacious; he prevailed on Dr. Lewis and Charles to ascend the mountain with him, early in the morning, before the sun had softened the snow. He pointed out to them the green plain below, and declared his intention of making the experiment of the descent himself, if they would await his return. He spread the skin of one of the guanacoes, which he had brought with him, on the snow, with the wool uppermost, and seated himself upon it, holding his knife in one hand, and his lance in the other. With these weapons to plunge into the snow, and to guide and check his descent, he set out, gliding down the steep.

The descent was gradual, and he proceeded on without accident, and reached the bottom, from whence he waved a signal of his safety. They waited long for his return, which was necessarily slow and tedious. In the first place, he remained a quarter of an hour below inspecting the locality; then, fastening the sledge to his back, he began his ascent, cutting steps in the snow with his knife, and resting on his lance. He reached his friends at last, very much exhausted with his toil; and it was some time before he was able to speak, and to assure them that the next ascent would be comparatively easy, for his steps formed a perfect ladder.

He described the valley below to be almost entirely free from snow, with tolerably good pasture, and some scattered low bushes and trees; there were two algaroba trees especially, in a sheltered nook, convenient for a frame for their tent, as there were no caves in the valley. He had also seen hares, and heard parrots; and he entreated Dr. Lewis to join him in endeavouring to persuade Mr. Merton to consent to the plan of the sledge.

Lewis had little hope of their inducing Mr. Merton to undertake such a wild adventure; but he endeavoured to convince him, on their return, that the project was safe and prudent; and, from Almagro's description of the lower valley, the change would be most desirable; but the parents were inflexible—the risk was too fearful.

Almagro was much dissatisfied, and lay awake for some hours planning the construction of a sledge which might have a more secure appearance to the eyes of the timid. In the midst of his reflections, he was disturbed by a great noise among the animals in the adjoining cave, accompanied by a deep growling which he knew did not proceed from the beasts. He was much alarmed, but remembered with thankfulness that he had, the evening before, rolled stones before the entrance to both caves, that the animals, as well as themselves, might be protected from nocturnal assailants. He trusted this precaution might be effectual, for he felt certain some beast, more danger-ous than any they had yet met with, was prowling near.

Rising from his bed, he looked through the spaces between the stones which guarded the opening, and saw with much vexation a large puma, digging in the snow, beneath which the guanaco flesh was buried, and turning away from time to time to growl at the entrance of the cave, where the animals, roused and terrified by the neighbourhood of their powerful enemy, were expressing their alarm by loud neighing aud bleating. The puma was too dangerous a visitor to be allowed to escape, and Almagro was determined to take the most ready way to despatch him. He therefore, pointing his rifle through the crevices at the entrance, by the clear light of the moon, took a careful aim, and shot the animal dead on the spot.

Roused by the report of the rifle, the alarmed family were soon assembled; and it was with some difficulty Almagro satisfied the females that they were not besieged by the Indians. After hearing the real story, they could take no more rest that night; and when the morning light showed them the large fierce-looking creature extended dead at their very door,

they trembled at the danger to which they had uncon-
sciously been exposed.

"Your alarm is greater than the danger demands,"
said Dr. Lewis, "for the puma rarely attacks mankind.
His favourite prey is the horse; and our faithful
Niger would probably have fallen a victim last night,
if Almagro's prudence had not saved him. This
seems a fine specimen, Tom; and you must preserve
his skin."

"I have measured him," said Tom, with the proper
gravity of a man of science, "and I find he rather
exceeds the common dimension of the puma, being
five feet six inches from the tip of his nose to the root
of his tail, and three feet high to the shoulder. *Felis
concolor*, the puma, or the American lion, as it has
been called, from its resemblance to the lion, is yet,
you observe, without the mane which distinguishes
that noble animal. Its prey is the guanaco or the
horse, especially the wild horse of the Pampas; its
habit is to crouch and glide silently along the ground,
usually beneath the shelter of bushes, till it is near
enough to its victim; then, springing on the shoulder,
it draws back the head with one of its paws, and dis-
locates the neck."

"After it is gorged with food," observed Almagro,
"I have frequently watched it cover the remains of
the carcase with bushes, and crouch down to watch it.
The condors would then descend in great force, and
dispute the prize fiercely with the destroyer, often
driving him from the field.

"And now, my dear Mrs. Merton," said Lewis,
"to escape from this puma-haunted valley, you must
suffer us to transport you a stage lower. This snow may
possibly indicate the commencement of an early winter,
and longer delay may render our removal more difficult. I propose that to-day we should make another
experiment with the sledge. Tom and I will, with
your sanction, accompany Almagro; and if we bring
you a favourable report, I trust you will not hesitate

to commit yourself to the guidance of our experience."

The fear of the pumas induced Mr. and Mrs. Merton to yield a reluctant consent to this trial; and the skin sledge, with some improvements, was again launched. The adventurers bound themselves to each other with thongs. Lewis and Almagro sat one on each side with a knife to plunge into the snow, to arrest their speed if necessary, and Tom seated between them held a long lance, with which he proposed to steer. The expedition was most satisfactory; they descended with ease, were pleased with the valley, and returned one after the other by means of Almagro's steps, with less fatigue than they expected.

It was finally agreed they should all descend early the next morning; and though some little doubts arose about the management of the beasts, yet all the young were sanguine. The day was happily spent in packing and preparation; and the next morning, as soon as day appeared, the animals were laden, and everything conveyed to the summit of the mountain, with the exception of the small remainder of the fuel and provender, and a bag of *charqui* and fat, which Mr. Merton begged might be hidden under the fuel, for the benefit of succeeding travellers.

They first allowed the baggage, tied together by ropes, to slide down the slope; then Jack, still rather lame, took his place between the two experienced travellers, Almagro and Lewis. He carried in his arms the young llama, a scheme of his own, which was perfectly successful; for the distressed mother, after walking to and fro for a few minutes, made up her mind, and set out in a winding direction after her young one, followed by the other llama, to the admiration of Nanny, who declared Master Jack was always an *umpossible* boy for contrivances. The llamas reached the valley safely; and after the mother had satisfied herself that her offspring was uninjured, they began to browse with good appetite on the herbage, now quite uncovered.

Lewis and Jack set to work directly to raise the tent and arrange the packages, while Almagro, after collecting a bundle of grass, ascended with the sledge. Charles and he placed the sisters between them this time, and Almagro, after allowing the famished mule and horse to smell the grass, fastened it behind the sledge. The poor animals looked wistfully at the banquet gliding away from them; at length the mule took courage, and carefully sounding the snow with his fore-feet, proceeded downwards, followed by the obedient horse. The mule accomplished his journey slowly, but successfully; but Niger, unaccustomed to the snow, after several slips and stumbles, finally rolled down to the bottom. He appeared somewhat stunned and bruised, but, in a few minutes, rising and shaking the snow from his rough coat, he joined his companion, and they began to crop the grass they had so long been deprived of.

Finally the most difficult part of the undertaking was completed, and Mr. Merton and his timid wife, with the scolding and struggling Nanny, were happily rescued from their dreary abode among the snows.

The temperature of this lower region was much warmer than the climate above, and revived the spirits and the hopes of the wanderers. They found scattered twigs and dry grass for their fire, and under the shelter of the tent refreshed themselves after the fatigues of the morning. As the poor animals needed recruiting after their long abstinence, it was agreed that they should travel no farther that day, which was spent in exploring the broad valley, and in climbing to the next ridge, from whence, though many basin-like valleys intervened, they obtained a view of the vast brown Pampas, which from that height appeared to be a wide ocean of plain, unmarked by any variation, except some threads of silver glittering in the sun, which Almagro told them were the rivers from the mountains.

Almagro's experienced eye had discovered a mule-

P. 136.

Charles and he placed the sisters between them this time; and Almagro, after allowing the famished mule and horse to smell the grass, fastened it behind the sledge.

track from the valley, and setting out early next morning, they made a long day, and reached a region of low trees and long rushy grass. Once more they heard the chattering of hundreds of parrots, and having become skilful in the use of the bolas, they caught as many birds as they wanted; glad to taste something rather more delicate than *charqui*. They now entered a gorge, shut in on each side by mountains; their path wound along the side of the rock, while below them rolled a mountain torrent, foaming over masses of rock which had fallen from the heights above. They were glad to lose sight of this tremendous torrent, though they long continued to hear its roaring.

Two days more they wound among the crooked paths of the mountain, and at length reached a broad and fertile valley in the lowest range of the Andes. Before them for many miles was extended, on all sides, a wide plain, bounded by the lowest chain of the mountains. The valley was covered with long grass, and scattered over with low trees and shrubs, not entangled, as on the west side of the Cordilleras, but growing in the beautiful order of Nature; a miniature forest, through which you might pass without difficulty, yet enjoy its shelter and shade. But an air of lonely gloom reigned over the valley; all was solitude, disturbed only by the sound of a rushing mountain stream, the discordant chattering of the parrot, or the sudden bound of the hare, or the agouti, with its long hind legs, alarmed in their undisputed domain by the unwonted presence of man.

There was a feeling of repose experienced by all the party beneath the rude tent stretched among the trees of that quiet valley; and the succeeding morning saw Lewis and Almagro early in serious council.

"What are we now to do, Almagro?" asked Lewis. "For my own part, to acknowledge the truth, I am so completely weary of this blind wandering; and I perceive that the whole party are so unequal to fur-

ther efforts, that, if you believe we are still far distant from civilized habitations, I would use every persuasion to induce Mr. Merton to settle on this quiet
spot, at least, for the approaching winter."

"I have often crossed the Cordilleras at this place,"
replied Almagro ; "I have descended to the Pampas,
and ranged, even beyond the misty mountains you
see at the east. I have chased the wild cattle and
the swift ostrich for leagues over the plain ; but near
this spot I have never seen the hut of man, nor the
trace of his presence. The way we have come has
only been tracked by the Indians of the far south,—
a cruel and savage race, who triumph in dyeing their
spears with the blood of the Christians. We must
avoid their path, which, till now, we have trodden
with impunity, and therefore you must urge our
friends to extend this tedious journey still for
some leagues to the north."

Lewis saw the prudence of the plan, and he proposed immediately to Mr. Merton, that after one
day's further journeying to the north, they should
select a convenient locality and build a hut, where
they might rest and recruit their strength in a pleasant and healthy climate.

"But, surely, Dr. Lewis," asked Mrs. Merton,
"you do not suppose that we can spend our lives in
this lonely desert, for ever in dread of attacks from
wild beasts or savage men ? "

"We will defy them all," said Jack. "Now just
listen, mamma. We will fortify our castle in such a
way, that neither savage nor wild beast can enter it.
Then we have arms ; Charles is a capital soldier, he
shall drill us, and see if we do not turn out a formidable force against any invaders."

"But how can we build a house ? " asked Mary.
"We have neither carpenters nor masons ; we have
neither bricks, nor beams, nor glass for windows."

"Mary," interrupted her sister, "you are speaking
of things you do not understand. A hut in this valley

must be, according to my notion, a mere log-house, such as we read are built by the North American settlers in the far west."

"No doubt such should be the plan," said Tom, looking round at the scattered trees, "but I see no timber here suitable for our purpose. The gigantic beech and pine of North America are used for those logs. Here is the algaroba, resembling a stunted oak, which even if sound, would furnish very poor logs. Here is also a kind of *espino*, too slender for our use. How valuable to us would be the noble Araucanian pine, which we saw on the west side of the Andes, and which I fear is not to be met with here."

"My young friends," said Almagro, "you must abandon these plans, and content yourselves with the Gaucho hut of the Pampas; the walls of wicker work, made of the pliant reeds which we shall meet with near the streams, and plastered with mud without and within. Trust to me to build a hut when we find a pleasant site, and when the good father shall agree to remain content under the humble roof."

As they moved gently along the level valley towards the north, they all endeavoured to prevail on Mrs. Merton to give up the idea of roaming still farther; and Lewis declared they should have to traverse the dreary Pampas for hundreds of leagues, before they reached the dwellings of men, an undertaking quite impossible in their weary and destitute condition.

"Not only must we cross the pathless desert," said Almagro, "but wide and rapid rivers lie in our way, dangerous, if not impossible for strangers to ford. With strong horses we might have a chance of crossing, but our worn-out animals could never safely do it."

"Nor would mamma ever consent to such an experiment," said Matilda. "But why should we not make a canoe? I have a perfect idea of how the thing should be done, and could sketch a plan for it."

"My dear child," said Mr. Merton, "your presumption gives me pain. You are totally ignorant of boat-building, and of mechanics in general. Be content to excel in feminine occupations, and leave your brothers to build houses and canoes."

"But I should really like to see Matilda's model of a perfect canoe," said Jack, laughing.

Matilda was silenced and mortified, but Lewis said her speculations were not to be despised, though she was apt to hurry too boldly to a conclusion. "We will consider the subject at our leisure," continued he ; "for we are now approaching a beautiful wood, and I propose that we enter it, and select a spot for our night's lodging. Who knows but this very wood may afford a pleasant site for our winter abode ?"

Mrs. Merton sighed at the allusion ; but the wood was inviting ; even Nanny declared that a house built among such bright green trees would look more like home than the jails they had been shut up in so long, and, influenced by Nanny's decision, her mistress resigned herself to her fate.

The wood crossed the valley, and extended up the mountains on each side. From the summit of the lower steep it continued in a gentle slope to the wide Pampas below. The tall trees afforded shelter from the noon-day sun and the night breeze, and the notes of thousands of birds promised a security from famine. They slept peacefully, and the boys, animated by the novel sight of abundant vegetation, rose early to explore the wood, and returned in high spirits to breakfast, loaded with gigantic pine cones.

"My dear Lewis," cried Tom, "I have found the tree that will be useful to us for all purposes ; and, though I have yet met with but one specimen, doubtless many exist higher up the mountain. See, this is the fruit, and here is the curious leaf of the *Araucaria imbricata*, a majestic tree of the Fir tribe, though, perhaps, this one is not so lofty and noble in appearance as the trees we noticed beyond the Andes. I recognized it immediately by the stiff, broad leaf, the branches growing in a circular form round the stem, and the long, leafy appendage which terminates the cone. This cone contains seeds which, I suspect, we shall find to be excellent food."

"At this season the seeds are in perfection," said Almagro. "In Auracania the tree is named *pino de la tierra*. The *pinones*, or seeds of the cone, are roasted, or boiled, or bruised, formed into a paste, flavoured with fruit, and baked in cakes."

The experiment was immediately made. One of the cones was opened. It contained nearly two hundred seeds, some of which were extracted and roasted; and after their long confinement to animal food, the delicate fruit, which tasted much like chestnuts, was highly enjoyed, and Tom received due praise for his sagacious discovery.

"This is not a mere luxury, but a valuable accessory to our stores," observed Dr. Lewis. "The *charqui*, and even the hare soups, will be more palatable and wholesome with this vegetable addition. I propose that we set out on a foraging expedition, to collect all the cones we can find fallen. They are best eaten fresh, but by preparing them into a paste, which can be preserved, we shall be enabled to augment our winter stores."

Charles was quite ready to join the party in what bore some resemblance to a sporting expedition; though he was greatly discontented with the plan of a hut in this solitary spot.

"You talk of stores, Lewis, as if we were not locomotive creatures," said he. "Now you may do as you will; but it cannot be supposed that I, with a noble fortune and a luxurious home awaiting me at Valparaiso, should be content to stay here, compelled to knock down a wild bull if I want a beef-steak for my breakfast, and to chop sticks before I can have a fire to cook it. I cannot even have a cigar here, which I

reckon to be one of the necessaries of life; and I
positively have to shave without soap, and to be thankful, even, when I can get water for the purpose!
Build your hut, by all means, and remain here, if you
can be satisfied to live on guanaco flesh and dropped
acorns or fir-apples, whichever they may be. But I
decidedly intend to proceed northward till I reach, as
I certainly must do, the haunts of men."

"But, my dear Charles, you would perish in the
wilds if you travelled alone," said Mrs. Merton.

"Nay, dear aunt, have no fears about me," answered Charles. "If I have my good rifle, and
Almagro for my servant, I can rough it for a week or
two."

"And leave us without guide or adviser," cried
Jack; "taking away our best head and hand. I say,
Charley, that is cool. And perhaps you would like
the mule for yourself, and Niger for your servant,
wouldn't you, now?"

It is probable that some vague plan of this sort had
really crossed the mind of Charles; but when Jack
spoke of it, and he began to consider the selfishness of
the act, he blushed, and was silent.

"Indeed, cousin Charles," said Mary, "if you desert
us now, after all our wanderings together, you are dis-
graced for ever,—a recreant knight! Even I, your
best friend and patroness, shall cast you off, and say,
'Never more be officer of mine.'"

"I really should be very sorry to leave you all, my
dear cousins," answered he ruefully; "but this sort
of existence is fearfully dull and fatiguing; and if Mr.
Merton proposes to sit down here for life, it is but a
chill prospect for us, who are young, to grow grey in
the wilderness,—'the world forgetting, by the world
forgot,'—with no society but the parrots. And when
our clothes decay, as they must do,"—and Charles
looked down with a sigh at his dilapidated raiment,—
"I shudder to think that, instead of going to my tailor
and ordering a coat of the latest fashion, I must shoot

a guanaco or a wild bull, and roll myself up in its skin, in any fashion. Eheu! eheu! the glory of Charles Villars is departed!"

"Go to the woods now, my children," said Mr. Merton. "We will not remain here without discussion and deliberation; and if it be considered expedient, we will agree to your plan, and move forward, my dear boy."

"I believe, uncle, I am a thankless varlet," said the penitent youth; "but I hope this sweet morning air will soothe my rebellious fancies."

"And to convince you, Charley, that the wood has better fruit than fir-apples, as you call them, see what a feast I bring you," said Mary, producing a basket of strawberries, which, even at that advanced season, she had found in a sheltered nook, near the encampment.

They feasted on the strawberries; and Matilda remarked that with such an immense quantity of fruit at their command, it would be prudent to make a stock of jam.

"And where will you buy your sugar?" asked Nanny, to the great diversion of the young party, and the annoyance of Matilda, who did not like to be convicted of a blunder.

"Why should we not find the sugar-cane?" demanded she stoutly. "Columbus found it wild in several parts of America."

"You labour under an error," said Tom, "in supposing that we should find this valuable plant growing naturally so far south of the equator. The cultivation of the *Saccharum officinarum*, from which the sugar is produced, extends to some distance beyond the tropics. It is even cultivated in Spain and Sicily, 35° to 40° north latitude; but no one acquainted with the geography of plants would expect to find the sugar-cane wild on the Pampas."

"Well, never mind," said Jack, "it all comes to this: we have no sugar, but we have lots of strawberries, so let us enjoy them."

CHAPTER XII.

The Wood and the River. The Ruined Hut. The Strange
Bird. The Spanish Girl. Maria's Story. Scenes in a
Guacho Hut. The Indian Attack. Maria's Escape and
Rescue from Death.

ARMED with bolas, lances, and rifles, the gentlemen
set out to explore the wood. Attracted by the murmuring of water, they penetrated through a grove of
thick trees, following the sound, and at some distance
from the encampment reached the margin of a clear
narrow river, pleasantly shaded by willows, and flowing from the mountains. They walked up the banks
of the stream, which they considered would be a guide
to lead them back from their wanderings in the trackless wood. The road was easy, pleasant, and scattered
with bright flowers; the air was fresh and pure, and
the chattering of the parrots, and murmuring song of
the humming-bird, enlivened the solitude. They
found the wild potato, and several other plants, which
were collected to be examined at leisure, in hopes that
some might be useful. At length they emerged into
an open glade of some extent, and a joyful exclamation from Jack directed their attention to the branches
of the tree beneath which they were passing, and
which were weighed down with ripe peaches.

"The hand of man has planted this tree," said
Almagro. "Let us proceed with caution, my friends.
We must be near the habitations of men, but we know
not whether they contain friends or enemies."

They went on in silence and anxiety, passing under
several peach-trees, all laden with fruit; then they
reached a plot of ripe maize. They stopped, and looked
round, with much agitation. Here were traces of the

industry of man; but still all continued silent and still: where were the hands that had sowed the maize and planted the fruit-trees?

Beyond the high stalks of the maize lay some scattered poles and sticks: Almagro bent over them and carefully examined them. "On this spot," said he, "has been the corral; it has been plundered and laid waste. But let us go on, the work of destruction would not end here."

Passing through another grove of peach-trees, they suddenly came on the charred and desolate ruins of a hut. The roof was entirely gone, and in the back wall there was a large aperture; the remainder, built firmly of boughs plastered with mud, remained entire. The door lay torn off, and half-burnt, and they entered, with dejected hearts. It was a melancholy spectacle: nothing remained to mark that it had been the dwelling of man, except some rude seats, formed of the skeleton of the horse's head.

"Here have plunder and murder done their work," said Almagro, at length, in deep emotion. "See! the everlasting stain of blood remains on the mud floor, the record of a savage massacre. Let us leave this spot, my good friends, which recalls painfully to my mind the never-to-be-forgotten horrors of my early days."

"But are we safe now?" asked Tom; "is there not some danger of the return of these barbarians?"

"We need have no fear now," replied Almagro; "these crafty destroyers return no more to the spot they have made desolate. They roam in search of new plunder, and of more Christian blood."

They left the melancholy scene, and continued, keeping the river in view, to ascend the woody steep beyond the hut, to search for more pinones; but they did not succeed in finding another pine-tree. They captured a hare and some parrots, and then began to consult on the expediency of cutting a portion of the ripe maize, which must waste in the desert if not appro-

L

priated.   They had decided that their necessity gave them a right to the food, when Jack, who had been rambling, for he could not bear discussions, returned to petition for the loan of a rifle.

"For what purpose?" Dr. Lewis inquired; for he considered himself responsible for the safety of his young friends, and he had some fears of the rash intrepidity of Jack.

"I have got a glimpse of a glorious bird," said he, "but it flits away at the motion of a leaf, and I shall have no chance of securing it with the bolas.   From its brilliant scarlet plumage, I conceive it must be a lory; we saw some of these splendid-looking birds in the Zoological Gardens, Tom."

"We did," said Tom; "and I am able to tell you that the lory is an inhabitant of India, one of the most beautiful of the *Psittacidæ*, and an extremely delicate creature; nothing can be more absurd than to fancy the lory living in the forests of the Andes."

"Your eye has deceived you, Jack," said Dr. Lewis, good-naturedly.   "Besides, my good fellow, we have already killed more parrots than is consistent with humanity; therefore we ought to spare this unknown bird, for we have no means of preserving it as a specimen.   There is another consideration—if the report of the rifle is heard at the encampment, it will greatly alarm our friends there.   We will steal up to the place, to endeavour to see this strange creature alive, but we will not wantonly destroy it."

Jack looked disappointed, but yielded to the counsel of Lewis, and they proceeded cautiously through the forest towards the spot where Jack had observed the scarlet wonder.   They looked round for some time in vain, and were about to return, when Charles made a signal for silence, and raising his rifle, pointed it towards a low tree, through the thick dark foliage of which they now saw the fluttering of some scarlet object.

"Stay!" cried Almagro, loudly, dashing down the

rifle, and springing towards the tree. They gazed after him with great astonishment; he plunged into the wood, and after an absence of a few minutes returned, carrying in his arms the insensible form of a young girl, clothed in a scarlet poncho.

"See, young man," said he to Charles, "you might, in carelessness, have slain this child. Even the sight of me has almost killed her. What a scene of misery is this! Bring some water, my friends, to pour over her."

The boys brought water in their hands and poured it over her. At length, she opened her dark eyes, and looking round in a distracted manner, burst into tears.

"This girl is, like myself, a Guacho, of Spanish origin," said Almagro, looking attentively at her beautiful features, darkened by the sun and exposure to the air. Then, addressing her, he said, "Do not fear us, unfortunate child, we will protect you; we are not Indians, we are friends and Christians."

"I, too, am a Christian," said the girl, in the Spanish tongue. "Oh, spare me! do not give me up to the wicked Indians!"

"Surely you have some friends, my poor child," said Lewis, addressing her in her own language. "Where is your home?"

"Here, in the forest," replied she; "I live with my murdered father and brother—they are lying behind the bush which I call my home."

Very much distressed by her words, Almagro and Jack went to the spot she indicated, and there, beneath the tree, piled over with brushwood, they found the decaying bodies of two men, who had apparently been murdered by Indian lances. Inexpressibly shocked at the sight, they returned; and Almagro asked the girl how the bodies were removed from the scene of slaughter, which he concluded was the ruined hut they had seen below.

"I brought them here," replied the girl. "I took

L 2

the bough of a tree which had been torn down by the
Indians, on this I placed the dead body of my father,
and drew it with toil and pain to this place; I then
returned and brought in the same way the body of
my brother. I chose a spot beneath the thick tree,
where I could hide my treasures, and watch them
night and day.   Then I collected branches to cover
and protect them from the attacks of the frightful
condors, which were continually hovering over us.   I
have spent many days here; but two days ago, I fell
from the tree into which I had climbed for safety, for I
had heard a rustling in the wood.   I hurt my foot
very much, and could no longer go to the cave for
food, nor to the stream for water, and I lay down
beside those I loved, that I might die near them."

"But you shall not die, poor girl," cried Jack, in
his imperfect Spanish; "you shall come and live
with mamma and my sisters.   My father shall supply
the place of him you have lost.   I will be your
brother; and Dr. Lewis will cure your foot."

The girl gazed wildly on Jack, scarcely comprehending his meaning, and looked back uneasily, as if she
wished to return to her hiding-place.

"You must remain no longer near the decaying
bodies of the dead," said Dr. Lewis.   "God has
recalled their souls, and we will remove the bodies
and bury them near the spot which they inhabited
when living.   If you will come with us, you will learn
to be good, and God will then permit you to join your
friends again in a better world."

The child wept; but, faint with pain and hunger, she
did not reply.   They carried her to the hut, and plucked
some ripe peaches for her, which she ate eagerly, and
then asked for some maize.   Jack ran immediately for
some stalks of the maize which was growing near; she
took them from him with pleasure, but said, smiling,
"There is still much maize in the cave."   They did not
understand her meaning; but, after eating some grains
moistened with water, she revived a little, and begged

them to carry her, through the opening at the back of the hut, into the wood. They bore her, as she directed them, some yards, ascending among the trees, which here grew closely together, until they reached a clump of thick shrubs, which grew against the face of a steep rock.

"Put me down on the ground here," said she. "I can show the young boy the entrance to the cave, though I cannot now creep to it as I used to do."

They seated her before the thicket, and she lifted the trailing branches, and pointed out to Jack, beneath them, a narrow tracked path, telling him he must crawl along this track, close to the earth, till he reached a dark stone, lying against the rock, which he must remove, when he would see a small opening, the entrance of the cave. Jack, delighted with the adventure, followed her directions, and entered a wide cave, in which he saw, by the dim light through loopholes half darkened by bushes, several bags of guanaco-skin; one, which was open, contained maize, and this he concluded had been the food of the young Spaniard during her residence in the wood. He brought away a handful of the grain, to prove that he had fulfilled his task, and left the cave; replacing the stone, and making his way out with some curiosity to have the mystery of the subterranean storehouse solved.

But the poor girl seemed now so exhausted, that Dr. Lewis determined they would return immediately to the tent, that proper restoratives might be administered to her, and her injured foot attended to. Almagro and he undertook to carry the stranger, Charles was charged with the guns and lances, and Tom and Jack, loaded with as many peaches as they could carry, went forward to relate the adventures of the morning.

"Here, mamma," said Tom, throwing some peaches into her lap, "I think you will now agree this will be an excellent place for us to settle at; besides this fruit, we have found abundance of maize."

"And something better than either peaches or maize," cried Jack; "we have brought you a pretty little daughter! I know you will take her to live with us, mamma; for she has lost her own mother, and her poor father has been murdered."

"What strange story is this?" said Mrs. Merton, in great alarm. "Who has been murdered? and who is the child you are speaking of?"

"You need have no alarm, mamma," answered he, "for Almagro assures us the Indians never return a second time to a place they have laid waste; so we are quite safe here, and the little girl will tell you how she escaped when she comes, and as soon as she learns to speak English to you, mamma."

Mrs. Merton had obtained but a vague and unsatisfactory notion of the adventure, when the rest of the party returned. Her sympathies were immediately awakened at the sight of the suffering little stranger, who was laid on a mattress, and had her swollen and dislocated ankle carefully attended to by Dr. Lewis. She endured all the pain attendant on the operation with patience and resignation; Lewis then administered a composing medicine, and they had soon the pleasure of seeing their new guest in a profound sleep.

"Your practice seems to prosper, even in this wilderness, Dr. Lewis," said Matilda. "I wonder how many more patients we shall discover for you. And now pray what are we to do with this lame girl, when we resume our wanderings; for papa and mamma must certainly have the horse and mule?"

"I propose," said Jack, "that we should build a sort of carriage or sledge, for the feeble or weary; I have no doubt the llamas might be trained to draw such a vehicle; though certainly not over such roads as we have lately passed."

"When we actually descend to the level Pampas," said Tom, "such a carriage might be convenient; but I could not possibly make one. Jack may have some knowledge of coach-building; but I decline the undertaking."

"Well," replied Jack, rather mortified, "I meant only a sort of sledge, made of interwoven reeds, upon which we could place the mattress and cloaks to form seats for mamma and the girls, and harness the llamas to it by twisted ropes of hide."

"The scheme is by no means to be despised," said Lewis; "we must not laugh at Jack, for it frequently happens that valuable hints may be obtained from rash speculations. When we have leisure, we will certainly try to attempt some useful invention of this sort. But the adventure of this morning induces me to propose that we should at once select this locality for our winter residence. The unroofed hut might soon be repaired, and rendered habitable; nay, with a little ingenuity and labour, even comfortable. It is pleasantly situated, and desirably secluded. We should have pure water, and a plentiful supply of maize and fruit; and in all probability the fish in the river would be as abundant as the game in the woods. What do you say to this plan, dear Mr. Merton?"

"I understand little about these matters, my kind and good friend," replied Mr. Merton. "You have led us safely through exceeding perils, and, under Heaven, I leave the disposal of myself and my family in your hands; secure that you will arrange all with a prudence and sagacity which I do not possess. My sole desire now is for a little repose, and leisure to study. I long to unpack my books, and am truly glad that, in our wanderings, I have been able to preserve the dear old friends it would have been so painful to me to lose."

"And to which we shall now probably add more," said Tom, "for I have a charming book in my head, to be called, 'Our Travels.'"

"Enriched with the scientific discoveries of Mr. Thomas Merton, and the wonderful and perilous adventures of Mr. John Merton," added Jack.

"But, do you really intend, Dr. Lewis," inquired Mrs. Merton, "that we should remain on a spot infested by those barbarous savages? I should never sleep in peace, from the dread of being aroused by the frightful cries described by Almagro."

Lewis repeated to her the assurance of the great improbability of the Indians revisiting a scene of murder, robbery, and ruin, when wide and unexplored tracts of the Pampas were open to them. He declared his belief that no spot they could select could be so safe from molestation. Mrs. Merton trembled as she thought on the dangers that surrounded her ; and it required many persuasions to compose her troubled mind, and to induce her to yield a reluctant assent to the plan of location for the winter.

In the mean time dinner had been made ready, and the young stranger awoke from her sleep. She ate some roast parrot, and then, as she looked round on the party with pleased astonishment, Dr. Lewis told her, that henceforward she was to become one of the happy family that surrounded her.

The remainder of the day was spent in discussing and arranging their future plans ; and next morning the little Maria, as she told them she was called, related her short tale of sorrow :—

" It is now two years since I lost my beloved mother. It was she who spoke to me of God, and made me repeat prayers to him. She taught me to weave the wool of the llama and the long hair of the guanaco ; to dye the cloth with berries and roots, and to form it into summer and winter garments. She was gentle and loving, but she was not strong as I was ; she could not roam in the woods, but would sit under the shade of the peach-trees, and sing sweet songs of the far-off country of her people, while my father played on the guitar. Bright and pleasant were the days of my childhood. I knew not the meaning of sorrow. My two manly brothers hunted the puma and the wild cattle, and sometimes they killed an ostrich, and brought the plumes to me to deck my hair. Our garden produced vegetables in the summer, and we reaped the maize to store for our winter food. On a very few occasions, my father and one of my brothers went to some far-distant station, carrying skins and the plumes of the ostrich. After many days, they would return with their lading changed for powder and shot, knives and spades, with some gay-coloured handkerchiefs for my mother and me; but *we* never saw a stranger.

"A day came when my father and my brother Fernando returned from the hunt without Gonzalo. They had encountered some travellers on the Pampas, and my eldest brother, a bold and athletic youth, had undertaken to guide these strangers across the Cordilleras. It was not the temptation of the handsome reward they offered, but the love of adventure, and the desire of seeing more of mankind, that induced my brother to forsake his home. My mother was ill-satisfied with this event; she wished that her children should ever remain around her; moreover, the autumn was advanced, and she dreaded the dangers of the mountain journey. My father and brother laughed at her fears; but they were just. We never saw Gonzalo more.

"When weeks and months passed, and he returned not, my father and Fernando set out to the Pass; the fallen snow obstructed their progress, but at length, lying half over the brink of the precipice, they found the skeleton of a mule; they recognised the saddle-cloth, which was the skin of a puma, fringed by my mother's hand; and they concluded that the mule had fallen on the frozen path, and precipitated my unfortunate brother into the frightful abyss, now half-filled with snow: from the position of the mule, this must have happened when he was returning alone, and could hope for no aid. They returned home sorrowfully to communicate the melancholy news.

"My mother's grief was deep and fatal. She spoke not of her bereavement; she wept not; but, day after day, pale and broken-hearted, she sat gazing on the snow-crested mountains in silent despair. My father

assured her, that when the warm suns of spring
should have melted the snows, my brother and he
would return to search the deep valleys for the body.
She shook her head, for she well knew the spring
would not return for her.   Before the stream was
swollen by the snows of the mountain, she had gone
to join the lost one, in that bright heaven of which
she loved to speak to me, and to teach me to seek.

" When the spring came, my father's sorrows overpowered him ; it was not till the end of summer that
he recovered sufficiently to send Fernando to search
the valley for his brother's corpse.   He could not leave
me alone in the hut, but he commanded my brother
strictly to abide by the directions he gave him ; and
cautioned him especially to avoid returning by an
Indian pass, many leagues to the south, lest he
should encounter any of the barbarians.   My brother
was young and thoughtless ; after searching the abyss
below the precipice, he continued his search from
valley to valley, forgetting my father's prohibition,
till he reached a path far south of our abode, by
which he descended to the Pampas.   On reaching
the open plain, he saw, with some alarm, a party of
mounted Indians, who were, however, at a considerable distance.   Instead of withdrawing to the shelter
of the woods, he trusted to the speed of his horse,
and fled, at full speed, along the plain.   He reached
the hut in safety, and told his tale to my father ;
acknowledging also, that the Indians might have seen
him.

" My father was disturbed ; he made a secret
entrance at the back of the hut, through which he
conveyed all our valuable stores for concealment to the
cave which he had some time before discovered by
accident.   He then proposed that we should abandon
the hut, and for the remainder of the summer live in
the woods.   But he was weakened by affliction, and
was not sufficiently prompt in action ; and on the eve
of our intended departure, as we lay sleeping, we

were roused by a wild and savage yell. Then we knew that our situation was hopeless, for the merciless Indians were at our door. My father gazed on me a moment, then removing the stone at the back of the hut, he folded me in his poncho, and ordered me to creep beneath the bushes to the cave; telling me they would follow as soon as they had secured their guns and bolas; but I had not reached my hiding-place before I heard shrieks and groans, and saw, through the bushes above me, that the roof of the hut was blazing. I feared that murder was doing, and unable to endure the horrors of anxiety, I lost my senses. How long I lay in this state I know not; but when I revived, I still heard the discordant shouts of the destroyers, and, impelled by the horror of a fearful death, or a still more fearful slavery, I made an effort to force my way, unperceived, to my hiding-place, through the low brushwood. I reached the cave and entered it, half-dead with terror, and sat listening with a throbbing heart for the approach of those I loved; but alas! they came not; I heard nothing but the lowing of the cattle, the neighing of the horses, and the ferocious yells of triumph, which proclaimed that the spoilers had succeeded in their bloody work.

" At length the cries began to recede, and I concluded they must be moving off. An hour of intense anxiety succeeded, and then I ventured to look out, and, by the gray light of early morning, looked on the ruined and still smouldering hut. I trembled with a sensation of strange and uncertain misery; I did not dare to think that I was left alone in the world; but it was long before I could summon courage to ascertain the extent of my misfortune. Then I ventured to approach my home;—all was still; the horses and cattle had been driven off by the robbers. The door of the hut was torn down, and, with a desperate effort, I entered, and sank down in long insensibility beside the mangled bodies of my father and my brother.

" God called me once more to life; I believed that
it was his will that I should still live, and I therefore
submitted.　　But I could not remain in the hut; I
therefore determined to wander about the woods
during the day, and sleep in the cave, if the nights
were cold, till God thought fit to summon me from
my dreary life.

" But I could not leave the bodies of my beloved
friends in that dismal hut; I could not dig into the
ground to bury them; but I thought if I could carry
them to the woods, I might sepulchre them in boughs
and stones.　　I moved them with difficulty, as I told
you, my kind friends; and it was with much labour I
tore down the boughs, and collected the scattered
branches to cover them.　　I had no want of food;
there was maize in the cave, and the trees, which the
Indians had not noticed in the darkness, supplied me
with peaches.　　But when I hurt my foot, and could
no longer procure food or water, I resigned myself,
believing it to be God's will that I should die of
famine in the wood.　　I am brought from pain and
death to a beautiful new life.　　I shall be glad to live
now, if God permits me; for you all look so happy,
that life must surely have many joys that I have
never known."

" Tell the child," said Mrs. Merton, " that I will
be her mother, and I hope soon to see her look as
happy as my own children."

Youth soon forgets its sorrows; and before twenty-
four hours were past, Maria was smiling with her
new friends, and endeavouring to learn English.
Dressed in some of Mary's clothes, with her long
dark tresses fancifully arranged by the sisters, the
young girl had a noble and picturesque appearance
that quite charmed her friends.　　She was, according
to her own account, about fourteen years old, but
looked younger than Mary, who had not yet reached
that age, and to whom the little foreigner had attached herself peculiarly, captivated by her warm and
ardent manner.

CHAPTER XIII.

The Family take possession of the ruined Hut. The Fortification. The Maize Harvest. The Wild Cow captured and tamed. The Capsicum. Spinning and Weaving. Walks in the Wood. The Cactus. The Hedge of Defence. The Alerse Pine.

In the mean time the whole family had been to inspect the hut, and notwithstanding the fearful adventure connected with it, even Mrs. Merton seemed pleased at the first sight with the peaceful seclusion of the situation, and the air of abundance produced by the appearance of the ripe maize and the laden peach-trees. She certainly shuddered as she looked into the hut, but the bold workmen promised not only to fortify it securely, but to change its present desolation into convenience and comfort. She agreed to wait for the completion of their promise ; and that no time might be lost, the tent was brought, and spread under the peach-trees ; all the property transferred to the same place, and then they began to work in earnest.

Their first task was to cut down trees, and Almagro shook his head as he saw the light axes which formed part of Tom's carpenter's chest. He had one strong axe which he had brought from his own hut, but the work could not be rapidly done with one hand. As soon as Maria understood their distress, she directed them to the cave for implements of work. They were glad to find there some excellent axes and spades ; and all hands working vigorously, they were able to bring to the hut, in the evening, a large stock of palisades ready for use.

Next morning they began to dig a deep trench, surrounding the hut and an area of about an acre,

which was to form their garden and pleasure-ground.
The corral was destined to be beyond the inclosure,
as they could not include it without more labour than
they had time, at present, to bestow. When the
trench was ready, they placed their palisades as close
as possible in it, and formed a stockade six feet high,
the palisades being pointed sharply at the upper end.
This defence cost all the able hands three hard days
of labour; but when it was completed, Mrs. Merton
declared she should now sleep in peace, especially as
the narrow entrance was protected by a huge stone,
which they rolled down with great difficulty from the
rocks above, and placed before the opening while they
slept, till they could make a door strong enough for
security. Almagro undertook to new roof the hut,
and to thatch it with slender dry branches and maize-
leaves; over which he pegged down hides of oxen, of
which many were stored in the cave. Thus the roof
was not only waterproof, but they trusted even fire-
proof, should it ever again be exposed to that terrible
ordeal.

Their next task was to partition the spacious hut
with slender interlaced branches, forming two small
dormitories, one each side, and reserving a large space
in the middle for the common sitting-room, of which the
floor was partly covered with skins. Nanny empha-
tically declared she now felt like herself, with a roof
over her head; and she forgot all her ill humour in
the pleasure of unpacking boxes, which they had never
before had opportunity to open.

And now they had time to gather in the maize
crop, which was done by plucking the ripe ears; in
which light labour old and young merrily joined.
These ears were accumulated in heaps, to be further
dried by the sun. Then the large grains were forced
from the pod by scraping the edge of a knife along it;
and these grains were placed in such casks and bags as
they could command, and deposited in the cave for
safety. Under the direction of Almagro, the boys

dug some holes within the inclosure, and lined them with dry maize-leaves; in these holes the remainder of the grain was stored, and they were then carefully covered with earth to exclude the air. The pods were stacked behind the hut to serve for fuel, and the leaves and stalks, after being left a little longer on the ground to be perfectly dried, were cut down, as well as the knives and spades permitted them to accomplish the tedious work, and were then stacked for the animals. This food, Lewis said, was wholesome and fattening for cattle, from the saccharine quality of the plant.

After the harvest they had each a little bed of fresh maize straw, covered with a skin and the blanket each had secured. Nanny declared, she did not see why her mistress should not have a four-post bed, as if she was in a Christian country; but more important occupations prevented the realization of this ambitious plan, and Mrs. Merton's mattress was, for the present, placed on a frame, made by planting four short poles in the earth, and stretching a skin firmly over them.

Some small openings were made in the mud walls, to admit light and air; the young people called them *windows*, but instead of glass, they were latticed with thin willow wands; and they proposed in the winter, if the hunters supplied means, to make curtains of skins for them.

The animals, which had fattened with ease and good pasturages, now demanded their attention, and a *corral*, or strong inclosure, adjoining the palisades, was soon formed to contain them, from the scattered palisades torn down by the Indians.

In the midst of these occupations the young men occasionally went to the woods with their bolas, and brought home parrots, or sometimes a hare; but the heavy labour being now accomplished, they set out one day early, to cross the hills and have a ramble on the Pampas; Almagro accompanying them on his mule. They were fortunate enough to see immediately a

herd of wild cattle.   They had never yet tried their
weapons on such large animals, and Almagro ordered
them to be very cautious and regular in their approach.   But, by good luck, a young cow had wandered to some distance from the rest of the herd, and
Almagro immediately galloped forward, and flung his
bolas so dexterously round the fore-legs of the animal,
that it fell on the spot.

"Stop, Almagro," cried Jack, as the Guacho was
about to despatch it with his knife, " we do not want
meat just now, and if we could get it home, and tame
it, Nanny would be so delighted to have a real cow!"

This was a very tempting plan, but not easy to
accomplish.   They succeeded in tying its legs in such
a manner that it could not run from them; but the
cow was absolutely determined not to move at all
with its legs tied, and all attempts to drive it forward
were found fruitless.   At length a strong lasso was
fixed round its neck, and, partly by main force, and
partly by goading it, it was brought by slow degrees,
and with violent resistance, to the wood near the inclosure, and there tied to a tree in. such a manner
that it could not reach the grass to feed.

However charmed Matilda and Mary were to possess a cow, they were much distressed that such painful
means should be necessary to subdue it; and but for
the extreme fear they had of its large horns, they
would have ventured to give it a handful of maize-
leaves.   After being tied up for twenty-four hours,
its lowing was so piteous that Mary could resist it no
longer, but approaching it cautiously, she held out
the straw at the end of a long forked stick.   The
animal greedily devoured the food, and then stretched
out its neck to her for more.   She took courage, and
ventured to stroke its huge thick neck, and to offer
the straw from her own hand, and water from a
wooden bowl.   The cow soon knew Mary, and lowed at
her approach; and Almagro's management rendered it
so quiet, that in a few days it was allowed to graze,

though still secured to the tree. A week after, the animal produced a calf, which soon became a great pet with the girls, and the mother, being gratified, as Mary said, with their kindness to her offspring, finally submitted to be milked, and Nanny triumphantly established a dairy in the cave.

And now the tent being finally struck, the family took possession of their new abode; which the chill night air from the mountains rendered a very desirable measure. Maria was perfectly recovered, and able to enter into their pursuits, and plans were talked of for regular daily employment.

" Permit me, papa," said Matilda, " to lay down the rules, so that the most profitable use may be made of every moment of time. I believe I have a talent for managing time well."

" And remember," added Jack, " you must all submit to the laws of Queen Matilda, on pain of the knout. The idle and disobedient, after a public reprimand, to receive a certain number of lashes, proportioned to their offence; to be inflicted by Nanny, as public executioner."

" Well, Jack," said Matilda, " at least give us your plan, before you ridicule mine."

" My dear children," said Mrs. Merton, " we will listen to all your suggestions, because we love you to acquire habits of reflection; and it is even probable some of your measures may be more practicable than my own, for my feeble health has subdued my energy; but your father and I alone must be rulers, supported by our prime minister and excellent counsellor, Dr. Lewis."

Lewis rejoiced to see Mrs. Merton had recovered some activity of mind, and the rules and laws of the little community were arranged and cheerfully submitted to, even by the abashed Matilda. Every one was expected to rise early, and assemble in the common room, where Mr. Merton performed the sacred service of the morning. The girls then assisted Nanny in milking,

M

and other household duties, and in making ready the breakfast of maize boiled in milk ; the young men, in the mean time, fed the animals in the corral with fresh grass, cut or plucked on the plain.   After breakfast, an hour or two was devoted to study ; then the hunters departed for the woods, the plains, or the river, on which they had constructed weirs, and, at this season, were enabled to take abundance of excellent fish. In the woods Tom frequently forgot the game in his eagerness to discover new plants, and it was with great pleasure he pointed out to Lewis one day, a low, dark-green, weedy-looking shrub, covered with capsicums.

"It is the *Capsicum frutescens*, the Chili pepper," said he, " one of the most pungent and wholesome of the pepper tribe."

They filled a bag with the capsicums for Nanny, who was glad to have some seasoning for her stews ; for though a small store of salt had been found in the cave, even that was nearly exhausted, and to eat meat without salt was an unpleasant prospect.   When Maria saw the capsicums, she took Tom to a spot in the devastated garden where this plant had been cultivated ; and he saw that the shrub, though broken, would revive in the spring, when they should have the produce always at hand for use.

" I don't know how it is," said Jack, " but I never make any botanical discoveries ; perhaps I have not patience to count the stamens or petals, or examine whether the leaves be serrated or lanceolate ; but I will tell you, Nanny, what I will do for you—I will make an oven for you."

" And if you say that, Master Jack," replied Nanny, " I'll trust you, you will do it ; you were always a boy of your word, and an oven is just the thing I want."

But Jack's oven, like all important undertakings, was not to be completed in a day ; many things intervened to delay even the commencement, though Jack did not forget his promise.

The morning, when the young hunters were absent, was spent by the sisters in acquiring from Maria the art of spinning and weaving the fine hair of the llama, and the coarse wool of the guanaco. The former, indeed, needed no spinning; it was merely drawn out, knotted together, and wound round a wooden spindle; but the wool was formed into a thread before it was wound. In both cases, the process was tedious, and Matilda declared she would certainly have a wheel made, but the unpractised workmen rejected the order. The simple contrivance for the loom consisted of four short rods placed in the ground before the hut, about eighteen inches apart, and four long rods, running along the top, from one to another, and tied to them. This was the frame, and the threads were stretched from end to end, and knotted to the rods. Then the young weavers, kneeling down, passed the weft from one side to the other, astonished alike at the readiness with which they acquired the art, and at the wonderful production of the stuff woven by their own hands. Even Mr. Merton was sometimes weaned from his studies to observe the rapid progress of the industrious little hands. And after dinner, the boys brought their carpenter's tools to the side of the loom, that they might converse with their sisters and obtain their sympathy in the many ineffectual attempts they made before they could produce anything tolerable, as a seat, or a table.

Towards evening the whole family went forth to ramble in the woods, to listen to the curious notes of birds yet strange to them, or to collect the last flowers of autumn. It was in these pleasant evenings that the good father loved to speak to his children of the charm and advantage of retirement from the evils of life.

" Here, my children," said he, " I should be contented to remain, and prepare my soul for eternity. Why should we ever stray beyond this wood? Here Nature, with her beautiful and inimitable propriety, prepares plenty for all seasons: the beasts of the field

and the fowls of the air, are alike bountifully fed by
the hand of God.   Here the sordid cares of labour
and acquisition are suspended, and man has leisure
for mental improvement, unbroken by the weary duty
of providing for the morrow.   How soothing to the
mind it is, in this blessed retreat, to contemplate the
wonders of creation which surround us, and to devote
ourselves to reading and meditation, undisturbed by
vexations.   Oh, my children ! God has led us to this
peaceful harbour ; let us remain here ; let us enjoy
this Garden of Eden, which shadows forth, in its peace
and beauty, that better world which God has provided
for them who love him.''

   " But we must toil a little, before we make you quite
comfortable in your abode," said Jack.   "And now,
papa, confess, if we had not been with you, could you
really have set about building yourself a hut ?"

   "In truth, my son," said the meek old man, "I
doubt it much.   I have small skill in mechanical
works, and should probably have contented myself
with the retirement of a cave, or with the simple
shelter of a sail spread over the lower branches
of a tree,—albeit that might have proved an insufficient protection against the attacks of the *Feræ*
of the forest.   Yet, had your mother been my companion, I might have essayed to construct some fabric
more suitable to her delicate health ; especially as she
has a feminine repugnance to abide in a cave.   Surely,
such an abode is gloomy ; yet we read that holy men
of old dwelt in caves to extreme old age unmolested,
save by their own sinful thoughts.''

   "I hope it is not sinful to think, papa," said Matilda, "that these devout men might have been less
exposed to evil fancies if they had been employed in
the useful labours of the world.''

   "We will try, my dear Mr. Merton," said Lewis,
"if we can, by God's help, successfully blend a life of
employment with a faithful attention to our sacred
duties.''

"You are ever right in judgment, my thoughtful friend," replied Mr. Merton; "for I now remember that the holy apostle Paul recommends that all men should work. Here our sphere of action is circumscribed; but it may please God to enlarge the boundaries of our utility. Waiting his time, I exhort you, my children, to help one another, and to fulfil, as far as human frailty permits, your duty to God and to those around you."

"And, after all, papa," said Jack, "I hope you will not forbid us occasionally descending to the Pampas, to have a scamper about, and see how the world looks outside our Eden?"

"Do let Jack go, papa," added Mary; "he is such a good boy, and he wishes so much to see ostriches and jaguars, and just to have a peep at the wonderful Indians; and he will take his lasso, and catch some wild horses, and then we can all ride. Let them all go; we are quite safe in our fairy bower."

"Certainly they must not go, Mary," answered her mamma, "if there is any possibility of encountering the terrible Indians."

"Not any probability, mamma," said Tom. "Besides, I have a plan to render our castle impregnable. Look here, Lewis, at this branch, which I deposited on this spot in the morning, when I returned from my climbing up the mountain. Is not this the cactus, described as so useful in forming the impenetrable hedge, that even the daring Indian shrinks from?"

"I recognize it at once," said Matilda, "as one of the Cacti, which are remarkable for their rapid growth, and for the spines, which render them so formidable. We must have a hedge; then dig a moat round our fort, and make a drawbridge, which will complete our security."

"What do you say, Matilda," asked Jack, laughing, "to our placing a row of cannon on our battlements?"

"In truth, my dear Matilda," observed Lewis, "you ought not to be offended with Jack's jest; for we might as well plan towers and guns, as a moat and drawbridge; we have not the means and appliances for such works. No: all thanks to Tom the thoughtful, the cactus hedge is the grand security for our peace; and I propose that *we*, the men of sinews and muscles, should set out to-morrow morning with spades and lassoes, to dig up, and draw to our fort, all the young cacti we can find."

They went off accordingly next morning in high glee, but returned with cross looks; for though they drew after them a great number of young trees, their hands and legs were bleeding from many wounds, received, as Jack said, in the battle with the Cacti.

"We will, however, convert our enemy into a friend," said Lewis, as he tore away the thorns from one of the leaves, and then bound it over the wounded hand of Charles, which certainly was dreadfully lacerated.

"Henceforward I give up the warfare," said Charles. "Give me but a sword, and, like the Paladins of old, I will cut my way through the most formidable obstacles; but it.is too much to expect a warrior to bind his prisoners with thongs, and then submit to draw them behind him."

"But I will not have you turn recreant," said Mary. "You must go out and conquer, that you may deserve the prize of a poncho I am weaving for you. In the mean time, receive these elegant gloves I have made, to replace those you sacrificed so soon after our landing."

The ingenious girls had been employed during the day in making a defence for the hands of the workmen, after a design given them by Nanny. She had described to them the mittens, as they are provincially named, used by the hedgers in Westmoreland; and these simple coverings they had formed very successfully from the skins of the hare and vicuna. They entirely covered the hand, having no division between the fingers; the thumb alone having a distinct protection. They were all much pleased with the gloves, which were soon put into use, for, immediately after dinner, the work of planting began.

Two of the party were employed in digging a trench outside the stockade, into which the other two placed the young trees, at a very short distance from each other, and then filled up the trench again. It was tedious work, and they did not complete many yards before they were quite exhausted ; but they were satisfied with their success, and ready to renew their labours next day. Yet it was not without some murmuring that day after day passed, and still the heavy task went on slowly ; at length experience taught them to improve their mode of labour. They secured the young trees by a lasso before they were dug up, and then placed them upon a sort of sledge, made by Almagro of some hides found in the cave, sewed together with threads of the same material. To this rude vehicle the horse and mule were harnessed ; and the trees were drawn to the enclosure, to the great relief of the workmen, allowing them to take a hare or some parrots to supply the table.

It was nearly three weeks before the great work was finished. The trees seemed all to take well, and the defence was already satisfactory ; for a double row of young trees completely encircled the enclosure and the corral, except a narrow opening for the entrance, which they planned to defend by as strong a door as their means permitted them to make. These trees were now about four feet in height ; but such is the rapidity of the growth of the cactus, that they hoped in time to see their hedge twelve or fourteen feet high.

"And now for our door," said Jack. "What do you say, Matilda? Shall we have a mahogany door, with a brass rapper ? or a heavy oaken portal with massy iron bars, like those in the mysterious castle of Udolpho ?"

"I am perfectly aware, Jack," replied his sister, "that in this solitude we can neither obtain iron, oak, nor mahogany ; but we have that tall pine or cedar that Tom pointed out the other day, and which Almagro calls the *Alerse*, and which he tells you is so easily parted into planks of any thickness. Why not cut down that tree to form a strong, narrow door ?"

"This time, Jack," said Lewis ; "the dictator Matilda is right. The Alerse is the very tree for our purpose, for with a single wedge we can split it into planks. We have still a good stock of nails, so that we can make our door doubly firm by nailing cross-pieces over it."

"And cover it with hide, to render it fire-proof," added Matilda.

"You are a skilful engineer," said Lewis, "and we will certainly adopt your plan. Come, boys, to work ! Let us to the woods. I have seen beeches, but they would be too hard to split up for our door ; and we must be careful to spare the valuable *Pino de la tierra ;* so we must try the Alerse pine, on the recommendation of Almagro."

The alerse was a noble tree, not less than ninety or one hundred feet high, and thirty feet in circumference. It was long before their efforts brought it to the ground. The short thick branches were then lopped off, and the trunk was hewed into logs, eight or nine feet long, for use. One of these logs was selected and split into thick planks by means of wedges, with less difficulty than they had anticipated. These planks were conveyed to the enclosure, and the door, strengthened by cross-pieces, was truly a heavy portal. It was attached by broad hinges of hide to strong posts, and secured by stout wooden bars ; and the young men had reason to be proud of their great work.

CHAPTER XIV.

Another Expedition after the Wild Cattle. The Wild Horses of the Pampas. Vixen and Pampero. The Cow, the Calf, and the Puma. The Successful Foray of the Young Hunters. The New Settlement named. Kitchen and Oven built. The Chase of the Ostrich, and Capture of another Young Colt.

"AND now, mamma," said Jack, "that we have placed you in an impregnable fortress, there can be no objection to our leaving Captain Matilda and Lieutenant Maria in command, and sallying forth ourselves, like good and worthy knights, in search of adventures."

"Or rather," added Lewis, "let us set out, as my dear countrymen were wont to do in olden times, over the borders, to make a foray on the stray cattle."

"I do not object to the expedition," said Tom; "but I confess my principal motive will be to observe whether the Pampas produce any plants or animals worthy of scientific notice."

"If you could meet with another cow," said Nanny, "we could do very well with her, for this young calf takes lots of milk; and you know, Master Jack, honey, you all like milk; and if you could pick up a few hens, honestly, it would serve to make things look like home."

Charles really liked the chase in a sportsman-like fashion; he was willing to slay pumas, ostriches, or even wild Indians; but to hunt cows for Nanny's dairy was a shock to his dignity; and he sighed as he observed that life on the Pampas was very *slow*. But the good feelings of Charles were soon recalled; and, after Mr. Merton's gentle admonitions, and Mary's persuasive entreaties that he would try to please poor Nanny, Charles was all kindness and generosity, and

would have scoured the plains for a whole day after a
solitary agouti, if he thought it would have gratified
his dear aunt and cousins.

" Well, I certainly had no intention of becoming a
herdsman, when I came out to South America," said
he ; " but I presume I must accompany you on this
gallant expedition.   Pray, which of the animals am I
to ride, the cow or the llama ? "

A few minutes elapsed before the question of
Charles was answered, for every one was occupied
with the unpleasant reflection of the inadequacy of
the stud for a hunting-party ; then a hearty fit of
laughter succeeded, and it was decided that Almagro
and Dr. Lewis should have the horse and mule, and
the rest of the hunters must necessarily be pedestrians.
Well provided with lassoes and bolas, which they had
now learned to manufacture for themselves, they set
out, through the woods to the right of the enclosure,
to ascend the hills and inspect the lower plains before
they descended.   They caught two vicunas in their
progress, to their great satisfaction ; as they knew how
much their sisters prized the fur of this pretty little
creature.   They reached the summit of the steep, and
there, after Lewis had surveyed the plains with a telescope, he gave the word to descend.

The descent was through a thick wood, which rather
impeded the progress of the horsemen ; and Jack first
emerged on the wide grassy Pampas, which, though
apparently untrodden by man, were certainly not solitary ; for he was astonished to behold, within a few
yards of him, an immense herd of horses, which,
sheltered by the wood, had been unnoticed from above.
Some were feeding quietly on the long grass ; others,
the young and playful, were careering round at full
gallop.   A young foal passed so near to Jack, that he
could not resist the temptation, but flung his bolas,
which, winding round the hind legs of the animal,
stopped its course, and, struggling violently, it fell.
Jack called on Charles to assist him, the rest were
already off after the horses.

"What a lucky fellow you are, Jack! You will have a horse of your own!" cried Charles, who was now all activity. He flung his poncho round the head of the prostrate animal, which, being thus suddenly blinded, ceased to struggle, and began to tremble violently; they then placed a halter round her neck, tied her legs loosely with a lasso, and disentangled her from the bolas.

In the mean time Almagro had taken another young animal, and, with the skill of experience, he immediately removed the bridle from the head of Niger, and forced the bit into the mouth of his captive; then he leaped at once upon its back. The horse, in great astonishment and dismay, reared up, and endeavoured in vain to shake off its unpleasant burthen, then it galloped wildly away, bending its head down, throwing up its hind legs, and endeavouring by any means to dislodge the bold and practised rider; but without effect. Finally it became quite exhausted, and he had no difficulty in bringing it up to the rest of the party. The whole herd of horses had taken to flight; and such is the attraction of society, that Lewis and Tom could scarcely restrain their quiet domestic animals from joining these wild, free denizens of the Pampas; and they had been compelled to convert a lasso into a rein to hold the excited Niger.

Charles and Jack had made no attempts to tame their captive, but had contented themselves with securing it by a strong lasso, by which they were enabled to drag it unwillingly after them. They now determined to convey their troublesome prisoners home, before they proceeded on the cattle chase; and, after much resistance from the led foal, and some awkward prancing from Almagro's horse, they brought them to the enclosure. Jack's loud whistle soon brought his friends out, whose delight and astonishment broke out in cries of joy at the sight of this miraculous addition to their stud.

"I shall name my prize Vixen," said Jack, "for she is an unamiable specimen of the worst properties

of her sex ; and if Charles and I had not been brave
fellows, and rather afraid that you girls would laugh
at us, we should have let her go long since, our arms
ache so with dragging her.   What is to be the name
of your horse, Almagro ?"

"You must ask my kind and noble friend and pre-
server, Dr. Lewis, to answer that question," replied
Almagro ; " I am proud to have captured so fine a
creature, that I may have the pleasure of presenting
it to him, when I have sufficiently subdued its fiery
spirit."

Lewis received the gift from the grateful Guacho
with a pleased satisfaction ; for he was truly attached
to the faithful Almagro, and declared he should be
very glad to mount the handsome horse, as soon
as it was safe for him to do so, without risking his
neck.

"I undertake to make you a saddle-cloth of skins,"
said Matilda ; " and you must call the creature
Pampero."

"A very appropriate name for such a wild fierce
spirit," answered Lewis ; " and I yield this time to
Matilda's imperious 'You must,' without a rebellious
feeling."

Matilda blushed at the implied reproof : she was
beginning to be awake to her prevailing foible ; and
made, occasionally, secret resolutions to endeavour to
subdue her desire for rule.

"My dear children," said Mr. Merton, " I behold
with gratitude the comforts and even luxuries of life
which your labours are collecting round us ; but it is
beyond my comprehension to discover the means by
which you have ensnared and brought into captivity
these fierce and savage quadrupeds, which appear to
me to possess that untameable nature which man
vainly labours to subdue."

"Have no fears about breaking in the creatures,"
said Jack ; " we are a set of clever fellows ; and before
long Vixen will be ready for you to mount ; and I

hope yet to make her gentle enough for mamma to ride, then I shall change her name to Dewdrop."

"We must now convey these unruly creatures to the corral," said Lewis, "and keep them without food for twenty-four hours, as a commencement of their subjection, but only strong will and perseverance can complete their education."

The young grooms, having fastened the heads of the prisoners to a beech-tree in the corral, so that they were prevented from reaching the ground to feed, left them in this unpleasant confinement, and returned to the Pampas to continue their day's sport. It was not long before they found a herd of wild cattle feeding near the edge of the wood. Lewis and Almagro dashed forward towards the herd, the young men remaining concealed at the skirt of the wood, watching for a favourable moment to sally forth.

The whole herd, alarmed at the attack, fled in various directions, tossing their formidable horns, and bellowing furiously. Tom did not like such opponents, and drew back under cover; but Jack, always fearless, sprung forward from the wood, as a cow passed, followed by a very young calf, and cast his bolas round the legs of the calf, which immediately fell, bleating piteously. The anxious mother stopped her flight at the sound, turned round, and made up to her calf, regardless of the presence of Jack, except that she evinced certain hostile intentions by the angry toss of her horns. Tom had now recovered his courage, and flinging his bolas, prostrated the cow which, however, made such vigorous attempts to escape that Charles came forward with his gun, in case extreme measures were necessary to secure their safety.

At that moment a monstrous puma sprung from the wood upon the struggling calf, seized its head with its large paws, and, drawing it back, dislocated the neck; then, flinging its victim over its back, it fled back to the woods with both calf and bolas, to the

great vexation of Jack. But, in this case, Charles
did not hesitate : he pointed his gun and shot the
puma through the head. It fell dead immediately,
and two victims being thus disposed of, they turned
their attention to the third, and with much difficulty
placed a halter over the horns, and tied its legs loosely,
so that it could not escape or do any mischief. In
the mean time the two equestrians, alarmed by the
report of the gun, rode up to them. They had lassoed
a very large animal, but it was so powerful that they
had been compelled to dispatch it, especially as they
were in anxiety about their young friends. When
they saw the puma, Lewis was quite satisfied that it
was no wanton waste of ammunition to rid themselves
of such a dangerous neighbour.

It was now time to return home with the produce
of their sport, but much difficulty arose in the disposal of it. Poor Niger was compelled to drag the
slain bullock, an immense animal ; but they decided to
carry away only the skin of the puma, leaving the
carcase a prey to the condors. There was much
trouble in inducing the refractory cow to move a
single step, the united strength of the three young
men being insufficient to drag her on against her will ;
and they were afraid they should be compelled to kill
her ; but when the body of her calf was laid across
the mule, she followed it voluntarily, lowing continually, in a piteous manner. Thus Jack and Charles,
guiding her by a lasso on each side, got the cow to
the enclosure, Tom bringing up the procession, carrying the skin of the puma. Heavy laden, hungry, and
weary, they reached home, very triumphant at the
success of their hunting-day.

"Here is your cow, Nanny," cried Jack ; "and a
gentle creature you will find her ! She has almost
torn off our arms with her struggles, but we know the
means of taming her fury now. Into the corral, my
good madam, and beware of corrupting our good
Brindle with your wild vagaries."

No sooner was the new cow tied up, than she was joined by her domesticated predecessor, which testified a little inhospitality at first towards her unfortunate sister, but they soon struck up a lasting friendship.

The replenishment of the larder was very gratifying to the anxious housekeepers—the hunters were promised a dinner of roast veal next day: Nanny was complacent, and was even brought to acknowledge, that if she had an oven, some bread fit for Christians to eat, and some pigs and poultry, the place was not *that bad* but it might do.

"But our settlement ought to have a name, papa," said Tom.

Mrs. Merton sighed at the word *settlement,* and looked at her husband with mournful inquiry.

"If it be God's will that we should remain here, my Lucy," said he, "and if our children are happy and healthy, we must submit with resignation."

"And, as it certainly is our own estate now," added Tom, "I think we might call it *Mertonville.*"

"Or *Lewis Grove,*" said Matilda; "for we should never have settled here, but for the suggestion of our dear friend Dr. Lewis."

"That is a capital idea, Matilda," answered Jack, "and I give up my plan, which was to name the place *Maria Haven,* for our dear stranger had the first claim on the property, and here found a refuge amongst us."

"I think," said Lewis, "we had better defer naming our retreat till we have finally resolved to continue in it. And now, whilst the nimble fingers of our young ladies are busied with weaving, can we not turn to some work?"

"There is some work ready, I know," replied Jack; "for in return for the poncho she is weaving for him, Charles probably intends to invest Mary with the skin of the puma he has slain."

"I will take the skin of the fore-legs to make the

fair child a pair of boots," said Almagro. "The skin of the hind-legs Charles may use himself, for the same purpose."

"My dear friend, Almagro," answered Charles, looking at his handsome legs, still adorned with Hoby's boots, of which he had not quite exhausted his stock, "you cannot surely believe that I could actually, in cold blood, plunge my legs into the skin just vacated by the rightful owner, and walk about in the fanciful attire of a puma's legs, as a pretence at civilized boots? I turn my right to the prize over to my friend Jack, who, bringing all things to the question of mere expediency, sees no wide distinction between the dress of an Esquimaux chief and a Parisian exquisite."

"I accept your gift, cousin Charles," said Jack, "with gratitude; but give me leave to say that a lion's hide, however ungraceful in form, is an appropriate dress for a hunter of the Pampas, and when your Hoby's fail, you will be of my opinion. And now, Almagro, initiate me into this new plan of boot-making."

Almagro cut the skin round the thigh, stretched it with pegs, and rubbed it with sand, to remove the hair. The lower extremity was then tied together, to cover the toes, the leg was introduced, the heel resting on the part which had surrounded the lowest joint of the puma's leg; and after drying a few days, and being rubbed with melted fat, Jack had a pair of boots impervious to the briars and underwood of the mountain forests.

They all remained two days at home, cutting up and drying the beef for charqui, of which useful provision they had now prepared a large stock for the contingencies of winter, of which they had had no experience. The new cow underwent a system of training, and was found much more tractable than expected: probably from association with her tamed kindred. She submitted to be milked in a very short time, and they had now such an abundant supply of milk, that Nanny murmured continually because she had no churn. They had made the experiment of putting the cream into a water-cask, and rolling it round, but though this produced amusement, it did not produce butter. The cask was too large, and the motion not sufficiently rapid, and after much labour they only obtained some clotted cream, which was, however, by no means despised.

They now determined to add a kitchen to the hut, for Mrs. Merton, seeing that they were happy in their continual employment, became reconciled to the retreat; and even agreed to have it named, in accordance with the united wishes of the family, ESPERANZA.

Then Lewis and Tom marked out a large square behind the hut: this they surrounded with poles of eight feet in height, which they cut down and brought from the wood. Between these they interwove the lopped branches till they formed a wall, which they finally daubed, within and without, with mud. In this dry climate a few days hardened the mud, and they had a firm and solid wall. Into this wall, while still wet, they fixed a number of stout wooden pegs, on some of which they designed to rest shelves, and the remainder were intended to hold their arms, or to be appropriated to other useful purposes. The roof was completed, like that of the hut, under the direction of Almagro; and at the end of a fortnight they had a large room, with a trellised window, and an aperture in the roof for the smoke.

The fire-place was merely a circle of rough stones, for they had not the means of hewing them; and on one side of the fire-place, Jack's long-promised oven was begun. But though Jack was the willing labourer in this important construction, it was to the information and retentive memory of Tom, that he was indebted for the plan; and it was Tom's judgment that pointed out the best mode of completing it. It was a simple contrivance, being merely a hole dug in the

N

ground, and lined with smooth, flat stones from the river. A single broad, flat stone formed the cover. When wanted, a fire was made in the oven till the stones were sufficiently heated; the ashes were then swept out; the meat placed on the hot stones; the flag was placed over the oven, and upon it a fire was kept up till the meat was thoroughly cooked. Nanny was so much delighted with the baked beef—her first experiment—that she proposed, without delay, to commence baking pies, puddings, and even bread.

And this undertaking, after laborious preparations, was successfully accomplished. The labour of pounding the maize was chiefly done by Jack and Dr. Lewis; the flour thus produced was by no means fine, but mixed with rich cream, it made excellent puddings and cakes; they had also peach-pies, and parrot-pies, which had raised walls of paste, for unluckily they could not contrive any baking-dishes.

"And now, mamma," said Jack, "just look round and confess that we have almost everything we can want at Esperanza. We have bread and milk, fruit, potatoes, beef in plenty, and fish when we will take the trouble to draw the nets these clever girls have made. We are as happy as kings and queens; and you, dear mamma, are so well, and can be so useful now in the kitchen and dairy, that after all it was a good thing those knaves put us out of the ship. And look out, mamma, at the two beautiful young horses, which Almagro has trained to be as gentle as lambs. We are going to mount them to-day, and make another hunting expedition; and depend on it, we shall bring home something new."

Mrs. Merton felt some trepidation when she saw the procession move off. Lewis and Jack were mounted on their lately-acquired prizes, Charles on Niger, and Almagro on the mule, all accoutred properly with saddles and bridles, neatly made from the hide of the large bullock they had killed; they had even spurs of the thorns of the cactus. As Tom could not have been mounted, except on a llama, a distinction which he declined, he remained at home to look after the fishery. The housekeepers wished him to go to the river and bring a large supply, as with the abundance of fat obtained from the bullock, they wished to bake and preserve as much as possible, before the frosts, which they anticipated in the winter, should close up their resources in the river.

Leaving Tom at the weir, accompanied by Nanny, who was groaning as she washed her linen in the water, at the pitiless devastations of time, the proud cavalry rode on, booted and spurred like gallant knights. They penetrated the wood directly east, instead of ascending the valley, and reached the Pampas at a considerable distance south of their last expedition. They rode forward some distance from the mountains, and spurred their noble steeds over the wide plains, with a freedom and enjoyment little known to men who ride over the beaten roads of civilized countries.

The mornings were already keen and frosty, and the air brought a rich odour from the pines. The sun shone brightly on the variegated foliage which clothed the mountain side, and glittered on the distant snowy pinnacles which seemed to pierce the clouds. For some time they pursued their way on the Pampas, seeing nothing but the agouti, bounding from its bushy retreat; or a solitary guanaco, the sentinel of the herd, perched on some little eminence, to watch and warn his friends if their enemy, the puma, appeared in sight.

"Shall we go after the guanacoes?" asked Jack. "But it is already too late, the sentinel is neighing out his signal of alarm, and see what a mighty herd are cantering off to the shelter of the next hill. Well, after all, we have meat enough for months; but the girls might have liked the wool to spin. We know their haunts now, and when we want fresh meat, we will pay them another visit. But look here,

Almagro! look at these monstrous eggs scattered about. Surely there must be the nest of an ostrich near."

" There can be no doubt of it," said Almagro, " for these scattered eggs are the *huachos;* they are never hatched ; but are reserved, it is supposed, for the food of the young birds. Let us draw behind these trees and watch. Ah! observe that noble creature marching from yon hillock of sand ; it is the male bird, and the young ones are following him. Make ready your bolas, and start at once ; we must surround them, and shall certainly take some."

The whole party dashed forward at once towards the astonished bird, which appeared for a few moments bewildered ; then uttering a deep hissing cry, it spread its sail-like wings, and fled with the swiftness of the wind, pursued by Almagro and Lewis. In the mean time Charles and Jack spurred their steeds after the young ones, which were following their parent, but less fleet in their movements than the old bird ; the youths overtook and flung their bolas round the legs of two birds, which fell, perfectly entangled in the snare.

" We will take them home alive, for I have always promised to give Maria an ostrich to tame, and this is a capital chance for me," said Jack.

" But, my good fellow," replied Charles, " how can we possibly lead or carry these great stupid, ugly birds ? They are scarcely even worth killing, for they have not a feather handsome enough to adorn our caps."

" I would certainly never place a feather in my cap," said Jack. " It would only entangle me in the branches of the trees ; but I do wish for a bird to give to Maria, and I think we might disable these troublesome, fluttering wings."

Lewis and Almagro just then returned from their unsuccessful chase ; and Lewis, seeing their captives, said,—

" Well done, my brave lads, you have had better

luck than we, for the swift racer distanced us. What do you propose to do with these large, struggling creatures?"

Jack explained his wishes, and begged assistance to subdue them. Almagro quickly drew his knife and mutilated their wings, an operation that made Jack shudder, and almost wish he had destroyed them at once, rather than subjected them to this pain; but Almagro assuring him that the wounds would soon heal, he was reconciled, and thought only of the pleasure his offering would give. The legs of the birds were released, and lassoes placed round their necks; these lassoes were attached to the saddles of the two conquerors, who thus led their captives in triumph.

They were considering the advantages of returning at once, for little more could be accomplished with such inconvenient appendages; but a herd of wild horses appearing in view, the two disengaged horsemen set out at full speed after them. More fortunate than in their first adventure, they succeeded in capturing a young colt, which Almagro mounted, as he had done in the case of Pampero, and brought him up to the party tolerably subdued. Jack was much gratified, as his brother could now accompany them in their hunting parties.

" This is glorious work," said he ; " now let us off home, and begin to build a poultry-yard."

They all laughed at Jack's notion of confining a a breed of ostriches in a poultry-yard; but Dr. Lewis assured him, as the birds were so young, they might be readily tamed ; and, if properly trained, he might be able some time to go out hunting on an ostrich.

They were now at a considerable distance from the mountains, when Dr. Lewis stopped to examine some tall, ragged, dry stalks growing on the plain.

" It is one of the *Linaceæ*, the useful flax," said he. " If we do settle in this solitary spot, we must try to cultivate the flax, that we may escape one of the evils of savage life—the want of linen. Fill the game-bag, Jack,

with the seeds; the very sight of which will raise up before
the delighted eyes of Nanny a vision of the hoards of
linen she pines for.   But much must be done before
these seeds are transformed into garments for our use.
We will, however, collect as many of the yellow
stalks as we can conveniently carry away, that we may
at once commence making some experiments in the
useful manufacture."

This was more "glorious work" for the active
Jack ; and though Charles, whose large portmanteau
still contained a good store of linen, ridiculed the idea
of their setting up a "spinning-mill," Lewis and Jack
were not deterred from their task ; and Almagro, who
had never known the luxury of wearing linen, kindly
assisted them in making a scanty collection of the
withered stalks, in binding them together, and tying
them on the back of the patient mule.   They were
preparing to remount, and Almagro was releasing the
captive colt, which he had tied to a tree, when they
were all startled by a rushing sound, and looking up,
saw a herd of deer bounding over the plains, about fifty
yards from them.   None of the party were mounted
but Charles, who, forgetting his unfortunate captive,
spurred his horse, and galloped after them.   The
young ostrich, unable or unwilling to follow the pace
of Niger, would certainly have been strangled but for
the warning cries of Lewis, which arrested the course
of the young hunter in time to save its life.

In the mean time the swift deer had fled beyond
pursuit, and Charles was inconsolable.   "Only conceive," said he, "for the sake of this ugly, awkward
biped, to lose such a magnificent chase, and the
haunches of venison into the bargain."

But Charles was laughed out of his vexation, and a
promise given that they would return to this deer-
haunted spot at a more convenient opportunity, and
carry home, if possible, the haunches of venison.
Now it was absolutely necessary to return with the
troublesome captives.

P. 183.

The cheerful voice of Jack singing " See the Conquering Hero comes," brought
the anxious party from the house in time to see the approach of the triumphal
procession.

CHAPTER XV.

Taming of the young Ostriches. Preparation of the Flax.
The Treasures of the Great Chest. The erection of the
Chapel. The Deer-hunt, and the Adventure with the Jaguar.
Another Expedition to the Salina. Alarm. An Encounter
with Lost Travellers on the Pampas.

THE cheerful voice of Jack singing "See the Conquering Hero comes," brought the anxious party from
the house in time to see the approach of the triumphal
procession, which had a most imposing effect, notwithstanding the neighing and curvetting of the wild colt,
the shuffling, waddling gait of the half-fledged strange-
looking birds, and the ignoble bundles of dry, yellow
stalks, which were piled on the back of the mule.
The girls laughed with joyful wonder at the sight of
the birds; and Charles, after all his vituperations
against his prisoner, presented it with a good grace to
his friend Mary; while Jack, in giving his bird to
Maria, added a promise that he would build a shed for
its residence, and collect roots and grass daily to feed
it.   All were pleased with their acquisitions.   Tom
was particularly gratified with the possession of the
handsome colt, which was a piebald; he chose to
give it the name of Maculato, and with the assistance of Almagro, he immediately set about taming and
training it.
   Tom, in his course of reading, had obtained a theo-
retical knowledge of the mode of preparing flax, and
Nanny had a practical acquaintance with the process;
therefore, after carefully reserving the seeds, in order
to sow a plot of ground on their own estate, the preparation was immediately set about.   The stalks were
first spread to steep in a shallow part of the river,
heavy stones being placed upon them, to prevent them

being carried away by the current.   This was a work of labour, and, the season now being cold, it was far from agreeable ; and they were glad to return to a hot dinner and a comfortable fire.

As Mr. Merton looked out at the two restless birds, which were tied to a tree, he observed : " My dear children, is there not much danger of our little state becoming too populous ?   Can we provide food and shelter for ourselves, and for so many living creatures depending on us ?"

" Why, the whole land is our own, papa," cried Jack.   " Let us build houses, and lay out fields and gardens, and form a complete colony.   Lewis must have a house first, for he has the best right to one ; besides, he is the eldest ; and we will all help to build it."

" In truth," said Mrs. Merton, " if it is resolved that we should settle in this strange solitude, and if Dr. Lewis is kind enough to forsake the world and remain with us, I certainly think he ought to have the comfort of a separate abode, and not be crowded in our over-peopled hut."

" I perfectly agree with you, mamma," said Tom ; " and I believe I shall be tempted to build a pretty snug place for myself, and lay out a farm."

" Very good, Farmer Tom," said his brother. " And with what sort of animals do you design to stock your farm ?   You must have fences six feet high, or you could never keep the wild cattle ; and what in the world could you cultivate, except maize, and the ugly, straggling flax, if it will grow ?"

" The flax is not ugly in the summer, Jack," answered Matilda, " as I hope you will see next year. Do not be discouraged, Tom.   See what treasures we have found to-day.   We have unpacked the large chest, which has never been opened since we took out the tea-service and the linen in the cave ; and besides all the silver spoons, we found the best dinner knives and forks, which we really wanted so much.   Then there are needles and thread to serve us for years, scissors, thimbles ; and, at the bottom of the box, were all these brown paper parcels. Read what is written on each of them."

Tom read " onion seed," " parsley seed," " turnip," " lettuce," " peas," " beans ; " then followed some smaller packets, marked " mignionette," " sweet peas," " stocks : " all the home flowers. It was Mrs. Merton and Nanny who had secretly prepared these packages, in order that they might surround themselves, in a strange land, with memories of home. In the trouble, dangers, and anxieties, which they had experienced since their arrival on the dreary coast, these packets had been wholly forgotten ; and they were now overjoyed at the unexpected sight of such valuable possessions. As Tom read the name on each packet, it was hailed with a cry of joy, and in imagination they saw their garden flourishing with all the useful and beautiful productions of their English home.

" If we had only been so fortunate as to bring some wheat," cried Matilda.

" Forbear, my child," replied Mr. Merton, " to encourage such unreasonable desires. Let us not be ungrateful to God for the blessings he has given us, nor pine for those which he, in his wisdom, thinks fit to withhold from us. Look around, my children, at the peace and plenty we possess, and be thankful."

" We are thankful, papa," answered Matilda ; " yet we may desire to extend our buildings,—to found a new town. Allow me to draw the plan. I have considered it well. The houses must form a large quadrangle within the stockades, and *the Church* must stand in the midst."

" But we have no land to spare within the inclosure for cultivation," said Tom, " and I wish particularly for a farm. I advise, that we should build our houses beyond the stockades, and each defend his own domain."

"My dear friends," said Mr. Merton, "you talk
of houses, as if you were really about to found a city,
instead of raising some very simple huts.   Most certainly these huts must be all within the inclosure that
you have so industriously formed, for your timid
mother and I could not rest in peace, if these de-
fences did not include all those we love."

"You are right, my good friend," observed Lewis.
"This fortress must be our stronghold.   Here we
must build, if the weather be not too severe to prevent it; if that should be the case, we must wait for
spring.' Tom and I have also a plan, but we are not
above taking a hint from the experienced architect
Matilda."

Matilda felt that she was reproved, and was penitent, but persisted in her petition for the church; and
Mr. Merton was so much affected at the idea of again
performing his duties in a temple, however humble,
which was consecrated to God, that the building of
the church was carried by acclamation.

And now the various plans for the dwellings were
brought forward, discussed, and one after another rejected.   The want of iron, and the scarcity of work-
tools, were formidable obstacles.   But as Jack observed, "We are ten times better off than the Indians,
or even the Guachos of the Pampas, and Almagro will
tell you, that they can get up very snug huts.   To
be sure, ours ought to have a more civilized look than
those of such rude fellows; besides, Charles, as the
great lord of the community, will, of course, expect to
have a castle."

Charles declared that he would at present content
himself with a hunting-box, for he protested against a
permanent settlement in the wilderness; but before
even this was begun, he begged that the horses might
have the comfort of a stable for the cold nights, which
would inevitably become colder.

This had been for some time a subject of thought, and
now without delay they raised within the corral, some

comfortable sheds for the cows, the llamas, and the horses. After this work was done, a plan was produced by Tom for the church, very neatly drawn, and fully approved by every one. They began to build immediately, in the midst of the area, between two peach-trees. The chapel was about thirty feet long; the walls, like those of the hut, formed of woven willows, covered with mud, and the roof was thatched with maize leaves. At the east end a large space was left as a window, which was neatly latticed with thin spars. A wicker door completed the exterior. Then they brought from the river large smooth, flat stones, which they laid down for the floor. This labour had occupied them about three weeks, when the frosts became more severe, and some slight showers of snow fell, which the sun soon melted; but this weather was unfavourable for building, and the workmen employed themselves within doors, and succeeded in producing some improved specimens of carpenter's work.

On fine days they went out to hunt; they added another foal to their stud, killed some guanacoes, and brought home about twenty ostrich eggs, which, sawed in two, gave to the kitchen a number of useful bowls and dishes.

The young ostriches had become perfectly docile, and now were allowed to stalk about the inclosure in freedom, feeding on the grass, and retiring to their own shed when the frost and snow came on. Their young mistresses were delighted to watch their habits, but Mrs. Merton, in some alarm, inquired how tall they would become.

" The ostrich of South America, *Struthio Rhea*," said Tom, " is, even at its full growth, not more than six feet in height. It is the largest bird of America, but much inferior in size to the ostrich of Africa, which reaches the height of ten feet."

" This diminution in size," observed Mr. Merton, " is a fact noticed in all the animal creation of the new world. The puma is a miniature lion, the jaguar, a small leopard, the monkeys are marmosets, compared with the gigantic creatures of Asia; and the birds, from the ostrich to the finches, are smaller than those of the eastern hemisphere. Nor can any other part of the world produce such a minute feathered creature as that miniature specimen of *Trochilus Fortificatus*, which, even in this cold season, is darting about after some wholly invisible insects."

"The American ostrich has, you perceive, three toes, each furnished with a nail," continued Tom; "the African ostrich has but two toes, like the camel. Almagro tells me, the flesh of the young ostrich is excellent food; but as we shall certainly not slay our pets to make the experiment, we must wait till we can take a bird on the Pampas. When this female bird begins to lay eggs, I can instruct Nanny ———"

"To blow them, no doubt!" interrupted Jack, "as we used to blow the sparrows' eggs at Winston. But we are all tired of the ostrich lecture; and I wish to know for what curious purpose the girls are splitting up these maize stems, which I had just brought up for Vixen."

"You must excuse us, Jack," said Mary, "for it is for something very useful. It is quite Matilda's plan; and remember, she has never boasted of it. We are making matting to cover the floor of the chapel; and when your ingenuity shall have furnished it with a reading-desk and benches, the building will be complete, and will look like a chapel."

"It will not be complete without a bell," said Jack, "but that, I fear we cannot make, and therefore I intend to be the *Muezzin*, and shall climb on the roof every morning to proclaim the *ezzan:* you shall hear how melodiously I shall chant the summons."

"I shall not permit such a mockery, my son," answered Mr. Merton; "I would not have a ceremony turned into a jest which is considered holy; though practised only by the mistaken followers of the impostor Mohammed. Remember, that the words of the Muezzin proclaim the might and majesty of the one true God, and that on hearing the solemn words, all fall down on their faces and worship, in spirit, that Great and Mysterious Being. Rather than mock at their ceremonies, I would counsel you all, my children, to imitate the humble spirit of devotion evinced by men who are yet ignorant of the Great Truth ; and with meek hearts worship him who has, to us, opened the way of salvation."

The reading-desk and the benches employed the industrious young men on the days when the snow whirled from the mountains, and the keen winds chilled the frame, till the family were thankful of the warm skins to line the hut, and the comfort of the cheerful wood-fire, to supply which they had previously collected a large pile of fuel behind the hut.

Fires were also made in the chapel till the walls were hardened ; then the desks and benches were arranged, and Mr. Merton performed the solemn ceremony of consecrating this simple temple to the worship of God ; afterwards they had daily prayers in the chapel. The cold flag floor was covered with neatly woven mats, and the sisters were now busily engaged in weaving, from the hair of the llama, a curtain for the window : Tom promising them, that in the spring, he would examine the cacti for the cochineal insect, that they might dye the curtain scarlet.

In various labours, the time passed rapidly, till the midst of winter, the month of July, arrived. The store-room still contained an ample stock of dried meat and maize, which, with milk, formed their wholesome diet ; but on fine frosty days the hunters went out, and seldom returned without a guanaco, a hare, or a vicuna,—a welcome addition to their dry food and their store of skins. In one of these excursions, when they had somewhat extended their researches, they were fortunate enough to discover a salina, or salt lake, over which was formed a complete table of pure

salt, crystallized in large cubes.   Many large pieces
were scattered round the shores of the lake, and they
were enabled to fill a bag to convey home for present
use ; determining to return to the spot and collect a
good quantity to store.

When Nanny was presented with a guanaco and a
bag of salt, she smiled graciously on the gentlemen.
" There's some sense in bringing such useful things
as this salt," said she, glancing invidiously at the
young ostriches, which were prone to mischief. " Now
we will have our meat cured after a decent fashion,
and this very day will I salt and smoke these two legs
of mutton, as we call it, though no mutton was ever
so poor ; but see if it will not eat better than these
dry chips of beef, that make one's jaws ache to chew
them : and to think of them poor ignorant heathens,
spoiling good meat by drying all taste out of it, when
they have salt growing, as it were, in their very
pastures."

The salt was highly relished, and the young men
promised more, but remained at home two days to
clean and prepare two guanaco skins, which were to
be used as carpets in the chapel this cold weather, one
being placed at the reading-desk, for Mr. Merton, and
the other was to be a warm rug for mamma's feet.

The frosts were now severe ; every morning the
ground was covered with snow, and the river was
frozen, but as the day advanced the sun dispersed the
frost, the river became daily augmented by the melted
snow, and the hunters feared it would soon become
unfordable.

" At all events," said Lewis, " before the swollen
waters entirely imprison us, let us have a chase after
the deer, which this cold weather will bring towards
the woods for shelter."

Jack sprung up directly, but Charles and Tom
thought it too cold, and excused themselves on the
plea that they were assisting the young ladies, who
were making a large net of slender thongs of hide,

with which they proposed to net the river, as soon as the spring had tempted the fish from their retreats. Almagro was in the woods, cutting down some trees, to build himself a hut, which was the next under-taking projected. The two friends therefore set out alone, mounted on their horses, and, crossing the river before the ice was melted, galloped forward to the plains. They soon met with the deer, and captured one, which was slain, and laid upon Pampero, and, a slight snow-shower coming on, Lewis turned home-wards.

" Come back, Lewis," cried Jack, " and tell me what that brilliant creature can be that I see through the foliage of that dark pine ? It must be climbing the tree."

" Quick, my dear lad!" said Lewis. " We must either make off, or prepare for action, for, by the splendour of the skin, that climbing creature must be the beautiful and dangerous jaguar."

Jack's rifle was ready in a moment. " I suppose the fellow will be too cunning to be trapped by the bolas," said he.

" If we attempted such a plan we should have the worst of it," replied Lewis. " But mark, how still the crafty creature is now. I am persuaded that he has seen us, and intends to have a banquet on us, or on our poor horses. Now, Jack, let me intreat you to retire, and I will take a shot at him, and then follow you."

But, before his prudent friend had finished his request, Jack had galloped up to the tree, and when within a few yards, had fired at the jaguar. The furious beast immediately made a spring from the tree upon the boy, and, to the horror of Lewis, dragged him from the horse, which fled like the wind, evidently conscious of its danger, and rejoicing at its escape. For a single painful moment Lewis hesitated : if he fired, the risk was great of shooting the boy, yet to leave him for an instant in the clutches of the powerful jaguar would be death. He snatched the bolas from his saddle, and whirling them with the rapidity of despair, sent them with such good aim that they entangled the hind-legs of the beast, which turned round in fury to attack the aggressor in the rear.

To the great astonishment of Lewis, Jack sprung up, apparently uninjured, leaving his poncho in the claws of the enemy, and began to reload his piece, but his friend, waving him on one side, fired at the head of the jaguar, and killed it on the spot.

"Let me have my poncho," cried Jack; "I hope the ill-bred creature has not rent it. Only think, Lewis, how lucky it was that Maria had made the opening so wide that I easily withdrew my head, when I found the savage beast had clutched my poncho instead of my ribs. But he would have had me, Lewis, at his second spring, but for your bolas. You are a capital doctor, for you never undertake a bad case but you save your patient; I should think there are not many doctors can say that."

"Remember, my dear Jack, I was only an instrument in the hands of God; you must thank him for your rescue from a frightful death," said Lewis. "And now, if you will wait till I skin this beast, that we may carry off a trophy, we will return."

The animal was skinned, and its coat was added to the burthen of Pampero, which was led home by its master, as Jack was compelled to walk, murmuring for the loss of his steed, though truly grateful for his escape.

"What a vexatious thing," said he, "that I must return in such an ignominious plight—dismounted and defeated, my poncho rent, and my horse lost! How the merry girls will laugh at me! I might as well have staid at home too, to weave fishing-nets."

But when they arrived at the entrance of the inclosure, they found Vixen standing quietly, but panting with her gallop, and evidently very glad when she found herself in her stable, escaped from the

P. 192.

To the great astonishment of Lewis, Jack sprang up apparently uninjured, leaving
his poncho in the claws of the enemy.

ing of the snow and the claws of the jaguar. The venison was well received, and the adventure of the jaguar created great interest; the heroes were applauded, and Matilda made a pretty speech, when the handsome skin of the animal was laid at her feet.

" The jaguar, rather than the puma," observed Tom, " should certainly be named the ' king of the forest ' in South America; he is the most savage of the wild animals, and Jack has had a most miraculous escape.   He is, as you would observe, nearly as large as the tiger of the East, though his bright yellow spotted skin resembles more that of the leopard : these spots on the back and neck, are ocellated black rings, with a black spot in the centre; the under part of the animal is white, with transverse black stripes.   He is truly a beautiful creature, but I trust, as the jaguar is a solitary animal, and usually frequents warmer latitudes than this, we need not fear having a nocturnal visit from another of these fierce creatures, which could easily climb into the corral and destroy all the stock.   I should rather have liked to see the jaguar living, if I could have done it in security; but to meet him alone would be a very undesirable shock to the nerves."

One more very important expedition was projected before the increasing waters of the river should imprison them.

They proposed to go at once to the Salina, and in the first place bring away several large bags of salt ; but they had still another motive for the visit, for they had observed, on the borders of the lake, an arborescent grass of great length, resembling the bamboo, which grew in entangled masses.   Of this grass or cane, they determined to collect a large quantity for the purpose of weaving the walls of the projected huts.

The morning was clear and frosty when they set out in good spirits prepared for a hard day's work, after the long ride to the Salt Lake.   On reaching the

o

lake, they broke the surface with axes, filled several large bags with salt, and then proceeded to cut down the bamboos, tying them up in bundles with thongs. These bundles were again tied together in one large pile, on which the bags of salt were laid, the whole to be drawn along by Niger and the mule, the most tractable of the animals in harness.

Tired with their long labour, they sat down to refresh themselves with some slices of beef they had brought with them, regretting that with that large space of water before them, they could not find any fit to drink. They were startled as they sat on that still spot by two pigeons flying from a tree near them; and Jack, persuaded that there must be a nest in some hollow of the tree, with his usual untiring activity climbed up to search for it. But, in a moment, he slid down the tree, pale and agitated, and exclaimed: " I see people coming towards us! Let us make ready, for they must, I fear, be the Indians."

" Most assuredly, if any people be coming this way," said Lewis, " they must be Indians; for, at this season, no one else would be crossing the dreary Pampas. But let us immediately ascertain their number, and the distance they are from us, that we may calculate whether we have time to escape ourselves, after concealing these traces of the presence of man," pointing to the piles of bamboo.

Almagro sprung up the tree to survey the plains, and came down with a look of wonder. " These are not Indians," said he; " they are the men of civilized countries, for they have carriages drawn by horses."

For a moment all were silent, mixed thoughts of pain and pleasure crossed their minds. Jack was the first who spoke.

" How unlucky!" said he, " There's an end of our Robinson Crusoe life. Who would ever have thought of people coming with their carts and carriages here, as if it was market-day; when we flattered ourselves we were in an untrodden solitude, and that the land was all our own."

"For my part," said Tom, "I shall not object to learn the way out of this wilderness. There is so much work before you can obtain the smallest comforts, and there are so many things, absolutely necessary, that we never can get here, that I am rather tired of such a hard life."

"We are really in a very unfit state to receive company," said Charles, "especially if there should be any ladies of the party. If it were possible, I would gladly withdraw; I feel so much ashamed of this rude, savage, ungentlemanly costume."

The lamentations of Charles, and the idea of ladies on the Pampas at this season, occasioned much mirth; but soon they all forgot their own feelings and fancies, in anxiety and watchfulness for the arrival of the party, which they now plainly saw slowly approaching the place where they were resting. As the carriages drew nearer, they discovered that they were two long covered waggons; the first, drawn by a single horse; the second, by two mules. Each of the animals was led by a person who seemed to have great difficulty in getting his charge to move onward with the ponderous waggons.

The friends now mounted their horses, and riding briskly forward, soon came up to the procession. "Thank Heaven!" cried a pale, emaciated man, in English, as they approached, "We are saved! for if you are Christians, you will not suffer us to perish in this interminable wilderness."

"We will do all in our power to aid you," replied Lewis. "Tell us who you are? and whither you are going?"

They were now joined by a tall fine looking man, who seemed likewise much exhausted by fatigue or privation. "We are brothers-in-law," continued the first speaker. "This is William Douglas; my name is Henry Carruthers. In this waggon are our wives

o 2

and an infant; the waggon behind is driven by our servant John Armstrong: this is our whole party. We left Buenos Ayres three months ago for Chili, intending to cross the Andes before the snows fell. Our purpose in visiting Chili, was, to work some mines in that rich country. We have been betrayed, robbed, and deserted by our guides; we have lost our way, and have wandered blindly over these dreary wastes, till we have been almost reduced to absolute famine. In another day our last remaining animals must have died of fatigue, and, with them, every hope of our escape. But God heard our cry in the wilderness, and has sent you to save us; His name be blessed!"

"Did I not tell you, Henry, to keep up your courage," cried a pretty little active woman, who, folded in a dark cloak, now descended from a door at the back of the carriage. "What was the use of falling into despair? And you see, as usual, I was right. My good strangers, your faces were never so welcome in this world as they are just now. I must have some talk to you; and, now William, take that poor horse out of the traces, and let him have a mouthful of grass,—such as it is. And you, Henry, just step into the waggon, and beg Eliza to give up that sighing and moaning, which is very bad for the child, and to cheer up, for we shall soon visit her, and introduce these charming kind young strangers, to her."

Having employed her husband and brother, Mrs. Douglas, as she proved to be, introduced herself to her new friends, and was soon on familiar terms with them.

"You must excuse my sister, young gentlemen," continued she. "She is delicate and nervous, and has almost fretted herself to death about our misfortunes; and would never hear me when I told her I felt sure that God would send us help, if we trusted in him, and used our own senses and energies. Poor Eliza! all she begged for was, that we should remain in one place till somebody came to help us, for she could not bear the jolting of the waggon. To be sure, I must allow, the motion is not easy, especially since we broke one of the wheels by driving over the fallen trunk of a tree. John Armstrong did his best to mend it, but he is no great workman; he certainly said he could have managed it, if he could have had a forge, but we could not wait till he set up a smith's shop on the Pampas. Oh! he made a sad bungling job of that wheel, which has never turned round since; so you may conceive how rough our travelling has been."

As soon as the voluble lady made a pause, Dr. Lewis inquired if Mrs. Carruthers was ill, as he was a medical practitioner, and would be glad to offer his services if required. Mr. Carruthers, who had joined them, accepted his offer with grateful acknowledgments, and conducted him into the long, clumsy carriage, which formed the lodging of the ladies; the gentlemen having been obliged to sleep on the piled luggage in the second waggon.

CHAPTER XVI.

The Adventures of the Strangers. Departure from Buenos Ayres. Delays on the Pampas. Separation of the Party. Suspicions of the Guides. Treachery, Murder, and Robbery. The Wanderings and Sufferings of the Travellers. Welcome to Esperanza. More acquisitions, and a new Mansion projected.

THE interior of the waggon was neatly fitted up, a mattress was laid on a sort of frame, upon this couch reclined a young, pretty, and very delicate-looking female; and by her side, in an ornamental, uncomfortable cradle, was sleeping a very young infant. After an introduction and a little conversation with the languid lady, Dr. Lewis inquired the circumstances which had reduced them to such a distressing state.

"It is now three months," said Mr. Carruthers, "since we left Buenos Ayres. We had then two carriages for ourselves, with six waggons laden with our property, and four guides. Besides these our party was augmented by twelve experienced miners we had brought from England, who were mounted on horses and mules. We travelled slowly, for the health of my wife would not permit us to go far in a day, and at night we either rested in our waggons, when our people formed a guard round us, or at the huts of the stations. About three weeks after our departure, my wife was unable to proceed; she remained two days at a wretched hut, inhabited by an aged couple of Guachos, and at the end of that time our poor baby was prematurely born. Our situation was most distressing; and, as the best plan we could think of, we proposed to Eliza, that as soon as she was able to travel, she should return to Buenos Ayres, and permit us to proceed to Chili; from whence I promised to return, and conduct her over the mountains, in the spring."

"Did you ever hear such an unkind and unnatural proposal?" murmured the invalid. "I was determined never to be separated from my husband. I would not listen to their plans. I insisted on going where Henry went."

"Alas!" said Mr. Carruthers, "it was an unfortunate determination for us all. The provisions necessary for so a large a party could not be procured at this lonely spot, and, after much deliberation, William Douglas and I agreed to send forward the miners, with three waggons and two guides, and we proposed to follow as soon as Eliza was well enough to travel. She recovered so slowly that it was a month before we left that dreary hovel, where we had been able to procure no provision except beef, and consequently our own excellent store was greatly diminished when we again set out. I discovered, after a day or two, that the guides had become sullen and discontented; they continually murmured at our slow progress, declaring that it would be impossible to cross the mountains if we did not reach them speedily, as the winter was actually begun. Douglas and I became alarmed at the dark and sinister looks of the men, and we determined, at the next station we reached, to endeavour to procure another guide, and dismiss these suspicious characters.

"From that hour we never reached an inhabited station: it might be that the men suspected our intention, or that they understood the English language, which I always believed they did, though they denied it, and had overheard Eliza and her sister talking of our plan of discharging them, and determined to thwart us. We were compelled, night after night, to rest in our waggons, and had now no guard except our faithful dog Wallace, but of his vigilance we never entertained a doubt. The dog had become attached to our chief guide, who caressed and fed him, and if the guides took a gallop over the plains after the wild cattle, Wallace usually accompanied them.

"One morning, when we arose from our anxious rest, we heard from the guides that they had been out early chasing some wild cattle; they had brought back the carcase of a young cow, but alas! Wallace had not returned with them. They declared that they did not discover his loss till they were on the road to the encampment, that they had then returned and sought diligently for him, but could find no trace even of his body. They suspected he must have followed the herd to some distance, and been gored by a wild bull. We were all deeply distressed, and Margaret Douglas freely declared her opinion of the treachery of the guides. She had brought up Wallace, and knew that he never wantonly attacked any animal; and he was too formidable in appearance, and too brave in defence, to have much to fear from any antagonist.

"Douglas and I remonstrated with the men on the

unsatisfactory nature of our progress ; we were persuaded that they were now leading us in a direction
which diverged too much to the south to be the regular
road.   Our accusations were received with insolence
and defiance ; my wife was in a fearful state from
terror, and at length we peremptorily told the men
that if they did not conduct us to an inhabited spot
the ensuing day, they must leave us immediately.   A
short time after, they came to us, assured us they had
diverged from the direct route to avoid some Indian
tribes, who were prowling about to watch for travellers ; but they added, they would certainly bring
us to a station the very next day.

"We were satisfied with this assurance, and slept
more peacefully than we had done for some nights.
I was waked by a loud cry from John, who occupied
the same waggon as Douglas and I, and had just left
it to rouse the guides and drivers, who slept in another
waggon.   My brother and I rushed after him, to the
open door of the third waggon, on the floor of which
we beheld the horrible spectacle of the two drivers
lying dead, bathed in their blood.   The villanous
guides, who had committed this dreadful deed, had
afterwards plundered the waggons of many valuables,
including an iron-box of money, and had then fled,
carrying with them our best horses, doubtless, with
the view of retarding our progress, for they left us only
the two worst horses and two mules.

"Stunned with this misfortune, we were for some
time incapable of thought or action.   The awful spectacle of violent death, and the fearful prospect of the
future, in these unknown wilds, distracted and un-
manned us.   What would have become of us I know not,
if Douglas had not decided on calling in his wife to our
aid.   She is a woman of a noble, vigorous, and enterprising mind : it was she who first projected our
undertaking, and it was she who rescued us in that
fearful extremity.   After the first shock of the dreadful intelligence, she recalled her energy, and arranged
and ordered everything. The waggon which contained

the two murdered men was closed—the door was even nailed up. After we had done this duty, we all knelt down, my brother and I were still plunged in despair, and that good and intrepid woman herself pronounced such portions of the funeral service as she could apply to that sad sepulture. The waggon was left on that blood-stained spot—the tomb of the two wretched men. Margaret then besought us all to be discreet, and it is only within the last ten days that Eliza has been acquainted with the whole of the terrible transaction.

" As we had but four animals left, we were compelled to abandon all but the two travelling-waggons, in one of which we placed the most useful parts of our property, and all the remains of our provision. Much was necessarily left, but a written notice affixed to the waggons, announced to whom the property belonged, and signified that if safely conveyed to Santiago, a handsome remuneration would be given. All this was Margaret's arrangement, and all was effected, and we had actually moved from the scene of horror, before Eliza awoke, when we made such explanation of the departure of the guides as satisfied her.

" But we were bewildered on the wide and trackless waste; we had no guide till we had the first view of the distant mountains, and our direct course was continually interrupted by deep rivers, or impassable marshes. For weeks and weeks we have wandered, seeking a resting-place, but finding none; our provisions exhausted, for days even without water, and our poor animals daily becoming weaker. At length one horse fell dead; we saw the rest could not long survive, and we had abandoned all hope, when we met you; but now I see you will aid us."

" Be assured that you will be welcome to the simple fare and accommodations of our little community," said Dr. Lewis. " We can offer you food, shelter, and rest; and the ladies can have the pleasure of female society, and a nurse for this poor delicate baby."

" How delighted I shall be to be restored to society,"

said Mrs. Carruthers, with some animation. "I hope your friends, Dr. Lewis, are not stiff, serious people ; my sister Margaret is so very rigid in her notions, that I am quite wearied with her lectures, and pine for the society of the young, for balls and amusements."

"But we really can offer you none of these pleasures," replied Lewis, laughing ; "moreover, by my medical authority, I forbid you all balls and exciting company, for some months. In the mean time, we can give you a desirable change from a broken vehicle, a short allowance of food, and a winter at the foot of the Andes."

Mrs. Carruthers looked disappointed ; she did not quite like the prospect of things ; but when the kind doctor again talked of herself, felt her pulse, prescribed restoratives, nursed the baby, and pronounced it to be a babe of promise, she became reconciled, and inquired when and where they were to go,

It was a question necessary to be settled ; but when Lewis and Mr. Carruthers left the waggon to consult with their friends on the matter, they found the energetic Mrs. Douglas surrounded by her assistants, and everything arranged. The obstinate wheel, repaired by the skill of Tom and Almagro, now consented to turn ; Niger was to be harnessed to the first waggon, and the mule to assist the wretched animals which drew the last. The bamboos were abandoned for another opportunity, and the young horses carried the salt-bags.

All being ready, the party set out cheerfully and moved at a tolerable pace towards their haven of refuge ; the gentlemen walking by the side of the laden horses, and soon becoming acquainted with each other's history ; while Mrs. Douglas alternately attended to her nursing duties in the waggon, and indulged in more cheerful conversation with the pedestrians. They found the river so much swollen, that it was already somewhat perilous to ford it ; and Lewis saw that if they wished to have the bamboos before the spring, they must go for them next morning, before the frost was dissipated, for another day's snow added to the river would render it impassable. The strangers were charmed with the secluded beauty of the valley which their new friends had chosen for their domain, and astonished at the strength and security of the fence, which had been planted but a few months. When they reached the entrance, which was always kept barred in the absence of the gentlemen, Jack, as usual, uttered a shrill whistle, which soon summoned the sisters to unbar the door and rush out, folded in their warm ponchos, to greet the hunters.

The astonishment and embarrassment of the young girls cannot be described, when they found themselves in the presence of strangers, and saw the two huge waggons at the gate. It was some time before the kind and frank manners of Mr. and Mrs. Douglas and Mr. Carruthers reassured them, and they were able to welcome their new guests; then Dr. Lewis opened the door of the waggon, and introduced them to Mrs. Carruthers; Maria shrunk back in silent wonder, the lady was so entirely unlike her first friends; Matilda was struck with admiration at the grace and beauty and the elegant attire of the stranger, and was overjoyed at the prospect of such an acquaintance; but Mary saw only the baby.

"Do allow me to be its nurse," exclaimed she; "it is more beautiful than any doll I ever saw. I will be very, very careful, if you will trust it to me."

"Oh! I shall be truly glad to be released from the distressing task," sighed Mrs. Carruthers. "I have been wholly unaccustomed to such menial employment, and my health has grievously suffered from the unusual labour. You appear young and strong, and have, doubtless, in your station of life, been accustomed to work."

"My dear Eliza," interrupted her husband, "these young ladies have been educated like yourself. It is only the unfortunate adventure which left them desolate in this solitude that has compelled them to labours to which they were not born."

"Besides that, we all like to work," added the little girl, "and I have been used to much harder labour than nursing this dear baby ; so come along, Maria, we will carry it to mamma;" and the little girls skipped away with their treasure, leaving Matilda half mortified at the contempt of Mrs. Carruthers, ashamed of her own coarse dress and laborious occupations ; yet pitying the weak and helpless lady whose beauty she admired so much.

Mary covered the baby with her poncho till she entered the hall, as they called their usual sitting-room, then placing the little creature on her mamma's lap, she cried out, "See, mamma, what a beautiful gift God has sent us !"

"Save the girl !" exclaimed Nanny ; "where can she have picked up that *fundling*, in this out-of-the-world place ?   I'll be bound it's no Christian ; and if we bring it up, who can tell but it may scalp us some day."

"But we are not to bring it up, Nanny," said Mary ; "its papa and mamma are here, and some other people.   Dr. Lewis is bringing them all to stay with us."

"What does he mean by such doings," said the irritable maiden.   "Where can we get meat for so many mouths ?   And may be they'll be fine folks, looking for their china plates and their drinking glasses."

"If they are in distress and need, Nanny," said Mr. Merton, "as they must be to have wandered to this spot, it is our duty to feed and shelter them.   I will go forth to meet these strangers, and to welcome them to our humble roof and frugal entertainment."

Mrs. Merton was at first confused and overcome by the news, but roused herself to assist Nanny, who, after she had scolded a little, busied herself heartily in preparation for her guests, casting many a side glance of compassion, in the midst of her bustle, on the pretty pale baby which Mary was nursing so tenderly. One of the best damask tablecloths was quickly thrown over the rough wooden table ; and a bright display of silver spoons contrasted strongly with the wooden platters, which were by no means round, and the drinking cups of ostrich egg-shells. The salt was on an oyster-shell, and the haunch of venison, which was making ready for the hungry hunters, was destined to be served up on a larger wooden platter. But a cheerful fire of wood was blazing, with as little smoke as could be expected ; and the room was light, warm, and home-like.

The large party soon entered, Mrs. Douglas leaning on the arm of Mr. Merton, to whom she had been rapidly sketching their history and adventures. Mr. Carruthers followed, bearing his feeble wife in his arms ; she was placed on one of the wooden seats, which, though covered with skins, were certainly not luxurious couches. Casting her eyes round, the lady uttered a faint cry, and, covering her face, cried, "Oh ! Henry, I had hoped that we were coming to some civilized people ! What will become of me ! I shall certainly die in this wretched hovel !"

Henry Carruthers seemed at once ashamed and distressed ; he spoke to his wife in a low voice, entreating her to be composed ; but Mrs. Douglas addressed her in a tone of remonstrance.

" Be silent, Eliza," said she, " or speak like a woman in her senses. Be thankful that you are not in a *wigwam*, or spitted for an Indian's supper, instead of being hospitably received by this worthy, warm-hearted family, who have, like ourselves, been unfortunate, but have had energy enough to shake off their despondence, and, by God's help, have created for themselves a peaceful home. You must pardon this sick, spoilt child, my dear Mrs. Merton ; you will learn, before we part, to know us all. And now, my good woman," addressing Nanny, who was regarding

her with much approbation, " Can I help you to take
that savoury preparation from the oven, for we have
tasted nothing better than biscuit this ten or twelve
days, and are all about famished.   John will help you
as soon as he has finished unloading the waggons, and
a capital assistant you will find him.   In kitchen,
house, or dairy, John is at home,—a good servant."

The venison soon smoked on the table ; Mrs. Carruthers pouted a little, but could not resist the savoury odour ; and though she shuddered at the platter
and shell goblet, she certainly did not make a bad
supper on venison and maize cakes.   Nanny in the
mean time fed the starved baby on warm milk, and it
was soon asleep in its cradle.

" Now, gentlemen," said the managing Mrs. Douglas, " as you seem too much engaged with the good
things before you, to think on the future, I must
appeal to our hospitable host and his intelligent
family, for advice and assistance.   What would you
counsel us to do ?   Can we procure mules and guides
to enable us to cross the mountains ?   And can we,
for love or money, obtain provision to support us on
the journey ? "

" My dear lady," replied Mr. Merton, " we were
compelled to cross these terrible mountains ; but it
was at the risk of our lives, even at a more favourable
season.   We can offer you no guide, we have but one
mule, and, it would appear, we are the sole inhabitants of this remote district.   I am not a man of
energy ; I love peace and repose, which I find here,
and offer to you.   Why should you attempt this dangerous expedition ?   Why not remain with us ? "

Mrs. Carruthers uttered a little shriek at this proposal.   " Oh ! Henry," cried she, " I could not live
in this dull place ; take me to some place where I
can have society, and, at least, the common necessaries of life."

" I fear, fair lady," replied Dr. Lewis, " that however our primitive style of living may offend you, you

must remain here for some months. The Cordilleras will not be passable till the spring is advanced; then, the passage may be effected without guides, but certainly not without fatigue, difficulty, and peril. Mrs. Merton, a lady, tender and delicate as yourself, has been compelled to rough it in the wilds, and I appeal to her to declare if her health is the worse for it."

"On the contrary, my kind and judicious friend," answered Mrs. Merton; "necessity, and your good advice, have induced me to use exertions, and brave difficulties, till I am no longer the feeble and helpless invalid I was when we left England. Then, I believed, that I could not exist if I did not recline half the day on a sofa; and now, having no sofa, I can sit on a skin-covered log, and have been glad even to find a stone for a seat. Stay with us, Mrs. Carruthers, and I trust that all your ailments will vanish under the care of Dr. Lewis, aided by our simple mode of living."

After the brothers had held a short consultation, Mr. Douglas answered for the party. "For the present, my good friend, we must inevitably fling ourselves on your hospitality; we have no means of proceeding, and are ourselves, as well as our poor beasts, enfeebled by famine. I fear we shall make large inroads on your winter stores; but, I trust God will repay you, for you are literally feeding the hungry. Both Henry and myself feel our health shattered by the mental anxiety we have endured, for the last ten days especially, and we shall be glad of repose for the mind as well as for the body. I cannot attempt to describe to you our utter bewilderment. I am quite persuaded that we frequently retraced the road we had gone over the previous day, when the sun, which was our only guide, was hidden in clouds. The rascally guides had carried off a box which contained a compass, with some other scientific apparatus: we were lost; and the despair produced by this conviction, nearly paralysed all our efforts. I communicated

my belief to Margaret, and I certainly believe that we
owe to her lively remonstrances, the courage which
enabled us to proceed."

"It was truly a situation of horror," added Mr.
Carruthers ; "and I shall never forget the gratitude
we felt, when, one evening, after fording with much
difficulty a river, and ascending a rising ground
beyond it, a mist, which had bewildered us all day,
was suddenly dissipated, and the beams of the setting
sun revealed to us a grand and glorious spectacle.
The mighty chain of the Andes, that marvellous wall
of Nature, which we had longed to see, though still
many leagues distant, was visible to us, darkening
with its gigantic shadow, the country below it. The
summits of the peaks, crowned with snow, glittered in
the beams of the sun, with a sublime beauty that
caused us for a short time to forget our desolation.
We then directed our course to the mountains, and
three days after, when exhausted hope and famished
nature refused further exertion, we happily encountered God's messengers of mercy, sent for our deliverance."

Supper being ended, Mrs. Douglas turned to Nanny,
and said : "Now, my good woman, as the child is
sleeping peacefully, let us think about the beds. You
will excuse me, Mrs. Merton, you are not very strong,
and I must be doing something. Come away, young
ladies, and help me to contrive ; " and Mrs. Merton,
with some wonder, but perfect acquiescence, saw the
bustling lady take all the trouble of the arrangements
for the night into her own hands.

"Very neat little cabins, upon my word," said she,
as she peeped into the small dormitories of her friends,
" but no spare beds I see ; we must bivouac in the
hall, and be thankful."

Almagro had been assisting John to unload the
waggons, and bring the contents within the inclosure,
through the narrow entrance of which it was impossible for the clumsy vehicles themselves to pass. He

now entered to suggest, that his small hut, which was already roofed, though not intended to be finished and inhabited till the spring, should be appropriated to some of the party. This was agreed on; a good fire was lighted, skins spread on the floor, and Charles, Tom, and Jack, with John and Almagro, took possession of the hut. The mattresses, cushions, and blankets were then brought from the waggons, and beds arranged for the wearied travellers, who were glad, after joining the family at their evening devotions, to retire to rest.

Mrs. Douglas appeared in the kitchen early next morning, " to look after breakfast," as she said. She found the three girls returning from the corral with large bowls of new milk from the cows; Nanny having been engaged in baking fresh maize cakes.

"Very nice looking cakes," said Mrs. Douglas; " but your flour is coarse, Nanny. How do you grind it ? "

"We just bruise it on a flat stone," replied Nanny. "A queer sort of mill; but what matter? We are glad enough to get coarse flour for ourselves,—and for them that needs it."

"All things are good if we can get no better," said Mrs. Douglas; " but if you can mend matters, the sooner you set about it the better. William!" she called, summoning her obedient husband from his couch. "We surely have the hand corn-mill in the waggon; will you go and inquire. You see, my dears, we were obliged to abandon half our property; but, I think, my mill was brought away. It was my own plan to bring it out; I did not know what strange spot we might settle on in the new country, and I determined to be provided against every emergency."

Mr. Douglas, at the command of his ruler, had issued forth in the keen, frosty air of the morning, and with the aid of John unpacked and brought up the mill, which Mrs. Douglas exhibited to Nanny with great triumph, and would have immediately tested its qualities, but the time was not convenient. The whole

P

party had now, with the exception of Mrs. Carruthers,
assembled; and Mr. Merton conducted them to his
chapel, where the travellers were glad to offer up
thanks for their preservation.

They returned to a breakfast of warm milk, clotted
cream, and new bread; the tea and sugar had been for
some time exhausted. Mrs. Douglas had sent for her
basket of china, and set out the table with cups and
saucers, instead of egg-shell bowls; a change which
delighted Matilda and Mary, and astonished Maria,
who now saw for the first time these luxuries of
civilized life.

"We have still half a chest of China tea left," said
Mrs. Douglas, " besides some of the *yerba*, used at
Buenos Ayres, to which Eliza took a fancy, but in
my opinion it cannot be compared to tea. Of sugar
we have but a small quantity, and the chocolate was
all used in the famine; but whatever is left must be
common property, so, my dears, I invite you all to tea
this afternoon."

The brothers being now satisfied that their further
progress must be delayed for a considerable time, the
prudent heads were all called together, to make such
arrangements as circumstances permitted for the
additional guests. It was decided that Almagro's
hut should be completed, and fitted up for the residence of John and himself, and that a larger habitation
should be immediately constructed for the rest of the
party.

"We have chests of tools," said Mr. Douglas; "and
I am no mean workman, having gone through a regular
apprenticeship as an engineer. Your woods offer us
material, and, with so many willing hands, we shall
soon run up a neat little hut, that we may rest in for
a few months."

This was joyful news for Tom and Jack, who were
ever ready for action. Not a moment was lost, all
Mr. Douglas's valuable chests of tools were transferred
from the waggon to Almagro's hut, which was to be

the workshop, and the contents of these chests seemed to the delighted boys to be inexhaustible.

" Only think, papa!" cried Jack, in a state of great excitement, " such boxes of nails, of all sizes! and we have wished so much for nails! And such a saw! And then, Maria, something you have never seen, something so useful, a wheelbarrow! If you will give me leave, Mr. Douglas, I can just run down before dinner, and wheel up one of the bookcases, for poor Maria has never seen a wheelbarrow, nor, indeed, a bookcase either, and she does love books so much since mamma taught her to read."

Jack was permitted to bring up the wheelbarrow, with the two small bookcases, which were placed in the hall, and both barrow and bookcases were duly admired by Maria. Jack would willingly have made another experiment with his new *toy*, as Matilda called the wheelbarrow; but dinner was on the table, and he was compelled to relinquish his amusement. Mrs. Carruthers was now reclining on a comfortable couch, made of mattresses, looking very miserable; her misery being somewhat increased by seeing that everybody else looked so happy. Mrs. Douglas was quite at home; she had won over even Nanny, and had made with her own hands the excellent dish of hashed-venison, seasoned with Chili pepper, which the famished wanderers were now all enjoying, except Mrs. Carruthers, who, though she had her own china plate, and drinking-glass, eat her dinner thanklessly.

The babe was already improved; it was a pretty dark-eyed girl, and Mr. Carruthers was very anxious that it should be baptized; therefore, after dinner, the whole party attended in the church; even Mrs. Carruthers submitted to be carried there by her husband, to witness the solemn ceremony, and to offer up thanks for her safety.

There had been some previous discussion about the name of the child, Mrs. Carruthers wishing it to be

P 2

called *Dolorosa*, indicative of its early sorrows ; Matilda, who had a taste for lofty sounding names, proposed *Cordillera;* Mary, who had never seen any child so small and pretty, thought of *Titania;* and Maria, considering only its present happiness, suggested *Felicia;* but Mrs. Douglas crushed all their proposals.

" Why should you not call the babe Martha ?" said she, " after our own good mother ; it is a respect due to her memory, Eliza, and if God had given me a daughter, Martha should have been her name."

But Eliza shuddered at such a plebeian name, and finally compromised the matter by calling the child Cecilia, after the mother of Mr. Carruthers; and Matilda and Mary, with Dr. Lewis, were allowed to be sponsors : though there was small probability of circumstances permitting them to fulfil the duties of their office.   Therefore, Mr. Merton, after baptizing the babe, in a solemn manner enjoined the parents to remember that they were left with the sole responsibility of the young Christian's education for eternity ; and even the thoughtless Mrs. Carruthers was awed by the words of truth and holiness.

In the evening, Mr. Douglas sketched a plan of the intended building, which was on a larger scale than the family could have previously attempted, with their limited resources.   The door was to open into a spacious hall, or dining-room, on one side of which, towards the front, was the ladies' sitting-room, and on the other side a study for the gentlemen.   The sleeping-rooms were behind these, and a door at the back of the hall opened into a separate building, intended for a kitchen, where John was expected to fulfil his several duties.   A colonnade was to extend along the front, around the wooden pillars of which were to be twined the beautiful creeping plants which abounded in the woods. In the front of the house, Mrs. Douglas proposed, with her own hands, to lay out a garden ; she had brought with her boxes of seeds of English vegetables, fruits, and flowers, and she promised her friends to leave behind her, as a memorial of her visit, the beginning, at least, of a pretty garden.

CHAPTER XVII.

Candle-making. The New Mansion and its Furniture. The Misfortune of the Ball-dresses. Another Expedition on the Pampas. The Fields and the Garden. The Alarming Observations of Almagro. Preparations for a Siege. The Well and its utility.

THE frost still continued, snow frequently fell during the night, and showers of rain in the day. There could be no hunting; but the building proceeded rapidly. Everybody was made useful, except the languid Mrs. Carruthers, who could only work at crochet or embroidery. She certainly could sing, and play on the guitar, and had brought her instrument with her, through all her distresses; but she had little pleasure in performing before such an unsophisticated audience. Matilda and Mary listened to her with delight, and Maria was perfectly enchanted; but the lady was accustomed to flattery, and though Charles Villars still retained some of the exaggerated expressions of the gay world, yet even he became weary of talking nonsense, and witnessing the indolence and affectation of Mrs. Carruthers.

"Pray, my dear Eliza," said her husband, "indulge us with a little music to-night; we really require some amusement after a day of actual hard labour."

"I cannot sing and play in the dark," replied she, pettishly; "all my own wax-tapers are consumed, and it is impossible to see with that very disgusting looking lamp."

The lamp was not brilliant, nor particularly elegant—it was invented and constructed by Nanny, and was merely an ostrich egg bowl, filled with melted fat, in the midst of which was stuck a peeled rush, which emitted a feeble glimmering.

"Remind me, my dear girls," said Mrs. Douglas, "early in the morning, and, if God spare me till to-morrow, we will have a candle-making day. Peel your rushes, Nanny, and have them ready; cotton is too scarce an article to be used for the wicks."

"But my friends," said Mr. Douglas, " I cannot help fancying you ought to have the cotton-shrub near you; but those knaves, who carried off my instruments, have left me in the dark about our certain position. At all events, boys, you must look about in the spring for the cotton-shrub, *Gossypium*—you will distinguish it by its large yellow flower, with a purple spot at the base of each petal."

"We are certainly not within the tropics," said Lewis, "beyond which I doubt the *gossypium* being indigenous. If we could procure the seed, I have no doubt we might be able to cultivate it in the long dry summer of this climate ; but, as that is not very probable, we must be contented with our rushlights, and thankful for any improvement Mrs. Douglas can suggest."

The next day Mrs. Douglas overlooked all the preparations for the candle-making. Nanny had a cask filled with the fat of the bullocks and guanacoes ; but this cask was an inconvenient utensil for the operation, and Mrs. Douglas despatched John to extract from the miscellaneous stores of the waggon a washing-tub. This was filled with melted fat, kept in a fluid state by being placed near a large fire. Then a number of peeled rushes of proper length were knotted along a straight pole, and suffered to hang down ; they were made smooth and straight by drawing a little tallow over them with the finger and thumb, and then the whole were dipped in the fat, which adhered to them. The rod was hung up in the open air till the tallow stiffened, when a second dipping took place ; the process was continued till the candles attained the desirable thickness, when they were removed, hung up in bunches, and a new set of rushes arranged. The manufacture was tedious, and by no means an agreeable employment; but John was an active assistant, Mrs. Douglas was never tired of useful work, and Nanny's exertions and approbation were extreme. The only drawback to her gratification was the prospect of losing the useful tub when the rightful owner should leave Esperanza; but Mrs. Douglas assured her that she waived all right to it, and that when they departed the washing-tub should remain—a *souvenir* to remind Nanny of her friends.

"After this success," said Mrs. Douglas, as they sat in the evening enjoying the comparative brilliancy of two rush candles, stuck in bamboos for candlesticks; "after this, I think we may venture to try making soap. I know the process; but I have always been able to send to the chemist's for soda; and I wish some of you gentlemen learned in chemistry to tell me how I shall now obtain it."

"The barilla, or soda of commerce," replied Tom, "is, I know, obtained from the *salsolæ*, which I have remarked frequently on the plains below the wood."

"The *salsolæ* is found in extra-tropical latitudes, scattered everywhere," said Mr. Carruthers; "but to obtain the pure soda for soap, I fear a tedious process would be required. The plants should be dried and burned, and should be rendered caustic by the addition of lime, which I understand you have not yet met with in the mountains. But perseverance and industry, such as you, ladies, have evinced, must overcome every obstacle; and you shall have all the assistance my small scientific knowledge can give you."

"But at all events," said Lewis, "the experiment must be deferred, for the barilla can only be collected at the end of summer; Mrs. Douglas must, therefore, write out the receipt for her young pupils."

In a month the neat dwelling for the strangers was built and thatched. Two small glass windows which had lighted the waggons were taken out, and fitted into the study and ladies' room.   In the midst of the hall was placed a small iron stove, which had also been used in the waggon ; it was of a new and excellent construction, and warmed the room perfectly, without the annoyance of the smoke which had offended Mrs. Carruthers so greatly in the parent dwelling of the settlement.

The skill and ingenuity of Mr. Douglas and John, who were assisted by the willing boys, furnished the house with tables, and seats stuffed with hair and covered with skins.   The bedsteads of hides stretched on four short poles were by no means despicable, and the whole of the furniture was greatly superior to the rude attempts which the slender appliances and unskilfulness of the first settlers had permitted them to make.   The study was furnished with a small bookcase filled with volumes on mechanics, mineralogy, and engineering, the property of Mr. Douglas, and a few works on natural history and natural philosophy belonging to Mr. Carruthers.   Writing desks, and a few useful instruments which had escaped the plunderers, completed the furniture of this room.   The ladies' apartment had a cushioned couch, and the furniture of the travelling waggon, a few shelves of French and English novels belonging to Mrs. Carruthers, and the small library of Mrs. Douglas, consisting of a cookery-book, a work on gardening, Hume's History of England, Shakspere, and a large bible and prayer-book.

It was on a fine clear morning that the whole community assembled on the festive occasion of opening the new house ; breakfast, on an extravagant scale, was set out in the hall, consisting of tea, cakes, pigeon-pie, and real butter, made in a small churn destined by Mrs. Douglas for Chili.   Even Mrs. Carruthers smiled as she took her seat at her own table, and looked on her healthy babe crowing in the arms of its father ; and, on the strength of this dawn of harmony, Mrs. Douglas ventured to say, "William Douglas, why should we risk a journey over these frightful mountains? Why can you not dig mines on this side of the Andes, or cultivate the ground in this peaceful valley?"

But William Douglas and his brother knew well that the golden treasure of the Andes lay far north of the settlement, and they sighed over the incompatibility of the acquisition of wealth with that charming life of ease so tempting in this world of labour; but, above all, Mrs. Carruthers protested angrily against a residence in the desert.

"How can you, Margaret, expect me to remain," said she, "in a place where I never see any one; where I cannot go to a shop for anything I want; cannot get a servant to wait on me; where I am compelled to eat hard beef and coarse bread, and cannot even have a glass of wine, so necessary in my delicate state. Above all, what was the use of bringing out ball-dresses from England, if I am never to go to a ball or a concert."

"You may well ask what was the use of bringing such frippery," said Mrs. Douglas; "better have brought a churn and a washing-tub, as I did, and see how useful they are to our kind benefactors. When you are a dozen years older, Eliza, you will know better the real utility of a ball-dress."

But Eliza wanted these twelve probationary years to complete her wisdom; she was determined that her ball-dresses should not be wasted, and she gave her strong vote for the journey.

Mr. Douglas himself had a great taste for rural life. Mrs. Douglas was delighted with the Mertons and their pleasant home; and Henry Carruthers, a man of refined taste and fond of study, would have been content to settle in this quiet solitude; but the ball-dresses turned the scale, and Eliza won her victory. It was agreed that the passage of the Andes should be attempted, as soon as the spring advanced.

In the mean time the ladies rode out daily. John,

whose talents were universal, made very good saddles covered with skins ; and Niger, Dewdrop (late Vixen), with the mule, were quite submissive to female control. Mrs. Douglas frequently rode out with her young friends, becoming more delighted with the charming scenery of the valley every day.

As the river continued swollen and completely impassable, the gentlemen set out for a long expedition along the banks, which they had not yet fully explored. After crossing the valley, the river wound along the foot of the hills for some distance to the south ; then, rushing through a narrow gorge, it poured its waters into a larger river on the Pampas.

As they passed along, Mr. Douglas pointed out to his young friends the rich soil of the land which lay by the river, and recommended them to enclose and cultivate it. "We can spare you as much wheat as will sow two acres," said he, "which in this fine climate will produce tenfold, and enable you next year to treble your space of tillage. You ought also to sow a quantity of maize in plots, and enclose and manure some portions for pasture and meadow. This virgin soil offers incalculable wealth to the industry of man ; more, I apprehend, than the mountains will afford to the miner. You know the oft-repeated observation : 'If you work a copper-mine, you *must* get rich ; if you work a silver-mine, you *may* get rich ; but if you work a gold mine, you will certainly be ruined.' Now, if our golden speculations are likely to become a snare and ruin to us, we will fly to Esperanza ; you will take us in ; and we will try to forget those temptations to evil, and seek with you the true treasures of the earth."

Henry Carruthers looked melancholy, for Mr. Douglas had spoken his own sentiments ; he loved to associate with the learned, scientific, and refined, and he had no sanguine hopes of such society in Chili. He had no abstract love of gold, nor much desire for the pleasures gold can purchase. If he had been able to follow his own wishes, life in the wilderness with the intellectual and happy Mertons would have satisfied him; but then there arose the antagonism of the ball-dresses.

They proceeded for several miles along the banks of the river till they reached the gorge; and passing through it, left behind them the mountains which inclosed their happy valley, and came out on the Pampas. They continued along the river till, about seven miles from the settlement, they reached its confluence with a wide and deep river flowing in a south-east direction. They found the plains to the south somewhat scanty of wood, but rich in grass, on which several herds of wild cattle and horses were grazing. The horsemen set out on the chase, and were fortunate enough to take two young horses, which, they planned should be trained for the use of the travellers. They also killed a large bullock and a calf, and turned homewards, well satisfied with their day's sport, and their extended knowledge of the country.

Mr. Carruthers inquired why his friends did not attempt to form a wooden bridge across the river, to escape their irksome imprisonment when the water was impassable.

"You do not consider," replied Lewis, "that we should, by doing this, afford access to any wandering Indians; these marauders, doubtless, haunt the Pampas, but the river is an insurmountable obstacle to them. We are therefore content to ford the river in the dry season, and to confine ourselves within its bounds, and rejoice in our security when it becomes unfordable."

"I can scarcely fancy this foaming torrent can ever be forded," said Mr. Carruthers; "its impetuous waters appear bent on continuing their course to the Atlantic."

"Of the many rivers which flow from the Andes," said Lewis, "few, if any, are supposed to reach the ocean. They spread over the level Pampas and form lakes, or, are absorbed in the heat of summer.''

" I could not help thinking, Lewis," said Tom, " when I looked on the large river which swallows up our own stream, that if we were again to set out in spring, and keep along its banks, we might reach the coast of the Atlantic, and the dwellings of civilization.''

" I should by no means encourage, or like to share the experiment, Tom," answered Lewis. " The difficulties of crossing the unknown Pampas, with a large party, and no conveyances, would be at least quite as formidable as those we encountered in crossing the Cordilleras. Moreover, we should be in constant danger of encountering the tribes of Indians scattered over the plains. We are safer in our fortress, Tom. But see, here is more sport; we must have a gallop after that drove of partridges.''

The partridge, or quail of the Pampas, is a very silly bird; these creatures are easily caught by riding round, driving them into a centre, and flinging the bolas or a small lasso. They soon caught nine or ten birds, and returned with some pride to show their spoil.

The weather began to improve, and while the young horses were training, the operations of agriculture and gardening were not neglected. Beyond the inclosure several large plots were marked out and fenced; ploughed with the large bone of a bullock,—for Mrs. Douglas had forgotten a ploughshare amongst her treasures, and then sown with potatoes, maize, or wheat. Some plots, covered with manure from the corral, were left for meadow. The gardens were laid out under the superintendence of Mrs. Douglas. Potatoes were first planted, that in case of marauders beyond the inclosure, they might not quite be bereft of this precious provision. Then rows of peas, beans, onions, turnips, and all the vegetables of Europe, were sown. Strawberries had in the autumn been transplanted from the woods; and all the flower seeds they possessed were sown, in hopes of some, at least, succeeding.

Maria described so vividly a flower she wished for, which she named *Fior di morto*, that they recognised it as the marigold ; and Jack sowed the marigold in Maria's garden, inquiring how it obtained such a mournful name. Almagro explained that the Araucanians, the Chilians, and the Mexicans, believe that it sprung originally from the blood of the natives slaughtered by the conquering Spaniards ; hence they named the flower *Fior di morto*, a name adopted even by the Spaniards themselves.

" I like the dear old English hearts-ease," said Matilda, " with all its quaint names, though some of them are perhaps melancholy."

" I think you are in error, my child." said Mr. Merton. " This flower of many names has truly no mournful allusions. It was originally named after St. Euphrasia, the interpretation of whose name signifieth cheerfulness. And its more sentimental appellation, ' Love in idleness,' recalls to us pleasant thoughts : the undying memories of Shakspere and the ' Midsummer Night's dream.' We see before us the glorious virgin Queen Elizabeth, turning aside the fiery shaft of love, and passing on, ' in maiden meditation, fancy-free.' Again, we mark,—

> . . . ' where the bolt of Cupid fell,
> It fell upon a little western flower,—
> Before milk-white, now purple with love's wound ;
> And maidens call it, *Love in idleness.*' "

" And though the French name of the flower, *pensée*, thought, or consideration," said Charles, " may have a somewhat dolorous sound ; yet it has still a merry association, for the modern knights of France, in adopting this flower for their device, add the motto : ' May it be far from thee.' "

" Then, Charles," said Mary, " I give the device

and motto to you,—the most *insouciant* knight I know; and in compliment to you, I will try to cultivate the *pensée* beneath my lattice, like one of the ladies of the days of chivalry."

The gardens now laid out were rich with promises of a perfect Eden, if the climate proved propitious. They only wanted roses; and the sanguine Mrs. Douglas did not despair, if she could have procured them, of cultivating roses among the Andes; and she promised, that if ever she should return to Esperanza, she would bring some roses to wind round the pillars of the colonnades.

But in the midst of the cheerful labours of the whole party, the keen eye of Mrs. Douglas had noticed a marked thoughtfulness in the countenance of Almagro for some days. He frequently held private conversations with Dr. Lewis, and the lady was persuaded he had some unusual care on his mind. He was still, however, continually employed, and having pointed out to Mr. Douglas the total uselessness of the waggons in crossing the mountains, he obtained permission to take them to pieces, and to bring them within the walls; the wheels being too valuable, he observed, to be exposed to the risk of accidents.

Mrs. Douglas reflected for a day on the change in Almagro; and then, with her usual promptness, set about discovering the cause. She entered the hut where Dr. Lewis and Almagro were engaged in some engrossing discussion, and said, " I insist on learning what conspiracy you two confederates are engaged in? I see something has gone wrong; and if two heads are better than one, three heads must be better than two. Therefore I pray you, my good men, take me into council."

Dr. Lewis smiled at her request, and speaking a few words to Almagro in Spanish, he announced to the sagacious lady that she was admitted into council.

He told her, that a few days before, Almagro had

visited the Pampas by the way of the mountain gorge, and that he had remarked, on the banks of the river, the regular track of a line of horses, with the trace of the lance dragging by the side, a certain indication that a party of Indians had recently passed. He thought it scarcely possible that the new settlement should have escaped the observation of these keen and crafty marauders; and he judged it expedient that the whole family should for some time seclude themselves within the fortress, and prepare for a vigorous defence, in case they should be subjected to an attack; but, at the same time, Lewis had advised that they should avoid unnecessarily alarming Mr. Merton and the ladies.

Mrs. Douglas received the information with firmness; only asking what steps they had already taken, and suggesting, that as these robbers usually made their incursions in the night, their first care should be to set a watch.

" That has been already arranged, my dear colleague," said Lewis. " For the last two nights, John, Almagro, and I, have watched alternately, for two hours at a time. On the roof of his hut, Almagro has laid a platform, from which he can observe the whole extent of the valley, being himself concealed by the branches of the cactus. We mount to this observatory every half hour, but have not yet seen any trace of the enemy. In fact, unless they should invade us with a very large force, I have no fear of our dispersing them, for we can muster a tolerably strong party, and, with the addition of your weapons, we are well armed."

" Quite right," answered Mrs. Douglas. " Decidedly we have nothing to fear but from a surprise. Yes; I approve of your prudence in keeping everything from the dear timid creatures, who could not help us in any way. But I see no reason why William and Henry should not be informed immediately. All ought to be in readiness, the plan of defence arranged, and the

commander-in-chief appointed. Our waggon still contains a little armoury, with powder and shot enough
to extirpate a whole tribe of Indians. Then why delay
an hour ? Why delay a minute ? Call up the forces,
and make ready !"

Though Dr. Lewis assured Mrs. Douglas he was in
no dread of an immediate attack, yet stimulated
by her energetic and prudent counsels, he called
Mr. Douglas and Mr. Carruthers, with the three
young men, into the hut, and made them acquainted
with the observations and suspicions of Almagro. The
intelligence caused a great sensation among them.
Mr. Douglas and Mr. Carruthers were concerned, for
they remembered their wives, and the baby. Tom
was rather annoyed to be disturbed in his studies and
pleasant rambles ; but Jack and Charles, it must be
confessed, forgot all their responsibilities in the charm
of an adventure, and the prospect of fleshing their
maiden swords.

"See how we will scatter the rascals !" cried Jack ;
" depend on it they will never pay us a second visit.
Now for our plans : what do you say, Charles, shall
we defend the fort ? or sally out, and put the besiegers
to flight at once ?"

"You will merely be steady, and obeys orders,
young men," said Mrs. Douglas. " It is very lucky
for us that we are not compelled to choose such
Hotspurs as you for leaders. I vote that Dr. Lewis
be appointed general of the forces."

The election was carried by acclamation, and Lewis,
bowing very gracefully, addressed his little army.
" My brave soldiers !" said he, " I entreat you to
remember that we are now placed in a deeply responsible, though honourable, position. It is not alone
our own lives and liberties, our own peace and wealth,
that are at stake, but the security and the lives of
those beloved friends who look to us for protection,
and must perish without it. For their sakes we must
be prudent as well as valiant ; and the remembrance

of our Christian profession will impress on us the duty of blending our valour with humanity. Let us never forget that these wretched heathen robbers are still our brethren ; and unless in defence of life, let us not take life. We must be firm, bold, and united, my dear friends, and, if possible, we must dismay, without destroying, our foes. Let ' Union and Discipline!' be our motto ; and may God defend the right!"

The speech was received with enthusiastic cheers, which brought out the ladies to inquire the cause of such unusual hilarity. It was for the gentlemen necessary to tell them that they were about to enrol themselves into a *corps*, and to undergo a course of drilling in the art of defence, in order that, in case of need, they might come out great warriors ; and, as the subject of the roving Indians was often discussed, this preparation created no alarm.

After the ladies had retired, Lewis said, " My first order shall be that John continue the work we have interrupted with our council, for, if our fears are realized, it will be a work of great utility."

John had been employed in making some neat buckets of hide, with handles of the same material, to replace the clumsy vessels of skin of their own rude manufacture, which the family had been glad to use for the purpose of bringing water from the river.

" We must immediately bring in a supply of water, and fill all our vessels," said Lewis; " for secure as our fortress seems to be, a determined plan of firing it might place us in great peril, and we must be prepared to subdue the first appearance of such a danger."

" But, allow me to speak now," said Mr. Douglas, " on a project I have long had in my head. From certain appearances in a particular spot, near the corral, where a bed of clay certainly exists, I hope we may find water within the inclosure. Come with me, this is too important a matter to be longer delayed." He immediately procured from his study a long iron

Q

rod, and, followed by the whole family, proceeded to the spot he had examined. He then bored the earth to the depth of five or six feet, and, on withdrawing the rod, the water sprung up, to the wonder and delight of the observers. Maria's astonishment almost partook of terror at the unexpected result; and Nanny declared there was something *uncanny* in Mr. Douglas seeing the water through the very ground; but Tom reproved their ignorance; adding—

"It is a well known fact, that an underground stream flows in a descending course, till it meets with a bed of clay, which stops it, as water cannot pass through clay. Then, if the ground be opened at the spot where it has accumulated, it *springs*, to use the common expression. I suppose, Mr. Douglas, we must now form a basin for this spring."

"Yes, my good lad," said Mr. Douglas, "we must just dig a well, and line it with flag-stones. A pump is beyond our mechanical powers and means. But amidst our stores we have some hose, or leathern-pipes, and John, from your stock of hides, will teach you to make more. These will be more serviceable than buckets."

"But now, the well! the well!" cried Jack, seizing a spade; then, putting it down, he added, "but I have forgotten, Field-Marshal Lewis has not given the word of command."

"But he gives the word now, and sets the example," said Lewis, beginning to dig vigorously. Working by turns, they soon formed a basin six feet deep, which was sufficient, as the water was so near the surface. Before night it was lined with stones, and the water had risen four feet in it. Then two large casks were carried up to Almagro's observatory, and filled with water, by means of buckets drawn up. A long, flexible leathern-pipe was introduced into each cask, from which, in a descending position, the water might be showered upon, or over the fence.

They worked so long and late, and slept so profoundly, that, even if the drowsy watch had not themselves been slumbering, they would have had much difficulty in rousing and assembling the forces, had any suspicious circumstances rendered it expedient; and Mrs. Douglas, who was the first to rise and observe the sleeping garrison, sighed over the loss of her faithful dog Wallace, which would have rendered any other watch unnecessary. Fortunately all remained quiet, and the refreshed troop assembled after breakfast to receive the instructions of their prudent commander, in case danger should arise; and while Nanny and her young assistants were testing the grand utility of the " wonderful well," the troop were undergoing a drilling, that they might be ready to perform their evolutions with promptness and regularity.

The day was so spring-like that the young ladies were anxious for a long ride, and even Mrs. Carruthers, who had been riding within the inclosure for some days, on a gentle creature which Charles Villars had named Mayflower, desired, on this day, to wear a pretty riding-dress from her well-supplied wardrobe, and, attended by Charles, to make an excursion. Lewis had some difficulty in warding off this wish of his fair friends without alarming them; but he determined that no one should leave the protection of the fortress for some days. At length Charles induced Mrs. Carruthers to be contented with a canter in that part of the inclosure which was not laid out in gardens; and the lady was so pleased with her exercise, and with her pretty palfrey, that she declared if she could not have a carriage for her journey, she should like to make her entrance into a civilized country on Mayflower, rather than on a heavy, ugly mule.

Mr. Carruthers observed to her that, besides the fact of Mayflower being totally unfit for such a difficult journey, she was the property of Mr. Villars, and must not be so unceremoniously appropriated.

Q 2

"If Mrs. Carruthers will do me the honour to accept Mayflower," said Charles, "I will train it for the mountains, before the unhappy day when we must, I suppose, lose you all."

"But why should you lose us, Mr. Villars," replied the lady; "surely you do not mean to waste your life in these dismal wilds? Come with us; you shall be our guide and protector over those terrible mountains, and you shall be our guest and our dear friend in Chili."

Charles smiled and thanked her, but did not accept her invitation; he was a little undecided on the subject; and he did not like to think about it.

CHAPTER XVIII.

The Night Attack. Wallace! The Brave Defence. Repeated attempts. The Water-engine. Dispersion of the Indians. Almagro's Discovery. Origin of the Indian Tribes. Preparations for the Departure of the Visitors.

THE night was so fine that Mrs. Douglas insisted on sharing the watch; and Maria, to whom she had confided the great secret of the suspected invasion, requested to be her companion. Warmly wrapped in their ponchos, they seated themselves on cushions on the observatory; and while Mrs. Douglas continued, with her usual volubility, to plan schemes of warfare, Maria, who had a poetic and enthusiastic imagination, was gazing on the stars, peopling them with countless multitudes, and lost in contemplation of the wonderful worlds her new education had revealed to her. Suddenly she started up, grasped the arm of Mrs. Douglas, and pointed in speechless terror towards a distant spot in the east.

"What has agitated you in this way, child?" said

Mrs. Douglas, "and why do you point at that dark, still wood?"

"Dear, dear lady!" exclaimed the excited girl; "see you not yon glimmering spot of light. That light is no star of heaven; it is the torch of the murderers, and we are all lost!"

Even Mrs. Douglas was silenced; she watched a few moments, and then believed that she also saw a strange light. She left Maria, begging her to be prudent and watchful, and descended to rouse the warriors, who were soon assembled and prepared. Lewis then joined Maria, and distinguished too plainly the moving torches.

No time was now to be lost. Mrs. Douglas undertook the task of preparing Mr. Merton and the ladies, and fortifying their courage with her own bold spirit. The guns were loaded, the stations appointed, and orders and signals arranged, before the regular tread of the horses fell on their ears. Maria still continued to act as sentinel, and rapidly communicated to those below the result of her observations. By the light of the torches she ascertained that the number of the horsemen was not more than twelve or fifteen. They were tall, dark men, clad in ponchos, and the leader was distinguished by long ostrich feathers streaming from his head.

A few moments more and all doubt was at an end; for then the shrill whistling shriek was audible, which ever precedes the approach of the depredators, and which, despite of all prudence, proclaims their hostile intentions. Great was the confusion among the besieged; there were palpitating hearts, faint cries from the house, and hurried preparations. At length all subsided into order, and they calmly waited the event. Maria announced that, after riding along a great part of the inclosure, they had halted, as was expected, before the door, which had previously, by the aid of the waggon stores, been secured by strong iron bolts and bars. Here the robbers dismounted, and attempted in vain to force the

narrow door, which, placed in a niche formed by the
enclosure, did not admit any more than two or three
to make the attempt.   Finding this mode of attack
hopeless, they gathered round the chief in consultation; and then, for the first time, the besieged party
heard a loud howling, followed by the sharp bark of a
dog.

"That is the voice of my Wallace," cried Mrs.
Douglas, rushing from the hut in great excitement
towards the entrance, where she stood crying out
loudly, "Wallace! poor Wallace!"

Apparently the dog recognized the voice, for he
barked more vehemently; and many strange voices
were mingled with the barking, encouraging the dog,
it seemed, to some feat; and this encouragement was
successful, for, with a tremendous bound, the creature
cleared the high door and alighted at the feet of Mr.
Douglas.   Nothing could exceed the delight of the
huge dog; he careered round his old friends, sprung
on their shoulders, and greeted them, in his rough
manner, with the earnestness of true attachment, and
soon comprehending the tie that united his people to
the strangers, he at once extended his friendship to
them.

In the mean time great confusion and astonishment
reigned among the Indians, who had evidently expected
good service from the dog, in dismaying or disabling
their opponents, and who appeared quite unable to
account for the joyful and familiar barking of the
ferocious animal, which they could not avoid hearing.

"I believe," said Maria, "that they fancy we are
necromancers, and that we have cast a spell over the
dog.   They are afraid of us, and are mounting their
horses and moving away."

But the Indians were not so easily discouraged as
Maria thought; they only rode round the inclosure,
inspecting it carefully by the light of their torches, as
if to discover a weak point.

As they passed the corral, the inhabitants of that

inclosure were roused by the lights and unusual sounds, and a great noise of bellowing, bleating, and neighing arrested the Indians, and probably inflamed their cupidity; for they once more rode to the entrance, now provided with large fragments of rock, with which it was plain they intended to force the door. This would have been a fatal disaster to the besieged, and the commander immediately placed Almagro and Charles to guard this important point.

A small loophole had previously been made in the fence on each side of the door, into which the ends of the rifles were introduced; and when the assailants had raised their arms to discharge the huge stones, Maria made a signal, Lewis gave the word, and the two guards instantly fired, one after the other, both barrels of their rifles. These were certainly random shots, for they could not see their foes; but, from Maria's report, two men fell and were carried off by their companions; she observed, however, that these men were only wounded, as, after a little time, they were able, with assistance, to walk to their horses.

A short time elapsed, and the resolute marauders again rallied, and rushing forward with several flaming torches, flung them into the hedge. This was the crisis Almagro and Lewis had dreaded; but they had fortunately prepared against it. Mr. Douglas and Lewis, mounted on the observatory, waited till the juicy stems of the cacti began to crackle and ignite, and all the Indians were gathered close to the spot to aid the progress of the flames; then directing the short iron pipe, which was fixed to the end of the hose, to the rapidly-igniting hedge, they poured such a volley of water down, that they not only extinguished every torch and every spark of fire, but half drowned the assailants, who withdrew to some distance with loud exclamations, uttered certainly in a tone of dismay.

The light-hearted young soldiery were greatly inclined to laugh at this comic and easy discomfiture of the enemy, but the commander called them to order;

and John pithily remarked, that it was better not to
crow till they were out of the wood.   And certainly
they were not yet " out of the wood ; " though half
an hour elapsed before the Indians had terminated a
long consultation with the chief.   Then Maria saw
the white plume coming forward again ; there were no
longer any torches, and it was not till the party were
close at hand that she saw, by the light of the stars, that
the enemy were on foot, and armed with long lances.
With these they began a furious attack on the fence,
cutting and tearing away the branches with their
hands, though not without many exclamations of
pain, caused by the thorns of the cactus.

And now Lewis drew up his whole troop in line
opposite the assailed point ; the rifles were introduced
through the branches, and two desperate volleys were
fired, immediately succeeding each other, followed by
three loud cheers from the brave little army.   Loud
groans and cries were heard, and Maria observed that
the chief had fallen, and two men carried him off with
mournful wails. Three men besides were borne away,
wounded, if not dead ; then the whole party mounted
and rode off slowly, carrying with them their wounded
and dead.   For a long time the victors, under the
command of their general, preserved a dead silence,
to be assured all was safe ; and once, they even
fancied they heard a groan, but Maria assured them
she saw every man, dead or living, leave the spot,
and as all continued dark and silent, they ventured to
leave their posts and enter the dwellings.

They found Mrs. Douglas engaged in attendance
on her sister, who had been in hysterics the whole
time of the action.   Dr. Lewis undertook to manage
the patient, and speedily cured her by the application
of a bowl of cold water thrown over her ; a mode of
treatment which was received by the lady with violent
indignation, succeeded by tears and lamentations.

" Take me away, Henry," cried the weak woman ;
" I cannot bear to live in this place, where no one has

any pity for me, and I run the risk of being eaten up by savages. I am weary of this dull, wretched, beggarly place, and I beg that we may set out to-morrow."

Henry looked much ashamed of his wife's foolish complaints, and endeavoured unavailingly to soothe her; in which pleasing employment he was left by the rest of the party, who proceeded to the dwelling of the Mertons, where they arrived in time to kneel down and join in the good man's thanksgiving to God for their deliverance from peril.

" Come, Nanny," cried Jack, " you must give us, brave fellows as we are, a second supper, or breakfast you may call it, for it will soon be daylight. And here is our dear little sentinel half frozen, must have some warm milk, and go to bed."

Nanny thought it no trouble to provide for all their wants; she called them her *bonny bairns*, her brave lads, a credit to Old England; and in her soft-ened state she even fed the gaunt, famished, gigantic Wallace; the dog ate voraciously, and was then taken to the important entrance and tied up. Mr. Douglas assured them they needed no other guard, for this was a duty the dog had been always accustomed to; and they were thus enabled to retire and obtain a short rest after their night of fatigue and anxiety.

Early in the morning Lewis and Almagro mounted the observatory to reconnoitre the valley. All ap-peared as tranquil as usual; but as they were about to descend, Almagro pointed out a dark object at some distance from the gate, and they both observed that it moved. They summoned Mr. Douglas, armed themselves, and cautiously unbarring the portal, pro-ceeded to the spot. As they drew near they saw lying a wounded horse, scarcely able even to turn its head. Lewis found in its shoulder a serious, but he thought not a fatal wound, and he humanely brought the proper applications, and dressed the wound of the suffering animal with as much care as if it had been a

human creature. The horse seemed conscious that
he was in friendly hands, and bore all the painful process with patience. The kind surgeon then administered a restorative mixture, and the animal soon revived sufficiently to rise, and walk with difficulty towards the stable of the corral.

It was a noble animal, and from its decorations,
and a long elegant spear which lay beside it, they concluded it must have been the horse of the fallen chief.
The bridle was ornamented with silver, and a saddle-
cloth of white leather was richly fringed with silver;
over this was the skin of a jaguar, as a saddle; and
Almagro declared that nothing but the terror and
confusion produced by the fire-arms, could have induced the Indians to abandon the valuable accoutre-
ments of their chief's horse.

When they got the suffering animal into the stable,
they made a bed of maize leaves for it; and Almagro
relieved it from its gorgeous trappings. As the young
men, who were now all assembled, were gazing with
admiration on the noble horse, they were startled by
a loud cry from Almagro, and turning round, were
shocked to see him leaning against the railing that
separated the stalls, pale, and trembling. For some
time he could not speak, but he pointed out to Lewis
on the embroidered saddle-cloth, the letters Z di V,
worked in silver.

" This is the work of my lost child," at length said
the agitated man. " Her mother taught her this
elegant art, and from me she learned to form these
letters; and thus have I seen her oft embroider her
poncho and her handkerchief. My Zara lives, but
where shall I seek her. Alas! alas! had I but suspected her fate when the robbers were in our power,
we might have secured them, and compelled them
to restore my child! "

They all tried to console their much-loved friend;
Mr. Merton even reprimanded him for ingratitude to
God, by whose mercy the life of his daughter had

been saved. And Dr. Lewis pointed out to him, that even if she were a slave, it was plain Zara was employed in no menial capacity, or she could not be able to practise the delicate art of embroidery. He encouraged Almagro to hope they might yet meet and be happy, for the Spanish girls were generally well treated by the Indians.

But it required time to compose the mind of Almagro, after this revival of his sorrow; and they left him alone, contemplating the work of his child, and returned again to the field of battle. Here they picked up two more lances, and to their great astonishment a small silver flask, filled with water. When Mr. Douglas saw it, he immediately claimed it, as part of the property which had been carried off by the unprincipled guides. How the flask and the dog fell into the hands of the savages was an enigma they could not solve, but they all agreed that the recovery of Wallace was of much more importance than that of the flask.

Though they were for some time cautious of venturing far from the fortress, yet the general opinion was, that the Indians would certainly not return after the experience they had had of the fire-arms of their adversaries. And they now enjoyed peaceful rest, relying entirely on the vigilance of Wallace. After a week of undisturbed tranquillity, the family returned to their usual pursuits; and though they could not forget the Indians had visited them, they no longer feared for the future.

" Is it possible, papa," asked Tom, " that these Indians can be in a purely savage state. Surely they must have some traditions of the great events of the Creation and the Deluge, if they are, like ourselves, the descendants of Adam. And if they were of the first people, how did they come from Asia to America? And how did they degenerate from the intelligence of the patriarchal times to this barbarous and degraded state?"

"You have broached a question, my boy," replied Mr. Merton, "that has long been asked deridingly by the ignorant sceptic. The faithful believer in the divine revelation sees, in all the works of God, the beautiful order and harmony that strikingly confirm the wonderful history of the creation, and which declare that we are all of one blood; as St. Paul says, God has made all nations of men. Truly, we are all the children of the first man, Adam."

"Then I suppose, papa," said Jack, "the people of Asia, the first inhabited part, would increase and spread to the east, and then they must have built ships, and come over to America."

"No doubt, Jack," said Mr. Carruthers, "you are right; but the first sailing vessels could hardly be called ships; they must have been rude rafts or skin canoes: the latter are used to this day by the half-torpid Fuegians at the south of America, and the scarcely more intellectual Esquimeaux at the north. But even these primitive contrivances would enable the restless or the inquiring inhabitants of the early world to cross the strait at the north of the two continents, which is so narrow that, from the islands which lie in it, you can at the same time look on Asia and America; and, in fact, these islands are so closely scattered, that it has been a question where Asia ends and America begins."

"I know an easier plan still for coming to America," said Jack, "and that is, over the ice of the frozen ocean."

"In the stern winters of the polar regions," answered Mr. Merton, "that cannot be a difficult undertaking; and the Esquimeaux doubtless visit both continents over the ice."

"But do not the features, the colour, the habits, customs, and language of the American Indians differ essentially from those of the people of Asia?" inquired Tom.

"In physical conformity," replied Lewis, "the races

of North-West America are identical with those of North-East Asia. From the north the people have gradually progressed southwards, losing as they descended, in their wandering and precarious life, the noble and intellectual qualities of their ancestors."

"But how strange it is, Dr. Lewis," said Matilda, "that men of one parentage should be of such dissimilar complexion."

"I believe, my dear Matilda," replied Lewis, "that the colour of the skin depends entirely on climate. In the regions of the tropics we find the native black races; the colder, temperate climates are inhabited by those of fair complexion, and the intermediate nations are brown or olive."

"Still, Lewis, I cannot see how the wandering life of these Indians should destroy their hereditary intellectual powers," observed Tom.

"We must ascribe their contracted intellect and their savage customs," replied Lewis, "chiefly to the wild mode of life they must necessarily be driven to, remote from all established seats of civilization; when the wants of nature being supplied by much bodily labour, but a small exertion of mental energy, the glorious powers of the mind become impaired for want of exercise, and sink into a dull or torpid state."

"Surely, Mr. Villars," said Mrs. Carruthers, yawning, "you do not feel any interest about these degraded creatures, whom I cannot recognize as belonging to humanity, and to whom any allusion makes me shudder."

"You must forgive me, Mrs. Carruthers," replied Charles, "if I feel a little curiosity about my fellow-countrymen; for I, like them, though a South American born, sprung from a race of civilized strangers; and who can tell but my descendants may, in the course of ages, become barbarous wanderers in these wilds, like our late dark-countenanced visitors."

"How can you speak in that alarming manner, Charles Villars," said the lady; "you, with your wealth, and youth, and gaiety, can never for a moment think of establishing yourself for life in these gloomy wilds. Return with us to the pleasures and even to the necessaries of life. I quite pine for my usual cup of chocolate and rusk before I dress in the morning, and for my glass of iced champagne and slice of pine apple at dinner. Margaret knows I never could eat beef or drink milk till necessity compelled me."

Charles evaded Mrs. Carruther's request, for though he had by no means decided to remain for life at Esperanza, he was far from wishing to be in attendance on the troublesome lady during her journey.

"Do not delude yourself, madam," said Mr. Merton, "with the belief that you are not of the same race as the wild Indian and the enslaved negro. All histories, natural and civil, testify the great fact, that mankind were descended, as the Mosaic records declare, from one family. All nations and all people still have a veneration for an unknown and Superior Being, and all preserve some wild traditions, too frequently distorted by time, of the world created from chaos, the first man, his sin and fall, the deluge, and the promise of a life beyond the grave. From one extremity of the earth to the other, all men, however contracted in intellect, believe in the immortality of the soul; all look forward to a future state; all hope that future will be a happier state. The unenlightened savage regards skill in hunting or success in war as the passport to eternal happiness. Still he acknowledges this reward for his merits as the gift of the Great Spirit. And thus did error, founded on truth, pervade the whole world, till God graciously sent his Son to redeem us by his blood, and to point out to us the way of salvation; commanding his ministers, from generation to generation, to go to all nations, and to pour into the heart of the heathen the light of the great mystery of love."

The winter had passed away rapidly and profitably, and spring now lighted up the valley. The deciduous trees, bursting into leaf, looked bright amongst the dark and gloomy evergreens. The river was swollen considerably by the rapidly-dissolving snows of the mountains, and confined the hunters within its bounds; but they daily netted, and brought out an immense quantity of fish. The wheat and maize had sprung up luxuriantly, and the seed potatoes were now planted in a small inclosure. The gardens were cultivated with care and neatness, and a promise of plenty cheered the young labourers.

But the parting with their friends was a melancholy prospect. Mr. Merton loved the society of the gentle and highly-educated Henry Carruthers; the young men were for ever at the side of the practical and active Mr. Douglas. John, the useful John, who assisted everybody, and played on the fiddle to amuse everybody, would be a great loss. Mrs. Douglas, busy, clever, and kind-hearted, would be regretted by all, even Nanny wept at the thought of parting with her; above all, Mary was in despair that she must lose her darling little Cecilia.

"Oh! you are welcome to keep the babe," said the careless mother. "What could I do with her on the journey, without a nurse? I, that am scarcely strong enough to dress myself."

Henry Carruthers looked deeply distressed at the heartless offer of his wife to leave her child; he took up the sweet babe and kissed it to hide his emotion.

"Make the best of it, Henry," said Mrs. Douglas, in her usual kind tone of authority. "It will be a sorrowful task for you to part with your darling; but better to reflect that it is well and happy than to risk its precious life in the journey. Let the good little nurse keep her pet; it will be another inducement for us to return to visit our hospitable friends."

"Henry can come after we are settled in Chili, and bring Cecilia to me," said Mrs. Carruthers, pettishly; "for my part, I shall certainly not return to this dull place."

And thus it was settled that the little Cecilia
should remain at Esperanza.   Mrs. Carruthers proposed that Matilda should accompany them to Chili,
assuring Mrs. Merton that she was committing an
act of great injustice in detaining a girl of Matilda's
age in such a solitude; it was quite necessary she
should be brought out, and this was her only chance
of being introduced into society. Mrs. Merton looked
at her husband in silent terror ; Matilda was much
agitated, and Mary and Maria burst into tears.   Jack
spoke first,—

" I cannot see any fun in balls and parties ; and I
know very well Matilda will say she would rather
dance on the grass-plot, to the merry sound of John's
fiddle, than be dressed up to dance among strangers,
who care nothing for her."

Matilda did not long hesitate.   " Do not look concerned, dear mamma," said she.   " Do you think I
could leave you ?   I am much obliged to Mrs. Carruthers ; but I could never be happy separated from
those I love."

The three girls embraced each other, delighted they
were not to be separated, and Mary said : " And I
know cousin Charles will not leave us either ; he
loves dear Esperanza too well."

And Charles was astonished to find that he really
did love Esperanza, with all its privations, too well to
leave it for a life of pleasure and ease. He declined
to forsake his friends, but Almagro, the ever-obliging
and unselfish Almagro, undertook to accompany the
strangers, and, with his experience and sagacity, to
assist them in overcoming the difficulties of the unknown and perilous route.   It was necessary to wait
till the river had somewhat subsided ; and while the
preparations were going on, Almagro undertook to
try the water daily, and to report when it might be
forded.

The two mules and the horse, which Mr. Douglas
had brought from Buenos Ayres, restored and invi-

gorated by their long repose and good food, were destined to bear Mr. Carruthers and the two ladies. Mr. Douglas, Almagro, and John, were mounted from the corral ; and Niger, with Almagro's mule, the steadiest and most experienced animals of the stud, were to be laden with the provisions and other necessaries for the comfort of the travellers. Mr. Douglas decided to leave his books and valuable instruments, till, the ladies being safely placed, he could return with proper baggage mules, to transport the heavy goods over the mountains. And thus, as Jack said to Nanny, they had the use of the wheelbarrow and the churn for an indefinite time.

Large skin bags, convenient for slinging over the mules, were filled with pieces of salted beef, charqui, maize cakes, and salted butter,—all the provision the settlers had it in their power to bestow on their friends. Water was never wanting in the Cordilleras, especially in the spring, when every crevice formed a streamlet for the melted snow.

When the bustle of preparation was past, the pain of parting became more oppressive ; but the river being now passable, the day of departure was fixed. Mrs. Douglas was quite overcome with her sorrow at the last moment, for she was truly attached to the Mertons ; she begged them to use her stock of linen and furniture, which she was compelled to leave behind her, as freely as if they were their own. Mrs. Carruthers insisted on taking her portmanteau and boxes, which were a sufficient load for one mule ; and the mattresses, blankets, and covering for a tent, which was intended to be raised on two long Indian lances, were a great addition to the provision-bags for poor Niger to carry. They had all lances, knives, and rifles ; and Mrs. Douglas, at her own particular request, was armed with a pair of pistols.

At the last, even Mrs. Carruthers was affected at parting with the pretty Cecilia. She wept bitterly, declared the journey would certainly kill her, and

R

that she should never see her babe more; and as her last injunction, she begged Matilda would teach the child music, even making the sacrifice of leaving her guitar for the purpose. Matilda had learnt to play tolerably well from the instruction of Mrs. Carruthers, the only benefit, since her arrival, that she had conferred on the community.

CHAPTER XIX.

The Departure of the Strangers. The Birds and Flowers of the Pampas. The Indian Chase, and the Escape across the River. The Gardens and Fields. Building a Brick Oven. The Hollow Tree and its Inhabitants. Hay-making.

ONCE more the old waggon was mounted on the wheels, that Mrs. Douglas and her sister might make a day's journey in it. The parting from Esperanza was painful; but the young men set out to escort them for some miles. Jack acted as driver, the others rode with the gentlemen; and on a balmy spring morning they crossed the rushing river, and passed over the high hills till they reached the Pampas. Thence taking a northern direction, they proceeded easily with two good horses, but in a melancholy manner, for about fifteen miles, when it was necessary to separate, that the settlers might return with the waggon. This was the most painful parting, for the wanderers literally knew not where to turn, nor what dangers they might blindly rush into. The ladies mounted their mules reluctantly, and Mr. Douglas proposed that they should still continue to traverse the Pampas to the north, till they fell in with some track that might tempt them to commence the ascent.

The homeward-bound party turned back dejected and silent; it was not the least of their afflictions that they must for an indefinite time be parted from their faithful friend Almagro, the most experienced and useful member of the community. But the charm of passing over new ground in a new season at length amused and consoled them. A fresh breeze wafted to them the reviving odour of the mint, scattered over the slopes, while beyond rose steep above steep; fragrant with the new budding foliage in the lower parts; and higher, rising to those mighty walls that seemed to shut out the world beyond them.

In the lower declivities, richly clothed with lofty trees bursting into leaf and knitted together with graceful llianes, were assembled multitudes of birds, of glorious plumage, sporting, chattering, and whistling, while the pretty, quiet-looking mocking-bird, was repeating like an echo all the various notes.

" I should like above all things to possess that curious creature," said Tom. " I suspect it is the *Orpheus Patagonicus*, the mocking-bird of the southern plains; I should be glad to observe it at leisure. Could we not capture, without destroying it ? "

" No, no ! " said Lewis, " We will not become slave-owners in this strange land. Let the pretty denizens of the woods sing in peace and safety. We have no more right to ensnare the mocking-bird for our amusement, than we have to kill one more creature than is necessary for our subsistence, or for our safety."

" At all events, Lewis," cried Charles, " Here is something that may be useful to us," pointing to a pair of ostriches on the plains. Away flew the two well-mounted hunters, but Tom and Jack, the charioteers, were compelled to remain with their charge; luckily, as they went slowly forward, they passed the nest of the ostrich, from which they took a dozen eggs, still leaving as many to hatch; and were thus more fortunate than their friends, who returned, somewhat crest-fallen, after an unsuccessful chase. They next sent their bolas after the parrots, and procured as many as they wanted for provision; and one

2 R

noble green bird, which was caught with no other injury than a broken wing, was carried off by Jack to present to Maria, who ardently desired to have a parrot to teach. Tom, in the mean time, collected large bunches of gay geraniums, the pink-wood sorrel, and the *œnotheræ,* to delight his sisters with the first spring-flowers of their new home.

As they crossed a little mountain streamlet, which, lower down, expanded itself into a miniature lake on the plain, they saw with much pleasure, on the rushy banks, various broods of water-fowl. There were several species of wild ducks, and flocks of a long-legged plover, which Tom and Lewis recognised as the *Hymantopus nigricollis;* the cry of these birds resembled that of dogs in chase, and diverted the boys greatly. Another bird had the cry of the peewit, and some resemblance to it; but Lewis, who said the bird was the *Vanellus cyanus,* pointed out as a striking distinction that the wings were armed with sharp spurs. The bird affected lameness, and flew about to draw the intruders from its nest, but they discovered it, and took some of the eggs, which Lewis assured them were as good as those of the plover.

In the pursuit of the water-fowl they had deviated considerably into the plain; and Lewis, reminding them of the anxiety of those at home, urged them forward; and taking out his glass to ascertain how far they were from the morning track, sweeping also the plains to the east, he suddenly cried out, " A large body of Indians are advancing, release the horses, and mount them. We must abandon the waggon, and gallop forward; we may yet escape an encounter.''

In a moment the horses were unhooked, the harness gathered up, the boys mounted, and galloping off; not without a pang at leaving their waggon, all the acquisitions of the day, and even the pretty parrot.

They fled with all the speed their wearied horses could use. seeking when they were able the shelter of the trees, and not even pausing to look behind them. They were within a mile of their own river, when the poor horses being totally overcome, they were compelled to rest under the protection of a clump of tall pine-trees ; and took the opportunity of reconnoitring the country between the branches. The youths were sanguine that they had distanced the Indians, for no traces of them were to be seen ; but Dr. Lewis was less satisfied. He was convinced that if the marauders reached the abandoned waggon, they would immediately track the fugitive owners ; and he felt great anxiety to reach the river. Seeing the horses were in a condition to proceed, he called to Jack, who was looking through the branches. " I am watching a herd of noble wild horses on the plains behind us," said the boy, " Do wait, Lewis, till I get a fling at them, with my bolas."

Lewis turned uneasily to look towards the spot ; and immediately cried out, " Quick ! quick ! to horse ! Our foes are upon us ! "

They sprung upon their saddles, and started off at full speed.

" This is a *ruse* continually practised by the Indians," said Lewis as they proceeded. " They suspend themselves by one arm round the neck of their horses, and hang crouched beneath them. The animals then have the appearance of a troop of wild horses, but the regular pace and order revealed to me that we were pursued. Have your rifles ready, my boys, but let no one fire till I give the word ; and then only one barrel. We must keep the second in reserve for the last extremity. God send that we may not need all our resources."

" I fear they are gaining on us," said Jack ; " they are terrible opponents on those swift animals."

" They are, indeed, Jack," replied Lewis ; " thus the horses which the cruel and mercenary Spaniards first introduced, now swarming over the Pampas in a wild state, form a powerful force against the very

descendants of the men who introduced them; and
the poor Guacho, in his lonely hut, suffers for the
sins of his fathers."

They had reached within a hundred yards of the
river, which Lewis was not sorry to observe was
greatly overflowed, when they saw the Indians, about
twenty in number, armed with long spears, sitting
upright on their horses, within fifty yards of them;
and they now uttered the extraordinary shriek which
proclaims their hostile intentions. Lewis called out
to his friends to hasten on; then suddenly wheeling
round himself, he took deliberate aim, and shot the
horse of the leader dead.

There was a momentary delay, for the Indians
crowded round to see if their companion was hurt;
and Lewis, profiting by the pause, fled after his
friends, and before the robbers came up, the young
men had plunged into the river, which at that spot,
where the banks were nearly level, was now about
two hundred feet broad, but not more than five feet
deep in any part. The wearied horses seemed to revive
when they entered the cool water, and plunging and
swimming they soon reached in safety the opposite
banks. The fugitives then rested a few moments,
and looking back, they saw their pursuers standing
gazing on the river, and chattering loudly and angrily;
but evidently having no intention to cross the water;
an exploit which Lewis was aware these people have
much fear of.

Jack declared that he recognised the white horse
which Lewis had shot, as one of the animals which
had been at the " siege of Esperanza." The light
colour had enabled him then to distinguish its form
and peculiarities, even in the dim light afforded by
the torches.

" I believe, indeed," said Lewis, " that these men
belong to the same tribe as our unpleasant visitors;
and I fear they must have their tents not far off, in
which case we may see them again. We must there-

fore only leave home together, and well armed; and we must caution the young ladies without alarming them."

" Do you not think, Lewis," said Charles, "that it might be possible to form an amicable treaty with the Indians? It is a vexatious annoyance to us, and a continual anxiety to our dear girls, to be constantly dreading these terrible visits."

" I wish it could be done, Charles," replied Lewis ; " but I see many difficulties. A deep feeling of revenge is implanted in their very nature against ' *los Cristianos*,' as the Spaniards, and with them all Europeans, are called. The implacable feeling is perpetuated from father to son, as they repeat the traditions of the spoilers and usurpers of their lands, who, it is too well known, slaughtered them without mercy, and tyrannised over those whom they spared for slavery. This hereditary hatred it will require ages entirely to subdue ; for even the pious and faithful missionaries, who have ventured fearlessly among them to teach the peaceful religion of Christ, have, in many instances, fallen martyrs in their sacred duties."

" We must just try to catch a young savage, and bring him up like Friday," said Jack; " and then we can send him back as the schoolmaster."

The youths laughed at Jack's plan as they rode up more leisurely to the inclosure. " A pretty figure we shall cut," said Jack, " slinking home, with the loss of our precious waggon and all its contents. Above all, to think of being robbed of that beautiful parrot. Charles, you may go first ; for I am ashamed to show my face."

They made the best report they could of their adventure, treating it lightly ; but still the dread it created, caused many an anxious hour, and many a sleepless night, notwithstanding their reliance on Wallace, who had been left with them, as his enormous appetite would have seriously drained the stores of the travellers. And even Wallace sometimes roused them to arms, when it was found out that the enemy was only a hungry puma, lurking about the fence near the corral.

A month passed away and Almagro did not return; but all continued quiet at the settlement. The wheat and maize were prodigious crops, and already in ear; the vegetables were excellent, and were daily brought to table; and the flower-garden was resplendent with the European favourites, and with the verbenas, the lovely yellow œnotheræ, and several graceful climbing plants which they had brought from the woods. The beds of scarlet strawberries were already ripening, and the groves of peach-trees were glorious with their purple blossoms.

"One might fancy oneself at Winston," said Nanny, as she placed on the table a couple of the wild ducks of the river, dressed with onions; and a dish of green-peas. "Only I never can get used to such topsy-turvy ways as peas and berries, and garden-stuff coming on, when we ought to be looking for Christmas."

It was impossible to give Nanny any notion of the cause which produced the inversion of seasons in the southern hemisphere, though Matilda laboured to instruct her; but she had become reconciled to the spot, and since she obtained a churn, perfectly contented. And but for the apprehension of the Indians, and a little uneasiness about the long absence of Almagro, the family would all have been happy. No one was ever idle; they had now, with the addition of the books left by their friends, a respectable library. Mr. Carruthers had also given them a quantity of writing materials, and they were enabled to pursue their studies regularly and profitably. Maria evinced excellent abilities for learning, and was the pupil of her sisters, as she called them. In the evening they played on the guitar, or danced to the music of the fiddle which John had left in charge of his pupil Jack.

They had collected a large quantity of the cochineal insect from the leaves of the cactus, these were pressed into cakes, and used for dying the wool they spun; and in this delightful season, the sisters had their loom in the colonnade, and were weaving a carpet, in stripes of black and scarlet, for the sitting-room of the new house.

" I am thinking, Charles," said Tom, as they stood watching the busy weavers, " that we ought to begin some new work. What do you think of making bricks of the clay which the receding waters have left on the banks of the river ? I mean, of course, the sun-dried *adobes*."

" You must really excuse me, Tom," answered Charles. " Doubtless the thing might be accomplished, but my education never gave me any notion of brickmaking, and I confess to having no taste for the noble art. Nor do I see the utility of the undertaking, unless you contemplate also the erection of a regular brick mansion."

" I don't think we could manage that, Charles," said Tom; " but I do believe, that if we could make the bricks, I could plan a proper oven, such as Almagro has described to us : but then, Jack and I could not do all the work ourselves.

" But we will all help you," said Maria; " Jack shall teach us, and we will spare no labour to have a real oven."

" I will willingly assist," added Matilda, " if Dr. Lewis thinks that bricks can be made here, and that our assistance would be proper and useful."

" Of course, Matilda, we can be useful," said Mary; " we can fill the little box with clay, smooth it with a flat bit of stone, and then turn the brick out to dry. I have seen even little children, in the brick-fields in England, busy at such work. Come, Master Charles, put on your gloves, and help the mechanics."

Charles soon agreed to join the labourers; Lewis pronounced the plan practicable; so the young men went to the carpenter's shop, and made some neat boxes of the proper size for the moulds. This was no difficult task for them now, for the instruction of Mr. Douglas and much practice had made them fair workmen. Early next morning they set seriously to work, and continued brick-making till they had spread out in the sun some thousands of bricks.

Then the spot for the oven was marked out on a piece of vacant ground a few yards behind the kitchen of the new house, and a few days having rendered the bricks sufficiently hard for their purpose they began to build. They formed a solid square of bricks, cemented with the moist clay, of about three inches high and four feet square. On this was raised the oven, which was of a cupola form, and was so difficult to construct that many failures ensued ; but the patient workmen persevered, and after much time was spent it was completed. An opening was left for the introduction of the bread to be baked, a smaller one at the side, for the removal of the ashes, and at the top was a sort of chimney. They suffered their erection to remain some days to dry in the sun before it was tried. Then Nanny made her cakes, though with much distrust and grumbling, while the young men heated the oven, by keeping up a fire on the floor of it, and closing the openings with bricks, which were removed when the oven was sufficiently hot ; the ashes were then swept away, the pies and cakes placed within it, and the openings again closed. In due time the viands were drawn out on a wooden shovel, made by Jack, and the baking was pronounced perfect. Nanny looked with pride on her young nurslings, and said, " None but Westmoreland lads could have done such a clever job. If I live another day, I'll try my loaf, and if that eats as it ought to eat, why then, we'll just bide where we are, mistress, and end our days at this bonny, quiet place."

But Matilda advised Nanny to defer the experiment of the loaf till the wheat was ready. She had not been accustomed to make loaves of maize; besides, they were all quite satisfied with the thin biscuits made from the fine flour which was ground in Mrs. Douglas's hand-mill.

The beaming sun of summer, though tempered by the cool breezes from the mountains, was so oppressive that they did not venture to quit the shade of the woods in the middle of the day; but the four younger gentlemen usually set out in the morning early, well mounted and armed, to procure game for the provision of the household; and they seldom returned empty handed; though the guanacoes were not plentiful, as they had sought the cool air, in the heights of the mountains; and they rarely ventured far enough on the Pampas to meet with the wild cattle. But hares, partridges, and pigeons were abundant, and Jack once more found a parrot for Maria; besides some ostrich eggs, which made excellent omelettes.

One day, all continued so still, that they determined on a longer expedition; they reached the spot where they had abandoned their waggon, and found the remains still lying on the plain. Every particle of iron about it, even the very nails, had been carried off, but the wheels still remained attached to the wooden axletree; and binding these firmly with thongs, the young men replaced the frame of the waggon, and placed the scattered pieces upon it. Then attaching two of their horses to the dilapidated vehicle, they succeeded in drawing it home, with the intention of putting it in such repair as their means would permit.

In the mean time the sisters ranged the wood beyond the inclosure without fear, relying on the protection of the river. They collected a quantity of strawberries, and brilliant flowers, quite unknown to them. And on this day the quick eyes of Maria marked the laden bees fly towards a particular tree, and she suggested to her sisters that there must be honey in the tree, of which they might take a part and still leave sufficient for the bees in winter. To take the honey was, however, an undertaking too formidable for the girls to attempt alone; but on communicating the discovery to their brothers, Jack valiantly volunteered his services for the enterprise, and the whole party set out to the woods to watch the bees.

"Now do, dear Jack," said Maria, "observe that bee which has plunged into the midst of the pretty yellow œnothera, it is quite buried in the flower; now it comes out slowly, covered with the yellow dust, and how wonderfully it brushes away all the dust from its body, till it forms a little mass, and now see the mass has entirely disappeared, the careful little bee has stowed it up in some unseen pocket."

"The mass is now hidden in the triangular cavities in the hind-feet of the bee," said Tom; "and the brushes with which it cleans the farina from the body, and collects it, are bushy substances which project from the fangs at the end of the four hind-feet."

"Then these fangs are actually the hands of the bee," observed Maria.

"You may, if you please, use that unscientific name for the useful fangs," answered Tom, "for without them the bees would be unable to cling to the branches, and to each other. You must distinguish, however, between the honey-gathering bee, which sucks the nectar with its proboscis, and the bee we have just observed, which is employed only in collecting farina."

"See! see! Tom!" cried Jack, "how they are buzzing round this old hollow tree; they certainly have a colony here, and let them beware of me! I am the man to slay the bees, and carry off the spoil of the battle. *En avant!*" and he was rushing forward, regardless of the cries of his sisters, when the firm and commanding voice of Dr. Lewis arrested him.

"If the bees have honey to spare," said he, "we will gladly share their abundance; but I am astonished, Jack, that you, who have exclaimed so strongly against the tyranny of the Spaniards in a strange country, should conceive you have a right to slaughter the bees, and take possession of their hereditary domain."

"But, my dear Lewis, how can we get the honey unless we destroy the bees?" asked Jack. "If we summon them to a parley, will they attend?"

"I fear not," said Lewis, laughing; "I believe, after all, we shall be tempted to use the power that might so often exerts over right. We must compel them to pay tribute to our usurping rule; but we will have no massacre. It is a measure which humanity and policy alike forbid. Let us examine their dwelling."

The tree, which was of large dimension, was a perfect shell, and they saw that the bees entered by several apertures. At the lower part of the tree was a large opening, and it was through this entrance Dr. Lewis proposed to storm their fortress; but, as some preparation was needed, they agreed to return next day.

Early the ensuing morning the whole family, laden with the apparatus, went to the wood; they carried a small saw, wooden shovels, and all the leathern buckets. Lewis had a long bamboo wand, to the end of which was attached a large piece of sponge, part of his toilet appendages. When they reached the tree, he wetted the sponge from a bottle, which contained some very powerful volatile, for he warned the whole party to keep at a distance, lest they should inhale the dangerous effluvia. He quickly introduced the wand through the opening into the hollow, and passed it up the tree. The loud humming of the insects gradually subsided, and finally all was silent.

Lewis then withdrew the wand, and called all hands to work; an opening was easily made in the frail shell of the tree, about four feet from the ground, and the curious work of the laborious colony revealed. The interior of the trunk was literally a column of comb, which they removed with wooden shovels, filling all the buckets they had brought. A slight movement announcing that some of the bees were recovering, the

signal for retreat was given, and the party marched off
with all expedition, and succeeded in arriving in safe
shelter, before the bereaved insects were sufficiently
recovered to pursue and avenge themselves on the
audacious robbers.

The spoil was deposited in the cool mountain cave,
which, closed by a rocky barrier, defied the attempts
of the despoiled to recover their property. A portion
of the honeycomb, with hot maize cakes, formed a
more luxurious repast than the family had indulged in
since they left England.

"See, my children," said Mr. Merton, "how bountiful our God has been to us. He has led us safely
through the wilderness, as he led the Israelites of old,
to a land flowing literally with milk and honey. I
rejoice exceedingly that I have been enabled to look
on the work of these wonderful creatures, for the study
of their habits has excited the attention of the sage
from the early days of the patriarchs. Aristæus, worshipped as a god, delighted still in his bees; and
Charles will not have forgotten the memorable description given of the recovery of his lost bees by the
first of the Roman epic poets, Virgil."

" Certainly not, sir," answered Charles, " and I also
remember that knowing old Latin, disdaining the idea
of female rule, gives the bees a king: ' Kings lead
the swarm.' I spare the ladies the original Latin
blunder."

Mr. Merton undertook an apology for his favourite
poet; but Mary interrupted him to ask if he thought
the Israelites had hives for their bees.

"Assuredly not, my child," replied he; "the bees
of the East, doubtless, then, as now, dwelt in clefts of
the rocks. In the Psalms we have this allusion:
'With honey out of the stony rock should I have
satisfied thee;' and in the song of Moses, recorded
in Deuteronomy, we have the words, 'He made him
to suck honey out of the rock.'"

The rich grass of the inclosed plots was now ready

for cutting; but the difficulty of accomplishing this simple operation of husbandry was very great. They had neither scythe nor sickle; Almagro possessed a long knife, but he had carried it with him for defence, hoping to return before the harvest. All the agricultural implements belonging to Mr. Douglas had been left in the waggons abandoned on the Pampas, to the great regret of the generous Mrs. Douglas; who had promised, however, if she could meet with any useful implement before Almagro returned, to send it for her friends. But of Almagro's return they began to despair, he had now been so long absent.

"Well," said Jack, "we must cut our grass; and we have the choice of a carving-knife, a spade, a hatchet, a saw, or an Indian lance. Which will make the best scythe?"

It could not be helped; they all set to work and hacked the grass with large and small knives, or any implement that would cut. The young ladies even plucked the grass with their hands, so determined they were to have hay; and a very neat, good-sized haystack was speedily made within the fortress; it was thatched with maize-leaves and thongs of hide; and the young farmers believed it might defy the rains of winter.

The beans were likewise cut and stacked, to serve as food for the cattle, or, in case of need, for themselves. The potatoes were excellent and plentiful, and the wheat was nearly ripe; but the prospect of reaping it in the same way they had done the grass was discouraging. They had gained the addition of a young llama and a calf to their stock, and they now turned the cows and llamas into the newly-cut grass-fields, which were securely fenced; and the animals fattened well on the fresh food. The dryness of the season was the single inconvenience they experienced; there had been no rain for some months, and though the dew fell, and partially refreshed the ground, they had to bring water from the river to irrigate the garden. This was

a great labour; but the well was so low they were
obliged to be economical. They had even to contrive
a plan for drawing up the water, which had sunk below
their reach. They planted on each side of the well a
short stout post, forked at the top; across these was
laid a rounded pole projecting beyond the forks at one
side, to serve as a windlass, to the end of which a rude
handle was fixed. The rope was formed of twisted
thongs, and a large leathern bucket was attached to it.
The machinery answered very well, though the workmanship was rough; and they were able to draw up
the water, deliciously cool, when they wanted it.
Occasionally they even indulged in the luxury of sherbet, made by mingling honey with the water, and fla-
vouring it with the juice of the strawberry, or with
that of the richer peaches, which were daily ripening.
Of the latter delicious fruit, besides their usual consumption, they dried a vast quantity in the sun for
winter provision. The family had, in fact, a profusion
of the necessaries, and even the luxuries, of life.
They had health, domestic happiness, and a peace only
alloyed by the absence of their faithful friend, and an
irrepressible dread of the Indian marauders.

CHAPTER XX.

The bountiful Harvest. Thankfulness. The Thunder-storm
and Conflagration. The Return of Almagro. His Story of
Sorrow and Trial, and Account of his Arrrival at Santiago.

THE maize was quite ripe, and the parrots and pigeons
were hourly visitants, the sisters being kept fully employed in watching and driving them away. At length
they began the task of plucking all the ears, which
were carried in baskets to the colonnade, where they
were shelled; the grains were stored in chests and hide
bags, and the husks built in stacks, behind the kitchens,

for fuel.   After this was finished, which occupied many days, the stalks were cut down, tied in bundles, and stacked for the cattle.   Some weeks before, a quantity of leaves had been collected to store for thatching.

Then came the important wheat harvest; the plot was small; but, with their inefficient implements, it took the young workmen several days to reap it; for they worked very cautiously, lest they should waste a grain of their precious corn.   When they judged the wheat was perfectly dry, it was conveyed to the workshop, on the floor of which the large sailcloth used for their travelling tent was spread, and a flail was soon constructed of two long poles united by a hinge of hide; then the corn was thrashed, winnowed, and stored in sacks of hide.   The produce was calculated to be about twenty bushels, and of this they proposed to reserve two bushels at least for seed.

How happy the young men felt as they looked round on their well-stocked farm; and all being finished, they assembled at church to return thanks to God for the blessings he had bestowed on them.   Mr. Merton concluded the service by a serious injunction to them not to put their trust in the multitude of their riches, nor incur the judgment of God, like the presumptuous men in the parable, by saying, "Soul, thou hast much good laid up for many years," but to be humble in the midst of their plenty, and remember all was the gift of God.

When they returned from church, Maria seemed troubled, and, addressing Mr. Merton, she said, "Do you think, my dear friend and father, that I am doing the will of God, by remaining in this happy valley without benefiting my fellow-creatures?   You have been a friend to Almagro and a father to me; and surely God sent me also into the world for some good purpose, but I have done nothing: I am negligent and idle, for I know many wonderful things that you have taught me, and I might teach them to the ignorant

s

savages, who are, like us, God's creatures, but do not, like us, know him."

"Your thoughts are just, my dear child," said Mr. Merton. "I fear I have too much neglected my mission on earth, but an unpardonable want of energy has prevented me from seriously contemplating my duties. I would gladly listen to any plan for opening a communication with the heathens, for I now feel the solemn responsibility of my situation."

Maria entreated that she might be allowed to go out and meet the Indians, who would never hurt a girl, and especially one who spoke Spanish ; which most of the tribes understood, from visiting the towns to exchange their skins. She was very sanguine that they would allow her to teach their children. Dr. Lewis, however, assured her she was very unfit for such a perilous mission; nor would he hear of Mr. Merton attempting any intercourse with the tribes, of whom they yet knew nothing but that they were savage and cruel. At all events, they must wait for the return of Almagro, before any mission could be planned, and day after day they watched and hoped to see their friend, but in vain.

The weather had been intolerably sultry for some days, when one evening, as the family were about to separate and retire to their several resting-places, they were startled by a loud peal of thunder. They went into the open air, and beheld, through the thick darkness of the night, the forked lightning darting along the heavens, like the fiery serpents of fable. Then came the terrific peals of thunder, which can only be heard amidst gigantic mountains. Mr. Merton and Dr. Lewis looked on with admiration, and pointed out to their youthful hearers the immediate causes, and the beneficial effects of these elemental strifes, so mysterious to human comprehension, like all the mighty works of the great Creator. The sisters clung to each other, trembling, and the family withdrew into the hall, agreeing not to separate, though they usually occupied both the dwellings, until this awful storm was past.

"Surely," said Mr. Merton, "I perceive some smell of combustion beyond that of the sulphureous vapours that fill the air?"

Convinced that this was the fact, they all left the house once more, and saw, to their great distress, the stack of maize-stalks in flames. Not a moment was to be lost, and Lewis, with his usual coolness and decision, appointed every one his work. Buckets and vessels of every description were hastily collected, and the young people formed a line from the well to the stack; Nanny drew the water, and the buckets passed swiftly from hand to hand, and were received by Lewis, who threw the water on the burning stack. Tom and Jack were left out of the line, and were employed in pulling down, and flinging to a distance, with the aid of two Indian lances, the bundles of beans which formed the next stack.

But, alas! the supply of water was scanty, the remains of the bean-stack soon took fire; and now all their concern was for the hut of Almagro, immediately adjacent, which contained not only their valuable tools, but many sacks of corn. All the supply of water was now directed to the thatch of the hut, but they saw with dismay that the flames must inevitably spread to it; from thence the fence against which it was built would also take fire, and not only all their possessions, but their very lives were in danger. Their arms were wearied with carrying the buckets, the water of the well was nearly exhausted, and Nanny, in despair, relinquished her occupation.

With aching hearts, they now hastily prepared to escape from this scene of desolation and danger; when suddenly, in a moment, the rain descended in torrents, quenching the fire, and driving them in, greatly relieved, to the shelter of the house.

Then, after many tears of joy, they knelt down, and, with fervent spirit and grateful hearts, offered up their

s 2

thanks to God, who had once more preserved them in the extremity of despair.

The thunder ceased, but all night long the rain came down with undiminished fury. The thick leather curtains of winter were suspended before the windows, and the whole family remained together watching all night, dreading that the thunder might again come on. When day broke, they looked out on the scene of desolation sorrowfully, but grateful for all that was spared to them; and wrapped up in skin cloaks, they all ventured out to see the animals, which were in the fields beyond the inclosure.

They found the llamas, crouched under the hedge, trembling with fear, the youngest animal lying dead by the side of the mother, struck by the lightning. The cows were quietly grazing, uninjured, and apparently heedless of the storm. The sisters wept over the fate of their little favourite, and removed the body from the sight of the distressed mother. They next proceeded to the corral, and found all safe, for the stables and sheds were left open, and the horses had taken shelter. The gardens were perfectly devastated: all the bright flowers were gone, and carrots, onions, and lettuces broken down and destroyed. But the loss was only for a season—they were still rich in stores; and they were filled with gratitude when they reflected, that if the storm had occurred a month before, all the crops must have been destroyed.

In a few hours the rain ceased, the sun beamed forth, and all nature revived after the terrible but health-bestowing dispensation. The young men then completed the survey of their losses: they found the stack of maize-stalks burnt to the ground, as well as all the beans, except some sheaves which they had thrown off before the stack caught fire.

"We still have the hay," said Tom; "and if the winter should prove severe we must spare some maize for the cattle."

"I propose," said Lewis, "that we make another

inclosure, into which we can turn the animals, and then try to raise a second crop of hay. This glorious rain will give new vigour to the parched soil, and vegetation will spring rapidly. And now, boys, set to work, for the sun has already absorbed the moisture from our lately flooded gardens, and we must have them put in order."

This was a work of great labour, for fragments of stone and pebbles had been washed from the rocks above and scattered over the whole valley. The gardens had to be cleared from these stones, the broken plants propped, and those which were torn up replaced. Then the beans which were saved were spread to dry, and it was found there would be abundance left for seed, though none for consumption. Finally, all the cattle were removed into the corral, till another plot of ground should be fenced for pasture.

The next morning the young men set out to procure poles and cactus plants for the fence. They had put the strong baggage waggon into order, and on this occasion they harnessed to it, for the first time, two oxen, which they had taught to draw. The river was greatly overflowed by the rain, but descending lower, they crossed it at a wide and shallow part. Then moving still along the valley for about a mile, they reached a spot where a gradual ascent enabled them to take the waggon within the shelter of the wood which clothed the lower part of the mountains. Securing the oxen, they sought for trees suitable to their purpose, and set vigorously to work. They cut down pines, and took up young cactus shrubs,—now an easy task in the moist state of the earth. With these they loaded the waggon, and then sought out and collected a large quantity of pinones. They found several trees blasted by the lightning, under one of which a bullock was lying dead. Some nests of young pigeons were lying scattered on the ground; many of the young birds were still living, and these they picked up, and wrapping them in the remains of the torn nests, placed them in the waggon, hoping to bring them up and tame them, that they might found a colony of pigeons within the fortress.

And now, their labour being accomplished, they sat down to take some refreshment previous to taking the road homewards. As they sat talking cheerfully over their plans of labour, Charles suddenly made a sign for silence. "Jack," whispered he, "be on your guard, for I certainly heard a movement among the low bushes below us; there must be some wild animal watching us."

The rifles were ready in a moment, and they were all cautiously looking out through the trees. A continuous low rustling was now plainly heard, but the thick bushes concealed the cause, till before an opening in the wood, about fifty yards from them, they caught a glimpse of a horseman. "It is Almagro!" cried Jack, springing impetuously down the sloping wood. The horseman, evidently alarmed, raised his rifle, and would certainly have fired, but for the well-known voice of Dr. Lewis crying out, "Almagro, we are here." He rode forward mounted on Niger to meet them, with a glowing countenance; he was followed by a train of six loaded mules,—a pleasant sight for the whole party.

The meeting was joyful and noisy; and so many questions were asked on both sides, that Dr. Lewis prudently requested Almagro to defer all explanation till they were assembled at home, where it was now desirable to hasten, with such a valuable freight. They proceeded therefore as rapidly as the slow movement of the oxen would permit, Almagro much amused with the new team, and the young men greatly delighted with the handsome mules, and not a little curious to know what their load consisted of. As they went along, Almagro heard the little history of the settlement since his departure; the encounter with the Indians on the Pampas, and the lucky escape.

Then they reported the work done, the rich harvest, the storm, and the conflagration.

Almagro had also experienced the storm, but had fortunately been sheltered with his mules in some caves he had found in the rocks; but he declared that he had expected every moment to be crushed by the rocks falling upon him, such were the fearful explosions, which seemed like the rending of the mountains above him.

When the sisters unbarred the gate, and admitted Almagro, the rejoicing was great; the girls clung round their dear friend with a thousand questions, and Nanny even, wiping her eyes, said : " God keep us all together now, for it is sore work parting with friends, when they are so scarce."

The mules were unladen, and taken to the corral, to be introduced to their new friends; and then, after supper, the impatient boys begged to know what Almagro had brought with him.

" Many useful and valuable remembrances from Mr. and Mrs. Douglas," said he ; " and, for the rest, I have done for Charles all I could effect, though not, perhaps, all that he wished."

This was a mystery, and all looked to Charles for an explanation, who, addressing Mr. Merton, said :

" You know, dear uncle, if I chose to visit Valparaiso, I should be a wealthy man, but having made up my mind to stay with you, I gave Almagro the bills and letters I had brought out with me, that if he reached any commercial town in Chili, he might get credit, and procure some little additions to the comforts of the family circle. I jotted down such things as I wished, rather than hoped for, and left him to make the best of it."

" Which I tried to do, Charles, for I honoured your good intentions," said Almagro. " But will you now inspect the packages, or shall I give you the details of our melancholy journey."

All were anxious to hear how the travellers reached

Chili; and though Jack and Mary looked inquisitively at some packages, the inspection was deferred till next morning; and Almagro commenced his narrative in Spanish, the language he spoke most fluently, and which the whole family now readily understood.

"When we left you," he began, "we proceeded towards the north, continuing on the plain in hopes of meeting with some track which might point out to us the pass over the mountains. For two days we pursued this solitary road, erecting a tent at night for shelter, and meeting with no inconvenience except the extreme uneasiness and the ceaseless complaints of Mrs. Carruthers, who declared that we were certainly lost, and should either be murdered by the savages, or torn to pieces by wild beasts. Mrs. Douglas, with kindness and energy, reproved her fears, and used every argument to divert her from them; but in vain. On the third day Mr. Carruthers pointed out some faint traces of a path on a gentle slope towards the Cordilleras. On examining the spot, I recognised with satisfaction the footsteps of mules, which convinced me this was not the track of the Indians, who always journey on horses, and ever at full speed.

"We followed the track for some time up the ascent; the path soon became stony; then we reached a ravine, in which we found a hut which we concluded to be a post-house, and hoped we should there meet with a guide; but we were doomed to be disappointed. The hut was a wretched abode, destitute of every comfort, and inhabited only by a deaf old woman and a stupid young girl. All my inquiries produced no other information than that the son of the old woman had left the hut some days before to guide some travellers. Miserable as this hut was, it was agreed, for the sake of the ladies, that we should spend the night there; and, though the only provision the dwelling contained was *charqui*, which we did not want, we had the refreshment of the pure water which flowed in a clear stream through the ravine.

" The beds which were offered to the ladies were but heaps of filthy and foul skins, from which they shrunk with disgust; but we carried into the hut all the blankets and mattresses to form couches for them; while the two gentlemen with John and I slept in the open air, and certainly had the most agreeable lodging; for no sooner had day broke than Mrs. Douglas came to us, declaring it was impossible any longer to endure the attacks of the millions of vermin that swarmed in the hut. She certainly had suffered greatly, for her face was absolutely disfigured by the wounds inflicted by the bloodthirsty little insects. She had left her sister weeping in great distress, and calling on us for the assistance which we could not possibly afford her. Fortunately the morning was fine, and abandoning the filthy hut, we breakfasted in the open air, and discussed the question of our proceeding.

" Mr. and Mrs. Douglas were of opinion that our most prudent plan would be to retrace our steps, and endeavour to preserve the mule-track to the last station on the Pampas, in order to procure a guide; but Mrs. Carruthers vehemently protested against returning, and moreover declared, she would certainly never again enter a post-station while she lived, words which were but too true!

" Mr. Carruthers, who was ever attentive to her wishes, entreated his brother and sister to proceed forward on the track which was now plainly marked. They reluctantly complied with his desire, and we went on, not knowing what dangers lay before us. Sometimes the track led us up a gentle green slope, sometimes through a ravine formed by some torrent, which, in part subsided, left a narrow path by the side. These were the pleasant scenes of the first two days after we left the hut, and the weather continuing fine, the tent was a sufficient night lodging.

" But on the third morning we entered a gorge, which lay before us a perfect labyrinth of huge fragments which had fallen from the mountains above. The gentlemen led the horses on which their ladies were mounted, and we followed each other closely, for if one by mischance was left behind, he became distracted at the disappearance of his companions, and the bewildering objects around him, and knew not where to turn.   I could not but fancy that such must the world have been, in the first days of creation, which Mr. Merton had so frequently and beautifully described to me, before the Great God had called forth the vegetation that gives it beauty, or the animals that give it life.   It was an awful solitude ; and even the peevish complaints of Mrs. Carruthers were momentarily hushed by the grandeur and terror of the scenery.

" A lofty mountain lay before us, which seemed to bar our progress, and defy any attempt to ascend it, but at length we made out a deep cut path, which carried us up to a pass which wound along the side of the mountain for some miles.   The fragments brought from the heights by storms had formed a sort of steep inclined plane, at the foot of which foamed a deep torrent.   It was on the side of this descent that the steps of the mules had formed a path which the hand of man had done little for, and which was in many parts fearfully narrow and perilous.   As we proceeded, the precipice on one side became more abrupt, while on the other hand rose a lofty and inaccessible wall of rock ; and far below us the rushing torrent sounded like a death-knell.   I held my breath for fear, and saw my dear friends grow pale with terror ; it was not for ourselves we trembled, but for the helpless females, who, seated on the *sillon*, had their feet frequently hanging over the precipice; for horse and mule alike fear the wall, and always choose to walk on the outer edge of the pass.   At length we reached a part where the path was not more than four feet wide, and was strewed with untrodden stones ; evidently brought down recently, probably by the melting of the snows.

" Half-way down the precipice on one side of us,

lay the dead body of a mule on a ledge of rock,—a signal of the dangers of the road. No sooner had Mrs. Carruthers caught sight of this painful object, than she became fearfully agitated, and uttered loud screams, which the rocks echoed back with a mocking sound. This alarm added to our peril; and I proposed that we should make this difficult pass on foot, first seeing the ladies to a place of safety, and then returning to lead the animals.

" All were willing to accede to this plan except Mrs. Carruthers: she would not be lifted from the mule; entreaties and remonstrances alike were unavailing. Mr. Carruthers endeavoured to persuade her to allow him to carry her in his arms, but she refused, which I did not regret; for the lady was so untranquil, I considered the attempt would be dangerous. We were compelled to comply with her unreasonable fancy. I took care the lady was tied to the *sillon*, and relying on the sure-footedness of my old mule, I felt some degree of confidence in our safety. We then dismounted, and Mr. Douglas agreed to lead our horses tied together in line; Mrs. Douglas with great resolution proposed to follow alone; then John was to join with the loaded animals, and last, Mr. Carruthers leading his wife's mule, as I knew the animal would not refuse to follow its companions, whatever might be the risk.

" For myself, I undertook, to guard against accidents, a scheme which I communicated to Mr. Douglas alone; and before the procession moved along the dangerous part of the pass, I descended the steep: it was an immense height; but accustomed from my youth to scale rocks, it was not so perilous as it would have been to an inexperienced person. I found a narrow path by the side of the river, and watched there, with my lasso prepared, in case any accident should occur.

" The procession had reached the narrowest part of the pass, which turned round the angle of a rock,

P. 268.

The mule in a moment was over the edge.

when a guanaco, which was perched on a ledge above, and was probably the sentinel of the herd, suddenly bounded down on the path directly before the mule. Mrs. Carruthers uttered a piercing scream, and struggled to extricate herself from the saddle. Whether the fright of seeing the guanaco before it, the struggling of the impatient rider, or some loose stone which had rolled beneath its feet, was the occasion of the fearful catastrophe, no one can tell, but the mule, in a moment, was over the edge. It clung for a minute by its fore-feet; and Mr. Douglas declared afterwards, that if the unfortunate woman had only remained still, John and he would have come up in time to drag up the animal, or to save her; but her shrill cries and struggles only hastened the catastrophe; and Mr. Carruthers still vainly pulling at the rein, was hurled, with the mule, down that frightful precipice.

"My first impression, when I saw the creature rolling over and over down the steep, was, that it was the baggage-horse laden with Mrs. Carruthers' portmanteau; and I shall never forget my horror when I saw that it was the mule. It dashed into the torrent, and sunk; I rushed down the banks, and in a few moments Mr. Carruthers rose to the surface; I flung my lasso, and brought him out at the first attempt, quite insensible; but I believed, not dead.

"I left him lying, after disengaging my lasso, and again ran forward, when I was astonished to see the mule swimming composedly towards me. It landed; and shaking the water from its sides, appeared uninjured, I scarcely dared to approach, for I saw the *sillon* was still on its back, and the lady tied to it : she was hanging forward, apparently dead, covered with blood, and her arms drooping as if shattered by the fall. It was a terrible sight, and I was greatly relieved by the arrival of Mr. Douglas, who had with great risk and difficulty made his way down the fatal precipice. We

P. 268.

P. 268.

The mule in a moment was over the edge.

immediately released the lady from the saddle; we found her face and head much cut, and we fancied her arms were both fractured; but she still breathed. I took off my poncho, on which we placed her, and moving up the stream we found an ascent less abrupt than that we had come down; and we succeeded, I can scarcely remember in what manner, in scrambling up with our senseless and mutilated burthen; and placing her in the charge of her weeping sister, we again descended to Mr. Carruthers.

"We raised him, and after a short time he opened his eyes, and gazed round with a strange, wild, expression. We were alone; for the mule had made its way up the steep, and joined its companions, apparently little the worse for the fall. Mr. Carruthers shuddered as he looked at the torrent, and without speaking, he turned his eyes inquiringly on us.

"'Eliza is much hurt,' said Mr. Douglas, 'but let us hope the best; she is now with Margaret, and you must try, if possible, to join them.'

"We found on examination, that most wonderfully the unfortunate husband had no bones broken. The descent was too steep for pebbles to rest on; and the melted snow flowing over it, succeeded by a hot sun, had clothed the hard rock with a short and scanty growth of grass, which had rendered the fall less destructive. Still he was much bruised and cut; but his anxiety to see his wife, induced him to strain every nerve to make the ascent. But he was struck dumb with horror when he saw the lovely youthful form, that not many minutes before was full of life and bloom, now stretched senseless, maimed, and disfigured with wounds. She still continued in the same state of insensibility; and we feared there must be concussion of the brain. We used every means we possessed to recover her, but in vain; and at length we agreed to move forward, as night was drawing on, and we could find no place on which to place our tent till we had emerged from this perilous pass.

"We continued on the winding road for about a mile; Mr. Douglas and I carrying the unfortunate lady, Mrs. Douglas walking by her side in deep distress, and Mr. Carruthers, scarcely able to sit on his horse, following us. The path then became more open; we reached a small plain covered with stunted pasturage, and on one side, on a little elevation, was a building which I recognised as one of the *Casuchas* of the passes, erected by the government for the use of travellers in case of snow storms. It was raised on a solid foundation about ten feet above the ground, and was merely one small room built of brick; the roof was arched, and covered with bricks placed so as to form two inclined planes, on which the snow could not rest. We entered it by means of a flight of rude stone steps, and gratefully took possession of it. It was only lighted by a few loopholes left in the masonry, but there was a table fixed in the midst, and in one corner a pile of firewood.

"In this miserable hut, on a bed formed of mattresses and cloaks, we rested the shattered form of the beautiful Mrs. Carruthers. We lighted a fire, and then, while John and I unloaded the animals, and tethered them so that they could not stray, Mrs. Douglas washed the disfigured features and bound up the bleeding wounds of her unfortunate sister. The application of the cold water revived the spark of life; she murmured faintly, 'Henry! Margaret!' They spoke tenderly to her, and inquired if she suffered; but she did not seem to have strength to reply; then Mr. Douglas brought a flask which still remained of his stores, and they administered to her a few drops of brandy. This cordial partially revived her; she again spoke: 'Mr. Merton,' she uttered, 'pray for me!' We entered the hut, and joined in the fervent prayers for the dying which Mr. Douglas offered up.

"The poor lady moaned feebly, and a few minutes after said, 'Margaret, I am then dying.' The sobs of her sister and the deep groans of her husband were her answer. 'Will God pardon me?' she said, in a broken voice; 'I have been very wicked; I have forgotten Him in my pride of beauty; will he now remember me?'

"Then Mr. Carruthers roused himself from the lethargy of despair, and spoke to the dying creature in words that seemed inspired by God himself. He told her of His surpassing love and mercy to sinful man, and earnestly besought her to pray faithfully, and to put her whole trust in him who freely offered forgiveness and salvation, and who could remove her by his will from that bed of agony to the mansions of eternal blessedness. The poor sufferer wept and prayed. John and I withdrew and spread our tent outside, and left the sufferer with her sorrowing friends.

"For twenty-four hours she lingered; but Mrs. Douglas told me her mind recovered the holy and pure character of her childhood; and her friends humbly trusted that she died in peace with God and man. I have dwelt thus on her death as a warning to the dear girls who are now weeping at the recital to avoid the temptations which haunt the paths of youth and beauty.

"The bereaved husband, who had struggled against illness while his wife lived, sunk down in a violent fever as soon as the excitement of attending her was passed. We conveyed him from the chamber of death to the purer air of the tent, and watched him night and day; but our means to allay the fever were few and inadequate. John, who understands all useful arts, opened a vein in his arm, and bled him freely. This ought to have been done immediately after the accident; but all our care and thought had been given to Mrs. Carruthers. We gave him the water which burst from the rocks above us to allay his burning thirst, and poured it over his head to cool and refresh him; and this was all we could do.

" For many days he raved with fever, and then sank into a stupor, which we feared would terminate fatally. By this time even the ample store of food provided by you began to fail; and though, in the dry mountain air, the body of the dead showed no signs of corruption, yet it was needful the rites of sepulture should be performed; and it was the wish of Mrs. Douglas that her sister should be buried in consecrated ground. We scarcely knew how to act. I proposed to go forward, to endeavour to reach some post where I might procure assistance; but I knew that I should find no post till I gained the west of the mountains; and the consequent delay induced them to reject my proposal.

" But in our great need God sent us help. A party of travellers from Chili arrived at the casucha. They were shocked and moved to compassion by our tale of misery, and offered all the assistance in their power. One of the party was a professor of medicine, going to Mendoza for the sake of his own health. He was a man of knowledge and benevolence; he told us Mr. Carruthers was now suffering from a nervous affection produced by a brain fever and great mental distress. He administered proper restoratives to him, and recommended us immediately to remove him from the scene of his affliction, supplying us with medicines and good advice.

" By the assistance of the strangers, who carried with them chests of tools, we made a coffin to contain the remains of Mrs. Carruthers, using for the purpose some deal boxes which had been filled with her dresses. Our kind friends finished by giving us clear directions for our journey, and we parted from them with gratitude and revived hopes. The coffin we suspended on one side of one of the baggage-horses, balanced by the portmanteau of fine clothes which the unhappy lady prized so greatly. This horse John undertook to keep behind, as far as possible from the observation of Mr.

Carruthers, whom we got placed on his horse with much difficulty; and during the first day's journey, which was necessarily very short, Mr. Douglas and I had to hold him up.

"But the next day he was a little stronger, and ate some boiled meat, though he still continued silent and deeply depressed. We met with scarcely any vegetation on this day, and the next morning we came on patches of snow. Another day and the snowy heights lay before us, which we must absolutely ascend; but Mr. Carruthers seemed to grow better in difficulties; and we began with stout hearts the zig-zag upward path, sometimes slipping back, sometimes clinging to the manes of the struggling horses; and finally we reached the highest point of the pass, and moved through a narrow passage between two lofty peaks, which led to the western descent.

"After a very cold night's rest, we proceeded downwards so rapidly, that before night we again reached the region of vegetation over a well-tracked road. Two days more brought us to wooded hills, and from thence we went on to a post station, the first dwelling of man we had entered since we left the filthy hut in the valley of the Pampas. This hut was clean, though it was a mean dwelling; and we rewarded the inhabitants liberally for a supply of milk, butter, and fruit. They directed us to a village lower down the hills, which proved to be only a few huts; yet the people were hospitable, and furnished us with food. We obtained a guide, who brought us in three days to the city of Santiago."

T

CHAPTER XXI.

Santiago.   Almagro displays his Treasures.   Jack and Maria
set out to search for Pinones.   The Encounter with the
Indians.   Jack carried off.   The arrangements for the Pursuit
and the Recovery of the Captive.

"I HAD lived only among woods and mountains, apart
from all my kind, and therefore to me the sight of the
crowded city of Santiago was wondrous.   I gazed in
speechless admiration on the innumerable houses, the
steeples of the churches, and the rich woods and gardens which half hid the city ; and I was so bewildered
and dazzled as to be absolutely helpless when we
alighted from our wearied horses before a spacious
hotel, which I believed was a palace.

"Mr. Douglas was soon surrounded by friends ; he
knew some English merchants who were settled in
Santiago, and through their means was enabled to
have the remains of Mrs. Carruthers deposited in
consecrated ground.   Proper medical advice was procured for the afflicted husband, whose health improved
daily ; but his depression of spirits continued unabated,
and Mr. Douglas saw that at present it was hopeless
to expect his aid in any commercial transactions.

"A few days after our arrival Mr. Douglas discovered
that all the contents of his abandoned waggons had
been safely brought over the mountains, and deposited
in the custom-house ; the officers of the department
having rewarded the men who had conveyed the property honestly and safely to its destination.   But there
was now little prospect of their being able to open or
work a mine ; the most skilful of the miners whom he
had brought out, after reaching Santiago, and waiting
long for his return, had finally engaged themselves to
some enterprising speculators, and embarked for Lima.

The rest of them, after depositing the tools with which they had been entrusted by the custom-house officers, had dispersed in different directions, hopeless of seeing their employers again.

" I was kindly treated by every one ; I was conducted over the whole city, and beheld with wonder the number, the regularity, and the cleanliness of the streets ; the elegance of the buildings, the display in the shops, and the noble cathedral, which was built, as Mr. Carruthers told me, in the Moorish style of architecture, and woke in my mind remembrances of the proud towers my father used to talk of, as existing in that country which he ever loved to call his own.

" I admired the gardens, blooming with flowers of exquisite hue and perfume, which occupied the courts of the houses. I wished to procure every flower to bring to Esperanza, but some, I was told, were too delicate to bear the journey or the change of climate ; yet, faithful to the promise I made to my friend Charles, I procured seeds of the most brilliant and fragrant of the annuals for the fair gardeners at home. Then I was taken to the rich vineyards at the *quintas*, or country-houses of the suburbs, and wished much that I could have transported to this spot the graceful plants, which were even then beautiful with the rich clusters of the unripened fruit. I consulted my friends, and Mr. Carruthers was of opinion that the grape might certainly be ripened in the long hot summer of this climate, and the vines protected in the winter ; at all events, that we might make the experiment. I have brought some young plants, carefully packed by the obliging friend of Mr. Douglas, who also wrote a paper of instructions for the cultivator.

" I then signified my wish to return to my best friends, who would I knew be anxious on account of my long absence. Mr. and Mrs. Douglas regretted that we must part, and Mr. Carruthers begged me to tell Mr. Merton, that he felt it now his duty to return to England, and to enter the church, his original des-

T 2

tination till his marriage, when the great objection
Mrs. Carruthers had to become the wife of a clergy-
man induced him to relinquish his intention, an act
which he greatly deplored, and he hoped for the future
to devote himself to study, and to the benefit of his
fellow-creatures.

" ' And tell my dear Mr. Merton,' added Mrs. Douglas, ' that I hope we shall, at last, all gather round
him at Esperanza, I see no reason now why we should
remain in this unhome-like town—I love the country ;
but William Douglas says it will take much time to
settle the affairs of his unlucky mining project. Then,
Henry must join us, he is anxious to do good, and
there is work enough to do among the heathens in the
wilds of America.'

" The good lady was indefatigable in collecting
useful remembrances to send to her friends ; and I was
compelled to remind her that I could not possibly
manage so many loaded mules as would have been
necessary for the conveyance of all her purchases, and
she reluctantly desisted from increasing them.

" When all was ready, I waited a few days to join
a large party who were crossing to Mendoza, as the
security of numbers was doubly desirable with the
embarrassment of riches which now weighed on me.

" Our separation was painfully affecting, for we had
been together through toil and sorrow. Mr. Carruthers, as a parting gift, presented me with his own
watch, a memorial I shall ever value. My passage
across the mountains was comparatively easy. We
had experienced guides, who saved us from many of the
inconveniences and dangers to which the lonely and
ignorant traveller is exposed ; and except the painful
recollections suggested by the sight of the lonely
casucha, and the perilous pass, where we had endured such affliction, the journey was cheerful and
pleasant.

" When we finished the descent from the mountains, and reached the Pampas, I parted from my

agreeable travelling-companions, and, to their great astonishment, took the road towards the south. They remonstrated with me on the madness of proceeding alone, with my valuable train of mules, on a track where I should hourly risk an encounter with the Indians ; but I scoffed at fear, and, by God's aid, have reached you in safety. I was certainly alarmed by the strange cry uttered by my dear Jack, whose voice I did not recognise ; but though I raised my rifle, I was determined that, only in the last extremity, would I shed the blood of a fellow-creature. And now, my beloved friends, that I am once more with you, I should be perfectly happy, were it not for the one melancholy and perplexing thought that ever haunts my mind."

" You must not be unhappy, Almagro," said Mary, " for Jack and I have considered several plans over for seeking Zara. We are all convinced she is living, and that you will meet again."

" May God grant it ! my kind-hearted children," said Almagro. " But see how late it is ! my long story has kept us beyond the hour of retiring. To-morrow you must examine my packages."

And then, after the evening devotions, they separated well pleased, after the labour and interest of the day.

The next morning was full of excitement, for all the novelties had to be inspected : there were several useful carpenter's tools, a scythe, and two reaping-hooks ; and the most conspicuous package was an especial gift for Nanny, from her old friend Mrs. Douglas. It was a large square basket, with open bars on one side, filled with real living poultry, six having survived the journey ; these arrived in good condition, and when they were turned into the little poultry-yard, and Nanny heard the crowing of the cock, and the clucking of the hens, she wept with joy.

A box, from Mrs. Douglas, contained handsome books, vestments, and a small silver communion service, for the use of the church ; and, by the order of

Charles, Almagro had purchased a large bell to be raised over the building. Mr. Carruthers had sent some books, maps, paper, drawing materials, a flute, and another guitar. There were some pieces of India calico and nankin, needles and thread, and a small hamper of crockery. A most useful present for Dr. Lewis of a well-filled medicine-chest, and a complete case of surgical instruments, was brought by the order of Charles, which had been augmented by the attached friends at Santiago.

There were many other useful donations to the community, procured by the liberality of Charles, including two copper-pans, a large quantity of tea and sugar, and a hamper of wine and brandy, which was by the desire of all immediately put in charge of Lewis, to be considered as medicine. Almagro had also succeeded in procuring some neat lamps, which could be burnt with animal oil; and as much ammunition as he could conveniently bring. A great quantity of seeds, cuttings of fruit-trees, with a number of trifles, all of great use, completed the cargo.

"I have but one package more—it is my own forlorn hope," said Almagro, as he produced a large packet of coloured beads. "These I hoped might aid me in my attempt to reach my daughter."

Nanny had in the mean time been arranging the kitchen, which she declared was now complete. "I defy her Majesty, Queen Victoria, to show me better pans, though, likely enough, she may have more of them. Master Charles is a gentleman; and, if it please God to spare me, I hope to dance at his wedding. To think of his sending all that way for such a grand red cloak and velvet bonnet for me, that I might go to church dressed like a Christian. And for him to think of the cheese-mould too! See what a cheese he shall have soon."

And Nanny spread her table, which was now a good, smooth, firm table, made by experienced hands, and she declared the table was a sight to see, set out with china plates, and the roast beef and potatoes on their " nat'ral dish." Then there was a real loaf of wheaten bread, an extravagance not usual; and fresh butter, such as Westmoreland dairy-maids can make; and she promised a peach-pie, baked in a proper pie-dish, on the anniversary of their arrival at the hut, which would be two days after.

After they had dined, and while the young ladies were arranging the books, maps, and all the new acquisitions, the active workmen fitted up the bell over the church. The erection was not a miracle of art; but it answered the purpose of suspending the bell, which would be useful not only to call them to prayer, but to summon the absent in time of need. They tried the sound, and were all satisfied with it.

" Truly we ought to be thankful to the good God," said Mr. Merton, " who brought us from the wilderness into this pleasant land, and has surrounded us with multiplied blessings. But, my children, we must not take our ease here in selfish indolence. God had some wise purpose in view when he placed us here. Let us act!"

Mr. Merton was not active himself; but he loved to preach action; and as he continued to enforce this duty, his words became powerful and effective, and the happy little party felt convinced that it was not their duty to live for their own enjoyment: the world had a claim on them.

" Yet the Swiss Robinson family," observed Matilda, " lived very easily and pleasantly, caring nothing for the rest of the world."

" As the story places them," replied Mr. Merton, " this inaction was unavoidable. But we are not left on an inaccessible island; we are amongst hordes of wretched heathens; we ought not to rest; our mission is to labour, to spread the blessings we enjoy among our destitute fellow-creatures; and God himself will surely point out to us the way to accomplish his ends."

"I am quite ready," said Jack; "what shall I begin to do first?"

"Well, if you please, Master Jack," answered Nanny, "As you were always a good-hearted lad, will you begin by getting me a great basket full of them —fir-apples—I call them. I never could abide to set them before Christians for meat; but if I had some now, I could roast and mash them up, and they would fatten the poultry famously; for young folks should be wiser than to give good meat to dumb animals." This latter remark was directed to Mary, who was scattering maize in the poultry-yard.

"Nanny is quite right," observed Lewis; "the pinones are certainly the most nutritious and economomical food we can give to the fowls, so we must all collect them in spare moments."

It was in pursuance of this counsel that Jack and Maria stole forth one fine evening with their baskets, not speaking of their intention to the rest of the family, who, weary with the labours of the day, had sat down to read or draw. For some time the absence of the lively pair was unnoticed, but when it was remarked, Mrs. Merton became uneasy; and Matilda suggesting the probability of their having rambled to some of the mountain woods for pinones, Lewis proposed that, instead of ringing the bell, which might summon unpleasant visitors, he and Charles should follow their track, and bring them home.

They set out, feeling no uneasiness, as they expected the young ramblers would have confined their search to the woods on their own side of the river; but when they reached the shore, they were vexed to see that the adventurous pair had placed large stones to form a temporary bridge over a shallow part of the stream, much lower in the valley than the settlement.

"The stream is already too low, from the absorbing heat of the last few days," said Lewis, "to be a secure defence to us; and we must certainly not permit this very easy mode of access to remain, to invite any passing Indian to visit our settlement. When we return, we must make the wild young pair assist us in removing their bridge."

"I think we might easily construct a moveable wooden bridge," said Charles, "which we could withdraw at pleasure, for it is really inconvenient and dangerous to cross the river on foot. I have often thought of the plan. We have tools, materials, heads, and hands, and we must certainly set about it."

After crossing the river, they followed the track to the wooded hills, which separated the valley from the Pampas—certainly a great distance for the young people to have strayed; but on these hills the pines were most abundant. They ascended the hills, and were taking the road down the descent towards some well-known pines, when they were struck with dismay by the sound of continued piercing shrieks. They forced their way rapidly through the wood till they reached the plains, and there, at a considerable distance, they saw Maria standing, her hands lifted up, while she uttered the loud cries which had caused them so much alarm. When they reached her, she gazed wildly at them, then, sinking down on the ground, she cried out, in a frantic voice, "He is lost for ever! We shall never see him more! What will become of my dear, kind mamma! And will she ever forgive me!"

Dr. Lewis in a firm tone commanded her to restrain her immoderate and useless grief, and to tell them the cause of it.

The girl made a great effort to subdue her feelings, then, in a voice scarcely articulate, she said, "The barbarous Indians have carried him off, and it was all my fault; my dear, dear Jack!"

"But when? and where?" asked Charles, hastily. "Point out the road the wretches have taken, that we may pursue them."

"Alas! it is long since," answered the weeping girl. "I cannot tell you what time has elapsed since, for I fell on the ground when I lost sight of him, unable to move or cry. It was long before I recovered ; and now they must be far beyond pursuit, for they galloped like lightning towards the south."

"And now, Maria," said Lewis, in great perturbation, " compose yourself, and tell us how this distressing event occurred ; for I see how useless the attempt would be for two unmounted men to pursue the Indians on their swift horses."

" We were in the wood, just above the plain," said Maria, " and had nearly filled our baskets with pinones, when I heard a rushing sound, and through the trees I saw a number of Indians on horses, galloping towards the south. I believed they were going to Esperanza, and that fear bereft me of reason, for though Jack made me a sign of silence, I scarcely noticed it, and could not forbear uttering a loud scream. The Indians stopped and looked round ; then Jack said, ' Hide yourself, Maria, and I will go and meet them.' He plucked a green branch, and, springing down the wood, ran across the plain directly to the man who rode at the head of the party, and who wore long white plumes.

" I saw Jack address the Indians ; but I was at too great a distance to be able to hear the words. I covered my eyes, lest I should see the barbarians murder him. Again I looked up, for I heard his voice : he now spoke loudly, and in English. ' For the sake of mamma,' he said, ' be still. Return home, and say I am safe.' I heeded not his request ; I endeavoured to follow him ; but my limbs were paralyzed with agitation ; and I could not extricate myself from the bushes. When I ventured to look up again, I saw my dear Jack mounted before a strong, fierce savage ; I saw also that his hands were bound, and that he was a slave. My strength returned, I rushed forward ; but alas! it was too late. The whole troop were flying over the plain, carrying with them my brave, my beloved brother, the victim of my rash folly."

The sorrowful girl burst out into new lamentations,

and it required even a degree of severity on the part of Lewis, to compel her to subdue these violent demonstrations, and to proceed homewards, where it was needful they should immediately return to communicate their distressing tidings.

"My dear Lewis," said Charles, "what shall we do? how shall we break the fatal event to our friends? and then how must we act to endeavour, even at the risk of our lives, to recover the noble and heroic lad? Consider some plan, for you have more prudence and judgment than I have."

"Prudence and judgment we must use, Charles," answered Lewis; "but even with these counsellors we cannot command success. Our first care must be to discover, if possible, the situation of our dear boy; but even then, I fear it would be alike dangerous and fruitless to attack the tribe openly with our small force. Our aim must be therefore, if he be living, to labour to effect his escape secretly."

"If they had not meant to spare his life," said Charles, "I do not see why they took the trouble to carry him off. These tribes of the Pampas are not cannibals, like some of the South Patagonians and Fuegians. I shall certainly set out to search for their tents."

"I believe," said Maria, "that the leader was the same chief who commanded at the attack on Esperanza. I remarked the same form of head-dress, with the silver band: and from the observation I was able to make by torch-light, I feel convinced that I distinguished again the same tall and graceful figure."

"I trust it may be so," answered Lewis, "as it indicates that the tribe cannot be very distant from us. Besides, I should be glad that the knowledge of our existence should, at all events, be confined to one tribe."

After crossing the river they removed the stepping-stones, and then, slowly and reluctantly, went forward to that pleasant home, of which they were com-

pelled now to disturb the peace, perhaps for ever.
Before they reached the gate they met Mr. Merton
and Mary, anxiously walking on to seek them.   No
sooner had he cast his eyes on the diminished number, than Mr. Merton turned pale, covered his face,
and said : " My boy ! my unfortunate boy is slain ! ''

" Not so, my best friend," said Lewis.   " He is
well, and I hope we shall soon have him with us
again ; but, for the present, he is removed from us."

They reached home, and then, with caution and
delicacy, Lewis revealed the sad fact to the family,
adding all the cheering circumstances of hope he
could venture to point out ; but no light of hope
appeared to the unhappy family, who were at once
plunged into sorrow, even into despair.

" His death I could have borne with more fortitude," said the hapless mother, " than this frightful
uncertainty of his fate.   We know these savage heathens are, by nature, cruel and revengeful ; and why
should they spare him ?   Perhaps they carried him
off but to torture, to put him to some cruel death,
or, at best, to consign him to a slavery worse than
death."

Dr. Lewis pointed out especially to the parents,
the advantage Jack possessed in being able to speak
Spanish fluently, for most of the Pampas Indians
understand that language, from visiting the Spanish
settlements, where they exchange hides and ostrich
feathers for iron and tobacco.   Then the bold and
frank address of the lad, his dauntless bravery, his
skill in riding and hunting, were qualities likely
to attract these uncivilized people, to induce them to
spare him, and even to be kind to him.

" And who knows what a blessing may arise from
dear Jack's residence with the Indians," said Tom.
" It may be, papa, that God has ordered it, to open
to us a way of communication with a people appointed to be instructed and enlightened."

" I am reproved, my son," replied Mr. Merton.

" The ordinations of God are ever just and merciful; and this, our first sorrow, must humble our pride and confidence. I will pray to be resigned. Follow me, my children, let us humble ourselves before God, and petition for his mercy and protection for our beloved lost one."

Surrounded by his afflicted family, the good father offered up those earnest prayers that are never offered in vain; and then, overcome with the painful excitement of the day, the family retired; not to rest, but to consider plans for the discovery of the unfortunate Jack.

" Now, my children," said the pale and anxious father, when they met in consultation next morning, " My duty and inclination alike call on me to seek my son. I will go forth, clad in the armour which God gives to his ministers,—Faith in his blessed word; and thus armed, I will preach the Gospel to the heathen."

" That, I fervently trust, you shall do, my dear sir," said Lewis; " but this is not your favourable moment, believe me. You are not able to gallop across the Pampas, to ford rivers, to travel night and day, regardless of food or rest, in order to search out the robbers and obtain restitution. Let the young and active undertake this duty; your hour will yet come, I feel assured."

" But I may, surely, be permitted to go and search for my brother," said Maria. " I can ride and endure hardships. I would enter the tents of the Indians, and entreat them to restore my brother to me."

" That cannot be, Maria," replied Lewis, firmly. " We know your ardent desire to aid us, but your presence would only impede our efforts; a female would sink under the hardships of our proposed journey, and could not possibly assist us. And now, my friends, I am of opinion, that out of the four who are really fit for this attempt, two must be left to protect the fortress. I leave you to determine who shall have the honour and responsibility of the adventure."

" May I speak, Lewis," said Matilda. " I will not direct, but I may advise. I think you, or Almagro, must be left in command of the fort ; for Tom is too *dreamy*, and Charles too hasty, for the office."

" My dear girl, you are quite right in this instance," answered Lewis. " And because our dear friend Almagro's feelings might become too deeply excited in any encounter with his foes, and discretion must be one of our strongest weapons, I propose to lead the party myself, taking Charles for my *aide-de-camp*. Almagro will carefully protect the dear family here ; Wallace will be a staunch and vigilant sentinel, and you, Matilda, must take care that Tom does not dream. And now, Charles, let us set out ; no time must be lost ; I will mount Pampero, and you must take old Niger, who is strong as well as swift."

The preparations were soon completed ; the saddlebags were filled with charqui and biscuits, some coloured beads, and a supply of ammunition ; bolas and lassoes were attached to the saddles ; each had a long knife in his girdle, a double-barrelled rifle for himself (and they did not forget to carry one for Jack), and across his shoulder a long bullock's horn suspended, to carry water. Each had a good telescope, procured by Almagro at Santiago, and each wore a warm poncho which was to form his bed at night ; for no hardships were to be regarded in this important undertaking.

CHAPTER XXII.

The Search for Jack on the Southern Pampas. The Indian
Bridge. Discovery of the Indian Huts, and Jack in Captivity.
The Indian Hunters. The Escape. The Destruction of the
Bridge. A terrible Nocturnal Visitor.

AFTER Almagro had received their last injunctions,
the two gentlemen parted from their mourning
friends, and continued to ride along the banks of
the river till they reached its confluence with the
large stream, which flowed to the south; then they
paused to consider whether they should attempt to
cross the river, or continue to travel towards the
south.   On the latter course they finally agreed; and
riding swiftly over the level plain, proceeded about
fifteen miles before they permitted their weary horses
to rest.   They then carefully examined the country
round them; they were on a grassy plain upon which
lofty trees were scattered with the graceful order of
Nature; but no trace of man appeared.   The agouti
was, bounding over the plain, the partridge springing
from the long grass, the parrot chattering on one
tree and the mocking-bird repeating the unmusical
note from another.   It was a beautiful solitude, and
the two friends sighed at the conviction that the
solitude had never been disturbed.

"We are certainly not on the track, Lewis," said
Charles; "and I regret now that we did not bring
the sagacious Wallace, he would certainly have tracked
his friend Jack."

"I had the thought myself," replied Lewis, "but
I was unwilling to deprive the fortress of its best
guard; and, moreover, I believe it would have been
an act of imprudence, for we could not certainly have

approached the tents secretly if the dog had been our companion, and open defiance would have been madness.''

Charles climbed a tall tree, and swept the country with his glass, but was unable to discover a smoke to guide them in their course; and after an hour's rest and refreshment, they once more mounted, and, travelling more to the south-east, accomplished fifteen miles more before excessive fatigue and the increasing darkness compelled them to desist. They selected the shelter of a large tree for their lodging, tying the horses to the tree with a long lasso, which permitted them to feed. Then, lighting a fire to guard them from the wild beasts, they ate a little food, and lay down rolled in their ponchos; and though the night was cold, and the solitude mournful, they slept profoundly.

They rose at daybreak, and after breakfasting on bread and water, which they had brought with them, for they had only continued a few miles on the course of the river, they again surveyed the country, and fancied that at a great distance towards the east they could distinguish cattle or horses on the plain. They concluded that the Indians would be most likely to settle on a spot frequented by cattle, and therefore set out in that direction, though Lewis was unwilling to go so far from the Cordilleras.

But this day passed, like the preceding one, without their meeting with any trace of man, or seeing the cattle, which had probably fled before them. They saw only the ostrich scouring the plain, which had now become undulating, and the grass now rich and thick, but, to their great distress, they reached no water. They believed that they were now about twenty miles from the Andes, though the lofty mountains appeared still close at hand, and they had travelled about fifty miles south from Esperanza.

The third day, the water they carried in the horns was exhausted, and they went on with languid frames and fainting hearts. Lewis suggested that their best plan now was to proceed directly south, by which means they must certainly reach one of the many rivers which flow from the Andes, and towards the evening they heard, long before it was in sight, the joyful sound of the rushing waters.

They set forward with new vigour, and at length reached the lofty banks of a noble river; but it was some time before they found a break in the rocky shores, which enabled them to reach the water, and enjoy the delicious draught, in which luxury the panting horses gladly participated. Then, reluctant to leave the long-desired acquisition, they lay down under a tall willow, close to the stream, and slept the sleep of the weary. It was not till the next morning that they were struck with the embarrassing thought of how they should cross the river. It was not more than twenty feet broad, but, confined between steep banks, it was deep and rapid. They did not dare to risk swimming the horses across the torrent, as besides being weakened by fatigue, the animals carried the precious stores of their provision and ammunition.

" Surely," observed Charles, " there will be a ford lower down; for the marauding Indians, in their excursions to the north, must necessarily cross the river."

" There can be no doubt of it," replied Lewis; " we must therefore ride down the shore, and shall thus, at all events, have no scarcity of water to-day. Besides, I think that I now observe a large lake lying to the left."

" There certainly is," answered Charles; " but tell me, Lewis, what are those curious gorgeous birds crowded on the banks?"

They rode up to the lake, which was a large salina, and in the beds of mud on the banks, the birds continued to wade about, careless of their approach.

" These bright creatures," said Lewis, " are flamingoes. Observe the long slender neck, and immensely long legs of the bird, which, though the body is not larger than a goose, stands as high as you, and at

U

a distance, when standing in a line, with their bright scarlet plumage, you might take a flock of these birds for a regiment of soldiers. They are now busy seeking for the worms which burrow in that briny mud of such ill-odour, and I think the flesh of the bird can scarcely escape the taint; so we will leave them to parade their beauty in unmolested peace, and content ourselves with our hard charqui; not even being tempted to try that extraordinary luxury of the epicurean Romans, a dish of flamingoes' tongues. See, Charles, these large crystals in the mud are gypsum, and these are sulphate of soda; I regret that we dare not encumber ourselves with them at present, but doubtless in the salinas near Esperanza we might discover the same deposites."

After riding about two miles down the river, they arrived at a sort of suspension bridge, of indifferent workmanship, evidently formed by untaught men, but truly welcome to their sight. Three short, strong poles were driven into the ground, about a yard apart from each other, to each of these was fastened the end of a thick strong rope of twisted hide; a sort of platform was laid on these three ropes, by attaching a number of transverse rods close together, twisting the ropes round each end and the middle. This platform was stretched across the river, and secured to three posts in the same way on the opposite side. The appearance of this bridge, which was much curved and very narrow, with no protection at the side, was alarming. Lewis walked upon it himself first—he found there was a dangerous oscillation; but there was no other resource, so they dismounted, and, one after the other, led the unwilling horses over the perilous pass. The poor animals trembled greatly, but, by keeping exactly in the middle of the bridge, they all got over in safety. Lewis then paused, and looking at the bridge, he said, " Charles, we must mark this spot, and take care to strike on it at our return, if God spares us to return."

They were now confident of the direction, and became more cautious, as they were certainly on the track of Indians; they even saw the marks of the horses' feet on the grass, and they were careful to follow the same track exactly, that they might leave no trace of their own. When they rested to eat their scanty meal, Charles mounted a tree, as usual, to take a survey around. " Come up, Lewis," he cried, " and tell me if you do not see smokes; I believe we are near the enemy now." The smokes were indeed within a mile of them, and it was necessary to use double caution and consideration.

On the right hand, about twenty yards from them, a thick wood extended far to the south, and riding up close to this protection, they proceeded onward slowly and watchfully, determined at the least alarm to take to the wood. When they arrived within a quarter of a mile of the smokes, they came in sight of a group of dark huts; then plunging into the wood, they made their way through thickets till they reached a convenient spot, where a little pasturage was left uncovered by bushes, and securing their horses, they sat down to consult.

" Our first endeavour," said Lewis, " must be to ascertain if Jack is actually in the power of this tribe; our next must be to open a communication with him. As this appears to be the nearest settlement, though it must be sixty or seventy miles from Esperanza, we have reason to conclude that these men must be the robbers."

" I have no doubt of it," answered Charles; " but you will see, my dear Lewis, that we must separate. It will never do to risk all our force at once; permit me then to take my rifle and go forward to reconnoitre."

" Thank you, Charles," replied Lewis; " but I have a fixed notion that I have the cooler head of the two. I will take the first chance, and if I fall, or am captured, do your best, my good fellow."

They shook hands, and the tears were in Charles's

eyes when he reluctantly agreed to remain in the
same spot till Lewis returned, or at least for some
hours. "At all events," he said, " I shall mount a
tree, and establish a look-out."

Lewis assured him he intended to follow the same
prudent plan, and took his leave. Firm as his nerves
were, and strong as the friendly motive which prompted
the attack was, it was not without an acceleration of
the pulse that he stole cautiously through the bushes
till he reached a narrow streamlet, which he crossed
with ease, and then found himself opposite to the end
of the cluster of huts, which were arranged in a semicircle, facing the south.

Lewis was not fifty yards from the huts, and could
see that these wretched habitations were merely formed
by placing three poles triangularly, tied together at
the top, and covered with the hides of oxen or horses,
a small opening being left at the side. The hut that
stood in the centre of the semicircle had a more
finished appearance ; it was of square form, and much
larger than the rest, but, like them, was only covered
with skins. Before the huts, a number of children,
quite naked, were rolling about, playing with two or
three spiteful-looking curs, the sight of which alarmed
Lewis greatly, lest they should scent the approach of
a stranger. Two or three women were standing watching the children. They were not ungraceful in form
or features ; their complexion was a clear brown, their
eyes dark and lustrous, and their long black hair,
which was plaited in tresses, hung down their backs,
ornamented with the coloured feathers of the parrot
and flamingo. Their heads were encircled with coloured
fillets, and a loose poncho, of coarse wool or skin,
was thrown over the shoulders, leaving the arms
uncovered.

Lewis had now ascended a tree of sufficiently thick
foliage to conceal him, and he thus obtained a better
view of the unconscious Indians. After a few minutes,
he saw a woman come from the entrance of the prin-

cipal hut. She was dressed with more taste and neatness than the rest: a poncho of bright scarlet flowed
down to her feet, and her head was gracefully ornamented with silver bands, and the waving feathers of
the ostrich. She was followed by a slight, tall figure,
clothed in a skin poncho, and leading a little child.
The fair hair announced one of a different race, and
Lewis felt immediately assured that this disguised
figure was Jack.

The woman, turning to caress the child, appeared
to be conversing with the attendant; a circumstance
which greatly delighted Lewis, who saw that Jack's
aptitude to accommodate himself to circumstances
had robbed his slavery of its worst features, restraint
and ill-treatment. The skin-clad attendant then caught
up the child, and began to sport with it, throwing up
a ball and catching it, and, by his graceful and active
movements, Lewis recognized with certainty the dear
lost lad.

After the game at ball had continued some time,
the female took the child, and retired into the hut;
but Jack moved to a distance from the rest, and stood
leaning pensively against a tree. Lewis thought this
a favourable moment, and he ventured to utter the
peculiar note of one of the shrikes, which the young
people at Esperanza frequently amused themselves
by imitating. This bird, *Saurophagus sulphuratus*, was
commonly heard near the shores of the river, which it
frequented in the autumn, when it was migrating from
the north, to catch the small fish. Its peculiar shrill
notes were always pleasing to Maria, who told her
friends that this bird was named by the Spanish
Guachos *Bien-te-veo* (I see you well), from its cry
resembling these articulated sounds. Jack looked up
at the first cry, and then resumed his melancholy
position and air; but Lewis repeating the notes more
sharply, he started, appeared to meditate for a moment,
and then answered in the same familiar notes. He
seemed at once himself again, understanding that

friends were at hand ; and he was about to cross over to the wood from whence the sound proceeded, when the loud discordant blast of a horn was heard. To this succeeded the sound of voices, and the trampling of horses, and a large body of Indians appeared galloping towards the huts, dragging after them their long spears, and the dead bodies of several bullocks, mares, and guanacoes.

At the sound of the horn, Jack had withdrawn into the hut ; but when the Indians arrived, he again appeared, with the lady in scarlet, and the little boy. A number of women rushed from the huts tumultuously, greeting their mates, and seizing the produce of the chase. They commenced, with long knives, to skin and cut up the animals, and the ground before the huts was speedily a scene of carnage. In the mean time the men led their horses to the corral, an inclosure that lay between the huts and the wood in which Lewis was concealed. The chief, however, who was distinguished by his silver diadem and snowy plumes, retired, with the lady and child, into the large hut, leaving his horse in charge of Jack, who led it to the corral, whistling loudly as he went, the familiar air, " Meet me by moonlight," to the great satisfaction of Lewis, who understood that Jack was making ready for the attempt.

Having turned the horse into the corral, the boy returned to the outside of the huts with the silver stirrups and trappings of the horse, and sitting down, he began to clean them with grass. Then putting down his work, he went forward towards the wood, gathering, as he went, some dry moss, as if for the purpose of rubbing the harness. He wandered on till he was not far from the tree in which his friend lay, and Lewis ventured to say, in a low, distinct tone, " Be prudent, prompt, and ready ; when can you come ? "

Jack, still stooping with his face to the ground, answered, " At midnight, if possible : they are all fatigued—they will not go out to-night. Do you want any provision ? "

" We should be glad of some slices of beef," said Lewis ; adding again, " be very calm and prudent."

" But, I had nearly forgotten one thing—the dogs?" said the boy, inquiringly.

" Give them meat," said Lewis, " over which you must strew this powder," and he flung down a paper containing a preparation, which was in fact intended for the jailer, if he had found Jack in confinement.

Jack hesitated, and then said, " I cannot kill them, Lewis, for I know them all."

" My dear lad, I promise, this will stupify, but not injure them," said Lewis.

Jack was satisfied, and, snatching up the paper, he concealed it under his poncho, and returned, with a handful of moss, to clean the harness. For some time a great confusion continued before the huts : the women cut long strips of flesh, which, with the skins of the animals, were hung up to dry. Then they feasted on the raw flesh, and washed their hair in the pools of blood. It was a revolting sight, and Lewis, who felt some interest in the female who appeared to be the mistress of Jack, was glad to observe that she, as well as the chief, remained in their hut during the noisy revels : and Jack, after he had concluded his task, took the harness into the same hut.

All this time Lewis had not dared to leave his concealment in the tree, lest some accident should betray him. At length darkness came on ; one after another the Indians retired to the huts, and all was still. Then, by the light of a young moon, he saw Jack steal out, carrying a large piece of meat, which he threw to the dogs, which were then noisily quarrelling over the fragments of the feast. They rushed on the new spoil, and soon tore it in pieces and devoured it ; a great satisfaction to Lewis, who was confident of the success of the preparation, which was a powerful opiate. In another hour all was silence and, he trusted, security.

He watched anxiously for several minutes ; then he

heard a rustling sound below the tree, and a whisper of " Lewis! dear Lewis ! "

The boy had actually crawled through the long grass, and, by the dim light, had been unmarked, even by the watchful Lewis.

In a moment he was down from the tree, and seizing Jack's hand, was plunging with him into the thick wood.

" Stay one moment, Lewis, and tell me, have you a horse for me ? " asked Jack.

" We have not, my boy ; you must mount behind Charles on Niger," was the reply.

" I have a lasso ; and I think I can take one from the corral unperceived," said Jack ; putting a large piece of beef into his friend's hand, and unrolling the lasso.

This was a dangerous undertaking, but the necessity was great; and though Lewis was aware Mr. Merton would not have sanctioned it, he consented to the experiment, determining to turn the animal loose when they reached home. So Jack crept quietly to the corral, and selecting a horse he knew to be swift and untiring, he led it out quietly, and brought it safely into the shelter of the wood. They moved onward without a word, till they reached the anxious and half-despairing Charles. No time could be spared for greeting ; they mounted without delay, and dashed forward over the plain, as nearly as Lewis could calculate in the track they had come on in the morning ; but the moon was set, and they had to rely greatly on the sagacity of the horses.

For five hours they travelled without rest, and morning began to dawn; still the river, anxiously looked for, was not in sight. The horses began to flag, and they proposed to take a short rest ; but just as they drew up, Charles exclaimed, " Hist! I fear we are pursued ! "

It was too true ; they could distinguish the rushing of the horses, and the cry of the pursuers through the clear morning air. They looked on each other with dismay: " On! on!" cried Lewis. " Let us only reach the river, and we may yet escape. We surely cannot now be far from it; and see, we are on the track that leads to the bridge."

In fact, the horses, even in the dark, had kept on the beaten road, and now, as if sensible of the danger of their riders, they pressed on vigorously. Charles looked back; he saw a dark moving mass at a distance, threatening destruction; a few minutes after he looked again; the Indians gained upon them; another quarter of an hour, and they were lost. " Lewis!" he cried, " all is over; the Indians are close at our heels."

" Hark! Charley!" answered Lewis; " listen to the music of the torrent! Now, my good fellow, I know you can swim the river; so be making ready, as we gallop on. You must save us!"

In five minutes they reached the bridge, and dismounted. " Now Charles," said Lewis, " you remain here till we lead the horses over. Give us your clothes, which you are better without. As soon as we have crossed, cut the ropes on your side; I will do the same on the opposite side. Then plunge in, and swim over. But first let me throw this long lasso round your waist, the end of which I shall attach to my arm; for we will not have you sacrificed for our sake."

All was accomplished with the speed of lightning. They crossed the bridge in safety; and while Jack held the panting, trembling horses, permitting them to drink, and feast on a mouthful of grass, Lewis and Charles at the same moment cut the strong ropes through at each end of the bridge, which was immediately whirled down the rapid stream, and was out of sight before Charles, holding his long knife between his teeth, had swam across. The Indians were now within a hundred yards of the river, shrieking loudly, and threatening with their long spears; and

though the young men were rather curious to see the
effect the loss of the bridge would have on their
pursuers, they thought it prudent to move forward,
though they now proceeded leisurely.

They looked round when they heard the loud cries
of the Indians on their discovery of the stratagem,
and saw that great confusion pervaded the party;
who, finally, rode off swiftly down the course of the
river.

"I hope they have no other bridge," exclaimed
Lewis.

"I have reason to believe they have not," said
Jack. "And it will take weeks to cut the wood and
make another. I think they are following the stream
in hopes of recovering the bridge."

"I trust they may go on," answered Lewis; "for
it must be a tremendous impediment that could
arrest such a cumbrous float; and it would take a
long time to replace it."

"I know that this bridge was formed when the
river was frozen over," said Jack; "and they were
thus able to cross it. None of this tribe can swim,
or would venture to swim their horse over a river
like this. But we must always be on the watch; for
I know we have many a weary league to pass before
we reach dear Esperanza."

They were all of opinion that it would now be
advisable to diverge towards the mountains, as the
woods which extended along the foot of the rocks
offered shelter, and many streams were to be met
with; besides they were certain of losing no ground
if they followed the sure guidance of the Cordilleras.
They soon fell in with a shallow stream flowing
directly from the mountains, and Jack proposed that
they should ascend in the water for some miles, and
thus disguise the track, which the Indians can readily
detect on the plains.

The plan being approved, they rode up the stream
for five or six miles; then entering a thicket of low

trees, they sat down to rest themselves and their weary horses. They even ventured to make a fire and boil some beef, for, hungry as they were, they could not eat it raw. Then Jack heard the story of the distress at home, and the anxious search made by his two friends."

"We must defer hearing your story till we get home, Jack," said Charles. "Only tell me, is that graceful, scarlet-robed princess, an Indian?"

"No, Charley; that is the very best thing in all my story," replied Jack; "but I cannot help telling it now. That is Zara! Almagro's Zara! And she knows her father is well, and is our dear friend. And she knew I meant to escape; but the tribe are all so ferocious she could not help me. Now I will tell no more till I get home."

"As if we did not know all now," said Charles, laughing, "How Zara is the wife of the noble-looking chief; and how she was divided between her duty to her husband and her father."

Lewis stopped Charles, declaring it was not fair to extort the story by anticipations and guesses; so Jack was allowed to preserve all that remained of his secret till he got home.

After dinner they accomplished another fifteen miles, still approaching nearer the mountains; then entirely worn out for want of rest, they unharnessed the horses, tied them to the trees, and wrapped in their ponchos, with their saddles for pillows, they slept profoundly. An unusual growling sound awoke Charles, who, looking up drowsily, saw two large eyes glaring through the bushes.

He was wide awake in a moment, and, seizing his rifle, was about to fire, when a large puma sprung across Jack, who was lying at the feet of Charles, and alighted on the unfortunate Indian horse, which Jack had tied close to his own sleeping-place. The huge beast seized the head of the horse, and drawing it back, dislocated the neck; and in a moment had plunged into the woods beyond with its spoil, and was out of sight. Charles was mortified that he had lost the opportunity of firing at the beast; but Lewis, who as well as Jack was waked up with the tumult, was only too grateful that they had all escaped, and that the puma had preferred horse flesh to human flesh.

CHAPTER XXIII.

The tedious Journey completed. The Alarm-bell. Skirmish with the Indians. The Destruction of the Hut. The Wounded Indian. Jack's Story of his Captivity, and the Account of the Indian Attack.

"AND now, Charles," said Lewis, "we shall be compelled to trouble Niger to carry double. There is nothing else for it; and the sooner we leave this puma-haunted wood the better; we shall enjoy our breakfast more at the next station."

Charles and Jack mounted the steady Niger, who evinced as much reluctance as they did to this undignified practice; but the case was urgent; and after obtaining a supply of water, they set out with some abatement of speed. They had not proceeded far when they came in sight of a troop of horses, and Jack begged to be allowed to mount Pampero, and lasso a horse for himself, an exploit he speedily accomplished, taking care to select one with the mane and tail cropped, the marks of servitude which proclaimed that it was broken in, and ready for use; for it is the custom of the Indians, as well as the Guachos, to turn their horses loose when they are fatigued, and lasso others from the troops which are scattered over the Pampas, half wild, and half accustomed to the bridle.

The horse was strong and swift, and Jack felt himself

a man once more. The friends now galloped forward cheerfully, and made a full day's journey unmolested ; but the necessary refreshment of the evening exhausted all their provision, and they had still two days' journey before them. Next morning they set out without breakfast, and travelled, faint and spiritless, for some hours, when fortunately an agouti crossed their path, which immediately fell a sacrifice. They were too anxious for food to proceed now, therefore, alighting, and looking carefully round to ascertain that no puma lurked in the bushes, they tethered their horses, and began their labour. Charles offered to be groom, and Jack to make the fire and broil the meat, if Lewis, who was more accustomed to such bloody tasks than they were, would undertake to skin and cut up the agouti. Indeed, Jack declared he should never like to see raw meat again ; he had been so sickened with the disgusting habits of his captors, who never cooked their food.

"I say, Lewis," observed Charles, "these fellow-creatures of ours require a strong pull up the ladder of civilization before they reach that step when they attain the grand distinction of man, and are classed as cooking animals."

"Zara was kind enough to permit me," said Jack, "to broil a slice of meat over a fire I made in some corner, while the men were out hunting. She had herself become accustomed to eat raw flesh ; but when I had persuaded her to try my cookery, she recovered her former taste, and said she would always eat her meat broiled, for it recalled the memory of home. I taught her to cook ; and I hope she will persuade the chief to eat of her cookery."

"And thus, you see, Charles," said Lewis, "the first step up the ladder will be accomplished. The work of civilization is continually progressing ; and whatever may be the secondary means, it must be accomplished, for God has ordained it."

As they talked, the agouti was skinned and cut into small pieces, which were spitted on a thin wooden rod and placed before the fire. The party sat round anxiously watching till the meat assumed some appearance of cooked food, and then eat it from the spit in a true savage fashion, without salt, and, unfortunately, without water, as they had met with none during the day. After dinner, they carefully collected the fragments and journeyed onwards, and before night they happily arrived at a stream, and refreshed their parched frames with the precious beverage.

Morning saw them spring up with joyful hopes; forgetting their weak and languid state, they ate their breakfast merrily, filled the horns with water, and then set out, careless of providing more food, and all thinking only of home. But a long day's journey completely wore out the horses, which now could only move slowly, even when the riders dismounted and led them; and Lewis frequently looked anxiously round, for now they had no chance of escaping pursuit. How relieved they felt when they caught the first view of the lofty green hills that bounded their sweet valley at the east! But the shades of evening had come on before they reached the banks of their own beloved river.

As they paused a moment to refresh themselves at the stream, Jack suddenly started, and with a pale and anxious countenance cried out, "Lewis! see here the recent traces of many horsemen. Let us on! the Indians have been here! Oh, my dear, dear friends, shall I never see you more!"

It was terrible to see Jack desponding; his buoyant spirits usually rose above every care and sorrow; but this fearful sight entirely overcame him. No more words were spoken; the wearied horses were urged on; the rifles were examined; all was made ready for the expected conflict. At that moment the sound of the bell reached their ears; they knew their friends were still safe, but calling on them for assistance, and this thought restored even Jack to hope. Then they heard the well-known, ever-dreaded shriek of the Indians, mingled with confused cries.

"Seek the shelter of the wood," said Lewis; "from thence we may surprise them, and they may not discover the weakness of our force; but let no one fire till I speak."

They arrived in sight of their fortress; and, heart-rending sight! they beheld the fence which they had trusted in as perfectly secure blazing furiously, and by the light they saw the dark countenances of a horde of mounted savages, who were continually flinging fresh torches on the fence to complete the work of destruction.

Lewis whispered a few words of instruction to his friends, then gave the word; they immediately set up three loud cheers, and at the same moment fired their three rifles at the back of the enemy. They had neither time nor necessity to discharge their second barrel, for the dismayed Indians, believing they were attacked by a numerous force, fled with precipitation, leaving one of their number lying wounded on the ground, still holding the bridle of his horse.

The shouts of the friends and the report of their fire-arms were music to the ears of the half-distracted family; and Maria, from her old station on the observatory, having proclaimed the retreat of the enemy, the gate was speedily unbarred to admit the welcome guests. But there was no time for explanation or rejoicing; the fire was rapidly spreading; and though the water and pipes were ready, there were no hands to work. The attack had been so sudden that, except Almagro, no one had possessed power to act. The cool presence of mind of Lewis, and the activity of his two assistants, were invaluable, they soon poured a torrent of water and extinguished the flames of the fence, but not before the roof of Mr. Merton's house had caught fire.

Every one was now employed, for even the females hastened to remove their valuable possessions from the endangered hut. Mr. Merton brought out all his books and papers. Nanny saved her churn, corn-mill, and pans. They brought away the chests of linen,

P. 304.

Charles and Tom brought the senseless form of the stranger to Almagro's hut, Jack
following them, leading the horse.

clothes, and crockery, and at last anything they first
caught up; but much was lost, for the old hut was
burnt to the ground before the conflagration was finally
arrested; and it was only the joy of seeing dear Jack
again that consoled the bereaved family for this
misfortune.

After the fire was extinguished, Jack's first thought
was of the poor Indian left lying on the field of battle.
Charles and Tom brought the senseless form of the
stranger to Almagro's hut, Jack following them, leading
the horse.   The Indian was a youth about sixteen
years of age, dark complexioned, with long black hair,
which was bound with a fillet of silver, indicating that
he was a chief, or the son of a chief. A scarlet poncho
bound round his waist, and boots formed from the
skin of the colt's leg, were all the clothes he wore.
A long knife was stuck in his girdle, and his lance was
lying by his side on the ground where he was found.
Lewis found that his arm was shattered by a shot; the
wound had bled profusely, and caused him to faint;
but strong applications were used, and he recovered
his senses, opened his large and piercing eyes, and
looked round with a glance of perfect bewilderment.
Lewis held a cup to his lips, and induced him to swallow
some cordial, the youth gazing on him with wonder
and awe.   "Do not be alarmed," said Lewis, in
Spanish, "you are with friends."   The lad seemed to
comprehend him, for he made an effort to speak, but
could not utter a word from his weakened state. But
Lewis, still concluding that he understood the Spanish
language, which many of the chiefs acquire from
trading, in their wanderings, with the towns of La
Plata, told him, in a few plain words, that his life was
in danger from his wounds and fractured arm; but
that, if he was patient and obedient, he hoped that he
might be enabled to cure him.

The young man evidently understood what was
said, for he shook his head, and closing his eyes,
stretched out his body to indicate death. Lewis

owing them, leading the horse.

P. 304.

Charles and Tom brought the senseless form of the stranger to Almagro's hut, Jack
following them, leading the horse.

examined the arm, and with the assistance of his young friends, reduced the fracture, bound up the wounds, and inclosed the limb in a frame of bark; he then enjoined the youth to swallow a cup of medicine, which he presented to him, for the purpose of composing him to sleep. The patient, who had never shrunk during the painful operation, received the draught passively, and in a short time was in a profound sleep, on Almagro's bed of skins.

Lewis assuring them the youth might be safely left, as he would not wake for some hours, the family all united under the roof that was still left for them,—the house built for their departed friends. Almagro took the precaution to place the kennel of Wallace near the breach the fire had left in the fence, and then they all sat down to hear the tale of Jack. Nanny placed before them the unusual luxury of tea, which was particularly grateful to Jack, after his long confinement to flesh diet; and gathered cheerfully round the tea-table, in the pleasant hall, the united family forgot for a time their late terrors, their losses, and the peril to which they were still exposed.

" Now, Almagro," said Jack, " look at me, and tell me if you can find out the good news I have for you ? "

Almagro was much agitated; he was scarcely able to utter in a tremulous voice the words,—" My child ! "

" Yes, my dear Almagro," replied Jack, " I have seen Zara; she is living, and well; and as happy as she can be, separated from her father."

Almagro covered his face with his hands; he did not speak for many minutes, and all respected his silence; then he said, " It is well, my dear boy; you have restored me to happiness. Now tell your story, that I may learn how this wonderful discovery occurred."

" When I left dear Maria in the wood," said Jack, " my great anxiety was to gain time, that she might

x

escape. I walked up to the chief, and addressing him in Spanish, I said, ' Great chief, I am not your enemy, therefore pray pass on, and leave me to gather pinones on these wide plains that God has given to all the world.' He smiled, and I do believe he would have let me go, but his people surrounded me, bound my arms, and one ugly fellow dragged me up, and placed me before him on his horse.

" You may be sure I was angry and a little frightened, especially about Maria, and I called out in English some words of comfort to her ; the Indians, I believe, thought I was imploring their pity, for they laughed contemptuously.

" The chief did not seem half-pleased with his men ; but the Indians are not slaves to their chief, and he has less of his own way than you would fancy. However, he rode up to me and said, in very indifferent Spanish, ' Fear not, Christian, you are my property, and I never slay but in battle.'

" We rode on for some days, sleeping on the bare ground at night ; and once in the day we rested, when an ox or a mare was killed for the occasion, and pieces were cut off, and eaten by the Indians on the spot, without ceremony, cookery, or seasoning. For my part, I had luckily preserved my bag of pinones, which was hung over my shoulder, and which nobody seemed to covet. On these I breakfasted, dined, and supped, to the great amusement of my captors, who doubtless considered me in the light of a two-legged hog.

" It was dull work, that long journey ; the tears often rose to my eyes, but I kept them down ; I did not want the rogues to fancy I was faint-hearted. Then I ruminated on plans of escape ; and on the schemes going forward at Esperanza, for I was sure of you, my good fellows. I knew you would find me, even if I was carried to Cape Horn. The Indians in the mean time killed lots of bullocks and mares, which were tied to the saddles and dragged after them; and at last the journey did come to an end, and in the midst of the imposing procession, I made my first appearance at the huts.

" The first sounds I heard were the tongues of women chattering loudly, children crying, and dogs barking; and in the midst of the strange multitude I was put down, to be stared at by the women, yelped at by the dogs, and tormented by the children, who pulled my hair, tore away my clothes, picked my pockets, and took my pinones for playthings. Then began the disgusting work of the shambles, and while all were engaged, the chief, after speaking in a tone of authority to the man who had been my guard, cut my bonds, and waving me to follow him, entered the principal hut of the group. He was met by a female, whose complexion and features were not Indian, and whose dress had a grace and neatness beyond that of the furies I had encountered at my arrival at the *toldos*."

" Do tell me what her dress was ? " demanded Matilda.

" I will tell you as well as I can," answered Jack. " She wore a bright scarlet poncho, thrown over one shoulder, brought under the other arm, and fastened round her with a long sash made of twisted wool, of very gay colours. Her feet and arms were uncovered ; but she had bracelets of silver, and a silver band, or diadem, round her beautiful black hair, from which hung a plume of ostrich feathers. She held by the hand a pretty boy, who was dressed much in the same manner as his father,—for he was the son of the chief, and the lady was his wife, his only wife ; some of the men had two or three wives. And this really lovely girl, the wife of the chief, was, as I see Almagro has guessed, his daughter, Zara.

" The chief spoke to his wife long and kindly in the language of his tribe, pointing to me occasionally. She looked on me with interest, and after the chief had left the tent, she addressed me in Spanish,

x 2

asked if my father was a Guacho, and where his hut was. I told her in as few words as possible our tale of misfortunes; then I described our happy little home in the wilderness, and the misery my dear parents would feel at my fate.

"She appeared greatly moved, and said, ' Yet such was my early history; I, too, was torn from my parents, and brought among strangers; but they were kind to me, and I learnt to love them, and to accommodate myself to their habits. Still I have never forgotten my dear home, my noble father, and my gentle mother, who would never, I fear, survive the loss of her Zara.'

" I was not at all surprised when she said this, for I was quite sure at first she would turn out to be Zara; but I said very quietly, 'Was the name of your father Almagro di Valdivia ? '

"She shrieked out, ' Do you know my father, boy; and is he living ? '

" I told her you were living, and were my very best friend,—one of our happy little community. She was greatly excited; she clasped her hands, and uttered rapidly many words of Spanish and Indian intermingled. I understood that she was asking me, in a distracted manner, many questions about you and her mother; and I thought the best answer would be to tell her your whole story, how we became acquainted, and all your anxiety about her, till you were visited by a gleam of hope on recognising her work in the embroidered trappings of the wounded Indian horse.

" Her eyes glistened as she said, ' Was it not a happy thought that I should embroider my cipher, as dear mamma had taught me to work it, on the saddle-cloth ? And I sympathized with Cangapol, when he regretted the loss of it so much, little suspecting that it had happily fallen into the hands of my own beloved father.'

" She wept much at the death of her mother, and

wished to see her father, but could not bear to abandon her husband. 'He is so kind to me,' she said, 'and would take no other wife; because the daughter of a Guacho must have her hut to herself. Besides that, my boy, my *Cacique Chico* forms another link to bind me to a strange people.'

"This irresolution appeared very strange to me; yet at first I was afraid to tell her what I thought; but after some days, when I got used to her, and saw she was kind and gentle, and liked to talk to me, I took courage and said, 'Zara, it is your duty to abandon the dark errors of this heathen people, and to return to your God. Your husband and your people abhor Christians, and you cannot worship God among these savages.'

"She wept at my words, and said, 'I have not forgotten the prayers my mother taught me; I repeat them daily, and have tried to prevail on Cangapol to join me; but he tells me, kindly, to pray in my own way; his God is a God of battles and slaughter, and loves only the brave, who, after their death, are happy in wide hunting fields, with plenty of food to eat. And I fear I had learned to wish that I might join that hunting field of the brave dead, and had almost forgotten the faith of my childhood, till your words reminded me that Christians worship a God of peace, who forbids them to shed blood; is it not so, boy?'

"I spoke to her with my best ability of the beautiful history of the Son of God, who walked on earth, enduring the hardships, the sorrows, and the sufferings of the world, that he might save the world. She listened with attention, and wished she could tell it all to Cangapol, who would not, she feared, condescend to listen to me. One day she asked me to speak of these wonderful things to Sausimian, the uncle of the chief, who was sick and infirm; and whom, she told me, the young Indians wished to strangle, because, when the toldos were removed, it would add to their labour to have to carry a man who was so aged that

he was wholly useless. ' I induced Cangapol,' added
she, ' to insist on the life of the aged sufferer being
spared.   He has no wife or child, and I have visited
him daily to take him charqui and cool water.   He
lies on his couch of death, seeing death before him,
and recoiling from it; in his old and feeble state he
does not believe that hunting-grounds can be a scene
of happiness.   Talk to him, good English boy, he
understands the Spanish language, and tell him of the
blessed rest promised by our God to them that believe
in him.'

"I went with Zara to visit the wretched Sausimian,
whom age and painful disease had bent nearly double;
yet his mind was clear and keen; he had been in
cities where he had seen civilization, and could speak
and understand Spanish.   He evidently doubted the
existence of the Indian paradise. ' I desire no longer,'
said he, ' to slay the puma, or to drink the blood of
the wild cattle.   I cannot dart over the Pampas on
my fleet steed, seeking to burn the hut of the sleeping Christian.   I desire only the sleep of the weary.
Can death be this sleep?   Tell me, young Christian,
what is death?'

"Then, papa, I tried to remember some of your
discourses, and to repeat them to poor old Sausimian.
I told him that, to the Christian, death was but the
passage to a heaven of peace, and love, and happiness;
and that the gate of this heaven was still, by God's
mercy, open to him.   I had in my pocket when I was
taken the little Spanish New Testament dear Mr. Carruthers had given me, and Zara had rescued it for me
from the thievish boys, for she had not quite forgotten
how to read, and was glad to see a book once more.
I now read from this book many passages of the life
and doctrines of our Lord to the afflicted man; he
seemed satisfied to hear me, and I visited him continually, till the night when I hoped to escape; then
I left my precious book to Zara, who will, I am convinced, daily read to Sausimian."

" May the book be alike precious to both of them, my son!" said Mr. Merton ; "and now I am fully repaid for all my sufferings during your captivity."

" Only think," said Matilda, " that Jack, who was always considered the dunce of the family, should actually have become the first missionary amongst us."

" Jack was a careless boy, Matilda," said Mr. Merton, " but was not a dunce, and you must now be satisfied that he had not neglected the best knowledge, and that he had the rectitude to make his knowledge useful. God grant that his one talent may gain many talents."

" But why, my dear brother," asked Maria, " did you not attempt to convince and convert the chief of the unmusical name?"

" Because, Maria," said Jack, " I fear I am not half a missionary, I lacked zeal and courage; for though Cangapol gave his brief orders to me with mildness, he was reserved, taciturn, and haughty. No one conversed with him but Zara, and I left him in her hands, feeling sure that God would help her ; nor do I despair, papa, of your being called upon to teach and convince the Indian chief."

" It will be a happy day to me, my son," replied Mr. Merton, " if God permits me the duty ; I have been useless for some time, and am anxious for labour."

" Now go on, Jack," said Mary ; " did you tell Zara your plan of escape ?"

" Certainly not," answered he. " It would have been madness. She would have immediately told it to Cangapol, as her duty commanded ; and he would have called a council of his warriors to prevent me, as his duty commanded. But I tore a leaf from my pocket-book, and wrote upon it in Spanish :—' I fly to my father and to your father. Come to us, Zara, bring Cangapol and the Cacique Chico, but no warriors. I leave with you the book of God's law, read it to Sausimian, and we will pray for you all.' I put this leaf in the Testament, and placed it where she must find it, the moment before I stole out, with a beating heart, to join dear Lewis; who is such a clever fellow that I do believe he could have won the battle of Waterloo as well as Wellington did."

" As my chief exploits have either been in ambuscade or in retreat," said Lewis, laughing, " you can scarcely judge, Jack, what sort of a general I should make if it came to a regular battle."

" What furniture had the Indians in their toldos?" asked Mary.

" Nothing in the world," replied Jack, " but some heaps of ill-dried skins, which served for beds, and some rush mats for seats. Across the poles which supported the roof were the long dry slips of meat which we call charqui. The water was brought from the stream in birch-bark buckets, made by the women, and the drinking-cup was the small end of the guanaco's horn. Lances, bolas, lassoes, and a few knives, obtained in exchange for skins, completed their possessions. The toldos are very dirty, and the smell intolerable to a civilized nose; but I suppose custom obliterates the delicacy of smelling, for Zara did not seem offended with these revolting circumstances; though she preserved some of the early habits of cleanliness, and daily washed herself and her child in the stream."

Almagro was deeply affected by the recital, and thanked his friend Jack warmly for his attempt to recall his daughter to the true faith. Lewis, wishing to turn the thoughts of the father from his anxiety, begged him to tell how the savages had surprised them.

" We had separated early, and I was sitting alone in my dwelling," said Almagro, " musing on my own sorrow, and the sorrow of my friends, and beseeching God's mercy for us all, when I was roused by the furious barking of Wallace. I knew at once it was no wild beast that had excited him, for there was no fear in the tone. It was a war cry, summoning us to battle. I ran to the hall and got the guns and ammunition in readiness. Maria, unbidden, ascended to her watch, and immediately cried out, ' Send up some buckets of water, the casks are nearly empty, and I see many torches approaching.' It was indeed an unpardonable neglect that in our false security we had not looked to the water-casks. We got out the buckets and set to work, even Mrs. Merton assisting ; but by the time the casks were filled the enemy were upon us ; and I charged Tom to fix the pipes, and make all ready in case of fire, whilst I defended the gate, which they were approaching with their usual discordant cries.

"They attempted several times, like our former assailants, to force the door, but, from its fortunate position in the niche, they could not succeed ; and a single discharge of my rifle prevented them from repeating the attempt ; but, as we feared, they only retired to bring all their torches forward at once, and cast them upon the fence. I expected the water to descend immediately, and waited a few moments ; it was too long ; before I could mount the roof, the flames sprung up and were raging along the fence, and the wind being east, drove them towards the house. I found that Tom, in his agitation, had not succeeded in attaching the pipes. I assisted him, and we had just finished, when your shouts and attack on the foe revived our hopes. It was Nanny who remembered to ring the bell ; but I had little hope that you would be within hearing of it. We are, at all events, once more together, safe and well, though we have suffered some loss. Let the God who saved us be blessed."

It was too late to talk more. They did not forget in their evening devotions a special thanksgiving for their deliverance, then, Almagro undertaking the care of the wounded Indian, they retired to rest.

CHAPTER XXIV.

The Effects of the Indian Visit. Projects for Repairs. The
Young Indian Chief. The First Convert. Alarm. Jack's
Grand Discovery. The Indian Encampment. The Fugitive
Family, and their Retreat in the Cave.

THE morning revealed a scene of distressing desolation. About twenty yards of the thick impervious
fence was completely destroyed; the hut was nearly
burnt to the ground, with everything it contained,
which they had not had time to remove. It was only
by slow degrees that they discovered the full amount
of their loss; but the disappearance of many useful
articles was soon manifest. In the small yard behind
the hut the stack of fuel, built up for the winter, was
burnt; and, still more distressing, the two pet ostriches,
which were always confined in this inclosure at night,
were found lying dead: they had been suffocated by
the smoke. Mary wept over the fate of her favourites,
more even than for the loss of her guitar; for the
flames had devoured the greatest part of Mrs. Douglas's
pretty gifts, and work-boxes, drawing-boxes, and writing-
desks were nearly all gone. The tables, seats, and
beds, the work of their own hands, and too heavy to
be easily removed, were lost; and by some mischance
the pretty wardrobe of the baby was all burnt; but,
except a considerable quantity of *charqui*, all the provision was happily saved.

"These Indians will certainly come again," said
Jack, "encouraged by the destruction of the fortress.
We must consider now, how we can defend it."

"We must go to the woods immediately for the
cactus," said Lewis. "Not only must we bring
branches to fill up the breach in a temporary manner,

but we must also procure a number of young trees to plant in the place of those which are destroyed. I scarcely expect the defeated men will return so soon; I am more afraid of a visit from your captors, Jack. The two parties certainly belong to distinct tribes; and as soon as our young captive is sufficiently recovered to bear any exertion, we must endeavour to extract some information from him."

Almagro offered to remain as guard and nurse to the Indian, whom Lewis pronounced to be going on well: the rest of the young men set out, taking the waggon with them; Maria promising to ring the alarm-bell if sentinel Wallace announced any danger at hand.

They soon completed the cargo of trees; and, in crossing the river on their return, Tom pointed to the pile of brick which still remained after they had finished building the oven.

"Why," said he, " should we not raise an indestructible fence round our domain ? A wall of brick, eight or nine feet high, would render the fort impregnable; and we have all the material."

"But the work, Tom ; how do you feel inclined for the work ?" inquired Lewis.

Tom shrugged his shoulders; manual labour was not agreeable to him; he loved to project, rather than to execute. "How much we miss Mr. Douglas and John," said he ; " they were such indefatigable workers. We only want servants to assist us, to render our little colony as secure as it is lovely. Would not the Indian captive make a useful hand ?"

"It might be so," replied Lewis, drily ; " but, at present, he has no hand to be of advantage to us ; but even supposing he had recovered the use of his arm, would Mr. Merton, as governor of the settlement, tolerate slavery in his dominions ?"

"There, Tom, down goes your plan, my boy," exclaimed Jack. " Fancy papa establishing slavery, and making this brave young chief his first victim, with Master Tom for overseer, armed with a whip to

make the stubborn fellow work, like the enslaved
Israelites, at the making of bricks."

"I did not mean that we should absolutely make
him a slave," said Tom ; "but we ought not to release
him to return to his own people and report the weakness of the garrison.   He must continue our prisoner;
and why should he not work as we do ? "

"Our best plan will be to try and make friends
with him," said Charles, "and then send him back to
tell his people what good fellows we are.   The Indians
do not like labour, even when it is voluntary ; and I
fear, Tom, our prisoner would consider a day's work
with us a cruel oppression.   But if aught of the divine
nature remains in him, he must feel a spark of gratitude for kind treatment, and surely would not turn
and rend us."

"I agree with you, Charles," said Lewis ; "we must
try the experiment of kindness ; it must do some
good ; it may, by God's help, do great good.   And
now, Tom, though your gigantic plan of inclosing the
town of Esperanza with solid walls is a little beyond
our power now, we will not forget it ; and, in the mean
time, as soon as the fence is restored to a tolerable
state of security, we will take the advantage of the
waning season, and get a good stock of bricks made,
dried, and stored in the fortress ; for I propose that
we should attempt to rebuild the paternal mansion
with brick."

This vast project was received at first with acclama-
tions, to which succeeded some doubts of the possibility of accomplishing it ; but the assurances of Lewis,
and the sanguine temperament of youth, restored their
confidence ; and they determined to begin brick-
making the very next day.

But it required a whole day to remove the charred
wood, plant the young trees, and fill up the vacancies
with thick, thorny branches.   After the fence was
restored to apparent strength and firmness, they slept
more tranquilly.   The succeeding day the captive was

much better; he had eaten some bread with great relish, but could not endure broth or tea. His usual beverage had been cold water; and he looked with suspicion at the cup when Almagro presented it, saying, " No fire! Bysanti does not wish to drink fire!" But an agreeable sherbet, flavoured with strawberry-juice, of which the young ladies had prepared a large stock with honey, was very agreeable to him. He seemed more reconciled to the new faces that visited him, and occasionally spoke a few words to Almagro; but he always appeared dejected, and frequently, when he thought he was alone, he was heard to murmur, " *Madre! madre!*"

The young girls, who spoke Spanish well, frequently accompanied Lewis to visit his patient; they took him sherbet, peaches, or fresh flowers; and sometimes asked him questions, which he always answered briefly and unwillingly.

" Have you refreshing fruit and sweet flowers at your home?" asked Mary.

" The Indian warrior," answered he, " has no draught so refreshing as the blood of his enemies. He scents not the flowers that spring on the Pampas, but the track of his foes."

" But here," said Mary, " you see how happy we are, for we love the fair gifts of God, and make war on none. Will you not learn, Bysanti, to love fruit and flowers; and above all to love all men, for all are God's children?"

" Bysanti can never love the fair man," replied the Indian. " The fair man is treacherous; he holds out the tobacco and the fire-water, and says, ' Come and take,' that the Indian may go to him and be slain."

" But, Bysanti," said Lewis, " these young girls do not offer you tobacco and fire-water; the fatal gifts which are destructive to the fair man as well as to the Indian. In the wide world, there are evil and good, Bysanti, among the fair men and the dark men.

You must hold out the hand of amity to the good, and avoid the evil."

The girls smiled, and extended their hands to the Indian, who looked amazed, but touched a hand of each; then turning to Lewis, he asked, "Has that made us friends?"

"I hope it has, Bysanti," replied Lewis; "and you must not war with your friends. When you return to your people, you must not permit them to come to this place and desolate the peaceful home of your friends."

The countenance of the boy became bright. "Shall Bysanti return to his people?" exclaimed he. "Shall the mother again see the son of her heart?" He sprung on his feet, then sinking down again, he added, despondingly, "But my horse is slain; and the Indian does not roam the plains like the ostrich and the white man."

"Your horse is ready to be mounted when you are fit to travel," said Lewis; "but you must remain under my care till you are strong, and able to use your arm; and in that time you will learn how happily the Christians live."

"The great Cacique, the father of Bysanti," said the boy, "was also a Christian. Good men came from a far land; they gave knives and bright garments to the Indians, and when the black sickness visited them, the Christians healed them as you would do. They taught the Cacique and his people to call on God, and God heard them, and made them happy. Then all the tribe were Christians. But other strangers came, who were Christians also, the evil men of whom you have spoken. They drove the people from their rich-wooded hunting fields, to the barren wilderness, where the cooling stream is not found; where the puma and the jaguar make war with man. But worse than the puma and the jaguar, the cruel strangers came in mighty multitudes, and massacred the betrayed Indians. The great Cacique fell, in the midst of his warriors, and his bereaved wife carried away her helpless infant, myself, far, far from the haunts of men.

"Some of the warriors escaped the slaughter; they followed the mother of the young Cacique, they taught the boy to ride, to hunt, to wield the lance against the foe. And when they saw Bysanti was tall and strong, they hailed him as their chief, and said: 'Bysanti is brave; let him lead his warriors to slay the Christian traitors.' But Bysanti is no warrior; he is a captive, and his people will scorn him."

The Indian covered his face, and was deeply agitated. Lewis endeavoured to console him, by representing that there was no disgrace in being conquered by people who possessed such formidable weapons of warfare as they did. And the girls tried to amuse the youth with stories of the wonders of the civilised world, and of the lives of good Christian men. When they became more acquainted, Mr. Merton sat by him for hours, and with gentle and persuasive words, won him to listen to the simple doctrines of Christianity. Suffering had subdued the haughty spirit of the Indian, and he heard Mr. Merton with interest and attention; still he could not be convinced that the men who believed these truths, could ever become robbers and murderers.

"My mother has told me, that when the Cacique was driven from the dwellings of his fathers, he said, 'The God of the Christians is a great and good God, but the Christian men are cowardly murderers.' And my mother has said to me, 'Go forth, Bysanti, and slay the evil race!'"

But when Bysanti was able to form one of the happy party in the hall; when he saw the useful habits, the mutual love, and the peaceful life of his protectors, he was moved to acknowledge the superiority of a belief that produced such happy results. He was pleased to hear them read, and wished to learn himself; he was astonished with their drawings, and charmed with their music. He went with them to the chapel, and though he could not understand the words, he was awed by the devotion of the little congregation. At length he begged that he also might be a Christian ; and Mr. Merton, after a course of instruction, baptized him, naming him Paul, after the saint whose life and labours he loved to hear of.

"My tribe shall never more war against my Christian brothers," said the youth. "But when can I go to my people ? My friends, I must go to them."

"I cannot let you go for some days yet," said Lewis. "Your arm might suffer, and I should not be near to aid you."

"Why are you so very impatient to leave us, Paul ?" inquired Mary.

He looked uneasy. "I cannot be happy," said he. "My people are restless ; they will call a council ; they will mount their fleetest horses, and come to seek the body of their chief ; or to snatch him from captivity. The Christian friends of Paul may again be in danger."

Lewis did not reply, but he was startled by the suggestion, and meditated for some time on the probability and the consequences of another attack in their present defenceless condition. Matilda watched his countenance, and following him from the hut, found him pacing to and fro in the garden.

"I know your thoughts, my good friend," said she ; "you believe we are in danger, and I think the same. What shall we do ? Ought we to dismiss Paul at once with the cure of his body and soul alike incomplete ? Such a step might save us ; but I think it would not be right."

"Certainly not, my dear Matilda," answered he ; "your heart prompts you to the true course of duty. We must risk a few days longer ; for it would be impossible for Paul to ride a considerable distance without endangering his arm, and probably his life. Nor can we trust that his presence among the turbulent and incensed savages would arrest their vengeance. I do not wish to alarm your dear parents, but in case we should be driven from this sweet spot, I think it would be prudent to secrete some of our stores in the cave of the rock. Do you think we could manage this quietly and discreetly ? "

" I will do it," said Matilda ; " I only ask that Almagro may be told. With his assistance we can easily make our *cache*."

Almagro was consulted, and he agreed with them that there was ground for alarm ; and as a commencement, he immediately removed the sacks of maize and wheat which had been deposited in his hut to the cave, in which he found Nanny had her stock of honey, salted butter, and some *charqui*, which had escaped destruction at the fire. It was desirable that more meat should be dried ; and it was therefore proposed to Jack and Charles that they should go out to try to kill a bullock or a guanaco, as the larder was low ; but they were strictly forbidden to go far from home. During the absence of the youths, Almagro and Lewis hoped to accomplish the removal of the greater part of the most valued property to the cave.

Jack and Charles set out in high spirits, crossed the river, and proceeded about two miles up the valley before they fell in with any sport. Then they saw a herd of guanacoes feeding on the green slopes below the mountain wood ; they gave chase, and pursued them half a mile along the valley, when suddenly the whole herd took to the mountain, plunging through the thick wood. The hunters were never deterred by difficulties ; they followed the game up the steep, and hearing the curious neighing cry of the guanacoes before them, struggled upwards, through a maze of thick underwood, which clung to the lofty beeches. After an ascent of half a mile they reached a ridge, and saw before them a wooded descent, below which lay a tiny, lovely dell, surrounded by tall trees and

Y

entangled bushes, pastured with long grass on which a herd of guanacoes were feeding, and watered by a little rivulet which flowed from some aperture in the rocks, crossed the dell, and again disappeared through some hidden channel.

It was no difficult task to capture the guanacoes now; and having secured two, they sat down to look round at the fairy spot. The side which they had descended was a gentle slope, but the rest of the little basin-shaped valley was surrounded by perpendicular rocks clothed with wood. The vale seemed to have been unvisited since the creation of the world, all was so fresh and solitary.

A pine, growing on a ledge of the rock opposite the slope by which they had descended, was loaded with pinones, which provoked the cupidity of Jack extremely, but they were beyond all reach.

" What a charming spot this would be," said Charles, " on which to erect a hunting-box! It is evidently quite unknown to the Indians; and we might gallop for miles over the plains, and return to sleep here; sure to be unmolested."

" I wonder how those pinones would taste, if we had a few to roast," said Jack, still gazing with desire at the pine, and trying to reach the fruit with his long lance. But the long lance fell short of the height of the tree, and becoming rather irritated by the jests of Charles, and his own ill-success, Jack hurled the spear at the tree, and to his great astonishment it disappeared entirely, through the bushes that covered the face of the rock.

" There must be a cave in the rock," said Charles; " let us try to find the entrance to it. It was lucky I did not take a fancy to tilt with the pine, for I have my lance still, and we must make a probe of it."

They tried repeatedly to find an opening, but the lance rebounded from the rocky surface. At length, close to the ground, Charles introduced his lance, which entered to its full extent.

"Give me my rifle," said Jack, "that I may slay the gnome who guards the magic cavern. I undertake the adventure of exploring this secret cave."

"But I am the eldest," said Charles, "and I claim the right of having the first peep into the mystery."

"I scoff at your right," answered Jack; "I am determined to seek my lance, so good bye, Charley— here goes!" and crouching to the earth, with his poncho over his head to protect him from the thorns, he forced his way beneath the bushes and disappeared, followed, however, by Charles, who was anxious for his safety. The entrance to the cave, thickly covered with entangled brushwood, was not more than four feet high; it was very narrow for a few feet, and then they emerged into a spacious and lofty cavern, or rather a series of caves, for small openings in the rock seemed to continue the line of grottoes. But the large cave they had entered was light and airy, from many small apertures, and the floor was scattered with a white efflorescent sand.

"Here is our hunting-box built and ready for our reception," cried Jack; "and what a delightful grotto it is! how different to the damp cave we inhabited on the coast, or the dismal dungeon on the Andes! It is really more like a ball-room than a cave! Look at the graceful festoons of creeping plants, coming through the openings and drooping above us! We must bring provisions here, and then surprise the family by escorting them to a gipsy party in our *casino*."

Charles agreed that it would make a charming summer retreat, if it were not infested by wild beasts; and, on examination, no traces appeared of such inhabitants. Several spacious caves communicated one with another by small openings, which appeared as if constructed by art. These caves were equally light and airy: pigeons and the bright little birds of the woods were fluttering about the openings, but no other animal was seen.

Jack was so much pleased with his discovery, that he

forgot the pinones, and, recovering his spear, which had fallen through an opening into the cave, they made their way back into the vale, and looking back, were struck with the perfect concealment of the caves. Jack declared, that but for the pine-tree which grew above, it would be impossible for them again to know the spot where they had entered.

They once more mounted their horses, which were tied to a tree at the foot of the slope; and, with a guanaco added to the burthen of each animal, they had some difficulty in making their way from this beautiful sequestered spot. They did not like to notch the trees, for fear the keen-sighted Indians might see and remark their track; but they made particular observations, that they might recognize the road. They descended into their own valley, covered with scratches; and galloped homeward, uncertain whether they should report the discovery of the morning, or reserve it as a surprise. But the temptation to tell the tale of wonders and difficulties was too strong, and they could not forbear describing the lovely retreat, and proving, by their lacerated hands and faces, the perils of the road.

"But, to-morrow," said Jack, "we will take a hatchet, and make a good road and a proper entrance to our new mansion."

"You must do no such thing," said Matilda; "wait till to-morrow, and I will tell you my plan, which will, I think, induce you to relinquish the hatchet."

"Ah, Lewis!" said Jack, "with all your skill you have failed to cure Matilda of her 'grand talent for governing.'"

"But this is only a proposal, Jack," said Lewis, "and not a command. Now, if the proposal be rational, it proves that the judgment is in a healthy state, and requires no physician."

"Thank you, my dear friend," said Matilda, "for doing me justice. If my proposal should prove impertinent, I am willing to be reproved."

Next morning Lewis and Matilda held a consultation with Almagro. It certainly appeared, from the report of the young hunters, that they had discovered a much more desirable place of refuge than the dark, chill, dungeon-like cave behind the old hut, which they had contemplated, in extreme need, might afford concealment to Mr. Merton and the females. The only objection to the hunters' cave was the distance from Esperanza ; but this might be obviated by retreating quietly to it for a short time, till any fear of an attack was past.

"And we will begin," said Matilda, "by transferring by degrees some necessaries to this newly-discovered retreat, that if we have to fly to it, dear papa and mamma may not be comfortless."

"I have thought of this too," said Lewis, "but Jack and Charles are indiscreet, and if we revealed our plans to them, they might alarm the family. We must only at present warn them to preserve the seclusion of the retreat, to avoid making any track; and we must allow them to convey what provisions they like, previous to the proposed visit of the family to see their discovery."

Next morning Jack and Charles set out again to their cave, their horses being loaded with two large panniers packed by Matilda, with a strict charge that they should not be opened till all the family were there. In one of these panniers she had packed the tea, sugar, and other little luxuries Mrs. Douglas had so considerately sent for her friends, filling up the basket with biscuits, butter, and dry fruit. The other pannier contained a kettle, pan, cups, plates, bowls, spoons, knives, and forks. "After all, Lewis," she said, as she showed her preparation to her friend, "if we are not driven from our beloved home, these things will be ready for the festival we shall enjoy in Jack's enchanted palace."

The young men contrived to ascend the wood by a more circuitous and less entangled road than on their first journey ; and allowing their horses to feed on the

rich pasture of the vale, they dragged with great difficulty the large hampers into the cave, which they now
examined with more attention.

"This large cave must certainly be our dining-hall,"
said Jack; "here are several small niches that will
make capital sleeping apartments, and that deep cave
behind must be the kitchen, for see, this little recess
will suit for the fireplace: it looks as if it had been
built for the purpose; and now, while I think on it,
I will climb up the hill to a spot where I saw a fallen
beech yesterday; I will tie up some bundles of the
branches for fuel, and roll them down the hill, and you
must drag them into the cave."

Away flew the active lad up the steep hill; he soon
tied up some bundles and hurled them down; but
before Charles could get them into the cave, he saw
his friend rapidly descending the hill. When he came
to Charles, he was much agitated, and said, "The
plain below is filled with Indians! I fear they are
going to Esperanza, and we are not there to protect
our beloved friends!"

Charles mounted the hill in a moment, climbed a
tree, and through his pocket-telescope surveyed the
valley below. He saw a great number of mounted
Indians scattered round, not more than four or five
hundred yards from the foot of the mountain. They
appeared to have halted, for women were busy unloading the horses which carried the poles of the tents;
and he concluded they were about to encamp for the
night on this spot. He returned to Jack, and said,
"We must by some means make our way home, to
warn and make ready; but how to get the horses
through the wood, unperceived by the Indians, I know
not."

"We must leave them," said Jack; "one of the
caves will make an excellent stable. Collect an arm-
full of grass for them, while I try to drag them in and
stable them."

The undertaking was extremely difficult, but was

accomplished; the animals were conveyed to a distant cave, the grass left with them, and their stable inclosed by placing a piece of rock before the opening. The fuel was then dragged into the cave, and the young men, taking their rifles, prepared to make the best of their way home. They kept, of course, within the shelter of the wood, winding along the steep mountain side, till having gone, with much delay and difficulty, about a mile from their retreat, and seeing they were now out of sight of the Indians, they ventured to descend to the valley. They then ran and walked as swiftly as they could, till, exhausted by fatigue, and overwhelmed with their evil tidings, they appeared before the family.

It was necessary now that everything should be openly discussed, and prompt measures adopted. Paul was not excluded from the council, and when he heard the description Charles gave of the people and their encampment, he said, "These Indians are my people: they have sought the aid of a friendly tribe whose encampments are not far from ours. They come to rescue me, or to avenge my death. But fear not, I will go out to meet my tribe: I will say to them:— 'These Christians are my brothers—I love them— they shed no blood. Leave them in peace.'"

This was a good promise, but Lewis doubted the power of the young chief to control the vindictive feelings of a savage horde who had assembled for the sole purpose of war.

"At all events," he said, "it would be prudent to remove Mr. Merton and the ladies immediately; especially as we know the Indians will now be engaged in raising the toldos."

"My people will not come here until the hour of darkness and silence," said Paul. "The Indian warrior loves the veil of night. But let my gentle friends depart; they will fear to see the dark Indian, who knows not that the true God has said to all men, 'Love one another.'"

As it was desirable to leave as many men as they could in the fortress, Charles undertook alone to conduct the fugitives to their retreat. Those who were left promised, if time permitted, to conceal in the cave all the moveables they were able to save ; and before they departed, Mr. Merton himself carried there all his books and papers, and Nanny placed in safety her churn, pans, and spinning-wheel.

They collected the blankets, mattresses, and everything they could conveniently carry, not forgetting a provision of charqui; and, to render a part of the journey less fatiguing, the mules were brought out and loaded, the ladies mounted them, and thus, accompanied by Tom and Jack, they went as far as they could safely venture along the valley ; then the mules were unloaded, and each fugitive taking a portion of the loading, the boys embraced their parents, and returned with the mules.

The fugitives must necessarily now ascend the wood, and Charles had a painful office in conducting the alarmed, sorrowful, and feeble party through the entangled bushes on the steep mountain side. Nanny, who had loaded herself with a great sack, which she carried on her back, was nearly borne down by it; Mr. Merton had, contrary to the advice of Dr. Lewis, carried away the large church bible and prayer book, which he refused to leave, even in the mountain-cave, and he was now very weary of his burthen. Matilda carried the little Cecilia, to whom Lewis had administered a gentle soporific, to still her during the perilous journey.

As they approached the point of danger, Charles enjoined the greatest caution; he climbed a tree, and perceived, through his glass, that a great confusion pervaded the newly-erected toldos, which had sprung up like a village. At length he discovered they were slaughtering animals, and judged that they were about to have a feast before they entered into action, which he was glad to see, as it promised a longer security to his friends at Esperanza, whom he was anxious to join.

At last he brought his weary and heavily-laden party safely into harbour; and, desponding as they all were, they were struck with the calm repose and beauty of the peaceful vale, and delighted and astonished when they entered the cave.

" Well, God be praised !" said Nanny.   " He can build such houses as poor simple folks like us could never equal.   This is far more like a church, to my fancy, than that ugly black place we saw in London, their grand St. Paul's !"

" And, by God's help, we will make it a church, Nanny," said Mr. Merton ; " where I trust we may be permitted to meet together, and offer praise and thanksgiving to Him."

Charles hastily pointed out to his cousins the several caves, enjoining them to procure some grass and feed the horses ; he promised that they should see the rest of the family, or hear from them before morning ; then, taking the road homewards, he made all speed to assist his friends.

For a few minutes after his departure, the party in the cave remained standing, silently gazing on the rocky walls of their retreat ; then, looking at each other, they wept together.   After some time spent in this abandonment to grief, Mary, whose lively spirits were seldom long subdued, said,—

" How very ungrateful we all are to be so unhappy, when we are securely lodged in this snug dwelling, while poor Charles is scrambling through that dreadful wood, with the Indians behind him, and unknown dangers before him."

Then the active girl unrolled the mattress which the good-natured Charles had brought upon his back, and spreading it on the dry earth, made her papa and mamma sit down upon it.

" And now," continued she, " let us unpack, and make our dwelling look something better than a prison.　First, I shall release my prisoners." Then opening a basket she had brought on her arm, she let out four full-grown chickens, which had been kept quiet by the enjoyment of a feast of maize, with which the basket was filled up. The feathered family stalked about their new abode, but finding nothing that suited their taste on the sandy floor, they perched on a rocky ledge, a few feet from the ground, and composed themselves to roost.

"The fowls set us a good example," said Matilda, "to make the best of it. And now, Nanny, as we cannot sit down for want of seats, suppose you begin to unpack the hampers brought here by Tom and Charles, whilst I find some resting-place for my precious charge."

The little Cecilia was deposited by the side of Mr. and Mrs. Merton, still enveloped in her blanket, leaving Matilda at liberty to assist Nanny.

"Aye, aye," muttered Nanny; "I reckon there will be a good deal left out that ought to have been brought. What should poor lasses like you know of what's wanted? Not but what it was a grand thought of Miss Mary to bring my poor bits of chicks out of the way of them black savages. There's no doubt they would have swallowed them up living, feathers and all, as they will do with them poor things that's left."

Nanny's opinion of Indian voracity created a diversion that was favourable, and they turned with more cheerfulness to inspect the panniers, which, being packed by Matilda, were filled with judgment. After the kettle, pan, and crockery were taken out, they spread a shawl over one of the panniers, and called it a table. Then folding their blankets, which had formed a great part of their load, for cushions, they sat down to rest. Nanny placed on the table a large pigeon-pie she had brought in a basket, but in the present suspense no one could think of eating. Night came on, but they felt too much fear of their neighbours to light a fire or candle, and an hour or two passed in cheerless darkness.

"Now Maria," said Mary, "we can steal out in safety, and cut some grass for the horses; for I promised Charles to feed them." So, each armed with a large knife, the two girls crept from the cave, and soon filled one of the emptied baskets with fresh grass.

"I feel a great desire to climb the hill," said Mary, "and try if I can see anything on the plain below. Come, Maria, no one can see us in the darkness."

They climbed to the ridge of the rock, from whence, by mounting the lower branches of a beech, they obtained a view of the level valley, which lay stretched far below them. A confused trampling and neighing of horses was heard, and the light of a hundred blazing torches dazzled their eyes at first; but by degrees they distinguished a crowd of dark forms, all mounted and armed. In the front, mounted on a white horse, was a figure clothed in a scarlet poncho, with a headdress of ostrich feathers; this figure, by the long braids of hair hanging down behind, they recognized to be a female, and concluded she must be the mother of Paul.

As the girls gazed silently at this fearful sight, the whole party moved off at full speed, uttering loud and discordant cries, in which the excited girls, in their agony and distraction, could scarcely forbear joining. In a few moments the warriors were out of sight, and nothing but a few dull fires, the chattering of the women, and the cries of the children, marked the position of the encampment.

Agitated almost to fainting, the girls descended, and with their basket of grass, entered the cave. Maria rushed up to Mrs. Merton, burst into tears, and cried, "The Indians are gone to Esperanza! Oh! dear mamma, what will become of my brothers? Why are we here in safety, while they are in peril?"

"Compose yourself, my child," said Mr. Merton;

" you agitate your tender mother. Your brothers are, like ourselves, under the protection of God. We will pray for them;" and kneeling down in the midst of the mournful family, Mr. Merton uttered a fervent prayer for the safety of the absent.

CHAPTER XXV.

The Arrival of the rest of the Fugitives. Account of the Assault. Paul carried off. The Flight. The Toldos removed. Expedition to the Ruins of Esperanza. The Ascent of the Cattle to the Vale of Refuge. Visit of Paul. His Story.

AFTER their devotions, they rose up, somewhat calmed. " Let us now make a fire," said Matilda, " which we may do in perfect safety, for it is absolutely impossible for the Indians in the valley below to perceive it; especially as we are inclosed in the solid rock."

The fuel provided by Jack and Charles was at hand, and a fire was soon made, which, in the wide and lofty cavern, greatly added to the comfort of the pensive inhabitants. They collected round it; and Mary and Maria going to feed the horses, found the saddles, which had been taken off and placed near. They brought them into the large cave to serve for seats; and having now a light, Mr. Merton read to them some select passages of holy writ; which engaged their attention in some measure, and enabled them to endure the torturing anxiety of their situation.

Mary looked at her watch; it was two hours past midnight. How much must have occurred since the Indians left the encampment; and how anxiously they longed to know the details. They felt no inclination for sleep; their nerves were too much excited by the frightful uncertainty; and it was in vain to listen, for no sound beyond the rock could reach them in their retreat. Another half hour of misery passed; then the voice of dear Jack was heard through the opening,—"All safe! All here! mamma!"

Mrs. Merton turned pale, and was almost fainting; but the sight of the party emerging, one after another, from the narrow entrance, revived her. They were all safe, and heavily laden with guns, blankets, baskets, and bags; but they looked pale and haggard, and after the first greetings, were silent for some time.

"Tell us the worst, my children; now that I see you all round me, I can bear it. Is it, that we have no longer a home?" said Mr. Merton.

"None but this, at present, certainly," replied Lewis; "and praised be God's name, who provided such a refuge for us, or what would have become of you, my beloved friends? But come, boys, we must not despair, put down your loads, and then Nanny will give us some supper, and we will relate our sad tale."

Jack went out to the stream for a pitcher of fresh water, and the pie was no longer rejected. They all took the refreshment they so much needed, and then Dr. Lewis said,—

"Notwithstanding the strong and sincere assurances Paul gave us of his influence over his people, I had doubts, and told him of them. I gave him the best advice I could for his conduct when we should be separated; I besought him, above all things, to remember the Christian precepts he had heard; and to hold fast the faith he had professed. He promised earnestly that he would never forget his friends or his God; and that if he was not permitted to remain with us, he would certainly return to us.

"That the Indians might be misled as to the mode of escape, should escape be necessary, we made a breach in the eastern part of the fence, near the corral, and turned loose through it, the two best cows and Almagro's mule, which I felt certain would voluntarily

revisit their old home; and if we should venture to
return, we might recover them.   The poultry we dismissed to the woods.   We then strewed branches
lightly over the breach we had made, and finished by
making up the bundles you see, which we placed in
the cave.   We had provided for the last emergency ;
but we determined to make the best defence we could.
Almagro mounted the observatory, with water ready
in case of a conflagration ; and we remained with our
rifles ready at that weak point of the fence, of which
the Indians were well aware.

" At midnight the distant torches and shrill cries,
announced the approach of the enemy.   The river is
unfortunately so low, that, as I expected, it did not
form an obstacle to them ; but we had our last hope,
and this was the moment to test it.   Paul mounted
on his own horse, after taking a mournful farewell of
us, and was let out through the portal.

" ' If I find my people will no longer hear me,' said
he, much agitated ; ' if I find they will raise their
hands against my brothers, I will speak in the words
of the language which my fair sisters taught me, and
proclaim my disgrace and despair.'

" We saw him join the rushing crowd.   There was
a short pause, succeeded by loud and angry dispu-
tation.   We hoped and feared ; but a few minutes
settled all our doubts, for the Indians rode furiously
forward.   Some attempted to force the door ; others
threw torches in all directions on the fence which
blazed in twenty places.   But in the midst of the confusion the clear voice of Paul reached our ears, crying out, ' Fly, my friends ! all is lost : I cannot save
you.'

" We tore away the loose branches from the breach
we had made, which they had not yet reached, so that
they might fancy we had fled in that direction ; then
firing a volley to lead them to suppose we intended
to defend the fort, and not to escape ; we retreated to
the dilapidated hut, raised the rock which covered the

secret outlet, and stole out into the wood, first replacing the stone; and we were soon in the old cave.
For a moment we contemplated remaining there; but
knowing how anxious you all would be, and trusting
that in the delight of destruction and plunder, the
Indians would not care to pursue us, we determined
to come to you.

"We crossed the river unperceived, and fled along
the valley till the lights at the encampment warned
us to take to the fatiguing wood. God be thanked
we have reached you, unseen and unhurt; and even
Jack the valiant allows that opposed by such numbers, it was not cowardly to beat a retreat."

"No, really, I think it was all fair," said Jack;
"for I had a peep at the villains from the observatory, and I shall never forget the sight. A great part
of them were entirely naked, and looked as wild and
furious as demons, and these would be, I suppose,
Paul's friendly tribe. His own people had some
scanty covering, and were led by the woman of the
scarlet poncho, who was certainly Paul's mother;
rather unlike our mother, I should say, Mary. Poor
dear Paul! he was surrounded by a band of armed
men, who did not join in the attack, but were doubtless placed to guard him. He looked very sorrowful,
and I am quite sure, if they do not assassinate him,
he will come back to see us."

"Then I hope he will not visit us in princely state,"
said Matilda. "I have no desire to see his court
round him. But I have many things to ask. First:
where is Wallace? Why have you not brought him
with you?"

"I wished it very much," said Lewis; "but sagacious as Wallace is, I fear we could not have made him
understand the necessity of silence and caution; for
you know that when he is let loose to walk with us,
he barks incessantly, and this would most certainly
have ruined us. I considered all this before Paul left
us; and as the dog knew him, I engaged him to

promise to be his protector; and I have no doubt he
will be able to do for Wallace what he could not do
for us."

"I am very weary," yawned Tom; "had we not
better go to bed?"

Tom's drowsy exclamation, and his quiet proposal
to go to bed, as if he was in a commodious mansion,
created a little diversion; and Jack begged to conduct
him to his bed-chamber. But Nanny had lighted fires
in two of the inner caves; and there, on such blankets,
cloaks, and cushions as they had been able to bring
away, the family retired to rest, too thankful to have
a secure sleeping-place to lament the want of mattresses.

It was late before the young people woke from their
heavy slumber; and they found Almagro had already
been reconnoitring from the summit of the hill. He
was of opinion, from the quiet state of the encampment, that the warriors had not yet returned to it, and
were probably ranging the country in search of their
lost victims. This was by no means a pleasant reflection; and the family determined to remain strictly
secluded so long as the toldos appeared in the valley;
they therefore breakfasted, fed the two horses, and then
began to set their house in order.

The cave which they named the kitchen looked certainly most like an inhabited place, for, besides Ma-
tida's forethought, the prudent Nanny had brought
more pans and kitchen utensils. In the panniers first
sent were the table requisites. Some smooth fragments of rock were selected and brought into the
hall, as they named the large cave, for seats, a larger
piece formed a table, and an emptied pannier became
baby's sleeping-cot.

Their provision consisted of a bag of maize flour,
some *charqui*, and the biscuit, tea, and sugar first sent.
They had also some candles, which, with the cloaks,
blankets, rifles, and heavy bags of ammunition, had
sufficiently loaded the young men.

"Here are the two lances we left the other day," said Charles; "so, with our knives and rifles, we have a tolerable armory, which I trust we may not need here; and we have two horses also, a most fortunate circumstance."

"I longed to have released my poor Pampero," said Lewis; "but I feared, if the savages found the corral emptied, it would incense them more against us."

"And my pretty Dewdrop's life is saved by leaving her here," said Jack; "for the wretches would inevitably have devoured her, as they do all the mares. Paul seemed astonished to see me condescend to ride Dewdrop."

The day after passed away very tediously, all being deprived of their usual employment, and unable to leave their retreat; and they were relieved when the darkness permitted them to venture from the cave, and to climb the hill to observe what was going on in the toldos.

They saw that all was in great confusion, many lights were visible, and the horsemen were coming in one after another; but the distance and the darkness prevented them from distinguishing their proceedings. But the refreshment of the cool evening air cheered the prisoners; and they looked round on the little quiet dell, so strikingly contrasted with the turbulent scene in the valley below, with pleasure and gratitude, and retired to the cave to thank God for their tranquillity, and to rest without fear.

The second morning's observation discovered to the anxious party the gratifying spectacle of the removal of their unpleasant neighbours. The women had already taken down the slight framework of the huts, and were rolling up the hide covers and placing them on the horses, many of which stood laden with the plunder of Esperanza. The men were mounted, their horses being decorated with the curtains and carpets woven by the sisters for their dear home. The war-

z

riors were waving their long spears in triumph, and
one was ringing a bell, which the Mertons recognized,
with vexation, as the bell of their chapel.

Finally the procession moved off, headed by Paul
and his mother.   Lewis observed through his glass that
Paul was leading a large dog, which he concluded was
Wallace, in a long lasso.   They applauded this act of
prudence; for if the dog had been at liberty, he would
certainly have tracked his old masters, and betrayed
their retreat.   All the Indians they now saw were
clothed; and from the diminution of numbers, they
concluded that the tribes had separated, to go to their
respective hunting-grounds.

It was with infinite satisfaction that the party on the
hill saw their enemies gradually disappear behind the
distant hills; and before the day was over, Lewis and
Almagro ventured to descend through the woods to
examine the site of the *tolderia*.   Nothing remained
to mark the spot where it had been, but the trodden
and cropped grass, the blackened traces of the fires,
and the blood and entrails of the slaughtered animals
on which the Indians had feasted the night before, and
on the remains of which were now perched some
hideous condors, gorged with eating.

The friends then returned to cheer the impatient
prisoners with the assurance that the search was abandoned, and their retreat secure.   The rest of the morning was passed in walking round the verdant little
basin, which seemed so wonderfully discovered for their
refuge.   In length it extended about a quarter of a
mile; but the breadth was not more than a hundred
yards, between the cave and the foot of the opposite
hill.   On the north, south, and west, the vale was
guarded by inaccessible rocks, and could only be
approached from the east.

"What a site this would be for a settlement," said
Tom. "How much more secure than Esperanza! We
have only to raise a high brick wall along the ridge of
the hill, and defy the lances and the torches of the

Indians. We have water and wood, and a fine situation for gardens and pastures."

"All this sounds very well, Tom," said Lewis, "but I am by no means sure that our good parents would like it so well as the spot that first gave them repose. Then I doubt much the salubrity of a place which must, in winter, receive a scanty portion of the sun's rays, and probably a large share of rain and snow. But above all, whatever may be the security of this remarkable hollow, I fear we might soon learn to regard it as a prison."

"No! no! Tom," cried Jack, "Esperanza for ever! We will rebuild our houses, fortify our walls, and never despair."

"That is right, Jack," said Matilda, "remember the tale of Lame Jervas: 'May good faith always meet with good fortune.'"

The little vale was certainly very beautiful. From the lofty heights above, the beech, the tall pine, and drooping birch looked down upon them, and a thick clothing of bushes covered the face of the rocks, forming an aviary for birds of gay plumage and musical notes; festoons of elegant creepers clung from branch to branch; and late as the season was, the crimson flowers of the fuschia shone through the dark foliage, and many of the bright blossoms of summer, scattered near the rivulet, lingered still in that sheltered retreat; whilst among the sedgy bushes, on the side of the water, the beautiful kingfisher had its nest.

Another day elapsed, the provision became scarce, the bread being quite exhausted; and Nanny declared, that if she had a certain iron plate which was secreted in the cave at Esperanza, she could bake cakes over the fire. Mrs. Merton trembled at the thought of the expedition; but Almagro agreeing to remain with her, she at length permitted the young men to set out, to ascertain the state of their beloved home.

They proceeded with caution, and after crossing
z 2

the river, they went through the wood to the rock at the back of the old hut, from whence they surveyed the scene of devastation. Ascertaining the perfect solitude of the spot, they descended among the ruins, and looked round in mournful silence. They crossed the garden, trodden down and strewn with charred wood and uprooted fruit-trees, and on approaching the church, were surprised to find it entire, except that the bell was removed. Either Paul's intercession, or a superstitious feeling,—for they could not attribute it to reverence, must have preserved it ; for not only the building was perfect, but it appeared to have been un-entered, for everything was in its place.

They were glad to have this good news to carry to Mr. Merton, for all else was destroyed, except a few patches of fence which had escaped the conflagration, and the brick oven which stood firm amidst the ruins of the pretty house they had been so proud to complete.

"If we had only had time to take out the glass windows," said Tom, " we might have saved them ; now, when winter comes, we must have the cold blast and the snow come drifting in through the openings which we call windows."

" This winter," said Lewis, " our mansion will be proof against storms, for we cannot leave our present residence at any rate before spring. Remember, we shall have to raise the houses from the ground, no easy task, and not to be attempted in winter."

The fences of the little grass fields were torn down, and the cattle taken away, as well as those in the corral ; but the corn-fields and the flax-plot were un-injured, and they hoped to sow them before long ; but such an attempt was not yet prudent.

They took from the cave the iron girdle-pan, a bag of charqui, and some mattresses and pillows, all they ventured to carry ; though Jack was tempted to catch some of the poultry which had returned to peck about in the old poultry-yard, but Lewis dissuaded him from increasing the cares of the establishment, when the fowls were better provided for in their state of liberty.

But Nanny was gratified to hear of the safety of the faithful flock, and to receive an augmentation of the scanty stores; but to prevent the necessity of such an act of inhospitality as devouring their inmates, the pigeons, the young men proceeded to the Pampas to look out for some fresh meat. They proceeded along the banks of their own river, where they could always obtain the shelter of the wood, and about two miles from their usual ford they at last caught sight of a herd of animals. They stole along, under the shelter of the trees, and, determined not to use the rifle except for defence, they held the bolas and lassoes in readiness.

Jack was considerably in advance of the rest, and they were surprised to see him stop suddenly, clapping his hands, and laughing loudly. " Here are some old friends of ours," he cried out, " come to greet us." And, in truth, the party of animals consisted of the two cows they had released before the attack, the two old llamas, and Almagro's mule. The creatures knew their friends immediately; the mule and llamas evinced much satisfaction at the meeting, running up to them, neighing and bleating in their several tongues; and though the cows showed less sensibility, they submitted with the rest of the animals to be driven to the foot of the hill beneath the vale of refuge.

The llamas and mule were driven or dragged through the wood with much difficulty; but to attempt to force the unwieldy and inactive cows up the ascent, was a task quite beyond the power of the drivers. They called Nanny and Matilda, the two most intimate friends of the refractory quadrupeds, and proceeded to tell them their adventure and their dilemma.

Tom suggested that the cows might be left to graze in

the valley below; and he had no doubt they would still consent to be milked as usual.

" I shall never try them down there," said Nanny, with her usual decision. " How, think you, could I *hug* a bucket of milk up that wood, that's little better than a wall-side?"

Nanny and Matilda then scrambled to the ridge of the hill, and saw the poor cows in the valley below, looking up, and lowing piteously after their departed companions. It needed only Nanny's well-known cry of " Cush! cush!" to nerve the obedient animals to make a vigorous attempt to ascend through the wood, and after much toil they succeeded, and were greeted by the dairymaids with caresses and a feast of maize.

At present the rich pasture afforded sufficient food for all the live stock, though it would be necessary to lay up some provision for them before winter. The cows, so well fed, gave abundance of milk, and Nanny observed, that there never could be a famine where there was a good cow. But by slow degrees they brought from their hidden store sufficient provision to insure them against famine during the winter; and as there had been no re-appearance of the Indians, they ventured to use their horses and the mule, and were thus enabled to bring Nanny's churn, mill, and spinning-wheel, with drawing, writing, and work-boxes, to give employment to the ladies.

At length they brought their carpenters' tools, and were soon able, from the trunk of a fallen pine, to make a table and some seats. In the mean time they daily collected all the pinones they could find fallen, or could knock down, to store for the cattle; but still they feared that the stock of maize must suffer, if the snow lay on the ground, for their faithful servants must at all events be fed.

A month elapsed, during which time they became reconciled to their rocky abode, which, lighted up by the good fires which the season required, looked cheerful; the bushes around the vale supplied abundant fuel; and they had no scruple in raising a blaze that shone brightly on the lofty glittering walls. Then the young men constructed an improved loom for their sisters, and after Nanny had spun the flax they had saved, they wove it into coarse linen; while the young carpenters worked at their bench, making tables, stools, bedsteads, window-frames, doors, ladders, and all manner of useful preparations for the houses to be built in the spring.

But the early part of the day was usually spent by the industrious youths at Esperanza, where they once more ploughed and sowed their little fields, in good faith that God might permit them to reap the fruits in due season. The miserable garden was dug, a few shrubs and bushes that were only broken, were trimmed and restored; the buried flower-roots were again planted, and spring was looked forward to in hope; they forgot the desolation: the spot was again " Esperanza."

Jack built a shed for the poultry, and scattered some maize occasionally, which induced them to frequent the place; and he was generally able to take home a basket of eggs; a pleasant addition to their diet.

Many an evening as they sat round the fire, working and conversing, they wondered they had never seen Paul, and hoped he had not forgotten them; but this doubt Mr. Merton would not allow. " Paul is a believer in God, my dear children," he would say, " and he will ever associate us with the happiness of his conversion."

One evening, as the party were talking thus of the young Indian, they were startled by a rustling among the bushes before the entrance; Jack seized his rifle, and was rushing forward, but Lewis laid his hand on him. " Stay, Jack," he said, " do not be rash; we are perfectly safe, for neither man nor beast can enter without our leave." For every night, before they retired, they rolled a huge piece of rock before the narrow entrance, which it was impossible to remove from the exterior.

A low whine, succeeded by a joyful bark, proclaimed who the intruder was; the rock was immediately rolled away, and Wallace rushed in, perfectly wild with joy, and careered round the cave with all the antics of a young kitten, to the great mirth of the girls. But their laughter was soon changed into astonishment and pleasure, when Paul followed the dog into the cave. Mrs. Merton certainly cast a glance of apprehension at the entrance; but Lewis having ascertained that Paul was alone, the stone was replaced, and the friends sat down to tell their several adventures. Paul looking round first at the prison-like walls so repugnant to the taste of the free Indian, said:

"It was Paul who drove his friends to this dark house in the rock! Why were the fair Christians so kind to him? why did they heal his wounds, and make him a son of God? Why did they not leave him to die, with parched lips, on the blood-stained ground, where he lay like a conquered slave? Then the Christians might have rested undisturbed in their peaceful huts; then the fair girls might still have sung like the bright birds of the woods, and danced on the grassy plains in happiness. It was Paul who brought to the home of his friends woe and destruction. Can they still hold out the hand of amity, and say, ' Paul, you are our friend?'"

As Paul stood folded in his poncho, he appeared to have added years instead of months to his age since they parted, and to speak the Spanish language with more of the idiom of his own than when formerly familiarly conversing with the friends who now encircled him, assuring him, with earnest kindness, that they loved him no less, though he was unable to restrain the aggressions of his people.

He told them that his mother had peremptorily

refused to hear his intercession for the Christians. She had, during his absence, assumed the command of his people, and her imperious spirit scorned the idea of concession. She rebuked him for his woman's heart, and ordered him to be guarded by some of his own warriors. By assuring the men that the God of the Christians would send down fire from heaven to destroy them if they entered the house where he dwelt, he terrified them into sparing the church. . But he had seen, with deep sorrow, the gardens, the shady arbours, the aviary, the pleasant halls of his dear friends, burnt, plundered, and demolished; and he followed his mother, silent and melancholy, while the Indians divided to scour the plains, to discover and murder the fugitives.

On their arrival at the tolderia, Paul, released from his durance, recovered his energy, and poured on the amazed ear of his mother his tale of the wonders, the charms, the sweet humanity of Christianity; and when the disappointed warriors returned, he harangued them on the guilt of bloodshed—on the excellence of peace. He told them, that by their unprovoked attack on the Christians, they had incurred the vengeance of the great God. Then, his mother, with a daring spirit, had answered:—" It was my will to go forth against the Christians; upon my head may the vengeance fall!"

" The tribe were all silent," continued Paul, " appalled by my mother's daring words. She still continued to lead the tribe when we departed for our own grounds, and chose to mount the noble and fiery Pampero. He tossed his beautiful head as the men arrayed him in unaccustomed harness, and spurned the ground when my mother mounted, as if he knew that he carried an enemy. When the procession moved, some of the men began to ring the bell, which I had forbidden them to remove, but the temptation had been irresistible; Pampero started at the sound, seized the bit in his teeth, and fled forward like the lightning.

I followed my mother in terror, but she waved me from her; she was a perfect horsewoman, and had never lost her seat.   Onward scoured the excited animal; still she sat firmly, and I trusted the horse would soon be exhausted.   Suddenly he fell to the earth, and I knew he must have trodden on a *bescachero*, an accident our trained horses avoid by scenting the spots where the animals burrow.

"My people, struck with fright, did not move; and when I reached the spot, I found the animal struggling over the prostrate and insensible form of my mother. I extricated the horse without much injury, and then lifting my mother in my arms, I saw, by the way the limbs hung, that one arm and one leg must be broken; what other injuries she had sustained could not yet be known.

"My people came up, and we placed her on a blanket, and bore her to a place where the toldos could be raised.   Then she was placed under the roof of her own tent, and the base impostors of the tribe, who practise incantations, and invoke the spirit of evil, came to her; but she had revived, and she dismissed them with stern and bitter words.   Her acute mind had detected their impostures; but her haughty spirit refused to submit to the true God.

"I bound her fractured limbs in shields of bark; I wetted her parched lips with cool water, as you had done for me. I prayed her to allow me to go in search of the wonderful medicine-man who had restored me to life; but, with her usual stern authority, she forbade me. 'The hand of death is on me,' she said. 'No medicine-man can raise me to life, and your friend would be slain by the tribe.   But can it be that the wife and mother of noble Caciques must die ignobly, because she disdains to submit to the God of the Christians?   Have the imprecations of the subtle white man brought this disgrace on our tribe? Speak, and tell me, Bysanti.'

"I did speak: I repeated the words you had spoken

to me; I spoke of the God of love and mercy, whose vengeance is terrible to the wicked, but whose love is happiness for ever to those who know him. I told her that even the sorrowful pains of death became joyful to the Christian, for he knew they would usher him into the visible presence of his God.

"I cannot speak as you can, good father, and my mother loved not to hear the word of instruction from her child. Long did her powerful and strong mind struggle against conflicting doubts. Daily her body became weaker—daily her mind became more enlightened: she listened with more attention to my earnest prayers. Her power on earth had been crushed in a moment; and at length she learned to aspire to a nobler future than the idle dreams of hunting-fields and wars. Slowly she woke to the conviction of her own useless waste of God's good gifts; she acknowledged with humility her unworthiness, and her last days were devoted to prayer, with faith in that mercy which you had taught me would be largely given, when faithfully prayed for."

CHAPTER XXVI.

The Death of Paul's Mother. The Visit to Esperanza, and Meeting with Cangapol and Zara. The Grand Reception in the Rock. Mr. Merton sets out on a Mission. The Siege of the Rock. The Slaughter. The Field of Battle.

" It was the last request of my mother," continued Paul, " that I, the Cacique of the tribe, should endeavour to make my people Christians like myself. She called round her the old men of the tribe, and told them her happiness in knowing the true God. They scoffed at the words, as the ravings of fever. She then imposed on them, as they dreaded a heavy vengeance, the promise never again to disturb the peace of the settlers at Esperanza. The whole tribe swore that, unless driven to it by aggression, they would never war against the fair tribe of the mountain valley.

"At the last hour, even the stern old men and the bold youths were awed by the sight of the noble woman's peace of mind in the agony of a death of suffering. The women wept, and said, ' Cacique, when death comes to us, bring the God of the Christians to us, that we may die thus.' I spent many days in mourning, and in endeavouring to win the men from bloodshed and robbery. Then I said, ' Brothers, I go to bring a messenger of God to speak good words to you. Listen to him—reverence him—and permit him to depart in peace.'

"This was pleasing to them, and I mounted my horse, leading also Pampero, on whom I cannot look with pleasure since my mother's death, though doubtless the accident was ordained by God to save her soul. I departed with no guide but Wallace, to seek you, for I was ignorant of the road to your retreat. But no sooner were we in sight of the wood, than he plunged into it; I followed him unwillingly, for I could not believe that any refuge could be found in the perpendicular steep before me.

"And now, beloved father, go with me to the tolderia, and show to my ignorant people the way of salvation. You are safe under my protection; still more, you are safe, for you are on the errand of God."

Mrs. Merton turned pale as Paul uttered this request; though she had anticipated it; but she still doubted the power of Paul to control his people. She pleaded that Mr. Merton was ignorant of the language of the Indians.

"Many of my warriors have visited towns," said Paul, "and understand the language Mr. Merton speaks to me; and I can interpret his words to the rest." But no objection would have deterred Mr.

Merton from going, he would immediately have set out; but it was agreed that Paul should remain with them a day or two, should visit Esperanza, and hear all their plans of restoration.

Two days passed, and on the Sunday they ventured for the first time all to go to Esperanza, and have divine service; and the good Mr. Merton's thanksgiving for the event, and for the safety of his little flock, was not heard without tears. On leaving the church, they were astonished and alarmed to hear the trampling of horses. They were unarmed, and except a spear or two left among the ruins, had no defence; they felt greatly relieved when they saw only two horses approaching. On the first, a beautiful white animal, was mounted a noble-looking Indian chief; the other animal was a small elegant bay horse, and as it drew near, they saw the rider was a female.

Jack recognized the strangers immediately, and springing forward, cried out, " Zara ! Zara ! "

But who can describe the feelings of the father when he saw, instead of the lovely innocent child he had lost, an Indian woman, the wife, as she believed, of a Cacique, with the dress, the habits, and he almost feared the creed of the Indian ? He leaned against a tree in painful silence; but the quick eye of his daughter soon recognized him among the strangers. She sprung from her horse, flew to his feet, and the lapse of time was forgotten. She was again the Guacho girl; and she murmured as she clung round his neck, " *Mi padre! Mi padre !* " And to the agitated father she was again the sweet child he had nursed in his mountain solitude; and he hung over her, forgetting the sorrows that had darkened his intervening life, crying, " *Nina de mi alma! Estrella mia !* "

In the mean time Paul had advanced to the Cacique; they were known to each other; their tribes were friendly, and their language the same. They spoke much, with the emphatic gestures and emotion

peculiar to the Indians, except when they assume a
cold and formal manner to confer with their enemies.
The family stood aloof, looking at the affecting meeting of the father and daughter; Lewis, with all his
coolness, feeling a little embarrassed with this adventure, for though it was very desirable to be on friendly
terms with Cangapol, he could not see exactly how
they ought to arrange for the reception of their
visitors. Already the secret of their retreat was
known to one who had been their enemy; but of the
fidelity of Paul there could be no doubt. But, he
considered, could they so surely depend on a Cacique,
whose tribe had evinced themselves on several occasions inimical to the Christians, whom they had per-
sonally injured, and probably offended deeply by
releasing his captive? Yet it was a duty to show
hospitality to their visitors, and they had no other
home than their retreat in the rock.

Almagro was at length conducted to the Cacique
by Zara, and while he was conversing with him, and
caressing the child, whom the haughty chief had condescended to hold while Zara greeted her father,
Lewis approached Paul, and consulted him on the
prudence of admitting Cangapol to a knowledge of
their retreat.

"Demand from him," said Paul, "a pledge of
secrecy; a Cacique, though he be not a Christian,
never violates his word."

Almagro was employed to negotiate the treaty, and
Cangapol readily promised that no consideration
should induce him to reveal the secret abode of
Zara's father, even to his own tribe; and that he would
never use his own knowledge of it, except for friendly
communication.

Satisfied with this arrangement, they set out to
return; the gentlemen walking, the ladies and Indians
mounted. From the constant use of horses by the
tribes, they are unable to walk far without great
fatigue; and though tall and muscular, with great
strength of arm, their legs are slender and weak.

Even Zara had lost her old habits, and could not possibly have walked three miles.

Cangapol regarded the apparently inaccessible mountain side with astonishment, which increased, when after winding through the labyrinthine path, he reached the ridge, and looked down upon the green vale below, with the cows and llamas quietly grazing.

But Zara's wonder broke forth when they entered the cave, and she looked on the neat and comfortable arrangement of the place; a fire was lighted immediately, and the bright glow gave an air of cheerfulness to the strange dwelling unknown in the dark and comfortless toldos of the Indians. A neatly-arranged dinner of cold roast beef and wheaten cakes was set out; and though the Europeans did not expect to see their visitors use their knives and forks like the inhabitants of cities, they were surprised to find how soon, and how successfully, they imitated the habits of their hosts.

The countenance of Cangapol was usually stern and haughty; but when he looked on Zara and his child, his features were softened, and displayed a noble expression. Though still retaining the habits of the wild savage life, the Cacique had seen cities, and trafficked with civilized men. These visits had opened his understanding; but it remained for the gentle influence of Zara to soften the savage manners, and develop the hidden affections of the untaught Indian. He still led out his people, at their desire, to slay and plunder; but he regarded deeds of blood as a duty in which he had no pleasure. As Mr. Merton conversed with his new guest, he saw with pleasure that there was material for a noble character. The good man turned the conversation on the aim and end of this life, and the glorious futurity offered to the Christian; and spoke long, earnestly, and powerfully, to his attentive hearers, on the doctrines of Christianity.

Cangapol was silent, yet his countenance displayed

thought and emotion; but Zara came forward, and kneeling at the feet of Mr. Merton, said, "Will God forgive me? I was in a strange land, and I forgot him; yet he has remembered me, and directed me to you, that I may become again a Christian."

Mr. Merton consoled the weeping woman,—promised her further instruction; and assured her that God would receive her, if she asked for pardon in his Son's name.

The day seemed short, as the large party conversed or listened to Mr. Merton. The girls answered Zara's numerous inquiries, and were amused with her astonishment; and the two children became great friends; though the rough caresses of the young Cacique, who was three years of age, somewhat alarmed the pretty Cecilia, now just beginning to walk and utter some words. Then the young Indian running round the cave, whirled a miniature set of bolas skilfully round a pigeon, and brought it to the ground, to the great wrath of Nanny, who extricated the victim, somewhat the worse for the rude pressure of the balls; and then bestowed a little gentle correction on the royal infant, whose cries declared he felt and resented the indignity.

"A young rascal!" said Nanny; "he's just like the rest of them dark villains. To think of his coming here to knock down our bonny tame birds, that live here like ourselves, and that not a body here would eat, if they had them set before them in a pie."

It was quite true that their fellow-lodgers, the pigeons, were regarded as part of the family; they gathered round the table to collect the fallen crumbs, and would eat from the hands of their friends; and the girls declared they would rather live on maize and water, than devour these trusting creatures.

Though the strangers could not comprehend this delicacy of feeling, they respected it: the boy was deprived of his mischievous toy, and amused himself with Cecilia and her doll. As the cavern had recesses that would have accommodated a whole tribe of Indians, and no couch but a skin and a blanket was needed, the arrangements for the night were soon made. The Indians listened with reverence to the prayers, and they parted to sleep in peace.

Next morning, Mr. Merton was to set out with Paul on his first missionary attempt, and it was agreed that the Cacique Cangapol should accompany them, Paul answering for the safety of his two companions among the wild horde; while Zara was to remain at the rock, to recover the habits of civilized life. Mrs. Merton insisted that Wallace should also go with her husband, as the dog was greatly attached to him; and at length, mounted on the steady old mule, and clothed in his sacerdotal vestments, the good man left his anxious family.

To Zara the economy of the little household was a wonderful spectacle; the order and neatness of the arrangements, the happy distribution of labour, by which every one was busily and suitably occupied, but never fatigued, seemed, in comparison with the alternate drudgery and sloth of the toldos, a marvellous triumph of civilization. " Teach me," she said, " fair girls from a far land, to fill my life with useful employment, as you do, that it may be pleasing to God and man."

The sisters persuaded Zara, in the first place, to resign her flowing poncho, and adopt the European dress in the house. She felt the constraint irksome for a day or two, but was soon reconciled to it, and looked very graceful in some of the best dresses of her friends. She followed the sisters round to their daily labours, she watched them milk the cows, feed the poultry, make the thin cakes of bread, and cook the meat and potatoes. Then they arranged their sleeping apartments, and afterwards sat down to spin, knit, weave, to sew, read, or draw. In the sunny part of the day, which was but short in the deep vale at this

2 A

late season, they played with the children on the grass, and collected piñones or fuel. Then the hunters returned with their spoil, and the evening was spent cheerfully; Jack sometimes playing on his fortunately preserved violin, while the rest danced, with light hearts, in that strange ball-room. When tired with this amusement, they sat down to talk, often on serious subjects, but always with happy feelings. Jack inquired one evening of Zara, if old Sausimian still lived.

"Alas! no, good friend!" answered she. "The angel of death has claimed his spirit. He suffered long, but was resigned and patient; only entreating me frequently to read to him of the sufferings and death of Him who died for us, that he might not repine at his own pains. He enjoined me to continue ever in the beautiful faith of Christ, and wished to see Cangapol. I induced him to visit his uncle, and he beheld with wonder the peaceful and even happy death of a man who had a Christian heart. Cangapol does not speak many words, he has more years and thought than the young and ardent Paul; but after much reflection he inquired of me, ' Shall none live after death but the Christians?' I could not answer him, but it was then I besought him to take me to my father, that the good and holy father of our young Christian captive might satisfy all his doubts. And I feel now, dear friends, that Mr. Merton will teach Cangapol to be a Christian."

Mr. Merton was not expected to return for a week; and before three days were past, Zara had acquired the habits of the sisters. She refused to leave Cangapol, but hoped to induce him to adopt the customs, as well as the creed, of the Christians. Mrs. Merton pointed out to Zara the necessity of her marriage being solemnized by the sacred rites of the church, and proposed that, if Cangapol would consent, the baptism of himself and his child, and his marriage with Zara, should be solemnized before they returned to the tribe.

As Zara was sanguine that Cangapol would consent,

the young party amused themselves with the consideration of names for the new Christians. Matilda and Mary had some favourite, grand, euphonious names, for which they warmly petitioned; but Zara, for her husband, decided on the name of Pedro. The little chief she allowed to be named by his sponsors, and they agreed that his name should be Albert. And, as there must be a festival on this great occasion, the hunters were ordered to provide hares and partridges; honey and wheat flour were brought from the rock at Esperanza, and Zara had the advantage of a new lesson, by seeing Nanny churn a quantity of butter for the grand festival.

A heavy fall of rain had kept them within the rock for a whole day, but the girls were busied in making pastry, and other unusual employments engaged the rest, so that their confinement was not irksome. Lewis looked out when night came on, and observing the dark and threatening state of the sky, they hastened to roll the heavy rock before the entrance, rather to exclude the wind, than from dread of any intruders.

An hour passed pleasantly; Zara was trying to learn English, and teaching her friends some words of the Indian language, when, in the midst of the laughter caused by their mutual blunders, a rustling was heard among the bushes, succeeded by the well-known bark of Wallace. "Papa! papa!" was the joyful cry, and Tom and Jack sprung forward to remove the stone.

"But why return so soon, and at this late hour?" said Lewis, with anxiety. "Wait one moment, boys, till I look out."

A ladder, made for the purpose, was placed to reach an opening in the face of the rock, about nine feet from the ground. Lewis ascended the ladder, and through the leafy covering of the aperture, he saw standing below six Indians, with flaming torches, armed with long spears. They appeared to have no

2 A 2

leader whom they chose to obey; but one man, taller and more muscular than the rest, of a peculiarly ferocious aspect, was haranguing the party and pointing out to them the spot where the dog had entered, and where he still continued whining for admittance. His hearers appeared rebellious, and he struck one man violently with the butt end of the spear; then crouching down himself, he followed the dog, and reaching the rocky barrier, he placed his shoulder against it, and attempted, with loud cries, to force an entrance.

The dog seemed now sensible that the man was an enemy; he growled, and then the party within were assured that he had seized the intruder, who uttered a frightful howl; but in his recumbent position, wedged in the narrow passage, and entangled among the bushes, it was difficult for his friends to assist him. At length the Indians seized his legs, and dragged him out, the dog still following, and holding him by the throat; and it was only by violent blows that the faithful creature was forced to relinquish his hold. The Indians then attempted to pierce the dog with their spears, but, darting from them, he bounded through an opening near the entrance, which was not less than eight feet from the ground, a feat Jack had taught him to perform a few days before; and his friends were rejoiced to welcome their brave defender in safety.

Two long spears were flung after the dog, fortunately without injury to any one; but the besieged party took warning and retired beyond the reach of danger, except Lewis, who kept his station at the opening, and reported his observations to his anxious friends. He saw that the poor wretch who had been attacked by the dog still lay on the ground, apparently desperately wounded, but able to speak, for he pointed to the rock, and uttered some words to the men around. They immediately threw their torches among the bushes that grew over the rock, following their usual destructive custom; but if the plan had even been successful, it could not have endangered the inhabitants of that impregnable fort. The bushes, however, moist with the heavy rain of the day, would not ignite, and every effort to cause a conflagration was vain.

The wounded warrior now seemed to urge on his companions the necessity of forcing the door; and three of the men, one following another, crept along the narrow passage to make the attempt, while one was left in charge of the horses, and the fifth bent over the leader, appearing to be stanching the blood that flowed from his wounds.

"We must now prepare in earnest for action," said Lewis. "If the stone gives way, Almagro, do you immediately fire through the crevice; and if those outside attempt to enter, I will fire from above; but let us not shed blood unless it be necessary."

The force of the three men, confined in the narrow passage, was wholly ineffectual in moving the rock; and Almagro called out that he believed all was safe; but Lewis did not attend, for at that moment his attention was excited by the horrible sight which the flaming torches revealed to him of an immense puma, which suddenly sprung from the dark wood upon the back of the Indian who was bending over his friend. The monster in a moment seized the head of the man, and swung him over its head with a violence that assured Lewis his neck must be broken, and was making off with his prey, when Lewis, involuntarily uttering a cry of horror, fired his rifle with such good aim that the beast fell.

Almagro, conceiving the cry of Lewis was intended for a signal, fired at the same moment, and a loud cry and groan proclaimed that his shot had been effectual. Two of the savages then withdrew from the entrance, dragging with them the dead body of their companion. They rose and gazed on it for a moment, then, turning, they beheld the puma, still struggling with its victim. They seemed appalled and distracted, and, rushing to the horses, they leaped upon them, and, followed by the man who had been left to hold the animals, the mounted men fled wildly up the hilly slope to the ridge.

"They are mad!" said Lewis; "they can never descend the mountain in the darkness of night; and ignorant of the road, they will be lost!" But the wind roared, and the rain fell, and they saw no more of the Indians.

"Something must be done for these wretches, who may still be living," said Charles, when Lewis had narrated the combination of fearful accidents which had preserved the innocent. "I, for one, will go out and look after these unfortunate creatures."

"We will all go!" was the cry of the young men; and, notwithstanding the terrors of the females, they took lighted candles, and all proceeded to the field of blood.

Wallace rushed after them, and would again have fallen on his old enemy; but Charles and Jack peremptorily called him off, while Lewis approached to examine the state of the wounded savage. He was lying with his eyes glaring round with a vengeful look, and as he saw them, he muttered some words in his own language in a tone of defiance. Lewis, addressing him in Spanish, told him he came to bind up his wounds, and to save his life if possible. As he bent over to examine him, Almagro saw the savage stealthily draw a knife from his belt; and he just succeeded in seizing his arm, and wresting the weapon from him, as he was making a lunge at the benevolent doctor.

"It is in vain to use humanity here; leave him to his fate—the death of a dog, which he deserves," said Almagro. But Lewis could not be dissuaded from doing his duty. He made Charles and Almagro hold the arms of the wretch, whose violence had caused a greater flow of blood, which rendered him weaker. Lewis examined the throat, and found it dreadfully lacerated; but as the artery did not seem injured, though the loss of blood was great, he thought, by proper care, a cure might be effected. It certainly was a fearful risk to introduce such a savage under their roof; but to leave him exposed to the tempest in this condition would be certain death to him. He began therefore to bind up the wounds, in order to render his removal less hazardous; but the struggles and resistance of the man were so great, that he succeeded with much difficulty; and as he finished, the ungrateful wretch endeavoured to seize in his teeth the hand that had saved him from immediate death. Fortunately he did not succeed; but, the moment his hands were released, he tore off the bandages with fury, and, raising himself by a violent effort to his feet, he sprung forward and snatched up his spear, that was leaning against a tree. But this exertion hastened his doom—the blood gushed from his throat and mouth, and he fell down in the agonies of death.

In the mean time Jack's first care had been to go up to the puma, which he found now, as well as its victim, quite dead. Tom and he removed the body of the man from the grasp of the ferocious beast, and laid it by the side of the Indian shot by Almagro, who was also dead. It was a fearful spectacle to see death around them; and the strong men could not forbear shedding tears over the disfigured corpses of their violent and unprovoked enemies.

When the last breath of the ferocious leader had passed, they looked upon the faces of these dark ruffians, and trembled to consider what would have been the fate of their happy circle, if the bolt of heaven had not fallen on the heads of the savage assailants. Still they could not abandon the bodies of these men, their brothers by creation, and the image of God, to be the prey of the unclean condor; and they were at a loss where to bestow these sad memorials of their victory till morning. At length they brought from the cave the sailcloth which had formed their tent in their early wanderings, and had been brought from Esperanza to use as a screen against the wind from the inner caves. They spread this covering over the bodies, and placed heavy stones upon it, to keep it down; then Tom stripped the puma of its handsome skin, and hung it up to be dried, before they finally entered and closed their retreat.

It was some time before the agitated community could be sufficiently composed to perform their evening devotions, which concluded with a special thanksgiving for their preservation from the savage beast, and still more savage man.

CHAPTER XXVII.

The Return of Mr. Merton and the Caciques. The Fate of the Indian Traitors. The New Converts. Departure of the Indians. The Caverns explored. The Ingot of Silver. The Visit to the Plains. Conflict with the Wild Cattle. The Peccaries. Tom's Accident.

THE repose of the family was disturbed, and they rose early to remove the fearful spectacle which deformed their quiet glade. The young men were not sorry to see the three horses of the slain grazing quietly; they were fine animals, with saddle-cloths of rich skins, and would certainly prove an acquisition to their diminished stud.

The morning was stormy, and the rain fell on the youths as they dug in a remote niche of the glen the graves of their enemies; but suddenly their labour was arrested by the sound of well-known voices, and they sprung forward to welcome their expected friends.

"Is all well?" asked Mr. Merton, in an agitated voice; and, satisfied with the reply, he lifted up his hands in thankfulness.

"These men," said Paul, looking on the grim features of the dead, " have received their just punishment. They were traitors to their cacique, cowards, and base liars. Nevertheless, you, good doctor, who love to save life, may find work on the plain below, where two of the cowardly fugitives lie, stricken by the hand of God."

The family then learned that Paul had discovered the absence of the six men, who were the most disobedient and savage of the tribe; he found also that they had not only stolen from him rich skins and silver ornaments, but had also carried off Mr. Merton's faithful dog. Alarmed at their flight, as he suspected their intentions, he communicated his fears to Mr. Merton and Cangapol. They had set out at a very early hour, well armed, and travelled at a speed which had alarmed Mr. Merton.

As they drew near the foot of the mountain, they perceived a dark group, and Cangapol made ready his bow, which he carried in preference to fire-arms; as he felt assured, he said, that the men were encamped on this spot. They soon saw that but one man was standing by the side of his horse, looking down on two recumbent figures. Paul, with the impetuosity of youth, rode up to the man, and denounced him, in the Indian tongue, as a robber and a traitor. The villain poised his spear with deadly aim against his chief, which Cangapol saw, and in a moment sent an arrow through the heart of the Indian. Mr. Merton was dreadfully shocked at this summary execution, and could never afterwards be convinced that the occasion justified the act of homicide.

On looking round, they found the other two Indians lying, apparently dying, their horses dead, and not far from them. From one of the unfortunate sufferers, Paul extorted some account of the proceedings of the previous night; he added, that in their frantic flight from the terrible puma, and more terrible fire-arms, they had rushed up the slope, not aware of the abrupt ridge of the mountain, for, guided by Wallace, they had come up by the winding path at the side, which they could not discover on their return. They had left the torches behind in their dismay, and being quite in the dark, and blinded by the tempest, they lost all control over their horses in the descent. The ground was moist and slippery with the continual rain; and the usually adroit horsemen were unable to prevent their horses from falling, and rolling down the steep mountain-side, through briers and brushwood, with fearful rapidity, till they reached the plain. One of the riders alone had been able to get clear of his horse, with little or no injury, but only to lose his life in the act of murder and treason; the others, bewildered, stunned, and lacerated, lost all consciousness; and recovered only to find their horses dead, and themselves dragged from the bushes by their uninjured companions, scarcely living, with limbs broken and lacerated, exposed to the fury of the storm through the long darkness of night, and expecting death every moment to release them from their agony.

It was impossible to remove these wretched sufferers without assistance; but no time was now lost; two mattresses were immediately carried down, and Lewis provided himself with medicine, bandages, and all needful appliances. He found, on examination, the fractured limbs of the men so much swollen and inflamed, that no operation could take place at present. The men were therefore placed on mattresses, and transported with all care up the difficult road, groaning with the anguish, which even Indian fortitude could not support unmoved.

All selfish considerations were waived, and the Indians admitted at once into the cave; but they were not in a state to notice where they were placed, and it was only the aid of powerful restoratives that prevented them from sinking immediately. Their limbs were dreadfully fractured, and Lewis had no hope of saving their lives, as assistance had been too long delayed. He gave them composing medicines to alleviate the pain; and Mr. Merton, with pious earnestness, endeavoured to awaken them to a sense of their wickedness, and to enlighten their ignorance. In their long hours of agony, during the darkness of the night, it was impossible to conceive a human mind so steeped in apathy or ignorance, as not to have made some reflections on the past; some speculations on the future; and the men seemed to be somewhat moved by the good priest's exhortations. But life was fast passing away; and though the charitable Mr. Merton always believed some ray of light fell on the souls of the dying men, none could judge of their state but that God into whose awful presence they were summoned in a few hours.

The day was spent in serious instruction and earnest prayer, and before evening Mr. Merton was satisfied to admit his new friends into the Church of Christ, by administering the rite of baptism. Early next morning the Indians were buried; and then, dressed in their fairest robes, the whole party set out for church, where Cangapol and his son were baptized by the names of Pedro and Albert, and the ceremony of marriage performed between the new Christian and Zara. Then Mr. Merton addressed a particular discourse in Spanish to the Indians, who listened to it with earnest and devout attention.

Notwithstanding the gloomy events of the last few days, the young people would not give up the festival; and when they were all gathered round the table, which was decorated with the plate, china, and glass brought from the hidden store at Esperanza, the happy and united family forgot all their dangers, and enjoyed Nanny's excellent dinner as much as she desired. The children were prettily dressed in white muslin frocks, made by the industrious sisters, who had also attired Zara in a rich blue silk dress,— a present to them from Mrs. Douglas; and Almagro sighed to think that his daughter, who now looked like a queen, must return to the huts of the savages.

"Do not be grieved, my father," said she; "is it not my duty to live with my husband and my child? and it is the duty of the Cacique to dwell amongst his people. See what a large work we have before us. I must teach the women to be clean and industrious; Pedro will persuade the men to become hunters or husbandmen; and when they are less savage, Mr. Merton will come to us, and teach them to be Christians."

This was a pleasant plan, and even the grave Pedro smiled at the enthusiasm of his lovely wife; nor did he altogether despair of such a result. At all events, he entreated the family to return to Esperanza in the spring; Paul and he engaging for the forbearance of their tribes. But Paul advised them to fortify their settlement, that they might be secured from the attacks of tribes from the west of the Cordilleras, who not unfrequently made plundering expeditions on the Pampas. From the still ruder savages of the south, they were protected by the great distance which lay between them; and the more civilized tribes of the north were less ferocious, and, if even they wandered so far, would rather desire to traffic with the settlers than wantonly destroy them.

The Indians remained a few days longer at the rock; the two chiefs hunting with the young men, and assisting them to obtain a considerable quantity of beef, to be dried or salted for the winter, now close at hand. The friends parted with reluctance, but it was necessary the Caciques should return to their people. Zara wept bitterly, and promised to come again if the snow did not fall; but the horses of the Pampas do not like the snow. Mr. Merton wished to retain the young Albert, to lay the foundation of a better education than he could obtain at the toldos; but the parents were unwilling to part with him, as Pedro said such a measure might offend the tribe.

Once more the family were left alone, to talk of the strange events of the last two months, and to

THE HOME OF THE WANDERERS.

prepare for their winter seclusion. No time was lost in bringing all the maize and wheat flour, which they ground on the spot, from Esperanza, leaving a plentiful supply of grain for seed in spring. Candles, soap, and potatoes, were also brought from the cave; and, trusting they had now sufficient stores for themselves, they turned to consider the condition of the cattle.

It was absolutely necessary to build sheds to protect the animals from storms, for it would have been a great difficulty, as they had previously experienced, to introduce the horses through the narrow passage into the cave; and to bring the cows into the same shelter would have been impossible. They soon raised two long low huts against the face of the rock; the end of one being close to the entrance to the cave, that the access might be easy in case the snow should be deep.

These huts were formed, like those formerly built at Esperanza, of poles intertwined with bamboos and plastered with mud; the roofs thatched with dry branches, leaves, and moss. The sun was still sufficiently powerful at noonday to dry the walls in a few days; and having collected dry grass and leaves for bedding, they completed the sheds by fixing to them substantial doors, obtained from the ruins at Esperanza, which they attached to the door-posts by hinges of hide; and hide straps, by which the doors were fastened every night, secured the cattle from the attacks of wild beasts.

Since the appearance of the puma, there existed a little fear in the family that more of the animals might be in the neighbourhood; and to satisfy Mrs. Merton, as well as to dispel some doubts of his own, Lewis proposed to the youths an expedition through the labyrinth of caves that existed beyond their own hall. With the precaution of carrying arms, and what Nanny deemed an extravagant supply of candles, they set out to explore these extraordinary hollows of the rocks. From one opening to another they

passed into a succession of caves, some totally dark;
others lighted by loop-holes above, so lofty and
artificial in appearance, that it was difficult to believe
they were not the work of man's hand. More than
once Lewis pointed out to Tom remarkable appearances on the wall, as if the rock had been cut away
by some instrument.

No animal but the birds seemed to have visited
these caves, and they terminated their search by turning through a lateral opening, attracted by the murmur
of water, and found the stream, which, pouring through
an opening above, had worn itself a channel through
the rocky caves, till winding through some unseen
passage, it again appeared on the green plain before
the cave. They pursued the course of the stream, and
as they passed along, the light carried by Tom fell on
some glittering object; he stooped to examine it, and
cried out, " Lewis, I verily believe this large mass lying
half in the water is silver."

It really was silver; and Lewis declared that he had
for some time suspected that these vast caverns were
abandoned mines, probably worked by the enterprising
Spaniards, when they held possessions on both sides
of the Cordilleras, and forgotten in the decay and
depopulation of the country.

" But what a fortunate discovery for us!" said
Tom. " We have only to collect as much silver as
we can transport from the spot, and our fortune is
made."

Jack burst into a loud laugh, which the echoing
caves returned with a mocking derision, very mortify-
ing to Tom. " You have forgotten the Swiss Robinson,
Tom," said his brother. " It was Francis, I think,
that wanted to carry away all the money from the
wreck. What use in the world could we make of
silver? Iron would be ten times more valuable."

" I should certainly not object to a pair of silver
spurs," said Charles, " like those our friend Paul wore at
his last visit. But I could not undertake to manufac-

ture spurs, nor indeed, if I had them, have I a pair of boots fit to attach them to," and Charles looked, with a sigh, at his worn-out boots.

"There were some capital bootmakers at Pedro's tolderia," said Jack; "they would have fitted you out in no time, Charley."

"I conclude the boots were merely colts' skins, dried and oiled," said Charles, with contempt.

"They had an improved plan," answered Jack. "They just drew the skin from the legs of the colt, and fitted it upon their own legs, warm and bloody, where it remained till worn out, a part of themselves, and a wonderful fit—Hoby himself could not succeed better. But now, Lewis, is it worth while to carry off this silver?"

Lewis left the decision to themselves; and Tom said, "Then we will take it. I acknowledge my blunder about the utility of the metal, but I should like to try the experiment of melting the silver, and moulding it into some vessel. You see the action of the water has already cleared away the earthy particles."

"Yes," said Lewis; "this appears to be a piece of virgin silver, and may be melted and used without further preparation. Had it been the amalgam, or compound of mercury and silver, in which mixed state it is usually found, we should have had to extricate the silver by a process which our present circumstances would have rendered difficult or impossible."

They continued along the stream, carrying with them their new acquisition, till in a cave adjacent to that they had used for the horses, the little rivulet disappeared through the rock.

"My opinion is," said Lewis, "that our most important discovery to-day is that of the source of the rivulet. Now we can always procure water, in defiance of frost or storm."

The piece of silver, which weighed two or three pounds, was admired by the young ladies, and curiously examined by Mr. Merton, who said, as he put it down, " Thank God, my children, that this shining metal cannot lead you into temptation. Fortunately, this lure to evil is useless to us. We have all the comforts of life without money, and money could not purchase for us the dangerous luxuries of life."

" It is clear," said Lewis, " that this mine has never been worked to any very great extent like some in the north of the Andes; one of which is said to extend three hundred miles."

" I trust," said Matilda, " that it may never again be opened, to desecrate this peaceful spot with fires and furnaces, and people it with worn-out wretches, torn from the freedom of their hunting-grounds to labour as slaves in the mines."

The young men procured from Nanny a large iron pot, and, in one of the interior caves placed the vessel, with the silver in it, over an immense fire, which was not an extravagance, as the woods supplied them plentifully with fuel. There they melted their silver, and in moulds made by themselves, formed two drinking-cups, even succeeding in placing handles upon them. Afterwards Tom engraved an inscription on each; denoting that they were presented to Mr. and Mrs. Merton by their children. These cups were by no means miracles of art; they were not classical in form, nor perfect in finish, but they were proudly used by the parents, and admired even by Nanny; who said, " There was some sense in making a cup that Wallace couldn't break, if he did knock it down with his *tantrums*." Nor was the remainder of the silver wasted, for they made saltcellars, fruit-knives, and several other pretty useful little utensils.

The wild fowl occasionally visited the streamlet, and the bolas supplied the table with an agreeable change from the charqui to which they had been confined while busied with the building and melting; but they proposed another hunting-day before the snow came on. This expedition was, however, deferred too long;

for on the morning they were to set out they rose to find the air darkened with falling snow, which already lay two feet deep on the ground. A path was soon cleared to the sheds, the cows were milked, all the animals were fed, and their masters rejoiced, as they secured the doors of the snug stables, that they had been able to complete this shelter for their faithful servants.

The snow continued to fall for several days, and the little glen was so buried among the high mountains, that at this season, even the midday sun did not reach it to melt the snow, which lay four feet deep, but became so hard that they could walk over it. The young men even climbed to the ridge, and looking down upon the plain, saw scattered patches of snow beneath the trees; but a large portion was uncovered, and groups of wild cattle were browsing on the stunted pasturage.

Charles was anxious for a chase, but Lewis dissuaded him, for the descent would be dangerous during the frost, and the family at home would be unhappy. The confinement to the cave was long, but they devoted many hours in the day to useful studies, perfecting themselves in languages, especially the useful Spanish. Lewis taught Tom and Matilda astronomy; Mary and Maria had greater enjoyment in reading history or travels; Mary had also a talent for drawing, and amused her friends with many humorous and skilful sketches.

After a month's confinement, the decrease of the snow, and a clear sky, induced Mr. Merton to consent that the party should visit the plains below; especially as the whole family were tired of salted food, and Dr. Lewis prescribed a change of diet, lest their health should suffer. They found the plains free from snow, but the air was keen, and the wild cattle were collected under the trees for shelter in rather larger herds than they liked to encounter; still they thought it would be disgraceful to return empty-handed, and

2 B

were riding up towards the herd, when a ferocious old bull made a charge against Field-Marshal Jack, who was always in advance, and was immediately followed by the whole herd.

The young men had proposed only to use the bolas, but had fortunately brought their rifles, and as this was no time for economy, Lewis cried, " Fire !" and they sent a volley into the midst of the astonished herd. The huge bull was wounded in the chest, but rushed on in his last agonies, gored Tom's horse frightfully, and then fell dead. The wounded horse, which was one of those belonging to the Indians, reared up, frantic with pain, and all expected he would fall back on his rider ; but Tom, by a sudden jerk of the rein, brought him down on his side.

" I fear my leg is broken," said Tom to his friends, who were gathered anxiously round him ; " but I am thankful to have escaped the death I expected, if the poor beast had fallen back. He is dying ; put him out of his misery, Charles."

Tom was extricated, and the horse shot through the head. The herd had scampered off after the death of their champion, leaving two of their number dead on the field, which were carried off by Almagro and Charles, who hastened homeward to break the sorrowful news to the family, and to bring a mattress and board on which to carry Tom.

In the mean time, with the assistance of Jack, Lewis reduced the fracture, and enveloped the limb in the bark of a tree, which they peeled for the purpose. He also bled his patient, who fortunately seemed to have received no injury beyond the broken leg ; and they then sat down to wait patiently for the return of the messengers.

" We should be in a pretty condition now, Lewis," said Jack, " if another army of those four-legged warriors was to take the field against us. What would be our best plan in such a case ? To make the best fight we could, as long as we could hold the ground? or to leave our poor horses to be gored, and run away on foot, carrying off our wounded hero?"

"No! no!" said Tom; "If there be any danger, you two must *tree*, and leave me to my fate. It is probable these wild creatures would hardly deign to notice such a poor prostrate creature as I am, especially if Lewis will give me his brown poncho in exchange for this unlucky scarlet, which doubtless offended the eyes of that irritable old bull."

Lewis laughed at Tom's precaution, but exchanged cloaks with him, for fear of accidents, and had scarcely done so, when Jack cried out, "Look out, Lewis, the enemy is upon us!"

Lewis did look out, and saw approaching a herd of hog-shaped, frightful dark animals, with long snouts, bristly backs and apparently no tails. There were not more than twenty of them, which rather abated the alarm of Lewis, for these animals, the peccaries or javalies, are dangerous when associated in numbers. With their large sharp tusks and formidable strong jaws, they will attack man or beast, and frequently gore the legs of the horses dreadfully.

"Don't be alarmed, dear Tom," cried Jack, "we will face the enemy and protect you. The bolas or the rifle, Lewis?"

"The rifle, by all means, Jack," answered his friend, "and we may need Tom's rifle as well, for these creatures have the hoggish nature, and are as obstinate as they are courageous. Wait till they are near, for we must not waste a charge. They have not seen us yet, for they are grubbing in the ground for roots. We must try to carry home some pork for Nanny; but at this season I fear it will be poor."

The leader of the herd, attracted either by its natural antagonist, the horse, or by the scarlet poncho, now grunted forth its orders to the rest, and set out in a waddling trot towards the foe. Lewis and Jack, marking their victims, fired, and the general and his *aide-de-camp* fell. But this did not arrest the course

2 B 2

of the herd, which moved on with dogged resolution. The friends fired the second barrels, and two more were killed.   The herd only grunted and screamed in a more angry tone, and came on to within twenty yards of their opponents.

"Lewis," cried Tom, "do you take my gun, and let Jack run up that beech-tree. I have my spear, and can keep the beasts off me for a little time."

Lewis took the gun, fired both barrels, and then prepared to drive off the animals with the butt-end, if possible, Jack assisting him with a spear. But the obstinate peccaries surrounded them ; and they were in great alarm for Tom, when fortunately they saw their friends approaching. They cried out aloud to them to hasten their speed ; and the good horsemen galloped on, and, speedily reaching the spot, with loud shouts they fired a volley on the ignoble, hoggish crew. The beasts, as much alarmed at the cries of their antagonists as at the destruction caused by their weapons, finally took to flight, with loud grunts of vexation at their discomfiture.

The first words were congratulations at their escape, then succeeded irresistible laughter at the nature of their enemies, in which even the suffering Tom joined, though he confessed he had been in mortal terror.

"Come, Charley," said Jack, " help to get this poor wounded fellow upon the mattress, and let us retreat before we have any more assailants ; though how we shall dare to show our faces to the girls I cannot tell, after crying out for help against an attack of swine."

"I can assure you, Jack," said Tom, "that the white-lipped peccary, *Dicotyles labiatus*, is by no means an enemy to be slighted, however you may loath its nature.   Yet its food is less disgusting than that of the domestic hog, being fruits, grains, and herbs when they can be obtained, and at this season the roots which lie in the earth.   It is said they will, in scarcity, eat fish, or even reptiles, but that scarcity can never exist in this land of plenty. Would it not be desirable,

Lewis, before you carry off the spoil, to remove the offensive gland, which will otherwise taint the flesh."

Lewis, with the assistance of Almagro who had met with the animal before in his rambles, carefully extracted the particular gland from the loins of the animal, which secretes a filthy fluid, of a nature so inodorous, that it almost vies with the zorillo in keeping all animals aloof from it.

The ground was strewed with the slain. The fierce old leader was abandoned as uneatable; of the remainder, six of the youngest were selected, tied in pairs, and suspended across the horses of Charles and Almagro, who carried Tom. Lewis rode by his side to see that all went on well, and Jack led the laden horses. The difficulty in getting the litter through the wood caused Tom much suffering; and many tears were shed by the family, who came to meet him, at the sight of his weak and fainting condition. But once laid on his own bed and a cordial given him he revived, and begged that no one would be distressed for by God's help, his good friend Dr. Lewis would soon cure him. "And, after all, mamma," added he, " it is better that I rather than Jack should be compelled to lie in bed for a month. Jack would have been wretched in confinement; but with books, and such employment as I can accomplish, I believe I shall rather enjoy my lazy life."

"And you see, my dear Mr. Merton," said Lewis, " I shall not lose my art for want of practice in the wilderness. I have had several patients, and tolerable success."

"You are very charitable, my son," said the good man, " to sacrifice the pleasures of the world to live here amid privations, dangers, and the dullness of solitude. I dare not expect you always to remain with us."

"I shall certainly not run away," replied Lewis; " see! Mrs. Merton and the young ladies actually look alarmed at the idea of losing such an important person as the family apothecary."

"The family friend, rather," exclaimed Matilda. "Never leave us, dear Dr. Lewis. If you go, we will all go ; without you Esperanza would indeed be a wilderness."

Lewis was much affected at the earnestness of his friends, to whom he was greatly attached ; he had no ties to attract him elsewhere, and in this salubrious air was in much better health than he had been before he left England. He was not only content, but determined to continue one of the family.

While Tom was left to repose, the rest assisted in removing the rough thick skin from the peccaries ; though Jack declared it to be a perfect waste of time, for the hide must be useless.

"I shall use some of the bristles for drawing-brushes," said Mary.

"The bristles, with a little ingenuity," said Lewis, "may be formed into several useful brushes. Nanny constantly bemoans her want of brushes, and we must try to make some. Neither is the skin to be despised, Jack ; it will make excellent saddles. We must cure and clean all the hides, for we shall need stout leather when we begin to work at Esperanza."

The pork was certainly not equal to the well-fed pork of Westmoreland ; but was an agreeable change of food ; some hams were salted for curing, and the fat melted for domestic purposes ; and after this large supply of meat there was no more hunting for some weeks.

CHAPTER XXVIII.

Plans for Rebuilding Esperanza.   The Coracles of the Indians.
The Breach in the Caves.   The Battle of Jack and the Condor.
The Spectre in the Cave.   The Happy Meeting.   Old Friends
assembled in the Cave of Refuge.

THE weather continued uncertain; showers of sleet
and rain during the day were often followed by frosts
at night; but the family were all happily occupied.
Tom was in a fair way of recovery, though still kept
in a recumbent position; but under his father and
Dr. Lewis he made great progress in improving his
mind.   He applied himself diligently to mathematics,
and acquired a taste for higher studies than those he
had been formerly engaged in.

The sun had now more power; the snow melted,
the little stream was swollen, and the rich mud
washed from the rocks above, spread itself over the
tiny glade to fertilize it.   Then the grass began to
spring, and the cattle were released to enjoy the fresh
herbage.   Tom was carried out on his mattress to
breathe the pure air, and the young workmen produced their plans, and proposed to commence their
building immediately.

" My plan is," said Tom, " that we should carry a
brick wall, nine feet high, round a space of ground
sufficiently extensive to contain our fields, gardens,
corrals, and dwellings.   Esperanza must be, in fact, a
fortified town."

" Might we not leave the side to the river open ? "
said Matilda.   " It is usually impassable to the
Indians; and we might have a drawbridge for
ourselves."

" No, my dear," replied Mr. Merton; " I would
rather have a wall.   Remember the lions and tigers

that have visited us. Moreover, some of the South
American Indians do cross rivers in coracles, which
vessels, if it could be effected with safety, I would
gladly see. I have an idea that they must be of classical form."

"Not a bit of it, sir," said Charles. "They are
no more like the coracles described by Herodotus, as
in use in Babylonia, than they are to a Roman galley.
The ancient coracle was of wicker work, circular in
form, with no distinction between prow and stern,
lined with reeds, and covered with leather, and 2,000
years have not effected much improvement in the construction of this vessel. The basket coracles are still
used on the Euphrates, precisely the same in form
and manufacture, except that instead of the covering
of leather, they have now a coating of pitch, within
and without."

"These coracles, then," said Matilda, "must resemble the Egyptian ark of bulrushes, in which the
infant Moses was placed, and which was ' pitched
within and without.' "

"Precisely so, my cousin," replied Charles. "But
the coracles of our neighbours, the Indians, are
merely hides, stretched out by rods within, and are
neither classical in form nor in association."

"However curious we may be," said Lewis, " to
observe the form of the Indian coracle or canoe, I
think the less opportunity we may have for the
observation the better. I agree with Mr. Merton
that it is expedient to wall our settlement, certainly
a formidable undertaking; but we are expert brick-
makers, have abundance of material, and are not
limited to time, for we can still retain possession of
this tolerably convenient lodging for an indefinite
period; therefore I propose that we no longer delay
our commencement."

All joyfully agreed to become labourers, and the
next question was the extent of ground to be inclosed. Mr. Merton thought the old boundaries contained as much land as they had a right to appro-

priate, that was, as much as sufficed for their wants. The younger party took a larger view of the future, and contended that when they were building they might as well secure an ample portion of ground, for the settlement might ultimately become a colony.

"And remember, papa," said Jack, "we are actually conferring a benefit on posterity, by bringing waste lands into cultivation, clearing the forests, slaying wild beasts, and civilizing savages. Indeed, I consider we are great philanthropists."

"I doubt it, my son," replied Mr. Merton. "I fear that we are merely actuated by the selfishness of fallen human nature; we seek our own profit, our own safety, and our own ease of mind; and the benefit of posterity is but a secondary consideration with us. Nevertheless, it may be prudent to enlarge our domain, for God may please again to send to us strangers in distress. Even the dear friends whose absence we so much regret may return to us, and it will be well to have accommodation for hospitality."

These preliminaries settled, Lewis, Almagro, Charles, and Jack, the working men, set out next morning, leaving Wallace as guard to the weakened garrison. They found all in the same state they had left it at Esperanza, except the garden-beds which were somewhat scratched by the fowls, which still roosted on the old spot; and the footsteps of the hare were also to be traced; but vegetation was springing, and the hand of the gardener and husbandman was needed; yet they agreed that they must have many thousands of bricks made before they could till and sow.

A number of moulds had been made during the winter, and the banks of the river now afforded them a plentiful supply of clay. They laboured diligently during the day, and returned at night laden with a basket of eggs, collected in the old poultry-yard, happy to report their progress, and enjoy the repose of the evening. After a week of hard labour they piled the bricks, already hardened, to be thoroughly dried by the sun, and turned to the garden. They sowed all their seeds, and put everything into order, hoping before the seeds sprung up to have a wall raised which would protect the plants from the devastations of the hare or the peccary.

Every day the spring progressed, and Lewis collected the first flowers one bright evening to present to the fair sisters. But they found a little agitation in the household, and had to put down the flowers till they heard the cause.

"About two hours ago," said Matilda, " as we were sitting quietly at work, we were startled by a tremendous noise. I fancied I felt the cave shake beneath us, and I concluded it must be an earthquake, and that we might be overwhelmed by the next shock. I considered for a moment, and then got Nanny and papa to assist us in rolling away the great stone from the entrance. I thought if we got mamma and Tom out as far as the slope opposite the rock, we might be in less danger. We removed the barrier and left the cave; then Tom said: 'It is no earthquake; the sky is clear and bright; the birds are singing, and all Nature is in repose. Depend on it, Matilda, the noise has arisen from some animal in the interior caves, or the fall of some piece of rock.' I thought it impossible that any animal should have caused such a sound; but it might be a fallen rock; and as mamma was very uneasy, I proposed that we should examine the inner caverns. She was very unwilling that we should venture; but seeing her actually tremble with agitation, we left papa and Tom with her, and set out with rifles and spears like heroines, with lighted candles which were of much more use, and walked forward boldly, though I own my heart palpitated as we got farther and farther from our own home. At length we saw daylight ——"

"Daylight! Matilda, are you dreaming?" cried Jack.

" No, indeed, Jack," continued she. " We actually saw broad, bright daylight, through an opening at the side of the rock, at no very great height above us, while in the cave lay a large mass of rock and earth, fallen from the chasm above. No doubt, the melting of the snow had loosened the earth, and probably the immediate cause of the accident had been a poor guanaco which had lost its life by the fall; but most wonderfully, a young one, which lay licking the dead mother, did not seem much injured. Maria took up the young guanaco, and we hastened to retreat lest there should be another fall. On our return I picked up some glittering ore, which Tom says contains much silver; and papa says is best left in obscurity."

" I perfectly agree with our good father," said Lewis; " we have more important objects to demand our attention just now than smelting silver, which, after all, we could make very little use of."

" Unless we cast it into bullets," said Charles. " I have heard of a tribe of Indians in the north who use golden bullets, gold being more easily attained than lead; and silver is much better. Nanny could tell you a silver bullet never fails to do its duty."

Nanny pledged herself for the efficacy of a silver bullet against " an uncanny body," and thought they might be good against " them heathen Indians," for they were " *surelie* uncanny."

But the silver was left unnoticed; the accident in the cave made the whole family still more anxious to return to Esperanza, and it required every moment of time to complete their great labours there.

Next morning a large piece of rock was rolled before the opening into the cave where the rock had fallen, and the workmen returned to their brick-making for a few days more. They found the corn sown in the autumn already sprung up, and the fences of the fields being still secure, they had no anxiety on that account.

" How much," said Lewis, " do I now wish for the

sound, practical head of our good friend Douglas, to aid us in laying out and fortifying our little domain. I have no hesitation in reclaiming any extent of land from the puma and the jaguar ; but to build so many hundred yards of wall, with only four workmen, would require much time now, when we ought to begin the dwellings. We cannot do both. Shall we build the house or the wall first ?"

" I know," said Jack, " that dear papa and mamma would never consent to return to an unprotected house ; they would rather remain in the cave, even during the hot summer. We must try either a wall or a moat ; which would be best ?"

" Let us have both," said Charles. " A wall, six feet high at present, which we can raise three feet higher when we have more time ; a deep ditch outside, and within a terrace formed of the earth thrown from the ditch. This terrace will form a pleasant walk for the ladies, and an immense advantage to us in case of a siege."

"Very well, my boys," said Lewis, " but this would be at least four months' work for four unpractised workmen."

" The girls will hand us the bricks," said Jack ; " we may reckon on good assistance from Maria and Mary who can work nearly as well as I can."

" The dear girls have occupations more suitable to them than building," answered Lewis. " I could not bear to see their hands plastered with mud. But what are you grubbing among the ruins for, Jack ?"

" I promised Tom that the *bee-tree* should be included in the inclosure," replied Jack. " Now, in his confinement, he has been making a new kind of hive, into which he designs to lure a swarm of bees, and he wished me to try and find some fragments of glass in the ruins of the dear old hall, that he might insert them into his hive."

They carefully removed the charred wood and scattered leaves from the interior of the melancholy walls,

which still remained standing, and found the frame of
the window, which, being partly burnt, had fallen
inside. Two or three panes of glass were still entire
—a valuable contribution for their intended mansion.
The fragments were collected and placed in a basket to
be carried home, where they immediately proceeded,
determined that very evening to settle the question of
the fortification.

They found Maria with her little nursling, the
guanaco, which she had brought out to crop the fresh
grass on the green, and Jack remained with her,
admiring the little creature, while the rest entered the
cave. "Look at that huge condor perched on the high
cliff," said Maria; "how he watches us with his cunning eye! I have no doubt, if we were lying as still
as my little guanaco is just now, it would have a peck
at us."

She had scarcely spoken, when the bird spread its
immense wings, and hovering over them for a moment,
pounced on the pretty guanaco, and began to peck at
its head. Maria shrieked, and Jack, who was without
bolas or lasso, threw his cap at the bird; but it merely
lifted its head a moment, with a look of disdain, and
continued its attack. Maria's distress affected Jack
much, and with his usual impetuosity he sprung forward and seized the huge neck of the creature with
both hands. It struggled, flapped its powerful wings
against the brave lad, and twisted its head that it might
reach him with its strong beak.

"A lasso! Maria! call Charles to bring a lasso!"
cried Jack; and Maria rushed into the cave, and
returned followed by the whole family. The animal
had succeeded in flinging Jack down on his back and
was beating him with its wings; but he still held it
manfully by the throat.

Almagro flung his bolas, which wound round its
huge body, and restrained its wings for a moment;
then the thick thongs of hide burst asunder with its
efforts, and the wings were released. But Charles and

Lewis, one on each side, pierced it with their lances ; the dark blood gushed out, the wings flapped slowly and feebly, and Jack, rising, dragged his ferocious antagonist from its poor victim, and then relinquished his iron grasp, and left the bird to die.

"A pretty thrashing I have had," said he, rubbing his arms, " and a narrow escape from that two-legged tiger, which would, I verily believe, if you had not come up at the right moment, have pecked out my eyes, as it has done those of Maria's poor pet ; for my strength was about done."

In that short time the condor had not only blinded the guanaco, but with its strong beak had penetrated the brain, and the animal died in a few minutes, to the great grief of its mistress. Tom measured the condor, which, with the wings extended, was twelve feet across.

"It is said," he remarked, "that the condor, *Sarcoramphus gryphus*, sometimes measures fourteen feet across, and from three to four feet from the back to the extremity of the tail. It is a hideous bird, especially when gorged with food, for then the bare, wrinkled, red skin of the neck is displayed in a most disgusting manner. It is bold as the eagle, and voracious as the vulture ; yet its talons are not formed to carry off its prey like the noble eagle ; but it pursues, secures, and then tears it to pieces, and feasts on it with a cruelty and voracity unparalleled among the feathered race ; and doubtless this creature itself will soon be devoured by its cannibal kindred."

This was actually the case ; before morning the bones of the destroyer were picked by his own friends, and Mrs. Merton shuddered as she hoped she should soon have a shelter at Esperanza, unmolested by pumas and condors. That evening they agreed that ten acres of ground should be inclosed—a large extent, but Lewis hoped, in a month, they should be able to raise round it a wall of six feet, and then proceed to the house-building. All this was measured and marked next day ; the area included not only the " bee-tree," but

P. 383.

" There is a man in the cave," she articulated with difficulty, bursting into tears;
" I saw his face above the large piece of rock."

several other trees, some of which were to be cut down and usefully employed, the rest to be left, as equally useful either for their produce or shade ; and these preliminaries arranged, they returned to the cave with the confidence that they had made a beginning.

"And we will have a supper of fresh eggs to celebrate the commencement of the great work," said Matilda. "The hens have selected the very extremity of the caverns for their roosting-place ; but as I have no dread of the genii of the caves, if Nanny will spare me a candle, I will bring the eggs," and taking a candle in one hand and her basket in the other, the intrepid girl tripped lightly through the gloomy windings of the rocks.

Matilda was perhaps less gentle and obliging in temper than her sister ; but as Lewis watched her disappear, he could not help thinking the foibles of his favourite, her impatience of weakness, and love of sway, were atoned for by her firmness and fearlessness of character. As these thoughts were passing in his mind, he was astonished to see Matilda re-appear, pale and trembling with agitation, and he sprung forward to assist her, and learn the cause of her alarm.

"There is a man in the caves," she articulated with difficulty, bursting into tears. "I saw his face above the large piece of rock you had placed before the cave where the opening was made."

Jack and Charles had seized their rifles, and were rushing towards the back caves, but the entreaties of the females, and the commands of Lewis, arrested them. "Do not be rash," said he ; "we will go together, prepared, but calm. I have no doubt the intruder is some animal, and no man. There is no cause for alarm, we will, if necessary, destroy the visitor, and then effectually close the communication with these remote caves.

Leaving the family tolerably tranquillized, the four able men marched first, followed by Tom, leaning on a short lance. As they drew near the spot, the countenance of each was marked by intense anxiety. The piece of rock which had been placed to defend the inhabited caves from the intrusion of animals, was about five feet in height; but above it, the evening light streamed from the aperture in the cave beyond. There was certainly no face over the rock now, and they stopped to consult on the prudence of removing the stone in order to examine the suspected retreat of the intruder, when they were electrified by the loud braying of a mule beyond the barrier. They burst into a loud laugh.

"To think," said Jack, "that the keen-eyed Matilda should actually take the face of a mule for that of a man. It has certainly fallen through the opening, and we must release it."

They removed the stone, and their lights flashing into the caves beyond, revealed the trembling form and pale face of a man, who, in a voice hoarse with agitation, exclaimed, in imperfect Spanish, "Spare me, noble Indians, I am only a harmless traveller; an accident brought me into the mine, and I have stolen no silver."

Lewis assured the panic-struck man that he was in no danger, and inquired if he was alone.

"Lewis," said Jack, "the man is neither Spaniard nor Indian; his Spanish is worse than mine."

"Oh! God bless you, young gentlemen," cried the man; "for them's the words of dear ould England for sartain."

"Then your are English?" inquired Lewis, gravely; but Jack disdained all dignity, and immediately shook hands with a man who certainly did not speak English much better than Spanish.

"Yes, sir," said the man. "I'se a poor Yorkshire lead miner fra' the Dales; glad to hear my own tongue. It's all along of this sappy mule, that knew no better than to tumble down t'shaft. Then t'mistress was sorely put about, for all her boxes had gone down too, and Jem Alderson, he cam' down, he's used to gan' down shafts; and up he comes, and swears he saw a spirit all dressed iv' white, wi' a lamp iv' one hand, and a coffin iv' t'other. And what s'uld sarve me, but I s'uld brag, that I'd come down, and send up t'mule wi' rapes. Master was fain to come his sel', but mistress has a bit of her own way, and she says, says she, ' Joe's a brave lad, Joe s'all gang ;' so down I cam, and a bonny fright I've getten," and he looked round him with terror.

While Joe was telling his tale, Jack had, unobserved, climbed up the inclined plane formed by the fallen earth, and disappeared through the opening above; and just at this moment they heard him utter a loud " hurrah!" Lewis and Charles were not long in following him, and emerging through the opening, they saw themselves in a hollow, surrounded by rocks, and in the midst of men, women, and laden mules. Jack was locked in the embrace of a fur-clad lady, in whom they soon recognised Mrs. Douglas, while good portly Mr. Douglas stood laughing; and even the pale and pensive Mr. Carruthers seemed to enjoy the scene.

" What! my dear, dear friends! " cried Mrs. Douglas, " are you all here ? Who could have expected you, one after another, to rise out of the earth, like gnomes, to help us in this Valley of Despair, in which we have wandered about for two days, without discovering any means of escaping from it. And now, Dr. Lewis, how are you all ? Why are you not·at Esperanza ? And where is Esperanza ? How can we get to it ? Extricate us, my dear friends, from this huge trap, which we have all concluded was to be our grave-yard."

" I cannot answer all your questions yet, my dear Mrs. Douglas," replied Lewis, " nor can I expect you to answer mine; though I am curious to know how you could possibly reach this inaccessible valley, unless, like Sindbad, you had each been tied to the

2 c

leg of a roc, a bird which Matilda declares must certainly have been the condor. Our first consideration must be to introduce you to our hospitable halls: and I can see no other mode to accomplish this introduction than by your descending, like your mule, into the bowels of the earth!"

" I am here with the long ladder," cried Almagro, putting his head through the opening ; " I have tranquillized all the ladies, but have not told them a word of the good news."

The re-united friends, accompanied by the two strange women, descended the ladder, John, their old servant, with Almagro and the two miners, remained to unload the mules and let down the baggage into the cave, and to leave the mules in their secure retreat, unless they could be induced to descend.

Loudly did Mrs. Douglas express her wonder, as they wound through the mazy rocks, till they reached the wooden door that inclosed the family residence; then the laughing Charles cried out,—

"On heaven and Our Lady call,
And enter the enchanted hall."

The door flew open, and disclosed a lofty, gothic-looking hall, lighted up with a blazing fire, on each side of which, in leather-covered easy-chairs, reclined Mr. and Mrs. Merton ; Nanny was spinning near them, and at a long table Matilda was reading, Maria drawing, and Mary, seated on a low stool, was teaching the little kneeling Cecilia an infantine prayer. This was a pretty and strange spectacle ; but the repose that invested it was soon dispersed. All were in motion ; laughing, weeping, and inquiries followed.

Mr. Carruthers lifted up the kneeling infant, and kissing her fondly, said : " This is my treasure, dear Mary ; I see again, in her features, my lost Eliza ; " and he covered his face when he recalled her sad fate. The pretty child, thinking he was playing with her, tried to pull away his fingers from before his face;

then playing with his hair, she turned to Mary, and said : " More papa ; " for Mr. Merton and Dr. Lewis were both called " papa."

" Bless us all ! " said Nanny. " How many more on you is there to come ? and ye'll want your suppers I reckon ; so I must just set by my wheel."

" Indeed you must, Nanny," answered Jack ; " for there is your friend John and two more hungry fellows to come. So bring out the ham, and cold round of beef you meant to give us to Esperanza to-morrow.

" That's not a bad thought, Master Jack," said she ; " but you'll have to fast for it. And where the beds are to come from for all of you I can't see."

Nanny was really glad to see her valued friends again ; but grumbled as usual about folks frightening you by coming in at back ways, as she set out her large table with beef, ham, butter, and biscuits ; but her murmurs died away in quiet enjoyment, when she saw the table filled with happy faces, enjoying the plentiful repast.

" You must not think," said Mrs. Douglas, " that we have fallen short of provision on our journey, when you see our mighty appetite now. But the truth is that for the last few days we have been too anxious and vexed to eat. And now, Dr. Lewis, as you are eating nothing, pray give us an explanation of the cause of your quitting Esperanza, to shut yourselves up in this magnificent dungeon."

Lewis gave a brief recital of all that had passed since they parted, and added the present project of restoring Esperanza, rather than selecting another locality for their settlement.

" Then we have just arrived at the right moment," said Mrs. Douglas ; " for you must give us and our followers portions in the new Esperanza, and in the mean time put us into some of these branch dungeons," following Nanny into some of the interior divisions, where she was already busy laying down skins and mattresses to accommodate the new guests.

The two men, with John and Almagro, now entered, rather amazed at the strange reception-room; but the sight of the viands dispelled all doubts, and after a warm greeting between Nanny and her friend John, they sat down to supper; informing Mr. Douglas that they had unloaded the mules, slung them down the shaft with ropes, and left them, with some fresh-cut grass in the back part of the caves.

CHAPTER XXIX.

The Return of the Douglas Family across the Andes. Encounter with the Araucanian Indians, Loss of Property, and Strange Admission to the Cave of Refuge. Restoration of Esperanza. New Pupils and Converts. The Harvest. The Pampero and its fearful Results.

AFTER supper the old friends drew round the fire, and Mr. Douglas explained to them the cause of their re-appearance in the wilderness.

" Almagro would relate to you," he began, " our fatal journey and the disappointment of all our proposed plans in Chili. Our miners were dispersed, much of our valuable machinery was entirely lost, and the delay and misfortunes we had experienced discouraged our hopes, and sickened us of the undertaking. Henry sailed to England from Valparaiso immediately, promising to return to us within the year; and I made the most I could of the remainder of my mining utensils and machinery; but I had invested a great part of my property in these preparations; I had advanced considerable sums to the miners who had disappeared, and had been robbed of a great deal by the rascally guides.

" I was now a poor man; and my cheerful Margaret, ever ready to accommodate herself to circumstances, proposed that we should return to you, with some labourers; cultivate the soil, and live contentedly on the produce of it. I did not see that we could do better; for Henry and his child were all the relations we had left; and we immediately set about selling the useless, and buying the useful.

"Just at this time, two of my best Yorkshire mechanics, hearing that we had arrived at Santiago, returned honestly to us, to offer their services, or to restore their advanced wages. I knew them to be ingenious, hard-working fellows, and used to agricultural labours, in the pastoral dales of their native home; and finding that one had married a respectable woman of Chili, and that Joe wished to marry an English laundress in the establishment of the consul, I explained to them our intentions, and offered them service with us. They had no wish to return to England, were all quiet, sober, honest folks, so we concluded our bargain.

"About six weeks since Henry returned, all anxiety to see his babe, if it were living; our preparations were complete, and with two experienced guides, and twenty mules, loaded with our whole fortune, we set out to cross the Cordilleras. You may conceive our journey was but melancholy from painful associations; but our guides brought us without loss or hindrance across the snowy summit, and we saw below us the ocean-like Pampas.

"On that day our spirits revived, we talked cheerfully of our future plans, and Margaret, for the first time, described to me all the pretty presents she was bringing for her young friends."

"Which I desire you will not allude to, William," interrupted his good lady. "It is a painful and vexatious subject. There is not a jot for you, my dears! If they had only left me the black trunks! Well! no matter; go on, my love."

"As we turned the angle of a narrow pass," continued Mr. Douglas, "I was confounded to see a long line of mounted Indians approaching. They were warlike, noble-looking fellows, with gay-coloured ponchos and plumed caps, glittering dirks in their belts, and long lances trailing after them. Resistance seemed madness; but some effort must be made to save our property, and probably our lives. I rode forward, waving a white handkerchief, towards the leader; and addressed him in Spanish, feeling encouraged by seeing there were not more than a dozen men. I requested him politely to allow us to pass unmolested. He looked on me with astonishment, and replied, in very good Spanish: ' The free hordes of Araucania allow no pale Christians to cross the mountains, to scatter desolation over the plains of freedom.'

" ' The Araucanians are brave people,' I said. ' I know their history; but we are no plunderers or traitors, we are harmless travellers; and if you refuse to let us pass peacefully, we must force our way; for we have women with us, whom Christian warriors are bound to protect.'

" ' Your women shall be our slaves,' he said, scornfully; ' but the bodies of you and your men shall be left to feed the vultures.'

" This was no pleasant prospect; I drew back under the protection of my white flag to consult my friends. We were well armed, and could soon have dispersed the men on open ground; but besides my reluctance to shed blood, the attack would be difficult on a pass where not more than three could safely ride abreast.

" The guides were of opinion that a vigorous charge would enable us to pass in safety, and we planned and formed our procession. My brother, John and I rode first, followed by the women and four baggage-mules, driven forward by our two men, who also led six mules attached in pairs behind them. Lastly came the two guides conducting the ten remaining mules, which were the most heavily laden.

" As soon as we, the vanguard, were within a few yards of our foes, we lowered our rifles, pointing them at the horses of the Indians, and fired. In the smoke and confusion, we galloped forward so suddenly that they had not time to gain their lances before Jem and Joe came up, who fired their pieces in the same way, and by good fortune we all passed in safety till the two guides reached the foe, when either from fear, or from wantonness, they fired both barrels of their pieces upon the Indians, and two of the number fell. But in a moment the Araucanians revenged themselves.

" The unfortunate guides, pierced by many mortal wounds, were hurled over the precipice, into a dark and fathomless abyss. We stood for a moment in dismay, and saw the Indians ride off with our ten valuable mules, carrying with them their wounded or dead friends. We thought of pursuing them, but our number was now diminished, the Indians were swift, and the females were so terrified, till we finally agreed to put up with our loss, and make the best of our way, lest we should be overtaken by a reinforced party.

" We had no longer any guide ; but for some time we followed the track of the Indians, till the fears of the women induced me to deviate, lest we should meet another party on the beaten road. I fancied we could not be lost while the Pampas. lay visibly below us ; but these bewildering basins and ridges, rocks rising here and there, shutting out the way you have come, and the way you have to go, confounded all my plans. We got into a perfect maze of mountains, and I thought we should wander there till our provision was exhausted, till at length having ascended a ridge, we looked into a gorge where a little stream was gurgling downwards. I fancied if we could reach this rivulet, and keep on its banks, we must arrive at the plain ; and we scrambled down, at the risk of our lives, and to the great damage of our baggage.

We rested and refreshed ourselves at the cool and pleasant stream ; we followed it for about fifty yards when it suddenly disappeared beneath a wall of rock."

"That was our river," said Tom.   "I know you would like the water ; it is excellent."

"Doubtless it is, my dear lad," continued Mr. Douglas ; "but I had no patience with the river just then for its treachery in leading us into such a trap, for we actually wandered two days in the valley, endeavouring in vain to escape from it ; for to ascend again the precipice we had come down would have been impossible with the laden mules.   We were resting before the dark hole in the rock, which we concluded was some deep chasm, when one of the mules grazing near the opening, the earth suddenly gave way under it, and it disappeared.

"I was sorely vexed to lose another mule, and Jem Anderson, who had worked in mines, looking down the shaft, declared that he could see the bottom ; and that if we would hand him a rope, he would go down and save the baggage.   I was unwilling, till I convinced myself the descent was not dangerous ; then we saw him safely down, but the appearance of Matilda terrified him so much that he renounced the attempt; and we owe our present happy meeting to the bravery of Joe."

It was a happy meeting, and thanksgivings mingled with the prayers which the re-united friends offered up that night.

"Now we are all ready for work," said Mrs. Douglas, next morning, when they rose from the breakfast-table.   "How are we to get out of this vault to go to Esperanza ?"

The stone was rolled away, and the strangers introduced to the little green valley with its rocky boundaries, which had afforded the family a winter's refuge.

"If we had never known the beautiful shades of Esperanza," said Mr. Merton, "I could have been content to finish my days here; but Dr. Lewis advises we should dwell in houses built by the hands of man."

"The doctor shows his judgment," replied Mrs. Douglas. "Who ever heard of people living in a cave, that had the use of their hands? Come along, good folks, and let us see how we can restore our old hall. I can work as well as any of you."

The horses were saddled, the stranger mules, brought through the tortuous passages of the cave, were again restored to day; and leaving Nanny with the two women to assist her in her increased household duties, the whole family set out, Tom now being able to ride.

"A pretty labyrinth!" cried Mrs. Douglas, as they wound down the wood. "Would that our houses were ready for us; but then, to think of my lost treasures, for when one does settle for life, one does like to have things comfortable. Oh! my dears! you have no conception of the pretty collection those grand-looking brigands carried off. Henry preaches resignation, and William laughs and says we can do without the things; and we must do without them here, for they can never be replaced. Just attend, my dears! there was pretty nearly my whole wardrobe. To be sure, I can go in a blanket, like our savage neighbours; but there were such nice silk dresses for mamma, such pretty muslins for you, girls, and gay prints for Nanny. Two large trunks, my dears—that's my first irreparable loss. Then came Mr. Douglas's mule-load of hampers of wine and brandy for good Mr. Merton, who needs something comfortable at his age."

"I thank you, my considerate friend," said Mr. Merton, "but the loss of the fermented liquors distresses me not. I love pure water, or the nourishing milk our cows so bounteously afford us."

"But I understand these things," replied the lady, "and I say, a glass of good wine would not have been a bad thing for you; but the robbers had swallowed it all before this time. Can we make our own wine, William?"

"I see no difficulty, my dear," answered he. "I have brought the vine cuttings in safety, and the climate and situation promise us success; but we cannot expect to drink our own wine for some years."

"I envy you your patience, William," said his restless lady; "I own my foible; I do love to see the grass grow. Well, at all events, there will be employment in the vineyard. Now, let me consider what more the robbers took. There was a large crate of china and glass, and a case of mirrors; for I knew you had no glass to show you how to smooth your pretty hair as it ought to be."

"Mamma has a small glass," said Matilda, "that has escaped all disasters; and Charles, when we put on our holiday dresses, lends us one from his dressing-case. So never regret the mirrors."

"You are good girls," continued Mrs. Douglas, "and are quite right. It is wrong to lament the loss of such luxuries; especially as we have saved a crate of window-glass for our buildings. But I must regret the books. Books to suit everybody; even new volumes of sermons for good Mr. Merton, and new medical works for our excellent doctor; and all the newspapers of the last year, with toys and trifles innumerable. But now I will think no more of my losses, for here is the river; and now for Esperanza."

As they crossed, with some risk, the swollen river, Mr. Douglas and Lewis consulted on the practicability of laying down a temporary bridge to facilitate the necessary and incessant communication with their present residence, and they agreed that they must immediately do it.

Mrs. Douglas wept over the ruins of her dear old hall, and then called on William to begin work; and Mr. Douglas proposed, that as the colony had increased so much they should inclose twenty acres; but Lewis proved the impossibility of their completing such vast labours in one season; and as every man would still have his acre to support him, it was decided that they should abide by the original plan.

Then the mountains of bricks were surveyed, and the mortar of clay inspected by the practical workman Jem, who suggested the improvement of a mixture of the fine sand from the floor of their cave with the mortar; finally, the whole party turned to the bridge. It did not require much time to fell three trees, tall enough to span the river, even in its present overflowed state. These were soon stripped of their branches, and laid across the stream a few inches apart from each other. A number of flat pieces of wood, collected from the ruins, were sawed the right length to be laid transversely and form a platform; all to be completed next morning, as weariness drove the workmen home before evening.

"Now we are progressing," said Mrs. Douglas, as they assembled in the cave. "Let me see, how many houses shall we want? The two Yorkshiremen must have their cottages; but as to John, it was in vain that his master requested him to select a wife, of any nation, when we were at Santiago. I assure you, Nanny, that he declared not one of them was fit to hold the candle to you. You are his choice."

"That's as I please," said Nanny. "I have plenty to do without looking after him, poor *wafflin* body! Let him bide as he is; he'll get on, I'll warrant him."

"But, Nanny," resumed Mrs. Douglas, "John is a good fellow, and I have set my mind on your being Mrs. Armstrong."

"Me, Mistress Armstrong!" cried the maiden. "Nay! Nanny I have been, and Nanny I *mun* be to the end of my days."

In fact, Nanny was right, every body had too much to engage them at this time to think about such trivial matters as marriages. The next day the bridge was completed by stretching a rope across, about four feet above the platform, to assist the timid; and now even the females crossed fearlessly, and no time was lost in fording the rapid and deep river. The brick wall was commenced; Jem was a famous builder, and though Joe excelled more in cabinet-making and turning, he was willing to take any work. While the wall progressed, Tom, unable to bear hard labour, worked in the carpenter's shop, and Mrs. Douglas, with the young ladies, laid out the garden. The vines had been planted in pots immediately on their arrival, upon a sunny slope facing the south and apart from the building.

After the labour of many days had raised a wall four feet in height, the completion was deferred, and the untiring workmen began the houses. Three small huts near the entrance, each surrounded by a garden, were soon built, and made habitable. One was for Jem Anderson and Isabella, the girl from Chili; the second for Joe and Mary Raine; and the third for Almagro and John.

The rubbish was then entirely cleared from the unroofed house, where Mr. and Mrs. Douglas had formerly resided; and the outer walls being firm and uninjured it was soon restored, and finished with boarded floors, with glass windows, and iron stoves brought from Chili; and so much pleased was Mrs. Douglas with her English-looking house, that but for the pain of separating from her friends, she would have taken immediate possession of it; for she had an insuperable aversion to a cave, the gloom of which did not accord with her vivacious spirits. But she usually spent the day at Esperanza, arranging curtains and carpets, with small remnants of crockery, saved from the spoilers, or planning the places for the tables and seats which were yet to be made.

In the mean time the great house was rising. To save time, it was built on the old plan, with substantial mud walls, but brick chimneys were introduced, and much greater accommodation made than in the old hut. There were a number of little dormitories, to enable them even to lodge visitors, and each had its small glass pane to admit light. The hall was large, with good glass windows; and a commodious kitchen and large brick oven, built by the master hand of Jem, completed the family mansion. The floors were laid and the windows fitted in, and then the family began to think of leaving the cave.

A day's labour repaired the corral, to which the horses, mules, and llamas were brought, and the cows, each with a calf, were to come with the family. A strong door plated with iron and fastened by an iron chain secured the entrance into the inclosure; and the female part of the community now began to fit up the new habitation.

They once more withdrew from the mountain cave the hidden hoards, which created much mirth as they were brought to light. The wheels of the waggons, iron pans and kettles, boxes of linen and clothes, garden-seeds, maize, beans, dried peaches, and honey. A light cart was soon made, and mounted on the wheels, and they were thus enabled to remove all their property from the cave of refuge with less difficulty than it cost to transport it to that happy retreat.

Once more they slept in a light airy dwelling, and returned to the various occupations of a large household. Tom brought forward all the productions of his long confinement; bed-frames of bamboo, chairs, worktables, chicken-coops, and many useful articles, besides the incomparable bee-hive, which was to be tried in the summer. To complete their furniture, they had materials and good workmen, and from day to day something was produced.

But now the grass was ready for the scythe, and while Tom looked after the garden and trellised the vines, John and Almagro, with some aid from the busy carpenters, brought within the inclosure hay to form two large stacks. The bean-field in the mean time was fragrant, and the flax brilliant in blossom; the potatoes were abundant, and the crops of wheat, maize, and oats progressing.

While the husbandmen pursued their labours, Jeu and Joe erected the frame of the third house, on the same plan as the others, with a colonnade along the front, the pillars of which were to be entwined by creeping plants, or by Mrs. Douglas's imported roses, if they would condescend to flourish at Esperanza.

The progress of this building was interrupted by many causes—hunting, bringing home cattle to supply the lost stock, laying out the inclosure in gardens and shrubberies, and inclosing and sowing fields for meadow and pasture, corn, or flax. And thus busily and happily the summer passed away; the evening being devoted to rational and improving pursuits, and ever concluded by united and earnest prayer.

Returning one evening from walking, they encountered a cavalcade, which, being led by their friend Pedro, created no alarm. Zara rode by his side, and the young Albert was also mounted on his own horse. Behind them rode four Indians; but, confiding in Pedro's discretion, the gate was opened to admit them all.

"See, good father," said Zara, displaying a pretty babe to Mr. Merton, "I have brought to you another young claimant to be admitted into the church of Christ. You must baptize my boy; and these young people also wish to become Christians, like their cacique."

Two young men, of intelligent countenances, and two females, came forward to Mr. Merton, with whom they could converse, as they knew a little Spanish. The softened manners of their cacique, and the gentle lessons of Zara, had induced the youths to desire to seek the good teacher who had changed the stern nature of their chief, and to hear from his mouth the wonderful truths of Christianity; as the women were to be their wives, Zara decided that they must also be Christians, and the girls readily consented to share the instruction of their intended husbands.

The Indian men were lodged in the unfinished house, and the women, placed under the care of Isabella, who knew something of Indian habits, were astonished with the sight of the order, neatness, and industry that pervaded the kitchen of the pale people ; and they ate with great relish the cooked meats and bread.

" I have been able to do little, my reverend friend," said Pedro, " since we parted, to prove that I am a son of God, and a ruler among men. I have said to my warriors that the great God has forbidden man to war with man, except to defend his property or life. They listen to my words, for I am their oracle ; they obey me, for I am their cacique ; but they thirst for action : they say to each other, ' Did God make man to sit in the tents with the women—to dry the skins and nurse the children ?' The old warriors scoff in their hearts at the peaceful doctrines of Christianity. I see in their eyes the fire of scorn. A message must come to them direct from the great Father of Heaven ; you are his minister ; come to my unbelieving people, and speak the words of Truth and Peace."

" Permit me to undertake this mission, dear Mr. Merton," said Henry Carruthers. " Though not eloquent, I am zealous. I am young and active, and besides the Spanish, I acquired from Paul some acquaintance with the Indian language, spoken by the tribes of the Pampas. I am a solitary being; save this little treasure, I have no one to cling to me ; and should I fall a martyr in the holy cause, I can safely leave her to her foster parents ; she will feel no loss. My plan would be to turn the desire for action among the Indians to useful labours ; to induce them to build permanent and comfortable huts ; to enclose and cultivate the ground ; to fill their corrals with cattle ; and to adopt the habits, as well as the arts, of civilized life. The early Christian missionaries on the eastern coast contended against greater difficulties and dangers, and,

by God's blessing, had happy success, till the hand of
tyranny drove them from their field of labour. I have
wasted much time ; let me now endeavour to fulfil
some of the duties of life."

When Pedro understood that Mr. Carruthers was
really a minister of the Church, he eagerly accepted
him in the place of the aged and timid Mr. Merton ;
and though grieved for the gap it would make in the
family circle, all agreed that Mr. Carruthers ought to
go.   The visitors remained several days, in which time
the Indians not only received religious instruction, but
were shown the means of being usefully and happily
employed.   They were astonished with the skill of Joe,
who turned on his lathe boxes and wooden cups for
them ; they saw the fruits of the earth repaying bounteously the labour of cultivation, and were inflamed
with the desire to acquire the useful knowledge of their
hosts.   The women, in the mean time, after assisting
Nanny as mere hewers of wood and drawers of water,
aspired to learn the higher culinary arts ; and when
the visit of the chief expired, his people begged to be
left some time to acquire the wonderful arts of the
Christians, that they might become teachers in their
turn.

Mr. Merton considering the Indians sufficiently
instructed, they were baptized at the same time as
the babe of Zara, who was named Christopher, after
the great Columbus, who first opened a way into that
new world to admit the light of Christian truth.

The parents were at length induced to leave Albert
for a short time, to receive the rudiments of education ;
and the child was delighted to remain at Esperanza to
play with Cecilia, to watch the workmen, and to listen
to the nursery stories of his young teachers.

Before the autumn came on, the third house was
ready to be inhabited, new stables had been built, and
barns for the promised harvest.   The flax was cut,
steeped, and made ready for combing ; then the abundant crops of maize were reaped and stored in the

barns; one plot of wheat was already housed, and all the rest of the corn and beans was cut and left out to dry before the Indians departed. Then the two marriages were solemnized; and the young people, with many presents, and much good advice, went to carry to their chief the tidings of his son's health, and to communicate to the tribe the vast knowledge they had acquired at Esperanza.

On the day that the Indians departed, all the peaches were gathered, with the intention of drying or preserving a large part; and the family proposed the next day to conclude the glorious harvest; but, on rising early for the task, they saw the sun rising behind lurid clouds, the atmosphere was gloomy and sultry, every one felt languid, and they remembered with sinking hearts the thunder-storm of the preceding autumn, which had swept away so much of their precious harvest. Heavy clouds rolled over the half-hidden Cordilleras, occasionally irradiated by vivid lightning, and the air was darkened by myriads of insects, all appearing to fly or be driven by some imperceptible wind towards the east.

The massy clouds grew darker and darker; and then Lewis with a vigorous effort roused himself from the oppressive languor that had seized on him, and intreated the able hands to assist him in preparations to save their property from the inevitable storm of the season. Two large skin tent covers, which Mr. Douglas had used on the journey, were drawn over the stacks and fastened down with heavy stones. The cattle were all housed, and a good supply of food placed in their cribs. The young vines, which were all potted, were placed in the shelter of the barn; and, finally, Nanny would have called together and secured her feathered family; but they had wandered off to the corn-fields, and it was too late to bring them back.

Then the whole community, including Wallace, whom they could not bear to leave out in the storm, assembled in Mr. Merton's large hall, determined to

2 D

remain together till the storm passed.   They looked anxiously from the windows ; the lightning grew brighter as the sky darkened, while hollow gusts of wind rolled down the mountains, heard before they were felt or the effects seen ; but soon 'they perceived more sensibly the rush of the hot gale, as it whirled from the forest above the lighter leaves and branches, and showered them on the ground.   To this succeeded a furious blast, tearing away huge boughs and fragments of rock, and overwhelming the blooming garden with scattered wood and stones, to the great sorrow of the fair gardeners.

A few minutes all was still ; then a noise was heard like the roaring of artillery from the mighty mountains. It was the Pampero ! which, bursting from the mountain holds, swept forward with terrible and restless violence, marking its course with destruction, till it should reach the Atlantic.

The family crowded together, the weak clinging to the strong ; but, though pale and trembling, they were resigned ; for they knew that it was the hand of God that directed the whirlwind and ruled the storm.

" I feel the walls totter and the earth shake," said Maria, as gust after gust shook the house.   "Do you not think, good father, that the end of the world is at hand ? "

"It may be so, my child," said the venerable man. "The inscrutable wisdom of God has hidden from us the hour appointed for that dreadful event.   But tremble not, my children ; put all your trust in him, and in the hour of death, and in the day of judgment, he will deliver you."

At that moment a noise, as if the mountains were torn from their foundation, was heard ; a shock, as if from an earthquake, was felt by all, and total darkness followed.   They were buried living ! !

For a few moments the silence of death prevailed, then the screams of the children and the low sobs of the females were heard ; but no one spoke.   Lewis first recovered from the shock; he drew from his pocket a match-box with a taper, which he lighted, and then asked Nanny to produce some candles to relieve the fearful darkness.

"I'll bring no candles, Mr. Doctor," said Nanny, in a low voice. "Folks want no candles in their graves. Let us say our prayers, and then lie quietly down till He sends his angels for us, for here we are buried till the day of doom."

"But, my good Nanny," answered Lewis, "God has not commanded us to lie down and die supinely, while he grants us strength and understanding; we will use the energy he has bestowed on us. Let me have the candles to see if all are uninjured, and what is the extent of the danger."

The candles were produced, and Almagro and Lewis raised the glass windows at the front of the house, and found that a wall of rock lay close against them, excluding light and air. Against the end windows, and those of the kitchen which opened westward, lay earth and stones, intercepting every ray of light. The doors they did not attempt to open, lest they should bring destruction on themselves, for they could not but believe that some mighty fall of the mountain had buried them in a mound of earth and rocks. It was impossible to think of any mode of escape, nor was it prudent to make the attempt now, for still the roaring of the wind was heard, though the sound was muffled by the mass around them; but the walls no longer shook, nor did the earth tremble beneath them, for they were now below the earth; and Lewis shuddered to think that another fall might bring the walls, so astonishingly firm till now, upon their heads.

"Read to us, good and holy friend," said he to Mr. Merton. "Read to us passages that may employ our thoughts on subjects beyond the perils in which it has pleased Almighty God to plunge us."

Amidst the dull howling of the unsubdued tempest the good man read the penitential psalms, the glorious

prophecies, the passion, the death, and the resurrection
of the Son of God; and from that sepulchre of the
living rose the incense of prayer, breathed in resignation to the will of God, and trust in his mercy; and
every heart responded as the reverend man concluded
by the words, " Lord, thy will be done!"

They waited patiently for hours. The roaring of
the wind sunk into hollow moans: a little longer and
all was still: darkness and silence brooded over them.
Again they examined the windows, even attempting
to raise one in the kitchen; but the rush of earth
through the opening showed the danger of the experiment. That the roof was covered was evident from
the strain upon the rafters; and it appeared marvellous
that they had not given way.

Lewis and Mrs. Douglas, both of sanguine and
active minds, cheered the rest, and pointed out faint
rays of hope. It was necessary to prop the sinking
rafters, they looked round for the means, and, finding some large chests of linen, they piled them on
end till they reached the rafters, and effectually supported the back of the roof. In the front part Lewis
observed that the rafters were unwarped, and he concluded that the rock which lay before the windows was
higher than the walls, and had protected that side of
the roof. This afforded some little consolation; and
he now insisted that the family should take food and
rest; for though their situation was painful and perilous, he did not think it desperate. They reluctantly
complied with his desire, took some refreshment, and
sought a short repose from their terrible anxiety.

CHAPTER XXX.

The Second Day beneath the Ground.　The First Ray of Light.
The Exploits of Jack and Maria.　The First View of the
Ruined Settlement.　The Escape from the Buried House.
The Second Restoration of Esperanza.　The Visit of Paul
and his Bride.

AFTER some hours of feverish rest they again assembled. Night and day were alike ; but they found from their watches that it was now midday, and twenty-four hours had elapsed since they were entombed. The props were examined, and all was found safe. Then an account of stores was taken. They had flour, tea, eggs, butter, and cold meat that would serve for a week, abundance of candles, which Nanny had recently made, and, greatest blessing of all, a large butt of water, which Nanny and her assistants had brought into the kitchen, on the morning of the storm, for the purpose of a great washing.

One consideration distressed Lewis greatly. The building was spacious ; but twenty people were now crowded in it. He fancied the air had already become close and pernicious ; what would it be in another day or two ? He ordered fires to be lighted in the kitchen and in the hall, to discover if the chimneys were open. There was not much fuel in the house ; but little was needed—they were too warm without fires. The experiment was first tried in the kitchen ; but it was soon obvious there was no vent for the smoke, which returned down the chimney. That of the hall was near the front wall of the house ; and Lewis watched for the effect of the fire with great anxiety. He saw the smoke hung round the grate ; but he was of opinion that part of it had escaped, and was convinced that some small aperture afforded a passage for the air. As they watched the flame, Tom more than once remarked a slight hissing sound, and asked Nanny if the wood was wet. She assured him it was perfectly dry.

"Then, I am certain," said the observing youth, "that a drop of water must have come down the chimney. Let us ascertain it."

A bowl was placed beneath the chimney, and they stood round, watching anxiously. In a few moments it was certain that a drop fell into the bowl; drop after drop following, in slow succession.

"See, mamma!" said Tom, "that drop of water is the olive-branch to our ark. We shall be saved!" And this augury of hope inspired them with spirits to move about, eat, and work.

"Leave the bowl there, Tom," exclaimed Mrs. Douglas. "We must have the water, even if somewhat muddy, it will do for our ablutions, for none must be carelessly used from Nanny's treasure-tub. And, by the bye, where are the peaches we gathered yesterday? or the day before? or . . . Bless me! William! I forget whether it is day or night; we shall have to keep a notched calendar, like Robinson Crusoe. Now, the peaches, girls?"

The peaches had been forgotten in the storm, and overlooked in the darkness. Several large baskets full were hanging up; they afforded a most agreeable and salutary refreshment, and enabled them to pass another day of darkness more cheerfully.

At an early hour of that part of the day which would be called morning in the world, Jack awoke Lewis, saying; "I must tell you something that I would rather no one else should know. I am going up the chimney. I helped to build it, and we left here and there a brick protruding for steps, in case we had to become chimney-sweeps. Help me to seek the small horn lantern which Tom made."

Lewis hesitated for a moment; but he satisfied him-

self with the reflection that Jack was light and active,
and the best fitted of the party for an undertaking on
which their sole hope rested.

They found the lantern, proceeded quietly to the
hall, and removed the bowl, which was now filled with
water, into which several stones and portions of earth
had fallen ; a gratifying sight, as they hoped this fall
might have enlarged the opening. Lewis gave Jack
a strict injunction not to venture to remove any earth
or stones from the top, which might endanger the
whole roof, but to content himself with observation.

The agile boy slung the lantern round his neck,
and springing up the chimney, left Lewis in a state
of intense anxiety, for he reflected that not only the
life of the boy, but the lives of all might fall a sacrifice to this undertaking ; yet every moment of inaction was a waste of life, energy, and resources, and
he satisfied himself that he had only fulfilled a duty.
He listened, with his head within the chimney, and
had speedily the pleasure of hearing the bold lad cry
out ; " Here I am, Lewis, safe at the top of the stair-
case. I can see the dark, gray sky, and feel the rain
pelting me, but the opening is a long *slit*, and my
head is too big to go through it."

" Come down, my good fellow," cried Lewis. " You
have done enough for the first trip." But Jack did
not come down immediately, and a considerable fall
of rubbish down the chimney was alarming ; but in a
few minutes he appeared, looking the better for a
taste of fresh air.

" Did I frighten you, Lewis ? " asked he, " I could
not help making a little experiment. The top of the
chimney is closed by a flat piece of rock, except a
narrow opening. Now, I considered that if I could
make the opening a little wider, as it is raining in
torrents, we might get a supply of water for washing
ourselves ; so I leaned my back against the side of the
chimney, and with both hands tried to give the stone a
good shove. And I really did move it about an inch and

a half, and then tried my head again; but it wouldn't
do; and I began to be afraid that if I did get it
through, it perhaps wouldn't come back; and I had
no wish to be gibbeted. But after all we shall get
more air and water from my expedition."

This was true, and by looking up the chimney they
could even see the speck of light; and the light, the
water, and the air cheered them through the third day.
But the council who discussed Jack's attempt, decided
that nothing more must be done till the rain ceased.
Jack was not one of the council; he arranged a plan
with Maria, who joined him early next morning, and
held a light below, while he again ascended the
chimney.

"I must try to move the great stone," said he;
"so I shall take the poker and this rope, which I
shall let down if I want anything, and you must send
it up."

"I could climb as well as you, if you think there is
room for two," said Maria.

"You are of more use below," replied he, "on the
great principle of the division of labour, as Philosopher Tom would say. Now watch for my signals."

After a little time several stones, and a quantity of
earth fell, which alarmed Maria; but Jack's assurances tranquillized her. At length there was a long
silence, and she determined to mount and discover
the cause; so throwing off her pretty calico dressing-
gown, she arrayed herself in a dark poncho belonging
to Nanny, and sprung lightly up the chimney, guided
by a faint ray of light from above. She reached the
top, and found Jack with his head through a small
opening, and his body in the chimney, and it was
only when she shook hands with him, that he discovered she was near him, and withdrew his head.

They could not help laughing at the grotesque appearance of each other; then Maria begged also to
have a peep into the world. "Come to this side,
Maria," said Jack; "but there is little to give you

pleasure. I cannot think how I could be so hard-hearted as to laugh after seeing what I have seen."

Maria's small head passed easily through the aperture; she was able to raise herself higher than Jack had done, and see the whole of the melancholy spectacle below.

"Oh! Jack!" cried she, "Our pretty shrubbery at the end of the house is quite covered up; and as far as I can see behind, there is nothing but stones, earth, and uprooted trees, covering all the slope up to the very woods; and, my dear Jack, I certainly see the end of a cask among the earth over the back part of the roof."

Jack gave a sudden cry as Maria said this. "I know it all!" cried he. "The dear old cave that saved your life; that protected all our treasures from the savages, and was our powder magazine, has been torn up. Only think; if the lightning had struck the barrel, we must all have been blown up."

"The ammunition is no great loss," said Maria; "but Nanny will lament the loss of her honey and salted butter; and I do grieve for the destruction of the cave. Now let us try to move the stone a little, which can be done with perfect safety, for it rests on the fallen rock in front, and on the great mound over the shrubbery at the end."

By exerting their united strength they moved the stone about two inches, which enabled them both to look round easily, but not to pass the whole body through. Then Maria sent Jack down for a wooden bowl, which they passed out, and left on the stone, for the heavy rain still continued, and they should thus be enabled to obtain fresh water.

"We can bring a tin cup and fill it when we choose from the bowl," said Maria; "for the water below is quite unpalatable, even when mixed with peach juice. And I have thought of something else, Jack. See, by removing the stone, we have uncovered a portion of the roof at the side of the chimney which has been protected, and is free from any covering of earth. Give me your knife, I will reach down and cut the hide-covering, and we will try to get an air-hole."

The strong and active girl was able to cut away a large square of the hide, for the chimney was very low; she then pulled away the maize-leaves beneath, and uncovered the spars which formed the roof. They washed their hands in the rain-water, and then descended to see the effect of their experiment.

To their great delight they beheld the rays of light streaming down; and Jack, fetching a long ladder from the kitchen, mounted, and cleared away the remainder of the thatch, making a perfect skylight, about six inches square. They then placed a table underneath the aperture, and arranged the breakfast things by the light of heaven. Jack could contain no longer. " Now, Maria," said he, " Let us give three cheers, and rouse the sleepers."

The cheers did effectually rouse the family, and in a very short time they all appeared, half dressed, in their anxiety to know what was the cause of rejoicing.

" Look here ! " cried Jack, in ecstasy, " see what we have done for you, idle sleepers ! "

" And who are *we ?* " asked Lewis, in astonishment.

" Maria and I, to be sure, the two geniuses of the family," replied he. " What could you do without us ? "

" Bless the lad ! " cried Nanny, " he was always a good scholar ! And to think that this poor thing," stroking Maria's glossy hair approvingly, " should turn out so sharp, when we catched her running about, and living among trees, like a wild cat. But, honeys, we needn't have our cups washed before we use them."

The rain was indeed falling into the cups, and precious as the water was, they preferred a drier situation for the breakfast table, so a tub was placed to collect the water. As they breakfasted, the adventurers described the desolation they had beheld, the gardens and shrubberies buried in earth, and the mighty ruin behind the house.

"And the new huts were all unthatched," continued Maria; "and our favourite beech-tree beside the gate is torn up, and lying across a haystack."

"Thereby saving the hay, I hope," said Tom.

"I believe the stacks are there," she added, "but covered with earth; and dear Mrs. Douglas's beautiful house is, like the rest, totally unroofed."

"And this tremendous rain falling!" cried Mrs. Douglas, in great tribulation. "All my pretty muslin curtains, my new carpets, and my polished stoves, will be entirely ruined."

"And your caps and bonnets, too, Margaret," said Mr. Douglas, laughing. "Confess that you were thinking of them; but I shall certainly not regret them, for your own pretty brown hair is much more ornamental than those strange combinations of frippery and artificial flowers that ladies choose to disfigure themselves with."

"Isabella can make straw-bonnets very nicely, and has taught us," said Mary. "We have our straw-work in some corner, and will begin a bonnet for you to-day."

"I believe," said Jack, "that if Jem, who is very strong, was to mount the ladder, and help us by pushing through the skylight, and Maria and I were to push at the same time from the chimney, we might move the stone more; the chimney would not hold two bigger than we are, so you must let us try, and if we do succeed in removing the stone entirely, we might all escape through the chimney."

"Impossible, my dear boy," said Mrs. Merton; "your papa and I could never climb a chimney."

"And consider what sort of climbing-boy Mr. Douglas would make," said his lady: and none of the party could forbear laughing, when they looked at the portly figure of Mr. Douglas, which could never have been forced up the chimney by any means; and Jack's scheme was unanimously negatived. "Besides," said

Lewis, " it is evident, that in the present rainy season, this dwelling, with all its inconvenience, is the
only place that could shelter us. It appears secure,
and we still have food, water, air, and some portion of
light. Let us spend the day usefully, and defer further attempts till to-morrow."

Every one therefore turned to some useful employment; and Jem, with some skill, enlarged the skylight as far as it could be done with safety, so that
the prisoners obtained a view of the dark, clouded
sky. Thus the fourth day of captivity passed cheerfully, and on the fifth morning the sky was clear, and
the rain had ceased. Maria was allowed to accompany Jack, and they once more ascended, Jem taking
his station at the opening below to aid their exertions. They succeeded in enlarging the opening so
far that Maria's slim figure passed through, and
mounted on the flat piece of rock, she surveyed the
dreary prospect. Then walking to the end where the
buried shrubbery lay, she descended by an inclined
plane of rubbish to the desolated garden.

She perceived that the front of the house was not
barricaded, as they supposed, by one huge rock, but
by two separate fragments which lay against the windows. Earth and stones hid the door, but sloped
down to the garden; up this slope Maria walked
with a broken branch in her hand, and as the upper
part of the *debris* was chiefly loose earth, she probed
it with the stick, and felt the door through not more
than a foot of earth. Overjoyed at this discovery, she
flew back to her companion, who, not being able to
pass through the opening as she had done, was looking round with a melancholy earnestness. " Let us
descend, Jack, I have a plan which I trust will release
us," said she.

They descended, and Maria, addressing Lewis, said,
" Pray, dear Dr. Lewis, unbar and open the door."

" Not on any account," said Mr. Merton; " the
heavy rocks and earth, might then fall forward and
crush us all."

" But hear me, good father," replied she ; and she narrated her observations.

Lewis and Mr. Douglas agreed that the experiment must be tried, and everything being first moved out of danger, and a force of strong men placed behind to prevent the door being forced suddenly open, it was unbarred, and allowed to open gradually ; heaps of earth and stone falling inwards. At length being quite ajar, a light shone on them from above the wall of earth.

" Now, my good fellows, for the ladder and spades," cried Lewis. The ladder was raised against the barrier, but only one spade could be found in the house. Jem took it first, and shovelled vigorously, throwing the earth outwards as far as he could. After a little had been removed, it was easier to work ; and they laboured alternately, hurling away the large stones, and shovelling the earth, till the opening was sufficiently large to be passed. Then Almagro and John made their way through the rubbish to the carpenter's shop, and extracted three more spades from under the ruins. The work then went on briskly, and throwing the earth to the sides, before night a free passage was made, and the hall cleared from all the rubbish.

The long secluded family, anxious to taste the pleasant evening air, passed in single file through the narrow passage ; and Jack, who was perched on the ruins above, cried out, laughing, " It is exactly the descent from the ark ; and see, Wallace and the two pet hens finish the procession. You must make a sketch of the scene, Mary."

" It has indeed been an ark of refuge to us, my son," said Mr. Merton, " for we must inevitably have perished in any other of these ruined houses. We ought to thank God for our deliverance, and I cannot have a ludicrous picture made of this merciful dispensation."

A loud crowing announced that some of the animals were still living, and Nanny saw, with pleasure, one of her old favourites, issue from a hut to greet his acquaintances. Struggling through the ruins they

made their way to the stables; many of the trees
which fenced the corral had entirely disappeared, the
roofs of the sheds were carried away, and of one cow-
house the wall had fallen inward, and killed a calf;
the rest of the animals were living, but miserably thin
for want of food, the supply given not being sufficient
for more than two days. The haystacks were overthrown, but still safe, under the well-secured covers;
and some hay was immediately cut for the exhausted
animals.

The roof of the church was partly injured, but the
walls remained firm; all else was desolate, there was
literally no resting-place for the sole of their feet,
and after milking the cows, they were glad to shelter
themselves again in their ark, which was no longer
regarded as a prison.

Next morning they visited the barn, the roof of which
was on its way to the Atlantic; but the walls had
fortunately fallen inwards, and thus kept down the
greatest part of the precious store, though some of
the upper sheaves had been carried away. In the
fields, where the corn had been left standing, not a
vestige was to be seen; the stubble was left as clean
as if it had been raked. And the destruction of trees,
amongst which were several valuable peach-trees, was
immense. They returned melancholy, for it was difficult to decide on the first steps to be taken.

" I say, let us have a drop of good water for breakfast, if it can be had," said Nanny; and thus the first
step was decided. The well had been fortunately
provided with a wooden cover, and the earth was soon
cleared from over it. The sight of the pure water,
and the enjoyment of a breakfast of tea and fresh
milk, restored them to cheerfulness and action; and
after breakfast, Mrs. Douglas declared it would be
better to get the shock over, so they would go and
inspect her unfortunate mansion. It certainly presented a scene of desolation. Part of the front wall
had fallen into the rooms, and the destruction of

glass windows, curtains, and cushions, was, as Mrs. Douglas had anticipated, tremendous. The carpets were covered with mud and moistened leaves, the heavy furniture turned topsyturvy, and a large table lay on what had been a bandbox, but was now but a a flattened board. Mr. Douglas looked at his lady with affected dismay, which caused a hearty laugh, notwithstanding the vexations of the scene.

Fortunately a small room which Mr. Douglas called his study, had escaped the general ruin, and the globes, telescopes, writing and drawing materials, and scientific apparatus, were preserved, and speedily removed to the more certain protection of the buried house.

"Now where will you begin work?" asked Mrs. Douglas. "I would say, put the small huts immediately into repair, for we are too many for this gloomy abode. It is really singular that, with my great antipathy to a dungeon, I should be again compelled to reside in a cave. But, my good men, could you not obtain us a little light? How did the early people of the world rear those buildings of massy stones, some of which are standing to this day. You men of science understand the means of levers and such mechanical aids; I leave it to you; but do remove these frightful rocks."

"It is disgraceful to us, Margaret," said her husband, "that you have to remind us of this duty; come, Jem, you must be leader; here is a strong force to assist you."

Jem examined and measured the pieces of rock, then from one of the fallen trees wooden levers were soon made. One of the rocks was not very broad at the base, and the workmen were able, without much difficulty, to remove it from before the window. The rock on the other side of the door was much larger, and it was agreed that they should not attempt the removal of it. They had now light into two rooms; and as it would be impossible ever to uncover the house, they proposed, at a convenient season, to build another in the front of it.

In a week, by a prudent division of labour, wonders were accomplished. Three huts were rendered habitable, and the barn put into repair. The ladies, assisted by Tom, cleared the gardens, and restored them to some degree of order and neatness. The vines, which had escaped destruction, but pined in their dark abode, now restored to the genial sunshine, raised their heads. Lewis doubted the success of a vineyard in a climate so subject to autumnal storms ; but they persevered in the experiment, which afforded, at all events, employment and amusement.

Effectual props were raised to support the roof of the subterranean dwelling, which the two families continued to inhabit till the Douglas mansion rose from the ruins, in outward appearance as neat as before, though certainly somewhat damaged in the internal arrangements. But brushes and water produced renovation in some cases, the broken furniture was mended, and the shattered glass replaced, as the crate was not yet emptied. After this, Mr. and Mrs. Douglas took possession once more of their own dwelling, with John and the two children, who were glad to escape from " the dark house."

Before any more labours were undertaken, Mr. Carruthers returned, accompanied by Pedro and Zara, with two more young Indian boys, to learn the truths of Christianity. Mr. Carruthers was satisfied with his visit : he had now the respect of the Indians, and had been able, among the young, to sow the seeds of the true faith. He had assisted the people to improve their huts, induced them to cook their food, to till some plots of ground, and to sow them with maize which he had given them. He was called the good father by the tribe ; and Pedro and Zara declared that there was a perceptible improvement in the manners of the people.

They were prepared to see some mischief at Esperanza, but had not surmised the extent of the destruction. The Pampero had extended so far south as to sweep over and scatter their huts; but these were more readily restored than the dwellings of their friends; and Mr. Carruthers shuddered over the recital of the danger he had not witnessed. The cacique and his wife were delighted with the improvement their child had made; he had already learned to read, and could speak English and Spanish fluently. He was glad to see his parents, but declined returning with them, unless "Cissy" would go; and Pedro was willing the child should remain, to fit him to rule a Christian tribe.

After their visitors departed, as the autumn was passing away, the workmen hastened to complete the buildings, and lay in stores for winter. The stones and earth scattered over the enclosure formed the foundation of a terrace, six feet broad, close to the wall, which it was proposed should, some time, be carried completely round. From the mass that lay above the house they succeeded in extracting, happily without accident or injury, the large barrel of gunpowder which had been in the cave that had been swept away in the vast slip of the mountain. They dug a deep hole in the earth for a powder-magazine, carefully covered for fear of accidents, and then turned to the consideration of building once more a family mansion.

"But, my friends," said Mr. Merton, "I confess to much fearfulness of nature; I tremble to dwell in another abode beneath these towering mountains. May not another storm produce similar consequences? and it would be presumption to expect that we should again be saved."

Mr. Merton was assured that an expedition had been made the previous day, to examine the rocks behind the house, and it was unanimously agreed that no danger now existed, those rocks which contained Maria's cave being the only parts of the mountains impending over the enclosure—now an inclined plane

2 E

spread for a quarter of a mile behind them, which was bounded by rocks rising like a perpendicular wall.

"Still we have lost the useful cave," said Matilda; "and should we ever again be reduced to peril and flight, we shall miss our store house; and therefore I have thought of a plan ;—but I will not speak till Jack promises not to laugh."

Jack did promise to be grave, and she then continued : "I think we might rest the back of the new house against these caverns, for such they now are, securing for ourselves a secret entrance to them, and a means of escape from them."

"It is a hint worth consideration," said Mr. Douglas, "though I see some difficulties, principally in the contrivance necessary to escape from the retreat."

"And one grand objection to the plan," said Lewis, is, that we should lose the advantages of light and air from the back of the house."

"But why not make the house face the south," said Tom, "and place the end against the ruins; we can then have light and ventilation as we wish?"

Tom's plan was adopted. The family removed the next day into the third house which had been built and called Dr. Lewis's house, and the mansion was begun and finished in a short time. A small back room contained the communication with the cave, which was in fact the door of the old house, with a strong iron bar added to secure it inside. The room was tapestried with furs, nailed firmly down, except at the door, where it was left loose to allow them to enter, and could then be fastened down from behind. The contrivance was perfect; but it was earnestly hoped it might never be needed.

In the interior of the cave they removed the front of the chimney, enlarged the opening on the roof till even Mr. Douglas could conveniently pass through it, and placed a ladder as an ascent. From the roof there was no difficulty in walking up the slope to the woods beyond. A large stone covered the opening, and rapidly-spreading creeping plants were planted over the buried house, which would in a few months cover all the *débris*, and no one could believe that the mass which spread from the mountains contained a spacious dwelling.

All useful stores were placed in the subterranean retreat, to which the ammunition was now removed, as no place could be more secure; and Mr. and Mrs. Merton slept peacefully, for they had a refuge in case of need.

Provisions were speedily accumulated for winter; but before the snow, Paul arrived, accompanied by a young Indian girl, who, he told Mr. Merton, wished to become a Christian, and to whom he wished to be united. Paul had requested his intended bride to be composed and silent, as became her dignity; but his charge was forgotten when she was introduced to the wonders of Esperanza. She uttered loud exclamations in a dialect of mingled Indian and Spanish, and touched the bright hair and neat dresses of the young Europeans with admiration. But Paul assured Mr. Merton that, though Ara acted like a child, she thought profoundly, and believed in the true God.

" Ara is the descendant of a race of warriors from the north," said Paul, " who have their tents at the foot of the mountains. Before she had reached her eighth year the warriors of her tribe met, and attacked us on our own hunting-grounds. My people fought bravely, and the cacique of the north and his wife were slain with many of his warriors; the rest fled, leaving the child of their chief weeping over the bodies of her parents. I was then a boy, and tender-hearted. I could not bear to see my people spear the weeping child; I took her upon my horse, and gave her to my mother, to whom she became a daughter. Yet I did not love the girl whom I had saved; she was proud and scornful; she spoke to me, a cacique, boldly, saying, ' The Indians of the south are like the puma and the jaguar; they hunt men; they love blood; they drink blood; they

2 E 2

bathe themselves in blood.   The noble warriors of the
north hunt for gold; with gold they buy cattle to fill
the corrals, and bright robes to clothe their maidens
and wives.   They eat meat, roasted by the fire, from
dishes of silver, and drink the *chica* or the fire-water
from cups of gold.   Their huts are dwellings for men,
but the toldos of the Pampas Indians are the dens of
wild beasts.'

"My heart swelled, for I knew the girl spoke the
words of truth; but still I loved her not.   Then God
cast me among new people, who taught me to love and
worship him: I returned to my tribe to tell them I
had become a changed man.   When our good father
came to deliver to my ignorant people the message of
God, the young captive listened in silence to the
words of wisdom; she thought on them long, then she
came to me and said, 'Death comes to all the world,
and one day the cacique, who loves her not, may choose
to wash his hair in the blood of Ara.   But Ara wishes
not to pass after death to the hunting-fields of her own
people; she would learn the way to that beautiful
world where the cacique himself will come—the heaven
of the Christians.'

"I spoke to the brave girl the words that had given
me knowledge, and she wept over the love and sufferings of the Son of God.   She prayed me to bring her
to you, that she might learn to be a Christian, and to
be patient and humble, although she was a captive and
unloved.   I said that Paul the Christian had no captives; she was free; my warriors should convey her in
safety to the tents of her own people.

"Still the girl wept more; she told me she would
die with my people, if I would permit her, and hide
herself from my eyes, if I loved not to look on her.
Then I said that I did love to look on her, and that if
she became a Christian she should abide in my tent,
and be my only wife; and now I come to you, good
father, to ask, Is it good that I should take my captive
foe to be my wife?"

"You will act like a Christian to do so," answered Mr. Merton. "If the young girl understands and believes the doctrines of Christianity, she shall be admitted into the Church, and I will unite you, trusting you may become the instruments of spreading around you the true religion."

The Indian stranger was a graceful girl, her glossy hair, bound round her head, was adorned with flowers and silver ornaments, and her throat and arms were decorated with bands of emerald and topaz. The girl had not forgotten among her wild captors the less barbarous habits of her own people; her poncho was arranged with a grace unknown among the Pampas Indians, and her whole appearance was dignified. Her mind was lively and intelligent, and she readily comprehended, and was deeply affected by, the beauties of religion.

Since they had last seen him, Paul had visited Buenos Ayres with some of his tribe, to dispose of a large collection of skins. His manners, dress, and facility in speaking the Spanish language had been the means of introducing him to the more honourable class of merchants, from whom he had obtained in exchange such iron utensils, china, and glasses as he had seen among his friends at Esperanza. He had also obtained for his fair sisters, as he called them, a guitar, to replace those destroyed; and this kind consideration deeply affected the family.

After a few days' instruction in household duties as well as religious doctrines, the marriage was solemnised, a great feast prepared, and afterwards John's fiddle was produced, and the great hall for the first time became a ball-room, even Mrs. Merton forgetting all her languor, and dancing merrily with the Indians and her children; and daily the reclaimed savages became more and more charmed with the life of civilization.

CHAPTER XXXII.

Paul's Proposal for a Second Settlement.   John's Love Affair.
Tom's Projects and Departure.   The Village of Amistad.
The Return of Mr. Carruthers.   The Fifth Anniversary and
its Plans.   The Conclusion.

BEFORE the Indians left Esperanza, Paul requested
his beloved friends to listen to his wishes.   " My tribe
is small," said he, " and my people are gradually
becoming weaned from their love of slaughter.   They
would still be hunters, and they see that the fair men
who cultivate the ground and eat the fruits of it in
peace, are not less brave in battle nor less bold in the
hunting-field than themselves.   They say, ' Why
should we not eat corn bread, and rich butter from
the cows ?   The whole Pampas are ours ; let us choose
a fertile spot, where our cattle can find grass, and there
raise our tents for many seasons.   Let us dwell near
the Christians ; they will not destroy our tents ;   and
we will swear, by the great and good God of the Christians, never to burn their dwellings, nor rob their corrals,
but to be their friends—the same people.'   I heard
them speak with joy ; yet I fear my Christian brothers
will say, ' the Indian is treacherous and bloody ; let
him dwell far from us.'   Give me words, good father,
to speak to my people."

Paul concluded, and there was a momentary silence.
Every one wished to speak ; but the duty and responsibility of answering devolved on Mr. Merton.   The
good man lifted up his hands, and said, " Blessed be
God, who may yet permit me to plant a church in the
wilderness ! and blessed be your example, my son, that
has won the stubborn heart of the heathens.   Come
near to us ; it is the command of God, and must be
pleasant to us."

All the family seconded the opinion of their father, and a grand discussion ensued about the locality, the huts, the gardens; but all decisions were deferred for the present; and Paul returned to his people with the invitation to become neighbours to the Christians, accompanied by his bride the new Christian, Anna, loaded with pretty gifts by her young friends.

The happy party at Esperanza spent the winter cheerfully in useful employment and improving studies. Tom, since his adventure with the peccaries, had lost much of his taste for hunting; he desired, like his father, to become a minister of the Gospel, and was now engaged in study to fit him for the office. The rain, sleet, and frost, came as usual; but with abundant provision, and warm, comfortable dwellings, every one was contented with his in-door life, and evenings of music and dancing delighted the young Indian pupils.

"Mistress," said John to Mrs. Douglas one morning, as he was setting out her breakfast-table, "I've gotten something on my mind."

"Then out with it, John," said his mistress, "or you will let my cups fall; and you must remember we have no china-shops at Esperanza. Now, what's the matter? Have the mules ate my linen from the hedge? or have you let the breakfast-cakes get scorched? Speak out, man; you look as if you were going to be hanged."

"Not so bad as that, mistress," answered he; "but, you see, it's Nanny. Oh! she is an uncommon woman —far beyond me!"

"That is the truth, John," said Mrs. Douglas, "for you are not an uncommon man, though you are a very good fellow, if one could get you to speak out. Here's your master—speak to him."

"Nay, mistress," said John, "it's you that must talk to her, if you will; and just *incense* her that it would be a good thing, so far as we both are fra' our nat'ral homes, that we should just come together and be married."

"A good thing!" said Mrs. Douglas; "why, you simple fellow, you know Nanny has a temper, and a quiet fellow like you would take ill to a termagant."

"Why, that's true, mistress," replied he; "she has her tiffs, poor body; but, bless you, its over in no time. She flies off like a sky-rocket, and splutters and roars, and there's no more on't. I'se used to her, mistress, and I just sits quietly till she comes right, and then it's always, 'John, my man, will' have a bit of supper?'"

Mr. Douglas laughed at John's boldness, but promised to use his influence with Nanny, and suggested that John should set about building a hut.

"It would be as much as my life was worth to name that to her," said the obedient lover. "Nay, we mun never set ourselves up to be householders. There's not a man living could wile away Nanny fra' her own folks. I can come here and *tantle* after mistress as usual, when she wants me, and then back to help Nanny a bit."

"With all my heart, John," said his master; "but how does Nanny receive your suit?"

"Why, she just tells me to hold my tongue, and go about my business, like an idle good-to-nought, as I is; but there's nought in that, sir," answered John. "And I'se be bound, if you would just give me a good character, she would come round."

So the master and mistress agreed to give John a good character; and though Nanny grumbled loudly and long at the hardship of having such a *feckless* fellow to look after, when her hands were filled with work, she relented at the intercession of the *bairns*, and the wedding took place with all proper solemnity and festivity.

And Nanny, notwithstanding her *chuntering*, as John said, made him a good wife, and he declared that he had never been so happy in his life, for he had no care but to do as Nanny bid him; and in the evening, as she really enjoyed music, he was permitted to sit down and play on the fiddle, often calming some little ebullition of Nanny's temper by playing one of her favourite tunes.

As soon as the frosts of winter dispersed, a site was sought for the Indian settlement, Dr. Lewis directing the attention of his friends to a beautiful spot he had noticed on his expedition in search of Jack. It was about eight miles from Esperanza, on the banks of the large river, abounding in rich grass and noble trees, forming a park-like scene. The whole party were charmed with the situation, which was not near enough to Esperanza for the Indians to become troublesome, and yet within an hour's ride, so that it would not be difficult for the young ladies to accomplish a plan they anxiously desired, of forming schools for young children, and devoting some time every day in teaching them.

A sufficient space was marked out to allow twenty huts to be built in a circle,—the number of the families of the tribe. Each hut was to be surrounded by a garden, behind which was to be a plot of ground for corn. The house for the chief was to occupy a larger space than any of the rest, and opposite to it a vacancy was left for a chapel, when they had time to raise it. The area in the midst, which included some beautiful trees, was to be appropriated to athletic sports, and the amusements of the women and children, and it was proposed to surround the whole with a moat, and wall of earth.

Paul arrived soon after with his whole tribe, who raised their tents near the chosen spot, that they might conveniently commence operations. The cacique was charmed with the locality, and was easily made to comprehend the plans his friends had drawn.

" I will go with many skins to Buenos Ayres," said he, " and obtain from the noble merchants there, in exchange for them, the cups and dishes of China, the silver forks and spoons from Peru, and the iron cooking utensils from Europe. Then my tolderia shall also be Esperanza.''

But Paul was told he must select some other name for his settlement, to distinguish it from the European dwellings. He was rather mortified that his tolderia could not be Esperanza, but finally decided that it should be named Amistad. He and Anna remained at Esperanza till the buildings were erected, improving in the society of their European friends, while Joe and Jem superintended the work, and taught and assisted the unpractised workmen at Amistad.

"And now, dear papa and mamma," said Tom, " since you are surrounded by so many friends, I will venture to petition that you will allow me to quit you for a season ; you know I am the least useful of the community now. I delight in theories, but I want energy to draw practical results from them ; yet I am not satisfied—I wish to do some good in the world. I wish to study divinity that I may fulfil a duty ; my scientific pursuits can still be my recreation ; and I might thus, among the untutored Indian, be able to turn my studies to the good purpose of advancing religion and civilization. We are no longer entirely cut off from the world, for our good friend Paul undertakes to conduct me, certainly by a long and dreary journey, to Buenos Ayres. From thence, if you will permit me, I will sail for England, receive such instructions as our means will allow, enter the Church, if I am thought worthy, and return to help you, dear father, in your missionary labours.''

It was with pain that Mr. and Mrs. Merton agreed to part with one of their children—the thoughtful, good, obedient son, who had always been so much the companion of his father ; but Mr. Carruthers represented to them the duty of consenting to God's will in this important matter, and even offered to accompany him to England, place him in one of the universities, and after transacting some affairs of his own, return to Esperanza to settle permanently.

"You must consent, dear mamma," said Jack; " see what treasures you will still have left. I declare myself a citizen of Esperanza for life, and Charles Villars intends to follow my worthy example—no despicable members of the community.   Then here is your fourth son, Dr. Lewis, an excellent fellow, determined never to leave home.   If you had remained in Westmoreland, the girls might have married men that lived hundreds of miles from us, and you would have lost them; but here their husbands must come, and we shall all dwell together like the patriarchs of old."

Mrs. Merton smiled at Jack's arguments, and when she reflected that her children might have been scattered in distant lands, instead of being gathered round her in health, plenty, and peace, she felt ashamed that she should regret parting with one, to fit him for the service of God.

Charles declared that Tom must be entered at Cambridge, at *his* college, which was a college of gentlemen, and clever fellows too, as might be seen by the specimen before them, and as to the money . . .

" Have we not some money, my dear?" inquired Mr. Merton of his wife, for the matter had been forgotten on a spot where money was useless.

It was then recollected that the Mertons had money sufficient for all expenses in Tom's college life. There was Mrs. Merton's little fortune in the funds, with the accumulated dividends; and Mr. Merton's rents since they left England.   In the mean time Mr. Carruthers would pay the expenses of the voyage, and Charles said :

" Remember, Tom, above all things to go directly to my tailor in Bond-street, and let him fit you out at once.   You would never recover your credit at Cambridge, if you were to appear in a coat made by Nanny, and a poncho woven by the girls.   And tell him to send me a new hunting fit-out next spring by Carruthers.   I want no full-dress matters.   I have a coat that I suppose I must wear when I am married, and then put it by till my eldest son comes of age. But still I shall give you a list of things that one does want even here, and tell the people to draw as usual, on my banker at Valparaiso, for the whole account."

Even Mr. Merton did not object to this arrangement, as he could not but perceive that the costume of Tom must undergo a reformation before he could appear in the polished society of England, and these minor matters arranged, many charges and counsels were given by the good parents. Then he was enjoined to visit Winston, and see all their old friends.

"You must see Dick Evans," said Jack; "I suppose he will be drudging on at R—— school. You can tell him what an old fellow I have grown, spending my days in hunting and shooting; knocking down a lion or a jaguar now and then; keeping half a dozen horses for my own riding, and thinking of building myself a mansion, and marrying a wife."

"And you will please, Master Tom," said Nanny. "to give a look after old Peggy Green, my aunt, if she be spared yet; and you may say I ha' no thoughts just now of coming over to Winston, for its an awful way to it; and I'se cannily off here. And you can just say, honey, that I've picked up a good man here, far away as it is. And ye needn't say ought but what's good on him, poor body, for the man's not that ill, if he'd stir himsel' a bit more."

"He's an excellent fellow," replied Tom, "and a good friend of mine; and depend on it, Nanny, I shall tell all the folks at the village what a sensible husband you have got, and what a good wife you make."

"Least said about that is best," said she; "for you know, Master Tom, it's not in t' natur of me to hold my tongue when folks aggravate me; and may be I say some hard words to him, nows and thens, but he never minds—not he."

It was a sorrowful morning, though the sun rose

on a prospect as fair and rich as the eye could desire, when Tom parted with his weeping friends, to pursue his way over the wide Pampas. He was accompanied by Mr. Carruthers, Almagro, Paul, and six Indians, all well mounted and well armed, carrying a tent to shelter the Europeans from the night air; the Indians, at this season, desiring no roof but the canopy of heaven, merely made a fire to keep the puma and jaguar at a distance, and lying down covered with their ponchos, to enjoy their sound and healthy slumber.

The work of attending to the rising buildings at Amistad, was salutary to the party left at home. At first the Indians had been quite unable to labour more than an hour or two without great fatigue; but they became gradually more accustomed to the muscular action, and more attached to the labour which produced such pleasing results. In the mean time the women were instructed in household matters by Matilda; Maria, remembering how she had herself been taught, chose to teach the elder girls, and Mary, seated on the turf, with a swarm of little Indians round her, undertook the difficult task of communicating to them the rudiments of religion, morality, and civilized manners. After a little preliminary discipline, she hoped to teach them to speak and read Spanish, which, as most generally useful, it was proposed should be the common language of the two settlements.

And thus busily employed, some weeks passed, and they had the pleasure of seeing Lewis and Paul return, bringing the good tidings of the welfare of the travellers, who had engaged a passage in an English vessel, and were enjoying the hospitality of Buenos Ayres when their friends left them. Besides satisfactory letters from Tom, Mr. Carruthers had kindly sent useful presents,—tea and sugar, the luxuries of the community, books for Mr. Merton, and silks and muslins for the ladies.

Paul's mules had exchanged their loads of furs for useful iron implements for agricultural and mechanical purposes, with seeds and fruit-trees for the new settlement, which, to the great delight of the cacique, now presented a most interesting appearance ; the houses were roofed, the workmen being now employed in fitting them up internally, with bamboo frames for bedsteads and tables, and benches for seats. Then the ingenious turners made a number of neat wooden platters, the Indians themselves forming cups of horn, and baskets of beech-bark. Many of the young men of the tribe became expert workmen, and succeeded in making neat articles of furniture for their huts.

The gardens were laid out by John, and the young ladies assisted in sowing seeds, and planting shrubs and fruit-trees. A number of cows were collected in a capacious corral, and Nanny and Mrs. Douglas with much difficulty induced the women to milk ; and Joe, having made churns and cheese-moulds, they were next initiated in the mysteries of making butter and cheese. The women, naturally disinclined to occupation and to cleanliness, were much less tractable pupils than the men ; but the persevering and indefatigable Mrs. Douglas finally reduced them to submission, and having once tasted the fruits of their labours, they became more reconciled to the exertion.

And when the labours of summer and autumn had filled their barns with stores for the winter, the Indians were rejoiced and grateful to their teachers ; and while hunting with the young Europeans, or assisting in their workshops, they acquired insensibly, from association, the manners, and much of the information of their civilized friends. One after another the young people came to Mr. Merton for the important instruction that was to fit them to be Christians, and week after week his little congregation increased, the church being already commenced at Amistad for the reception of Mr. Carruthers.

Thus the winter passed away in improvement and cheerfulness, and summer brought Mr. Carruthers again to his anxious friends. Amidst the noisy greetings of the happy party, from the loud bark of the delighted Wallace to the sweet tones of Cecilia, it was some time before any details could be heard of dear absent Tom.

At length they had the satisfaction of learning that he had already succeeded in obtaining honourable distinction in his college, that he was well and happy, and sanguine in the hope that he should be permitted to return to them to work good. Then came the satisfactory account of the visit to Winston, and the great rejoicing of the villagers, many of whom would actually have come out to join their beloved pastor in a far land; but Mr. Carruthers did not conceive himself authorised to incur such a responsibility in the infant condition of the settlement. He had been compelled, however, to undertake the charge of many little remembrances from the poor villagers, several pairs of warm woollen knitted stockings for " the master," and a number of pots of blackberry jelly for " the mistress." There was also a large supply of fishing-flies from Jack's friend, Dick Evans; and two young kittens—which in the course of their long journey had become cats—for Matilda and Mary, from Nanny's aunt Peggy, happily arrived in safety.

Besides the charge of these gifts, Mr. Carruthers had fulfilled the request of Charles, and brought over large packets of useful articles for himself and the family; and to these he had added, on his own account, a good supply of the cutlery of England for the use of the colony at Amistad, and slates, pencils, and books for the schools, which he rejoiced to find had progressed so wonderfully. He now devoted his time principally to instructing the Indians, and performing the services daily in the church of their settlement, and had the satisfaction of believing that his labours were attended with success.

The young Albert, under his many instructors, was receiving an excellent education; he was a quick and intelligent boy, and his father consented that he should remain entirely with his European friends, to be accomplished in every branch of learning and science; Dr. Lewis intending even to cultivate in him a taste for all studies connected with the medical art; for nothing would be more likely to command the respect and attachment of his people than this useful branch of knowledge.

On the fifth anniversary of the first settlement of the Mertons at Esperanza, a large and happy party assembled at the new house. Paul and Anna, who were daily visitors, were of course there, and Pedro accompanied them with Zara, and the little Christopher, always welcome guests. Pedro had been inspecting with astonishment the thriving colony at Amistad, and he now said to Mr. Merton :

" My heart desires to be near you. Are not you the father? Are not these the brothers of Pedro and Zara? But the Indians of the Pampas are proud of their independence; they love not the Christian's law of obedience. The old warriors of my tribe are meek-faced and treacherous as the jaguar which crouches to spring on its prey. Shall I bring the spear of destruction to the dwellings which have sheltered my child? Shall the songs of my sisters, the songs which rise to heaven like those of the forest birds in the summer morning, be changed to the wail of mourning or the shriek of despair? It shall not be, dear father; my people shall remain in the far south, till death calls the old warriors, and the young men have been taught by their European friends that the true God is a God of peace."

Mr. Merton was affected at the discourse of his reflecting friend Paul, yet he felt well pleased to hear that he did not intend to bring his numerous and formidable tribe into the neighbourhood, for the good old man could never entirely overcome his dread of the wild rovers of the Pampas. Mr. Carruthers promised to make frequent visits to the tents of the south, and doubted not that a few years would bring the peace of Christianity to the tribe.

The dinner was set out on the lawn before the house, and the happy parents looked round on the smiling faces of their children with joy and thankfulness. One alone was wanting, and he was, they hoped, happily and worthily occupied.

"I fear I am a selfish old man," said Mr. Merton, "for I cannot contemplate the separation from another of my circle with composure ; and yet, my Lucy warns me, I must not expect the young, the adventurous, the ardent spirit to submit to this life in the wilderness. The repose that is the bliss of age, is irksome and revolting to youth. Tell me, Lewis, my faithful friend and counsellor, ought I to ask that you should all remain here, far from the pleasures, the improvements, and the duties of society ?"

Dr. Lewis looked round at the smiling countenances of his young friends, and read the wishes of their hearts.

"We are not your captives, my excellent friend," answered he, "but your devoted subjects. We have the means and the liberty to leave Esperanza when we choose ; but I do not see any one anxious to avail himself of the privilege. I cannot answer for the young ladies, who are no longer children ; they may perhaps wish to see more of the gay world before they take upon them the sober duties of life. What does my fair philosopher, Matilda, say ? Has she no desire to try the charms of fashionable circles, and find a new home in one of the gay cities of America?"

"This is my home for life ; you cannot doubt it, Lewis," said Matilda, a little reproachfully.

"If that be the case," said Lewis, "I trust, my dear father, you will make me indeed your son, by bestowing on me your good and beloved daughter, Matilda. You will thus secure two certain retainers at Esperanza."

"My dear friend," cried the astonished father, "you cannot be in earnest! These children are too young to think of marriage."

"Why, papa," answered Jack, amidst the general laughter of the circle, "Matilda is nearly twenty; and we are all of mature years, and, with your consent, we all intend to found separate houses. Maria agrees to take me; indeed, she has no choice, for Charles, as everybody knows, has long been engaged to Mary."

"Wonderful!" said Mr. Merton; "and I really never expected such events to take place; neither, I suppose, did Lucy; but probably she was in your secret. Still, my dear children, this is a most terrible prospect for your mamma and me. We shall be left quite alone."

"Nothing of the sort, papa," said Jack; "our tents will surround yours, like those of the patriarchal age, and you will be the head of the tribe of Merton. I conclude you have said 'yes' to us; so now, Charley, it is your turn to speak."

And Charles did speak, to the astonishment of Mr. Merton, for no one could ever have believed that the day would come when Charles Villars should petition to remain for life at Esperanza. But his dear lively Mary had won him from his taste for the pleasures of fashionable society, and rallied him out of the little conceits that he had been led into by affluence and indulgence; and naturally amiable, and attached to his guardian, he was now perfectly contented with life at Esperanza.

"Now I will not have you speak another word of nonsense, my good friend," said Mrs. Douglas. "It is quite plain the dear girls must be settled; and I am quite ready to assist them in managing their household matters. We must have the houses built and furnished, the wedding-dresses made, and the weddings celebrated before winter; so, the sooner we begin work the better. Come, my dears, let us walk round and fix our plans, and then just run over my things and see what I can spare you."

Still, notwithstanding the impatience of the managing lady, it was some time before Mr. and Mrs. Merton could reconcile themselves to the sudden step from childhood made by their children; but they were finally persuaded that the arrangement was not only reasonable, but most fortunate, as they should thus secure the settlement of their children around them. And then Mrs. Douglas stepped forward, in all the bustle of management, and as she sewed carpets and curtains, delivered profound lectures on domestic economy to her happy and much-amused young friends.

It is always painful to take leave of a pleasant family with whom you have been long intimately associated; but our time is come. We must not even wait for the festivities of the weddings, nor for the return of Tom, rich in academic honours and pious hopes. We will leave the Indians progressing in civilization and true knowledge; while the calm old age of the good Mr. and Mrs. Merton was blessed by the sight of the prosperity and happiness of their children, satisfied that the reflecting mind will deduce from the simple narration, that perseverance and good faith must ever be rewarded with success and peace.

FINIS.

PRINTED BY COX (BROS.) AND WYMAN, GREAT QUEEN STREET.

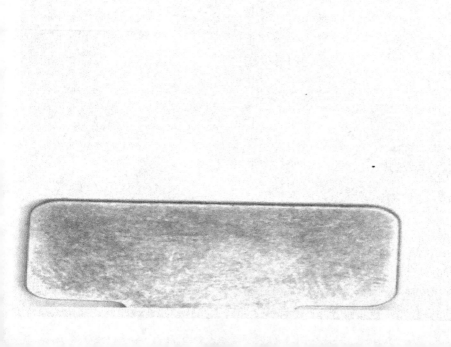